DEAD CENTRE

DEAD CENTRE

The inside story of the mysterious disappearance of
Peter Falconio

ROBIN BOWLES

LAKE PRESS

LAKE PRESS

Lake Press Pty Ltd
5 Burwood Road
Hawthorn VIC 3122 Australia
www.lakepress.com.au

Thanks to the Northern Territory Supreme Court for
access to and use of transcripts and court photos.
Transcripts have been edited for clarity and brevity, but
remain true to the words spoken.

This book has been previously published.
This edition printed in China 5 4 3 2 1
LP22 179

A catalogue record for this
book is available from the
National Library of Australia

DEDICATION

Dedicated to my beloved husband, Clive, who has put up with a lot during the writing of all my books, but no more so than during this epic.

His practical and caring support is a contribution words cannot acknowledge. Without him, this book would not have been possible.

ACKNOWLEDGEMENTS

More than 150 people have contributed to the writing of this book. I met them in all kinds of locations – pubs, cattle stations, universities, windswept beaches, dark coffee lounges, police stations and private homes – or spoke to them by telephone. I thank everyone for sharing and trusting. Those who wish to remain nameless can relax, but among those who can be named, a few people stand out.

My special thanks to Chris and Annie Tangey, Glenn Morrison, Frank Thorne, Mark Wilton, Vince Millar, Helen Jones and family, Les Pilton and family, Rick and other Barrow Creek Hotel staff, Lindy Chamberlain, Tammy Hackett, Shane Ride, Val Prior, Brad Murdoch, Julie* and Jazz*.

Several police have helped me with my inquiries – though most didn't want to make a statement. My thanks to former Northern Territory Police Commissioner Brian Bates, Superintendent Colleen Gwynne, Superintendent Bert Hofer, former Deputy Police Commissioner (South Australia) Jim Litster, police in Broome and many others who have spoken to me off the record.

Dozens of media representatives have also shared their experiences with me, including Fleur Bitcon, Narelle Hine, Jason Scott, Edith Bevin, Mandy Taylor, Tracy Andrews, Genine Johnson and Penny Doust.

Thanks too for the generous contribution of various experts in their specialised fields – forensic psychologist Dr Tim Watson-Munro, senior psychiatrist Clifford Boland, psychologist Professor Dianna Kenny, DNA expert Professor Barry Boettcher, forensic photography expert Associate Professor Gale Spring, forensic scientist Joy Kuhl, forensic anthropologist Professor Machiej Henneberg, forensic criminologist Wayne Petherick, barrister Grant Algie now a QC, solicitor Mark Twiggs, Northern Territory Director of Public Prosecutions Rex Wild, QC and Assistant Director of Public Prosecutions Tony Elliott.

Anna*, Kathleen*, John Turahui and Ted Egan gave me insights into the complex Aboriginal culture in the outback. Thank you for opening my eyes a little wider.

Excerpts have been used from Martin Bashir's interview of Joanne Lees for ITV's *Tonight* with Trevor McDonald; a documentary made by Scottish TV; various newspapers, in particular the *Centralian Advocate* and the *Australian*; Northern Territory police media releases; transcripts from the South Australian Supreme Court and the Northern Territory Supreme Court; *Criminal Profiling* by Wayne Petherick, *Mindhunter* by John Douglas and Mark Olshaker, and the Cross Borders for Law Enforcement Investigative Report on the Commonwealth Attorney General's website. Interviews with John Bryson and Neville Dawson were sourced from the Guardian Unlimited web site (interview with David Fickling, 2002). My thanks especially to the staff of the *Centralian Advocate* for their contribution to the photo section and their generosity in providing access to their staff, their photo library and their archives.

Names followed by an asterisk when they are first used have been changed to protect identities. In some cases, the transcripts of court hearings have been condensed for the sake of clarity and brevity, but I have remained true to the words spoken.

Sincere thanks to my first publisher, Jane Southward at Random House, who believed in me and this book, and David Horgan at Lake Press; proofreader Danielle Hampshire; lawyers Nic Pullen and Alex Wade; CJZ, the producers of the Ch7 telemovie 'Murder in the Outback', and my trusted friend and editor, Jenny Lee.

And finally, thank you to all the readers who write such wonderful messages of encouragement to me. This book is for you.

Robin Bowles
Melbourne
www.robinbowles.com.au

CONTENTS

INTRODUCTION

*'The aim of science is not to open the door to infinite wisdom,
but to set a limit to infinite error.'*

Bertoldt Brecht

This is the third edition of *Dead Centre*, originally published in 2007. The story has evolved over the years. Various 'champions' of the convicted alleged killer of Peter Falconio have raised a raft of reasons why Bradley John Murdoch should not have been convicted for the murder of Falconio and the assault of Peter's girlfriend. From time to time I have come up with some of those reasons myself, as you will read.

What has fuelled my ongoing interest through all those years is the way the investigation and trial were conducted, which resulted in a 28-year sentence (twenty-year mandatory and an extra eight years because the judge was upset with Murdoch for allegedly telling lies about Joanne Lees, saying that Murdoch's actions were 'cowardly in the extreme'!). So, I'm not necessarily a Murdoch supporter, rather a campaigner for truth and justice. This is a conviction with no body, no weapon, no cause of death, no witnesses, no obvious motive and no tangible evidence!

The story was updated two years ago, as you will read in the Epilogue. Up until that chapter, you are reading the book as it was published in 2007. Murdoch has new champions now – his choice – so I haven't spoken to him in a couple of years, although I keep across all new developments!

However, these have been few and futile. The Northern Territory government – and especially the Northern Territory Police – do not want Murdoch's unsafe conviction questioned or overturned. The most common refutation of any new evidence or request for further investigation is, 'We don't want another Chamberlain on our hands'. It's all too hard and, as the judge commented at sentencing, it's likely Murdoch will die in jail.

Robin Bowles
Melbourne, 2022

◆ ◆ ◆

I first heard Peter Falconio's name in July 2001, when I was attending a murder trial in Western Australia. One of my friends rang from Melbourne, asking if I'd read about the disappearance of the British tourist and the miraculous survival of his girlfriend, Joanne Lees.

'You should do a book about it,' my friend said. 'It's got everything, wicked gunman, murder of innocent backpacker, brave girl eludes boyfriend's murderer, rescue by passing truckie, police crashing round destroying the crime scene, and the Barrow Creek pub acting as police headquarters.'

I knew the Barrow Creek pub, which is the fond reference to the otherwise known Barrow Creek Hotel. I'd driven past it a couple of times, but never been tempted to go in. A seedy-looking roadhouse, spaced about a petrol tank's distance between two equally seedy establishments, beside the long straight Track that runs through the Northern Territory from Alice Springs to Darwin.

During a couple of weeks at the WA trial, I'd heard nothing about the NT incident. After tense days in court, the stale news of daily newspapers held no attraction for me and I reached my accommodation too late for the TV news.

I said, 'Perhaps Falconio's just gone missing. About ten per cent of people who disappear in Australia completely vanish – either they end up dead, or don't want to be found. That's about 3000 people a year. Maybe he's one of those.'

My friend said I should buy a paper and read all about it, like everyone else in Australia.

Despite the near hysteria of national and international news stories about the incident over the months that followed, I wasn't convinced that the disappearance of Peter Falconio and the skill of a media-shy Joanne Lees in evading a vicious killer was anything more than grist for the tabloid mill.

However, something happened on 28 August 2002 that changed my mind.

A 45-year-old drifter named Bradley John Murdoch was arrested at gunpoint in a supermarket parking lot in Port Augusta, South Australia. His immaculately packed rig was fitted out for an independent life on the road. And an arsenal of weapons was found hidden among his possessions. He was carrying a serious firearm when arrested. Murdoch was charged with the abduction and rape of a Sedan woman and her twelve-year-old daughter.

Within days, the Northern Territory police had asked their southern colleagues for a sample of Murdoch's DNA, obtained under protest (but legally) from Murdoch at the time of his arrest. At the time, it was unclear what was behind this request. Murdoch's counsel vigorously opposed the 'gift' of this DNA on the grounds that Murdoch had not committed a crime in the Northern Territory; the Northern Territory police had no warrant out for Murdoch and they had no jurisdiction in South Australia.

The papers didn't know then that, in May 2002, James Hepi, Murdoch's former partner in drug running between Sedan in South Australia and Broome in Western Australia, had named Murdoch to the Northern Territory police as 'the man who did Falconio'. This community-spirited gesture was made in return for a negligible sentence for his own criminal activity of trying to sneak four kilos of hydroponically grown marijuana into Broome to sell. Hepi suspected Murdoch had dobbed him in and, in the time-honoured criminal tradition, this was payback time. Unfortunately, after receiving this little jewel of information, the police had a name; they had 'unidentified male DNA' on the back of Joanne Lees's T-shirt; but as they had no idea where Murdoch was, they were unable to test Hepi's claim. They'd searched for four months, but Murdoch had gone to ground. He'd heard the rumours and he was a man who knew how to stay out of sight – at least until 28 August 2002.

The publicity following Murdoch's arrest, both in the local media and on the internet, became impossible to ignore. I deliberated about how the story had changed, from being 'Brave Pommie girl eludes sadistic gunman, boyfriend disappears, believed murdered' to one with more layers than an onion. Was Murdoch guilty of the abduction and rape in SA? If so, this could be an indication that this was just one of a pattern of other vicious crimes against women. Would the alleged rape of a minor (most recent incident) take judicial precedence over the alleged murder of a British tourist (a year ago); that is, which charge would be heard first? Would the trauma to the child be considered more pressing than an internationally notorious murder?

I became interested in discovering the answers and wrote to Murdoch asking him to see me. To my surprise, he agreed. Murdoch was acquitted on the SA rape and abduction charges, but two years later was found guilty of murdering Falconio and abducting and assaulting Joanne Lees, made possible mainly by the presentation of expert, but controversial, low copy number DNA evidence. What followed that visit in March 2003 to this day in 2011 has become woven into my own life. *Dead Centre* was my fifth book, but possibly the one I learned most from. It connected me with high-octane criminals, international forensic experts, seedy drug underworlds, worldwide media networks and the fascination and frustration of a high-profile, high-stakes legal process. There would be no winners. Even the NT prosecutors, although they 'won' the case, have copped a lot of criticism since the verdict was delivered in 2005. And continue to do so.

Part One

THE VANISHING

The story is so bizarre it's almost impossible to believe.

Commander Bob Fields, Northern Territory Police

PROLOGUE

The heavy transport rig bored south through the darkness, following the highway south across the Northern Territory desert. Vince Millar and his co-driver, Rod Adams, were so familiar with this run that they could do it in their sleep. Almost did, sometimes. From high above the road, the beam of their double headlights lit the middle distance and dissipated in the scrub along the edge of the road.

Vince was driving while Rod caught some sleep. They were coming up to their next changeover at the tiny settlement of Barrow Creek when the headlights caught something moving beside the road. Moments later, a young woman was standing in the middle of the highway, about twenty metres in front of the truck, hands together and arms outstretched, trying to wave them down.

Vince swerved violently. 'Jesus H! What the f--k was that?' he yelled.

'Are you OK?' asked Rod, who had been woken by the commotion.

'Some sheila just jumped out at me, mate,' said Vince. 'I f--kin' nearly hit her. Maybe I did.'

Vince knew the front of the truck had missed the woman, but he was worried that one of the trailers had collected her. You don't feel much in the cabin of a road train if you hit something.

Rod said, 'If she was black, mate, just keep goin'.'

For a moment, Vince considered driving on in case it was a set-up, but his concern for the woman overcame his fear. The airbrakes hissed as the mighty truck slewed to a standstill. It eventually stopped in the middle of the highway, blocking both lanes.

'Do you want me to help you?' Rod asked.

'Nah, go back to sleep. You're drivin' from Barrow Creek. I'll just go and do a tyre check.'

Vince flicked on his hazard lights and jumped out of the cabin. He walked to the rear of the rig, checking to see if the woman was caught up under one of his three trailers, but he couldn't see anything in the blackness.

Then, from the other side of the truck, he heard a female voice say, in an English accent, 'Help! Help! Someone's trying to kill me!' Seconds later, a girl crawled from under one of the connectors and threw herself towards him.

'Shit, lady! Where did you spring from?'

She struggled to reply. Vince stared at her. She had dark hair, a white face and enormous eyes, which gave her the look of a startled nocturnal animal. Although the desert night was cool, she was wearing only a pair of pale green shorts with a light blue short-sleeved top.

'What's the matter?' Vince asked.

'Oh, you've got to help me find Peter. Please!'

Vince was flummoxed. He'd never encountered anything quite like this. 'Look, love, just calm down and tell me what the f--k's happened.'

'Someone's trying to kill me. I escaped out the back of his car. I want my boyfriend! I want my boyfriend! I can't find him.'

Vince saw that her hands were tied together. He put his arm around her and led her to the front of the truck, where he could see her properly in the headlights. Her hands were bound with plastic electrical ties, and silver duct tape circled her neck like some weird punk necklace. She had fresh grazes on her elbows and knees, her nose had a slight smear of blood on it as if she'd wiped it with something, and there were a few smears of blood on her top, above her breasts. He thought they might have come from her elbow grazes.

'Rod! Rod!' he called. 'Wake up, mate! We've got some sheila all f--kin' tied up, mate.'

While Rod got the wire-cutters and freed the girl's hands, she gasped out her story to Vince. 'My boyfriend ... I can't find him ... My car's gone ... The man was looking for me with his dog and his torch ... He's gone ...'

Rod cut off the silver tape around her neck and pulled it carefully out of her jaw-length dark hair. She told them, 'I've got more on my ankle.' Vince removed that as well.

While they were freeing her, she told them that a man had stopped her and her boyfriend, Peter, on the road. She was afraid Peter might have been killed. The man had tied her up and put her in the back of his car, but she'd escaped and hidden in the scrub. The man and his dog had searched for her for a long time. Finally, he'd given up and left, but she stayed hidden in case he came back. She didn't know where Peter was, and she couldn't find their Kombi van.

At first, Vince was unconvinced. So this sheila is driving up the highway when some bloke jumps her, kills her boyfriend, ties her up and forces her into his car; then she manages to get away and the bloke drives off? It all seemed too far-fetched.

But in spite of his doubts, Vince collected all the bits of tape, put them back in the toolbox and locked everything into the rocker box, where truckies keep their bits and pieces. 'I'm keepin' this stuff for evidence,' he told Rod. 'This is gunna be big.'

Chapter One

THE HIGHWAY

In all directions stretches the great Australian Emptiness, in
which the mind is the least of possessions.

Patrick White

In the late 1860s, the South Australian government decided to build a telegraph line from Adelaide to Darwin, almost 3200 kilometres away. From Darwin, the line would join up with an underwater cable from South-east Asia, linking Australia with the rest of the world. In 1871 a party of explorers with packhorses and camels was sent out along the track that would become the Stuart Highway, searching for suitable sites for telegraph stations. They followed a route blazed by John McDouall Stuart, the first European to cross Australia from south to north. Returning from his first attempt at a continental crossing in 1860, Stuart had found a promising waterway and named it Barrow Creek in honour of J. H. Barrow, the treasurer of South Australia.

In September 1871, Barrow Creek was chosen as the site of a repeater station. Construction of the station had begun by January 1872, and later that year the telegraph line was opened. The station was 'a good substantial stone building', made from local rock. Tellingly, it was built like a fort, with narrow slits for windows, to resist attacks from the area's traditional landowners, the Kaytetye (pronounced 'Kattich') people. Eventually, the station would have a house, a wagon shed, a smithy, a butcher's area and a cool room.

James Stapleton, head of the crew at the repeater station, reported that Barrow Creek was 'one of the prettiest sites of the overland telegraph and will, I trust, soon be the nucleus of a thriving settlement'. But his optimism was misplaced. The creek was brackish, its supply unreliable. Though it could be used to irrigate fruit trees and vegetable gardens, drinking water had to be hauled from fifteen miles away. There were also tensions between the operators and the Kaytetye, who speared several of the telegraph station's cattle. In an attempt to prevent these attacks, the government stationed a police officer at Barrow Creek early in 1874.

A few days later, on the evening of 22 February, the Kaytetye stormed the telegraph station, killing Stapleton and a linesman, John Franks, and wounding the second-in-command, Ernest Flint. When news of the deaths reached Adelaide, the *Adelaide Advertiser* called for retribution to be 'sharp, swift and severe'. In fact, it went on for months. Police from surrounding outposts were summoned to the district and rode through the bush slaughtering dozens, if not hundreds, of the local people, whether or not they had been connected to the attack.

Barrow Creek would never become the 'thriving settlement' of Stapleton's vision. Although cattle stations followed the telegraph line, by the mid-1890s many pastoralists and their families had had enough of trying to carve a life from the unforgiving heart of the world's driest continent. Even the wealthy Barrow Creek Pastoral Company abandoned its station, and smaller landholders simply walked out, abandoning most of their possessions and hundreds of head of cattle.

By 1899, a well had been sunk beside the creek, providing a more-reliable water supply, and from 1914 a new wave of landowners tried again to tame the neighbouring country. George Hayes, a former drover and telegraph linesman – both lonely jobs in the vast open spaces – took up the lease on the old Barrow Creek Pastoral Company station, a holding of about one million acres, which he renamed Neutral Junction.

Violence continued to mark the relations between settlers and indigenous people in the region. In 1928, the dismembered body of a dingo trapper, Fred Brooks, was found in a rabbit hole near Coniston station. Reprisals by the mounted police produced 'fearful results', killing at least thirty-one Warlpiri people – but not, it seems, Brooks's killer, who escaped and lived to an old age out west at Yuendumu. An official inquiry in Adelaide gave the police only a token reprimand. Privately, it was said that the death toll was far greater, but in those days a black life didn't count for much, so thirty-one it was, for the records.

In 1930, the Barrow Creek telegraph station became home to the local constable and his wife, who operated it as both a post office and a police station. Traffic along the Stuart Highway was increasing, and in 1932 the Kilgariff brothers, building entrepreneurs from Alice Springs, opened a hotel about 200 metres from the telegraph station. It was constructed from the Kilgariffs' signature concrete bricks with a wavy pattern on the facing side.

As the only stopover between Tennant Creek, 224 kilometres to the north, and Alice Springs, 285 kilometres to the south, the Barrow Creek pub enjoyed a healthy trade. It had barely opened when gold was discovered at Tennant Creek, precipitating a rush that lasted for several years. Then, during the Second World War, the pub became the watering hole for an army camp thirty-two kilometres to the north. The telegraph station now doubled as a telephone exchange, and new wood and fibro-cement buildings were erected around the original stone outpost.

The Kaytetye played a part in these developments. They stayed around Barrow Creek – or Thangkenharenge, as they knew it – working in the construction industry and in the mines, building their dwellings around the pub and the telegraph compound. In time, they began to resume possession of their land. In August 2002, after years of lobbying, the Thangkenharenge Aboriginal Land Trust received the deeds to 12.5 hectares of land around the town, in a ceremony conducted at the old telegraph station.

I first heard about Barrow Creek in December 1997, when my husband, Clive, and I were travelling south on the Stuart Highway. We stopped for a late lunch at a Tennant Creek roadhouse, attracted by the large collection of road trains parked outside. We planned to continue to Barrow Creek, permanent population eight, and stay the night. But when we mentioned our plan, the staff and customers at Tennant Creek warned us to give 'Barrow' a wide berth.

'What's wrong with it?' I asked.

'It's a dreadful place. Rough as guts, missus,' a truckie said, looking at me as if I were some exotic plant who would wilt in an outback bar.

'Yeah,' someone else said, 'blackfellas everywhere, drunks hanging round the veranda – not a good place to spend the night.'

'The accommodation's pretty basic, too,' added the girl behind the counter as she handed us our mountainous steak sandwiches.

'I wouldn't stay there.'

'We camp most of the time,' I said. 'What's the camping area like?'

'Dangerous,' someone growled.

Back in the car, Clive mumbled through the tomato sauce.

'Better keep going to Gemtree. It's not much further – we can camp there instead.'

But we did stop off to visit the disued Barrow Creek telegraph station. When we opened the car doors, the heat hit us like a wall. It was about 46 degrees Celsius. Stony ground shimmered in the heat, and the silence was only occasionally fractured by screaming crows or the whoosh of a vehicle on the highway.

Carrying my little dog, because the ground was too hot for him, I walked over to the telegraph station. I peered through the small windows into the Spartan interior, imagining the isolation, the heat, the sheer hard labour the operators had endured.

The Northern Territory government had attempted to preserve the remnants of their labours, but it seemed to have made little headway. The buildings looked neglected, and there were traces of camping and squatting. Before the station was padlocked against unauthorised visitors, Aboriginal people had been drawn to the shade of the stone buildings. The newer timber and fibro-cement buildings were now a resource centre, a Community Council centre and Kaytetye dwelling places. The detritus of daily living was scattered about.

Huge stony buttes rose behind the settlement, overshadowing the site as we walked across to the low-walled graveyard. Our elongated shadows fell like caricatures across the graves of Stapleton and Franks, and I thought about those two men who had died so violently, with no family or friends to mourn them.

'It's so lonely,' I said. 'How must it have been then? How brave they were!'

'It's a big country, Rob,' Clive replied. 'Until you get out here, you have no real appreciation of how big it is. You could drive off the highway into the bush and be lost in half an hour.'

'Ugh! Let's get back to the car,' I replied. 'I'm starting to feel desiccated.'

We walked back to the car across smooth dark-red soil, streaked by wind gusts here and there. A group of drinkers lounged in the shade of a spindly tree. An old black woman with impossibly yellow hair watched, her eyes like currants pushed into her pleated face, as we slid into the air-conditioned comfort of our car. Then she returned to her beer, and we rejoined the highway.

'Do you want to go into the pub for a drink?' Clive asked. I replied, 'No, I don't think so. Let's push on.'

I've often regretted that we didn't stop. But we had no inkling then of what an important place Barrow Creek pub would become in a few years' time.

◆ ◆ ◆

The Stuart Highway today is a well-travelled route. There are semitrailer drivers earning their living; 'grey nomads' spending their super funds pulling caravans around Australia; fast cars carrying people in a hurry; dusty utes full of panting dogs and middle-aged tools; and slow old vans bearing backpackers on the well-worn tour around Oz.

Joanne Lees and her boyfriend Peter Falconio were two of the many young travellers on working holidays in Australia. Peter came from a large, close-knit family of Italian descent, and had recently graduated from Brighton University with a degree in building and construction management. Joanne and her younger brother had been brought up by her mother, Jennifer, and stepfather Vincent James. Joanne was twenty-seven when they left England, and Peter was twenty-eight. They had met in their home town of Huddersfield, and Joanne had left home to be with Peter in Hove, near Brighton, while he worked as a building contractor and completed his university degree.

Joanne was pretty and vivacious, and seemed very much in love with Peter. After he disappeared, she said, 'Pete was my best friend. He meant the world to me, really. Because I lived away from my family, he had to be everything – family, boyfriend, best friend. He's the nicest person I've ever met.' They made a handsome couple.

Long before they embarked on their 'world trip' in November 2000, they had discussed every place they wanted to visit. Joanne worked at Thomas Cook, the English travel company, and did most of the planning. Their first stop was Kathmandu, where they spent a few days trekking. They next toured South-east Asia – Singapore, Malaysia, Thailand and Cambodia – before going on to Sydney, where they spent six months working to finance the next leg of their travels.

Joanne took a job at Dymocks bookstore in the centre of Sydney. The manager, Gary Sullivan, said, 'She was very attractive and popular, and soon became almost like the social organiser for all the staff.' Meanwhile, Peter found work at January Design, a furniture factory that assembled imported Italian components into upmarket office furniture. His workmates remember him as a 'lovely chap', fastidious about his work and easy to get on with.

Peter and Joanne both quickly made friends and adapted to the casual lifestyle of Australia's backpacking community. They socialised together and separately, according to several of their friends. It seems Joanne threw herself into the Sydney scene. She met with a circle of friends for coffee breaks at Earl's Café behind Dymocks, drank with Peter and others at the nearby Angel Bar and partied at clubs, pubs and nightclubs.

Paul Dale, who worked with Peter at January Design, describes him as 'a loyal, trusting guy who liked to party hard. Both him and Jo liked to party really hard – it was hard to keep up with them. I'd have to leave to go home because I was trashed, but they'd carry on. They were not what I'd describe as addictive people, but they did take pills and they enjoyed life.'

Joanne had fallen in love with Sydney and was reluctant to move on. 'I was really settled in Sydney and didn't want to leave,' she said later. 'It was Pete – he bought the camper van. I really didn't want to leave.'

Paul Dale told me Peter was restless. 'He didn't want to get stuck in Sydney. He reckoned Australia was a big place and he wanted to see as much as possible while they were here. He had plans to drive across through Adelaide to Western Australia, up through the Kimberley and back through Darwin and down the centre.'

In May 2001, Peter and Joanne headed off in an ancient orange Kombi camper van with a white pop-top, bought from another adventurer for $1200. Paul Dale and Peter had spent their weekends working on the Kombi, replacing the lining panels, rewiring the lighting and putting in new shelves. But Paul was still dubious about the van. 'The Kombi was way underpowered for the trip Pete had planned,' he told me. 'And he was the wrong kind of engineer to be good with automotive stuff. But we turned that old van from being really cruddy into something pretty comfy.'

In spite of their refinements, it did not turn out to be a good investment.

◆ ◆ ◆

The couple's first stop was Canberra, the national capital. From there, they visited Katoomba in the Blue Mountains before embarking on the long haul through Melbourne and Adelaide to Coober Pedy, Ayers Rock, Kings Canyon and Alice Springs. They kept in regular contact with Peter's family, sending postcards along the way. The one Peter sent from Coober Pedy, received only days before he disappeared, read:

> *'Dear Mum,*
> *We are currently in Coober Pedy. Then we are on up to Ayers*
> *Rock and Alice Springs and Broome. The weather has been*
> *cold ...'*

They travelled part of the way in company with a hitchhiking couple, Canadian backpacker Izabelle Jetee and her partner. On 10 July, they arrived in Alice Springs. After dropping their hitchhikers at Melanka Lodge, a backpackers' hostel, Peter and Joanne parked their Kombi nearby, in a quiet street, where they planned to camp. Then they went into town to do a bit of essential washing and send emails home. Peter also found time to submit his income tax return. During their four-night stay in Alice, Peter and Joanne spent most of their evenings partying at Melanka Lodge until late.

Unlike its owners, the Kombi was feeling its age. Its performance had been worrying Peter on their drive up from Adelaide. Soon after arriving in Alice Springs, they went to Alice Auto Craft in Railway Terrace to have the most urgent repairs done.

Joanne stayed in the van while Peter went in and spoke to mechanic Rod Smith. Rod's reddish-haired dog greeted Peter as he approached.

'Nice dog,' Peter said, bending to give him a pat. 'What kind is he?'

'He's a blue heeler – cattle dog,' Rod told him. 'Everyone has one up here.' He explained that Australians often called red-haired dogs (and people) by the nickname 'Blue'.

'Heelers are trained to chase cattle, but they don't usually bite, because a bite can do a hamstring on a cow,' he said. 'They're not big barkers either, because barking can stampede a mob of cattle. There are blue-grey ones too,' he went on, 'but they are called Queensland heelers, not blue.'

All this seemed to confuse Peter, who began listing the Kombi's ills. The engine was leaking oil and missing badly, making the van backfire and lurch from time to time. Rod lifted the rear hatch and peered in at the engine.

'The exhaust system's probably stuffed – that's why it's back firing,' he told Peter. He checked the odometer. 'It's got nearly 90,000 miles [just under 145,000 kilometres] on the clock, and that's probably the second go around. It's twenty years old, after all.' He moved around to the front.

'And who's tied that bit of rope around the tie rod? Don't tell me you got towed using that as an anchor point?'

'No, another mechanic did that. We've had trouble with it on the way here,' Peter told him.

'Doesn't sound like much of a mechanic. Anyway, if you bring it back first thing in the morning, I'll have a go at it for you.'

'How much will it cost?' Peter asked, mindful of every penny.

'Oh, a hundred and five dollars should get you out of trouble. How far are you going?'

'Darwin,' Peter told him cheerfully.

'I wouldn't risk it if I were you. It's a long way between garages.'

They brought the van back the next morning. 'Come back later on today and it'll be ready,' Rod said. 'Just leave it over there, will you, next to that ute?'

After parking the Kombi, Joanne and Peter went off to look around town. When they returned, Rod noticed that Joanne was in a huff. 'She stomped off to the van and got in the passenger side, slamming the door as she got in,' he told me later. 'He was very cranky and surly and just asked for the bill.'

Rod handed him a bill for $115. 'I changed over your fan belt, mate,' he told Peter. 'It was completely buggered. I don't reckon you would've got out of Alice with the old one. It was only ten bucks, so I just did it.'

'You shouldn't have done that without asking,' Peter told him crossly. 'I shouldn't have to pay for that if it wasn't part of the quote. How do I know it was no good?'

'Look, mate, if that's the way you feel I'll take the friggin' thing off and put the old one back on,' Rod retorted. He started across the workshop to retrieve the worn-out fan belt.

'Oh, all right, I'll pay it,' Peter told him. 'I just don't like people taking advantage.'

'Like I said, mate, I don't reckon that van would've made it out of Alice with the old fan belt – and I'm willing to take a bet now you'll never make it to Darwin.'

The next day, Friday 13 July, Peter phoned his family and Paul Dale, saying he was having the time of his life and was planning to 'go up-country' next day.

He told Paul that he'd cancelled the planned trip to the Kimberley, as he was not sure that the Kombi was reliable enough to take on the isolated roads. Instead, they planned to head north. As they were now taking a more-direct route, they thought they might have a few weeks in Sydney before leaving Australia on the next leg of their trip.

On Saturday 14 July, the annual Camel Cup was run at Blatherskite Park. It was a hot, dusty day, and the roar of the crowd almost drowned out the thunder of camel hooves as the winners crossed the makeshift finishing line with loping, ungainly strides. The event was attended by just about everyone in Alice Springs. Locals and tourists mingled together, out for an afternoon's fun and a few beers. Some of the spectators' photos and amateur videos captured Joanne and Peter as faces in the crowd.

Joanne described that afternoon and all that followed in an interview with Martin Bashir on Britain's ITV1 a year later.

'We decided to stop at the camel races on the way out of town. It reminded me of the galas we used to have in my home town.'

It was quite a detour. Peter and Joanne were planning to head north toward Tennant Creek, but Blatherskite Park is south of Alice Springs, on the road in from Adelaide. They left before the Cup events finished, but far too late to reach Tennant Creek in daylight.

Joanne continued, 'I drove between Alice Springs and Ti Tree. Pete was asleep. We drove into a small community, listening to music as I drove. There was a petrol station and a lay-by, so I decided to stop. We recorded the purchase and our mileage in the log. We kept a record of all our petrol and mileage.'

It was 6.22 pm when they bought the petrol at Ti Tree, 195 kilometres from Alice Springs. This suggests that they had set off at about 4 pm, well before the camel races finished, but a very unusual time to begin a long journey in a mechanically dodgy van on a remote, unfamiliar road frequented by feral cattle and suicidal kangaroos.

Chapter Two

JOANNE'S STORY

Mate, this is about as true as it gets.

Vince Millar

D ark descends quickly in Central Australia, and the sense of isolation at night is difficult to convey. Beyond the highway outside the Ti Tree roadhouse, the sun was melting into the red-ochre desert.

Joanne told Martin Bashir that she and Peter had coffee and watched the sunset. 'It was very spectacular,' she said.

When they left, Peter took over the driving. There were hardly any other cars.

'Just as we were leaving Ti Tree, there was a fire beside the road. Pete swerved and then said we should go back and put it out. I didn't want to. I had a strange feeling … there's bushfires and fires beside the road, but that [fire] seemed to be lit deliberately. I had a bad feeling – I can't explain it.'

From Ti Tree, it was ninety kilometres to Barrow Creek, then another 225 kilometres to Tennant Creek. The only stop between those two settlements is the Wycliffe Wells roadhouse, a surreal place famous for UFO 'sightings'.

The highway stretches out of sight, two lanes bordered by rough gravel. On each side are stunted mulga trees and clumps of needle-sharp spinifex grass. In search of anything more interesting than spinifex, the local cattle often roam across the road. They are a deadly traffic hazard, especially for vehicles travelling at high speed. There's no contest between a small sedan and a 500-kilo cow. It's like hitting a brick wall. Bloated cattle hit by road trains lie along the highway verges. The stink of their decomposition is sucked in by the air conditioning long before the carcasses appear.

There is no speed limit in the Northern Territory, and cars travel at up to 160 kilometres per hour. After dark, kangaroos hop across the bitumen and are dazzled by the high-beam headlights.

Huge pupils glow momentarily; the animal freezes, or jumps erratically at the last instant, often colliding with the car. Kangaroo bodies too litter the roadsides, lying swollen and scavenged by predators. Although tourists sometimes brave the highway's hazards, Territorians rarely drive at night.

Joanne recalled that after Ti Tree, 'Pete kept driving, I'd change CDs, feed Pete sweets. Occasionally I'd point out kangaroos darting across the road and he'd slow down. It was pitch black.' The moon had not yet risen.

Some time after 7 pm, they passed Barrow Creek. On their right, the pub was lit up, brimming with locals and visitors who had gathered to watch the big Rugby Union match between the Australian Wallabies and the British Lions being played in Sydney that night. Territorians take their sport (and the accompanying beer-drinking) very seriously. Joanne said they did not stop, but continued up the highway.

She says they saw no other cars until Peter told her someone was behind them. He said a car had been following them for some time, although Joanne had not noticed it.

It was about 7.30 pm, and they were eleven kilometres past the Barrow Creek pub. Joanne told Martin Bashir what happened next. 'Pete slowed down and said, "I wish this car would just overtake us." Then the car pulled alongside. The interior light was on. I could see a man and his dog. He was pointing at the back of our vehicle and motioning to us to stop. Again, I didn't want to stop, but Pete loved his camper van so much and we'd had trouble with it before, so we stopped.

'I got a clear view of the man. He was forty-plus, a local man, I would say. It was a four-wheel-drive utility truck.'

Peter stopped, and the truck parked behind them. Peter got out, taking his cigarettes, and spoke to the other driver. They were standing at the back of the Kombi, between the two vehicles. Peter told Joanne to wait in the van.

'It was cold. I was in shorts and a T-shirt,' she said. 'Pete came back and told me to rev the engine, so I moved to the driver's seat. He said everything was OK. Pete said to the man, "Cheers, mate, thanks for stopping." I could hear them talking in friendly tones. He sounded like a nice man.'

But she remained uneasy. She caught glimpses of the man – through the window or in the rear-vision mirror, she didn't say – and made eye contact. 'I felt nervous again as I looked in his eyes. I can't explain it. He was taller than Pete, about six feet, not particularly broad, but bigger than me. The man said sparks had been flying the whole time he'd been following.'

What happened next has been the subject of countless speculations.

As Joanne described it, the man and Peter stood on the gravel verge, looking at the engine while she revved it. It is not known whether the four-wheel drive's headlights were on or off, although it is likely they were on, to enable the men to identify the problem. Joanne said she heard a 'bang' that sounded like a backfire.

She stopped revving the engine and turned to the window beside her. The man was standing outside the driver's door, his right hand holding a handgun pointed at her head. He looked 'very big and very calm'. He started to open the door.

'Switch off the engine and move over,' he said. She was frozen with fear and couldn't move. He told her again to switch off the engine, but eventually he reached in and did it himself. Joanne was shaking too much to turn the key.

'Move over to the passenger side, put your head down and your hands behind your back,' he said. She remained where she was.

He repeated his instruction roughly, this time putting the gun to her head. Joanne realised that resistance was futile. The man got into the cabin, pushing her across to the passenger's seat. She did not say if he was holding anything other than the gun.

She couldn't understand why Peter didn't come to her rescue. She was calling his name desperately, expecting him to appear and save her from this nightmare. The man pushed her out of the car onto the ground, and this made her livid with anger.

She said, 'He tried to tie my feet together. I kicked and kicked and kicked and he couldn't do that so he hit me, threw a punch to the right side of my face. I was stunned, thinking I'm going to die. Where's Pete? This is over.'

While she lay on the ground the man bound her hands behind her back with four cable ties, one around each wrist, held together with two more linked in the middle. He tried to put silver duct tape across her mouth, but she swung her head around frantically, and the tape wound around her neck and into her hair instead. He gave up and dragged her to his vehicle, lifted up the side of the canopy, got a sack out and put the sack over her head. He then pushed her through the passenger door.

Then, for some reason, the man left her there and went around the side of the vehicle. Questions raced through her mind. Where was Pete? What was that bang? Could Pete have been shot? What did the man want? Was he after money? Was he going to rape her?

She told police the next day that she decided on a desperate attempt to escape. She managed to get the bag off her head, wriggle through a space between the bucket seats and across the tray of the utility, and drop over the tailboard onto the road.

Six months later, she recounted a different version of these events to Martin Bashir. She said that, when she was sitting with the bag over her head, she told the gunman she couldn't breathe.

'I don't know if he let the sack come off, but it did. His dog was there, which didn't make a sound. And he pulled me and grabbed me and pushed me into the back of his vehicle, which had some sort of bed in there.'

Then the man went around the side of his vehicle. He seemed distracted. She kept shouting, 'What have you done to Pete? Is he hurt?' The man told her to shut up or he'd kill her.

She decided to make a break for it. 'I thought: this is it. This is my chance. I'm going! And just slid down the truck, down the base to the tail, jumped out and then just ran into the bush.'

She ran into the darkness with terror-driven speed. 'I couldn't see anything. I knew he was behind me – I could hear him behind me. I tripped over a few times. I knew I couldn't outrun him so I just crawled into a bush and hid. I didn't go very far – thirty to forty metres. I had no energy left to run. My hands were still tied behind my back.' In the desert silence, every move she made seemed to produce a deafening noise. She could hear her heart beating.

'I heard his footsteps crunching the branches and I saw the torch – very close – he came past me three or four times, shone the torch above me in the trees. I put my face into my knees and covered my legs with my hair and held my breath. He was three to four metres away, maybe closer. I've no idea why he didn't find me. I just believe someone was looking out for me that night.

'I heard the man drive away in our van. I thought, he's going, he's leaving, just wait. I just waited, but then I heard him come back on foot. I remember thinking, is this ever going to end?'

He was slamming the doors of his truck, and seemed to be dragging something heavy. She thought it might be Peter, maybe being dragged into the bush near her. At last she heard the vehicle drive away. 'I really wanted to come out, but didn't,' she said. 'I didn't know what to do. So I thought it's best to just stay there hidden really well. I felt safe in my little hiding place.

'I was too scared to move. I was in agony, with my hands tied behind my back and my head between my knees. I'd been like that for hours … All the time I just thought Pete was close by and injured and I just wanted to get to him and get help.'

At last a sliver of moon rose, producing enough light for Joanne to see the white line marking the edge of the highway. It was now early morning; moonrise that night was 12.23 am. Joanne crept out, crossed the road and hid in a clump of grass near the verge. Both the Kombi and the four-wheel drive had vanished, and there was no sign of Peter.

She lay listening to the sporadic sound of passing vehicles until she heard the unmistakable roar of a road train. 'I picked that truck because it was the only truck that I'd seen go past. I hoped that it wouldn't be the man, that they'd be working people, lorry drivers ... I ran alongside it and I thought it wasn't going to stop, but it did.'

◆ ◆ ◆

Vince Millar was a truckie with more than sixteen years' experience driving big rigs. On Saturday 14 July, he left Darwin at 4 am, in a Bull's Transport road train – a prime mover and three trailers. The rig was about fifty metres long, and fully loaded it weighed about 140 tonnes. It was fitted with a speed governor, which limited its speed to eighty-five kilometres per hour. His co-driver, Rod Adams, was not his usual partner. They took turns to drive, about three to four hours each. They also had to follow strict rules about log keeping, taking rests at prescribed times and not driving for more than twelve hours in twenty-four.

Vince said in his police statement, 'We had arrived at Tennant Creek at approximately 8 pm, where Rod and I had to unload a pan. We left at about 8.30 pm. I was driving and Rod was asleep in the back. We were due to change over at Barrow Creek.'

Vince knew every landmark along the Darwin–Adelaide run, because he drove it every week. They had just passed the sign marking 300 kilometres to Alice Springs when Joanne jumped out on the road.

After untying her and hearing her story, Vince helped her up into the cabin of his truck. Then he walked back to Rod.

'What are we gunna do, mate?' Vince asked.

Before Rod could answer, Joanne began crying, 'I want my boyfriend. I want Pete.'

'We better go and have a look,' Vince decided. 'Just in case he's hurt or somethin'.'

Rod agreed. 'Yeah, we can unhook the prime mover and go back to where she says it happened, I suppose. Have a bit of a look around.'

Vince moved the rig to the side of the road, then jumped out to help Rod uncouple the trailers. Joanne sat quietly between the two men while Vince did a U-turn and headed back to where he had found her.

Vince spotted a pile of dirt near the white line at the side of the highway. 'Is this where it happened?' he asked.

'I'm not really sure,' Joanne whispered.

He stopped and peered through the windscreen. There was a freshly dug hole beyond the gravel verge, and the dirt from the hole seemed to have been piled about ten centimetres high over something dark on the road.

'Don't know what that is,' he said as he moved off. Privately, he thought it might be blood. 'There's nothing else here. We'll go up the road a bit and have a look round.'

Joanne said, 'I heard the Kombi start up and drive off. I want to find my car.'

She was insistent, so Vince thought he'd do a bit more looking. About 400 metres further north, Vince spotted a track on their left, leading into the bush, with recent marks from a single set of car tyres.

'Hullo, whaddaya reckon that is? Let's go have a look.' He drove about 200 metres on loose dirt, following the tracks, which came to a skidding halt at a wire gate.

'Don't get us bogged out here, mate, or we'll be lost,' Rod said. 'Looks like he's chucked a uey here,' Vince guessed. 'But where's the f--kin' Kombi?'

They peered into the dark, but could see nothing. The big prime mover was awkward to manoeuvre on the narrow track.

'Maybe Pete's in the Kombi. The man might have put him in the Kombi,' Joanne said quietly.

'Where do you think he is?'

'I haven't seen him since the gunshot at the back of the car.'

'What f--kin' gunshot?' Vince demanded. 'What makes you think he's got a gun, this bloke?'

'Because he held it to my head before he tied me up.'

In all the excitement, this was the first time that Vince had registered the fact that the attacker had a gun.

'This is f--kin' stupid!' he said. 'What are we doin' drivin' around here in the f--kin' dark, maybe muckin' up evidence with me wheels? That bastard might still be out there, runnin' around wavin' his gun. Darlin', let's get the ball rollin'. We need to get to the cop shop.'

He looked at his watch. They'd already wasted nearly an hour.

Once they got moving, Rod Adams turned to Joanne. 'What's your name, anyway?'

'Jo.'

Rod said, 'Hi, Jo. I'm Rod, and that's Vince.'

The girl turned to Vince. 'Hi, I'm Jo.' Vince got the feeling she was trying hard not to cry.

Vince returned to his trailers, and the men hitched them up. 'We're going to have to take you down to Alice,' Vince told her.

'I think I saw a police station at Ti Tree,' she told him.

'OK. We'll go there, then.'

Joanne sat quietly, hunched over, occasionally murmuring 'I want Pete.' Once she said, 'I want my mum.' Vince felt a bit tearful himself at that point.

At Barrow Creek, the pub was still lit up. A few diehards were commiserating about Australia's loss to England in the Rugby. Vince looked at his watch. It was 1.45 am. 'Might as well take her here,' he said.

'We're best off going to Ti Tree,' Rod argued. 'There's at least a police station there.'

'He'll probably be in bed,' Vince said. 'I'll go in and ring him up.' 'If you ring him up, we'll have to stay here all f--kin' night.'

Joanne did not want to go in. Vince got out, telling her to stay in the cab with Rod. 'I'm gunna go inside and sort things out,' he said.

Les Pilton, the Barrow Creek publican, looked up as Vince burst in. Les was a bit of a legend along the Stuart Highway. Quite a small man, with a developing paunch and a big smile, he ran the Barrow Creek pub with easy-going authority.

'We've got a girl in the truck with us. She's been in a bad blue,' Vince told him as he approached the bar. 'We've gotta get her inside and get on to the cops.'

Mindful of the stragglers in the bar, Vince lowered his voice to tell Les the story. He described the pile of dirt on the road. 'I think it was covering some blood, mate,' he confided.

'Oh, go on,' Les scoffed, peering out at the truck. 'I've heard some tall tales, but this is laying it on a bit thick.'

Eventually, Les agreed to phone the Ti Tree police station. The answering machine took the call.

'Bugger,' Vince said. 'I knew the bastard'd be in bed.'

'Ring Alice, then,' Les advised. It was now about 2 am. The remaining drinkers had drifted off, leaving Les and Vince alone.

Alice Springs and Tennant Creek were both at least two-and-a-half hours' drive away. Vince called Alice Springs and told his story to the constable on duty.

'You fair dinkum, mate?' the constable asked.

'Mate, this is about as true as it gets,' Vince reassured him.

The constable told Vince to wait by the phone while he got a senior officer. Between calls, Vince ducked out the back to wake Cathy Curly, a girl he knew who worked in the bar, and ask her to take care of Joanne.

After a bit of phoning back and forth for additional details, Senior Sergeant Geoff Sullivan, the newly designated Search Master, told Vince to wait at Barrow Creek until someone arrived. Vince, Rod and Joanne should stay exactly as they were, Sullivan said – no changing clothes, washing or anything that might destroy evidence.

Unfortunately, this instruction came too late. Rod Adams had recently completed a first-aid course, and without saying anything to anyone, he had used alcohol and Betadine from the truck's first-aid kit to clean Joanne's grazes.

When Les walked out to the truck at around 2.30 am to persuade Joanne to come inside, he found her hunched over her knees, still perched on the engine casing.

'Why don't you come along in?' Les said. 'We'll look after you. Come on, love. We've called the cops – now let's get you warmed up. You must be freezin'.'

Eventually Joanne allowed herself to be led towards the pub. On her way in, she almost tripped over a canvas mailbag that was leaning against the steps. In the bar, the overhead fans gently stirred the stink of beer and sweat, and the smoke was thick enough to rest your elbows on. Rod propped Joanne up on an empty bar stool.

The bar had a jokey-blokey feel. The walls were decorated with old clothes, male and female, interspersed with photos and smart-aleck graffiti. Travellers' cards, army memorabilia, letters, notices and poems were attached in layers, yellowing at the bottom and fresh-inked on the top. Bras of various cup sizes hung from the ceiling, seemingly attached by thick cobwebs. Along the shelves behind the bar were various poisonous reptiles, preserved in jars of alcohol to embellish tall tales.

Joanne started to shiver. Vince went back to his truck and pulled out the blue sloppy jumper he wore on long cold hauls.

'Here, put this on,' he told her when he came back. She pulled it on over her T-shirt.

Les offered Joanne a nice stiff drink, but she said she'd rather have a cup of tea. Cathy Curly arrived in time to hear this and went out to the kitchen to boil a kettle. Rod went back to the truck to get some sleep. It was his turn to drive, and he assumed they'd be leaving soon after the police arrived – if they came.

Around this time, a police officer from Alice Springs rang, wanting to get details from Joanne. After a short conversation, she hung up, indicating that she didn't think the police believed her story.

Les stoked up the fire and settled her down in front of it with a hot, sweet cup of tea. When she had finished, he shepherded her into a nearby room to lie down.

'The cops can't get here any quicker than they can get here,' Les told her with impeccable outback logic. 'You get a bit of rest.' She asked him to leave the door open and the light on.

Les went back to tidy up the bar. The chinking of china and glass punctuated the silence of the deserted pub. When he went to check on Joanne, she was lying on the pale blue chenille bedspread, one arm thrown across her forehead, eyes shut, tears sliding into her hair.

'I want Peter,' he heard her sigh.

Chapter Three

THE FORCES ASSEMBLE

That piece in the pool room, her boyfriend's been murdered.
Cathy Curly, Barrow Creek Hotel, 15 July 2001

The phone calls from the Barrow Creek pub signalled the beginning of what Northern Territory Police Commissioner Brian Bates would later call 'the most puzzling case ever'. From Alice Springs, the police called stations all over the Territory and summoned all available Aboriginal Police personnel in the outlying Aboriginal communities.

Before leaving Alice Springs, Geoff Sullivan strapped on his sidearm and took a pump-action shotgun from the locked cupboard. For all he knew, there was a crazed gunman lying in ambush somewhere in the bush.

The Ti Tree police were woken by the shrilling of their phones and ordered to block the highway going across the South Australian border near Kulgera, almost 600 kilometres south. The two officers struggled into their uniforms, buckled on their side-arms, took their rifles and hit the road.

'What are we looking for?' one asked the other.

'No idea, mate. Awaiting further instructions. S'pose we stop every vehicle until we get more info.'

'Why don't they send the Alice Springs mob? They're much closer.'

'Dunno. They're heading north, I think.'

'Oh, right. That makes sense,' his partner replied sarcastically.

The constable in a small Aboriginal community near Katherine was woken and told to stop anyone attempting to leave the Territory on the

Victoria Highway. His partner turned over in her sleep and said, 'Don't be back late.' They were supposed to be in Katherine later that day for the town's seventy-fifth anniversary celebrations. He would be gone for the next three days.

Police were alerted all along the Stuart Highway, and roadblocks were in place within a couple of hours. Quick response is the golden rule for any investigation. Homicides are best solved within the first twenty-four hours. After that, leads become cold, little mutations of facts occur, witness statements become contaminated by others' versions, and things get 'tidied up' or put away. In this case, the gunman already had a head start and a vast area in which to lose himself and evade his pursuers.

Some locals were critical of the police response. According to one, no use was made of the police at Yuendumu on the Tanami Track, a four-wheel-drive track that runs across the desert from twenty-one kilometres north of Alice Springs to near Fitzroy Crossing in Western Australia. 'They were on stand-by for hours but not deployed until some ridiculous time later.' Elsewhere on the Track, police did not alert the security staff at the Granites mine or the publican at Rabbit Flats roadhouse, the most isolated pub in Australia.

Ted Egan, the well-known Australian folk singer from Alice Springs, was stopped by police on his way back from Camooweal, just over the Queensland border. 'At Avon Downs I was stopped by a roadblock manned by Queensland police. They told me, "There's been a bit of trouble at Barrow Creek. Are you a local?" I explained who I was and showed my ID. "Well, watch out on the road," they told me.' He drove past Barkly Homestead roadhouse and stayed overnight at Three Ways, north of Tennant Creek, but saw no police at either of those places. He woke at 4 am and drove through Tennant Creek without being stopped.

'I drove straight past Barrow Creek, noticing a fair bit of activity there, but the first police I saw were at Ti Tree, stopping everyone, armed to the teeth with guns and rifles. A policeman told me,

"Someone's been shot at Barrow Creek." I explained I had to get through to an appointment, and another officer said, "That's Ted Egan", so they let me through.'

Later reports criticised the delay in getting roadblocks established, the seemingly disorganised use of resources, and the overlooking of smaller exits from the highway that could have been used by someone escaping in a four-wheel-drive vehicle. To be fair, though, more than six hours had passed before the police were alerted, and it was several more hours before they had a description of their suspect. By the time the constables from Ti Tree arrived at Kulgera, they knew what to look out for – but by then the gunman could have been a thousand kilometres from the crime scene.

◆ ◆ ◆

Time dragged at the Barrow Creek pub while everyone waited for the police to arrive. Joanne had been unable to sleep and had returned to the safety of the main bar. Cathy offered to take her to the bathroom to freshen up a bit. In the corridor, they were greeted by Cathy's dog, Tex. 'What sort of dog is he?' Joanne asked, staring at the chunky, speckled dog with a black patch over each eye.

'He's a blue heeler,' Cathy told her. 'Crossed with a staffie. Looks more heeler, though.'

'Is he friendly?' Joanne asked.

'Oh, yeah – he wouldn't hurt anyone.'

Joanne bent to fondle the dog and said quietly, 'I can't believe this is happening to me.'

They gave Joanne's face, hands and legs a wash and returned to the bar.

'Can I get you anything?' Cathy asked.

'A cup of tea,' Joanne answered, without any please or thank you. 'Stuck-up bitch,' Cathy grumbled as she went to make the tea.

Meanwhile, Les had gone up to his house to wake his partner, Helen Jones. Helen had come to Barrow Creek as a tourist some years earlier after her husband died. She fell in love with the place, and with Les, and stayed.

As soon as she heard what had happened, she pulled on some clothes and rushed down to the pub to help. Joanne was sitting on a two-seater couch near the pool table, watching Cathy walk to and fro, making tea and toast for Vince and the others. Joanne's feet were bare.

'Oh, your feet must be frozen!' Helen said. 'I'll get you some warm socks.'

She went back home and returned with some thick white sports socks. As she helped Joanne put them on, Helen noticed that apart from a couple of fresh grazes on Joanne's knees, her legs were free of scratches and cuts and her feet were not cut or bruised. 'Not a mark on them,' she would say later. In fact, the few visible signs of her ordeal were hidden by Vince's jumper.

'She was quiet, a bit distant, almost off-hand about the whole thing,' Helen recalled later. 'Although she did seem frightened about being left alone.'

About 5 am, the police began to arrive. A sergeant took Vince Millar aside and asked him to describe what had happened. Helen went to wake Rita and Rick, the other hotel staff.

Rita, a well-travelled outbacker in her fifties, emerged to find the pub full of police. She walked through the pool room to help Cathy in the kitchen, and recoiled at the sight of the pool table covered with guns.

Joanne was still sitting on the couch. Rita smiled at her and said, 'Hi.' Joanne seemed to look straight through her.

'What's going on?' Rita asked Cathy.

'Someone's been murdered. That piece in the pool room, her boyfriend's been murdered.'

'Go on! She doesn't look it. She don't have a hair out of place!'

'Yeah,' Cathy agreed. 'If it was my boyfriend ...' She left Rita pondering as she sailed off with the first of many servings of bacon and eggs.

In the bar, Les briefed Rick.

'The poor girl!' Rick said. 'I'll check her out, see if she needs anything to calm her down.' He made his way to the pool room and sat beside Joanne, but she didn't want his help, so he left her to herself.

A police officer came and told Joanne they would need all her clothes, underclothes included. She protested, as she had no others.

Helen took Joanne to her house and found her a black-and-white flannelette shirt, a pair of tracksuit pants and some thongs. Rita, who was about Joanne's size, found her some underwear. All Joanne's clothes were bagged and tagged and kept safe for the forensic pathologist, Carmen Eckhoff, who was expected to arrive from Darwin later that day.

The police hierarchy sorted itself out, with the most important police interviewing the most important witnesses. The pub phone on the wall was in constant demand. Denise Hurley, head of the police media unit in Darwin, was alerted; at 7.45 am she issued a media release, warning drivers not to travel through the Territory that day, and announcing that there had been an incident at Barrow Creek involving two tourists and an armed and dangerous offender. This was picked up by the media, and soon the phones were ringing in the police media units in Darwin and Alice Springs.

Joanne had by now described her attacker and his vehicle. Her description was sent to all police stations and radioed to the officers who were speeding to establish roadblocks:

- *Alert to all stations. Abducted: two tourists, by offender believed to be armed. The alleged offender is described as:*
  - *forty-to-forty-five years, possibly older*
  - *dark, straight hair to the shoulder with grey streaks*
  - *long thin face*
  - *droopy grey moustache with corners tapering down below mouth*
  - *heavy bags under his eyes*

- *medium build*
- *deep voice, Australian accent.*

He is believed to be wearing:

- *black baseball cap with motif on front (yellow colouring on motif)*
- *dark T-shirt with long-sleeved [shirt with] small black and white checks over top*
- *heavy jeans or canvas-like pants.*

He is believed to be travelling:

- *in a white four-wheel-drive utility with bucket seats*
- *the utility has canvas on the back with clear open space at its rear with possibly a blue heeler dog.*

This information was sent out to the media at 10.45 am. There was an unusually large contingent of senior journalists in the Territory that day because a Territory election was imminent, and Prime Minister John Howard was due to arrive to drum up support for his party's candidates. Soon hire cars and chartered choppers full of journalists were heading for the much more interesting story at the Barrow Creek pub.

At Barrow Creek, the police put a protective cordon around the pub in case the gunman was still nearby. A group of police headed north to look for the location of the incident, following Vince's directions. By now, Vince had gone more than thirty hours without sleep. Rod was still sleeping inside the rig, but Vince couldn't get a minute to himself. Joanne had been isolated in the pool room until she could make a full statement. Helen was looking after her, doing a passable imitation of a mother hen.

After about three-quarters of an hour, the search party returned. 'They can't find a thing, Vince. You'll have to go out and show them,' one of the police told him.

Reluctantly, Vince put down his sixth or seventh coffee and went out to the waiting police car. He took them to the 300-kilometre marker on the southbound side of the road.

'I was just past this,' he told them. Then he saw the track. 'Hey, that's where we went down lookin' for her van.' The three cars slewed to a halt and everyone peered along the track.

'There it is!' Vince yelled. 'Off to the left, along the fence line. I can see the white top. She said it had a white pop-top.'

Drawing their guns, the officers formed a line across the dirt track. They told Vince to stay back and squat behind one of the cars. The police started advancing carefully, then froze when Geoff Sullivan called out 'Stop!'

'Who has the car keys?' he called out.

Someone patted his pocket and held them up. 'Here, sir.'

'Give them to Vince,' Sullivan ordered. 'Now, Vince, you keep your head down. If there's any trouble, jump in the car and drive like the clappers back to Barrow Creek and raise the alarm.'

Vince was beginning to feel he'd wandered onto the set of a horror movie. He wasn't sure he'd be able to drive the police car if shots did ring out. Every boy's dream – to drive a speeding cop car – and he'd probably be shaking too much to find the bloody ignition. Crouching down, he peered through the car windows, watching the police advance. *The gunman must have driven along the fence line*, he thought. *That's why I couldn't get the van in the headlights last night. Too much of an angle on the truck.* He wondered if Pete was inside. *Hope the poor bastard didn't bleed to death in the night*, he thought. *I'd never forgive myself.*

From the lack of excitement when the police reached the van, Vince could tell Peter was not there. In one sense, he was relieved. *She never saw his body*, Vince told himself. *Maybe he's still alive.*

Two police stayed to wrap crime-scene tape around the trees surrounding the Kombi while the remaining officers returned to the cars and drove slowly south, searching for the place of the alleged attack.

Vince peered along the highway. 'There!' he said. 'See that flat patch of dirt on that other side? I saw that last night. Looked a bit suss to me.'

They pulled over and gathered around the pile of dirt, which was flattened out to the size of an irregularly shaped dinner plate.

'It was about five inches high last night,' Vince said. 'It's been run over by traffic. I shoulda got out and looked at it, but she was more worried about findin' her van.' He pointed at a fresh disturbance beyond the gravel verge. 'See that twisty sort of hole where he's dug the dirt from?'

The police conferred. 'Looks like blood under there,' said one. Others agreed. Two more police remained at the spot, and the rest returned to Barrow Creek.

Vince was keen to get back on the road. 'I got refrigeration on me rig,' he said. 'Me boss'll be spewin' if the stuff gets spoiled. We're f--kin' late, mate.'

At the pub, the police held a huddled conference.

'She could be telling the truth,' the searchers told those who'd stayed behind. 'The Kombi's there and there's blood on the road. Someone's tried to disguise it.'

'Well that's something,' said someone else. 'We've all been thinking she must've just seen Brad Pitt in *The Mexican*.'

Everyone laughed nervously. 'Why?' asked Sergeant Sullivan.

'Well, sir, it's the descriptions. A real 'baddie', just like in *The Mexican*, and even the gun she's described is a dead ringer for the pistol in the movie – got a fancy handle with whorls on it, like a typical pearl-handled revolver. Who'd carry something like that in the outback?'

'Well, whatever happened out there, we have a victim in the next room, there's blood on the road, and we have a possible homicide to investigate. Let's get on with it.'

Geoff Sullivan took Joanne aside and told her quietly that there was a strong possibility that she would not see Peter alive. She became very upset. 'How am I going to tell Peter's family about this?' she sobbed.

Rod Adams and Vince were finally allowed to leave, after being fingerprinted and providing DNA swabs. Vince also gave a written statement. Gratefully, he crawled into the sleeping cabin as the rig pulled out from Barrow Creek.

'Gotta go to Alice and tell 'em about lendin' her me jumper, mate,' he murmured sleepily to Adams. 'I forgot when I gave me statement.'

'Not while I'm driving, we don't,' Adams said. 'We're late enough already. The boss'll be goin' spastic.'

It occurred to Vince that the police hadn't looked inside their truck. They could have put Peter's body in the refrigeration unit and no-one would have twigged.

Soon he was fast asleep. Rod got to the South Australian border before being waved down by a police roadblock.

Chapter Four

THE SEARCH BEGINS

You don't get haystacks much bigger than the
Northern Territory.

Commander Bob Fields, Northern Territory Police

B y early Sunday morning, a command centre headed by Sergeant Geoff Sullivan had been established at the Barrow Creek Hotel, with CIB Superintendent Kate Vanderlaan in charge from Alice Springs and Commander Bob Fields of Southern Command (Crime) in overall control.

Kate Vanderlaan was brought up on Groote Eylandt, east of Arnhem Land. Her family later moved to Western Australia, but Kate remained in the Territory and joined the police. 'She was one of the early female trailblazers,' says her former boss, Brian Bates.

'She was terrific at her job – she was my assistant for quite some time. She had every academic qualification you could think of, but not a lot of field experience. You need that for good leadership. So I told her that if a job in the field came up and she wanted it, "you let me know and it's yours".'

Shortly afterwards, the job of head of CIB in Alice Springs became vacant and Kate Vanderlaan put her hand up for it. Now it was about to become the hottest seat in the Territory.

It was agreed that everything should be thrown at the investigation. At Ali Curung, an Aboriginal settlement seventy kilometres north of Barrow Creek, Sergeant Gert Johnson was woken before daylight and summoned to assist with roadblocks at Tennant Creek, 150 kilometres away. He roused Constable Tony Peterson and they sped up the Stuart

Highway, receiving further snatches of information as they travelled.

Thinking it was likely to be a long day, Tony Peterson phoned a mate in Tennant Creek to ask him to bring out some coffee and sandwiches. About 9 am, his friend approached the roadblock in a white four-wheel drive and wearing a black baseball cap over long hair.

Gert dropped into a firing stance.

'Don't shoot him!' Tony yelled. 'He's got our breakfast!'

'Oh, boy,' Gert said, lowering his rifle. 'Do you look like that fella we're on the lookout for or what? I hope you have an alibi for last night,' he joked.

◆ ◆ ◆

At the incident scene, the police commenced a line search through the scrub. Metre by metre they advanced, looking for signs of a struggle, a heavy object being dragged along the ground, a panicked flight through the bush, footprints, cigarette butts, anything left behind the previous night – including the body of Peter Falconio.

They did not find any of those things, but they did find Joanne's lip-balm lid lying under a small bush, as well as a broken branch and three partial shoeprints, which may have matched her sandals. Other police combed the roadside, collecting debris, packets, cans, anything not part of the natural environment. Four hundred metres further north, they searched the ground around the Kombi. There had recently been a grass fire, and the ground was covered with powdery ash, but no footprints were visible. Some police wondered how the driver could have left the scene.

The crime scene was worked and reworked. Evidence technicians and police scoured the road, the gravel edges and the surrounding bush until nothing remained except the hope that they already had the clue they were looking for.

Over the day, more than a hundred police, a contingent of volunteers and eight aircraft, some privately owned, joined in the search. A ten-square-kilometre area was divided up into sections and searched on foot. The wider search extended over nearly 5000 square kilometres. Airspace above the search area was closed to all other flights, and police in nearby parts of New South Wales, Queensland and Western Australia were placed on high alert.

Aboriginal trackers were summoned to help. Trackers were once widely used in the Territory, where they helped to solve many important crimes. In recent years, however, there has been less money for employing them; a few were kept on in a part-time capacity to be called upon when required, but many now live in far-flung Aboriginal communities. Senior women are often the best trackers, with a legendary ability to see signs 'invisible' to whitefellas.

Gert Johnson and Tony Peterson returned to Ali Curung and went looking for as many trackers as they could find. Five or six trackers were mustered and sent down in a car with Aboriginal policewoman Gwen Brown. Unfortunately, the trackers couldn't find much either, apart from the boot prints of the police involved in the line search. One identified two sandal prints left by Joanne Lees near the blood on the road. Another said the car being driven by the gunman might have had a flat tyre or had a tyre changed. They could see no footprints of the gunman or Peter Falconio.

The trackers looked up at the sky as well, searching for circling scavengers – the hawks, eagles and crows that feast on carrion in the bush. They saw nothing unusual for miles.

They did notice signs of the bush being recently disturbed. There were twigs broken from branches, trodden-down grass clumps, disturbed rocks and plants, and little patches in the scrub where someone might have crouched down or run through. But were these disturbances caused by the police line-search, a fleeing girl or a man and his dog? No signs of a dog were found – no prints, no excreta or puddles left on the red sand, no hairs caught on low-growing mulga. Not a whisker.

Around Sunday lunchtime, the phone rang at Outback Vehicle Recovery in Alice Springs. Tammy Hacket took the call. The police needed a tow-truck to move a vehicle from a crime scene near Barrow Creek. When Tammy contacted her partner, Russ, he said he'd come out and help load the van, but she'd have to bring it back herself, because he had another job further north. By then they'd heard the early news around Alice – the gunman, the abduction the possible murder – and Tammy was reluctant to go alone.

'Don't worry,' Russ told her. 'They've already caught the bloke. Otherwise they wouldn't be bringing in the van.'

They set off in convoy about 3 pm. At Ti Tree they were stopped by armed police, who searched both their trucks. Tammy was a bit cross. Then she saw police snipers hiding in the bush at the side of the road, and her irritation turned to fear. This guy must be a real baddie, she thought. I wish I wasn't doing this job.

They arrived in the dark and were told to drive a few metres past the track where the Kombi had been found. Then they bush-bashed through the scrub in their tow-truck, approaching the Kombi from its rear. They pulled on their standard-issue gloves and manoeuvred the tilt tray so they could get the van on board without having to get in and steer it. Russ tied a chain to the Kombi's towbar, and it was loaded without any drama.

'We're sending an officer back with you,' a policeman told Tammy. 'He's been here since the early hours of this morning, so he'll ride with you.'

Tammy was pleased. She'd been dreading the slow trip home on her own with the gunman still at large.

Constable Trent Abbott climbed in and soon fell asleep. He didn't say much on the journey, but Tammy gathered enough snippets to realise that she was participating in an important case. She delivered her cargo to the police workshop, where she'd arranged for another employee to help her offload.

While she was standing around, she heard two police discussing a call-out to the Melanka Lodge the previous night. Apparently, two backpackers were involved in an 'almighty blue'. The police seemed to think the Kombi belonged to the same people.

By the time Tammy left, it was about midnight. She was spooked by the dark, knowing the gunman was still at large and she would be going home to an empty house. Unable to sleep, she stayed up until dawn, then went to work and waited impatiently to share her bits of inside knowledge with Russ.

When she told him her story, he said, 'Whoa! Be very careful what you say. We don't know what the police will give out. Make sure you listen to the news and keep reading the papers, so you know what they've made public before you say anything to anyone.'

She saw the wisdom in that advice, but couldn't resist telling her stepsister, who was employed at Melanka Lodge, the story about the backpackers' 'blue'. Her stepsister was not surprised.

'They did. I heard it. The whole place heard it – a real screaming match.'

Back at Barrow Creek, Joanne was questioned relentlessly. All afternoon she went over and over her story. As Commander Bob Fields said a couple of days later, 'The story is so bizarre you can hardly believe it.' And there were a lot of doubters in those early hours at Barrow Creek.

Even the discovery of her lip-balm lid at the scene did not convince everyone. She could have left it there deliberately to give credibility to her story, some said; and how could an experienced bushman with a torch and a dog fail to find her in such sparse scrub? More importantly, if the gunman had killed Peter Falconio, why would he give up the search for the sole witness to his crime? After all, he had all night to look for her. Few people in the outback will stop if they see two cars parked beside the highway. They might stop for a single car, in case the occupants are in trouble, but two cars would rarely attract attention.

For her part, Joanne urged the searchers to keep trying to find Peter. She was certain she hadn't seen his body, and she thought he might still be alive. She had also provided a fairly detailed description of the four-wheel drive, including its chrome bull-bar.

Joanne was still in shock and had not slept for nearly twenty-four hours. She was angered by the constant repetition and the way some questions seemed to indicate doubts about her story. Outside the hotel, a media throng was gathering, and she dreaded having to go through the same story again with inquisitive reporters. She had had enough.

The police said she could go back to Alice Springs, but they refused to let her take any of her clothes or her mobile phone from the Kombi, as all its contents had been impounded. She wanted to speak to people she knew and cared about instead of being surrounded by insistent strangers. She clung almost desperately to Helen, saying she was frightened to be alone.

Late in the afternoon, Helen and Joanne got into a waiting police car. The police had agreed to let them go to Les's parents' house in Alice Springs. The media would have a hard time tracking her there, and she'd be in the caring hands of Judy and Bill Pilton, who were like parents to Helen as well.

But when they reached Alice Springs, the police took Joanne to the hospital. She was there for some time, having her DNA taken and her injuries catalogued and photographed. The sum total was − grazes on each knee and elbow, a bruise on one ankle and minor bruising around her wrists. Her right eye was slightly puffy. She refused to have vaginal swabs taken. 'I wasn't sexually assaulted,' she said.

From the hospital, she was taken to the police station for further questioning. It was after midnight when she and Helen arrived at Judy and Bill's. Bill, who was in his eighties and quite frail, was already in bed, but Judy, a bright, chirpy little woman in her mid-sixties, was awake and waiting.

'You poor girl! What can I get you?' 'A cup of tea,' Joanne replied.

She took it with her to the room Judy had prepared and sank onto the bed. The nightmare was far from over, but she desperately needed sleep.

◆ ◆ ◆

Halfway around the world, in front of a television set in Huddersfield, Joanne's mother and stepfather were watching the evening news. With mounting apprehension, they listened to a report about two young English tourists who'd been held up in the Northern Territory by an armed gunman. 'Murder, abduction, police searching for a body' – the words struck like darts. They had not been officially notified, but somehow Joanne's mother knew.

They phoned Peter's parents. 'Have you heard the news? Could it be them?'

Peter's brother Paul later told *Daily Mail* reporter Richard Shears: 'It was only when Joanne's parents were watching the news that they put two and two together and feared it could be her and Peter. We wouldn't have known anything if Joanne's parents had not rung us.' Joan Falconio, Peter's mother, later told the ABC, 'Joanne's father telephoned to say had we seen the television this morning. A couple had been attacked on the Stuart Highway. I thought, it can't be them. Can't be. We couldn't get any information.'

She said that Joanne's stepfather, Vince James, had gone to the police station to see if it could be true, and police confirmed the worst.

'I just fell to my knees when he told us,' Joan said.

The next day, the Falconios held a conference and decided that Peter's father, Luciano, and his two brothers, Paul and Nick, would all go to Australia. Paul told Joanne they were coming.

But Nick was worried about his mother. 'Me mum, she just collapsed on the floor. I couldn't leave her like that,' he said later. So it was agreed that Paul and Luciano would go while Nick looked after Joan.

By now, Joanne had managed to phone her parents. She was in tears, but coherent. Once more she went through the details of the event, trying to play down some of the worst of it to protect her mother. She assured them she had not seen Peter's body and said he might still be alive. Everything was being done to find him. She was safe and in kind hands.

Joanne and Peter had left all their belongings in a room at his parents' house. Every time Nick walked past the door, he felt a pang of distress. He dealt with his sorrow by pretending that Peter would still be home on schedule. 'He's still on holiday, still travelling,' he told himself. 'Hopefully, I will see him in November.' He vowed Peter's things would not be disturbed until he returned.

Joan Falconio told the media, 'The worst thing is in the morning when I get up, because I know it's night time in Australia. And I'm looking at the clock all the time and as soon as it gets to morning in Australia, I feel a bit better, because I think, well, there'll be more happening and the police will be out and hopefully something today will happen …'

Speaking to Richard Shears on the phone, Joan said her family was 'going through hell'. Close to tears, she said, 'Peter is a very outgoing man who lives life to the full. He is the kindest boy in the world.'

Her choice of the present tense reflected her hope that Peter was still alive.

◆ ◆ ◆

Journalists from all parts of Australia were converging on Barrow Creek. The police had already taken over the ten beds inside the pub, and the extra visitors had to sleep in swags in 'Les's Folly' – a partly completed motel out the back, with concrete floors and a roof, but not many other mod cons – or camp outside the hotel. The tourist camping area was south of the hotel, but the journalists didn't want to miss a thing, so they set up camp in front of the telegraph station, where they could see police coming and going between the incident site and their 'Command Centre' at the pub itself. Soon their camp would cover the area from the Telegraph Station graveyard to the hotel's petrol pumps.

Over that day, the police issued three media releases, each more detailed than the last. The first was the warning to drivers issued at 7.45 am. At 10.45 am, police released Joanne's description of the man, his dog and the vehicle, and at 4.30 pm they provided a bit more information about Joanne and Peter and outlined the positions of the roadblocks – Kulgera in the south, Avon Downs near the Queensland border, Katherine in the north and Top Springs in the west, just off the Victoria Highway. Locals pointed out that there were no roadblocks on the Plenty and Sandover highways or along the Tanami and Oodnadatta tracks.

Chapter Five

ALICE SPRINGS

... the type of lead you champ at the bit about.

Superintendent Kate Vanderlaan, Alice Springs

Alice Springs, population about 29,000, is surrounded by sparsely vegetated sand plains and rocky buttes. Stark red dirt stretches for miles; wind-blown dunes bear dead gum trees, their white bones etched with precise, inky lines left by insects sucking out whatever nourishment remains.

The town is unusual in having a permanent water supply from a chain of waterholes in the Todd River. For thousands of years, the river was a focal point for the Arrernte (Arunta) people of the region. It was not until the overland telegraph line was surveyed in 1871 that surveyor W. W. Mills discovered the waterholes. He named the spot Alice Springs after the wife of Charles Todd, the Superintendent of Telegraphs, and the site was duly chosen for a telegraph station. The telegraph line and the accompanying track soon formed an umbilical line for explorers, pastoralists and prospectors, an inland red-dirt route offering both water and safety.

Fortunes were made and lost along the Track, as the Stuart Highway was colloquially called. Speculators took up pastoral leases in the area. The land was dusty and barren throughout 'the Dry'. Then came the intolerably humid 'Build-up', followed by 'the Wet', when dry creek-beds turned to raging torrents that cut roads for days or weeks. There was talk of building a railway, particularly after the discovery of mineral deposits in the MacDonnell Ranges.

The operators at the Alice Springs telegraph station received occasional supplies by camel train, but otherwise they grew their own fresh food or managed without. Not far from the telegraph station, a small township named Stuart was proclaimed in 1888. Its first pub, the Stuart Arms, was built in 1889. By 1901, Stuart had nine buildings – a pub, three breweries, three stores and two houses. Every item to come to the town, from beer barrels to honky-tonk pianos, dress materials and farm tools, had to be hauled in by camel. The breweries soon closed down; it was rumoured the brewers drank most of the beer before it ever got to the pub.

The railway from Adelaide finally reached the town in 1929, and the European population had grown to 250 by 1932. Stuart was now the administrative capital of Central Australia, but it was not much more than a dusty, ramshackle outback town. The Stuart Arms was still its only pub. When the beds inside were full, visitors bunked on the veranda.

The settlement was still widely known as Alice Springs, and in 1933 the government made this official. During the Second World War, army recruits were 'desert hardened' in the outback before being sent to North Africa and beyond. To speed the movement of troops, the Stuart Highway from Darwin to Alice was sealed in 1943, but the long stretch between Alice Springs and Port Augusta remained unsealed until 1987. Until then, it was almost impassable to any but four-wheel-drive vehicles, ensuring that the outback kept its mystery, adventure and isolation.

These days, not much remains of the old Alice Springs – the quintessential outback town, a Mecca for people trying to disappear for any number of reasons. For much of the year, the town is inundated with tourists. There are trendy outdoor cafes, new air-conditioned shopping malls and souvenir shops galore. Early risers can sip their lattes, and night owls can party till dawn in the nightclubs. Groups of Aboriginal people sit under the trees outside the municipal chambers and the library, taking advantage of the shade to carry on their traditional meeting, talking and socialising.

In July 2001, the town's population was swelled by almost a hundred of the world's media, rushing to cover the story of the brave young English girl who had eluded a murderous gunman, surviving an ordeal beyond all odds.

◆ ◆ ◆

On the evening of Sunday 15 July, police from Alice Springs accompanied forensic scientist Carmen Eckhoff to Ti Tree police station, where she was briefed by crime scene examiners. From there, they travelled to the crime scene in the dark, arriving at around 8.30 pm.

Eckhoff examined the area near the pool of blood on the roadway for blood spatter, but found none. She also tested the Stuart Highway for body particles. As well as the small pool of blood that had been covered with dirt, she found three other slight bloodstains on the bitumen, suggesting that someone might have walked through the puddle of blood on the roadway – or even upended a container of blood and flicked it to empty it out. She collected a number of bloodstained rocks from the roadside. But there were no drag marks to indicate that a bleeding body might have been dragged off the road.

After taking samples of gravel and dirt from beside the road, Eckhoff returned to Alice Springs to inspect the Kombi van, which was being kept under lock and key at the Crime Scene Unit. Its windows were shut and the passenger and side doors locked, but later she could not recall if the driver's door was locked. Starting at about 11.30 pm, she swabbed the van from front to back and tested it with ortho-toluidine, a substance that shows the presence of blood not visible to the naked eye. Her report stated, 'No blood was found in the vehicle.' She also examined the rear bumper bar and engine cover for blood, brain matter and gunshot residue. There was blood under the front right wheel arch and more under the rear bumper. She took samples from the passenger seat, using a sticky strip of tape to lift off left-behind DNA or other particles.

Samples of Joanne Lees's DNA and the test results from the van were sent off to be analysed in Darwin as soon as possible. The pressure was on to find any evidence that would indicate a third party had been at the scene.

At about 9.45 that night, Andrew Head had arrived for his shift at the Shell truck stop on the Stuart Highway north of Alice Springs. It's a big centre, where drivers fuel up before leaving Alice. Diesel pumps on one side cater for road trains and trucks; cars use the petrol pumps on the other side, bowsers, as we call them in Australia. The pumps are a fair way from the main building, and the complex has continuous video security in case people fill up and take off without paying.

When Andrew came in, he was called into the office, where Val Prior, the security manager, was talking with security guards and police.

The police had asked the day manager and the technician who installed the camera to check for anyone who resembled Joanne Lees's description of the gunman. 'They'd taken some images from the previous night's footage,' Andrew told me later, 'and they showed them to me. They asked me, "Do you remember serving this guy?" I remembered him quite well.'

Andrew had seen a four-wheel drive pull in around 12.40 am, while he was stocking the fridge with drinks. 'I authorised the pump – it beeps when the person picks it up and you can see which pump it is on the security monitor. The man bought a lot of diesel, $115 worth, and I was a bit worried he might take off, so I crossed the building to get a closer view and write his number plate down, in case. I wrote the number down and had a good look at the truck from the rear. It had a canvas canopy and it looked like you could roll up the back. The police asked me if I saw a dog, but I didn't. When the man started walking towards the building to pay, I think I threw the paper with the number plate in the bin. I didn't tell the police about writing down the number plate, but after they left on Sunday night, I went through all the bins to see if I could find it. But the day staff had cleaned up.

'The man bought some iced coffee. He also stocked up on ice and bottled water and paid cash for the lot. They found the transaction on the register tape, which tallied with the time shown on the video footage.'

Andrew didn't notice anything unusual about the man. 'He was normal height; didn't say much, just paid for his stuff and left. Probably the only reason I even remembered him that well was because it was a really quiet night.' He didn't think the man was a regular – but Andrew didn't always work the night shift.

The police had found this footage almost by accident. Val Prior had often helped police with enquiries about car thefts and other offences. That Sunday evening at about 6 pm, she had received a phone call at home from Wayne Hartley of the Alice Springs police.

'Sorry, Val, but we've got an urgent case on,' he told her. 'We need to view last night's footage – like now.'

Reluctantly, Val agreed to help, although it was supposed to be her day off. The gear would have to be set up in a locked office, and she had to be there.

'We had only recently upgraded the whole system,' she told me later, 'and it was all in a new digital format. The police sat for hours watching real-time replays of the night before, and finally thought they identified someone matching the description given by Joanne Lees. They wanted to take our system and copy the footage, but I couldn't allow that.' The cameras had been out of action while the police were watching the replays, because the system couldn't record and play at the same time.

The police brought in video recording equipment and some new VHS tapes. The copying went on for several hours, assisted by the security staff. 'I think they left with about twelve tapes,' Val recalled. 'Several hours on either side of the bloke that interested them.'

This was 'the type of lead you champ at the bit about', as Kate Vanderlaan said later. The police took the tapes back to their office at Alice Springs police station, where for some time they sat in an in-tray, unseen and not reported to senior officers.

Alice Springs has a very effective 'bush telegraph'. It was not long before staff at the *Centralian Advocate* heard a whisper that there was a video containing images that might help identify the gunman. The *Advocate*, the local arm of Rupert Murdoch's News Limited empire, only comes out on Tuesdays and Fridays, so its staff are always keen to get good 'mail' in time to meet their deadlines. If a big story breaks on Wednesday, it's fish-and-chip wrapping by the time the Friday edition appears.

Knowing their patch would soon be swamped by out-of-town journalists, the *Advocate*'s reporters were keen to get the front running. Mark Wilton, a senior reporter with the paper, phoned his police sources and came up with denial after denial. It seemed the police were genuinely unaware of the existence of any tape.

Mark was confused, and he was under pressure from his superiors in Alice and beyond. Was there a tape or wasn't there?

Early on Monday 16 July, Helen Jones took Joanne Lees to a shopping-centre cafe where Helen's eldest son, Justin, was the chef. Helen wanted Joanne to have breakfast before her next session with the detectives, but Joanne did not want anything to eat. Pale and withdrawn after an almost sleepless night, she only wanted coffee. She was still wearing the track pants, checked shirt and thongs lent to her the night before.

When they'd had their coffee, Helen left Joanne at the CIB, where she spent most of the day answering more questions.

◆ ◆ ◆

That day, the media trickle into town became a flood. All were anxious to secure the interview with the girl who had outwitted the gunman. The British dailies were already blaring 'Britons ambushed by gunman in outback' and 'Briton's blood on outback road'. The police had no media strategy in place for such an event. Mark Wilton said later that Denise Hurley of the Darwin police media unit was 'running round like a rabbit in headlights. The police were blown away by this – totally out of their depth at the beginning. They just couldn't cope.'

Orders came from the top that Joanne Lees was to be treated as a victim, not a suspect. Fears were already being voiced at senior levels. The last thing the police wanted was to be involved in 'another Chamberlain disaster'.

The 'Chamberlain disaster' referred to the disappearance in 1980 of baby Azaria Chamberlain, said by her mother Lindy to have been taken from their tent near Uluru (Ayers Rock) by a wild dingo. The case turned into a national witch-hunt against Lindy Chamberlain, a seemingly emotionless Seventh Day Adventist, who was accused of sacrificially murdering her baby. The humiliation that followed when her conviction was overturned was etched into the collective memory of the Northern Territory police.

Chapter Six

THE SCOOP

We've got Lees! Mark Wilton, our man, got Lees.
Jason Scott, chief of staff, Centralian Advocate, 17 July 2001

Police management had decided that information would be 'drip fed' to the media through written releases and periodic press conferences – a tactic perfected by a former Queensland premier, Joh Bjelke-Petersen, who called it 'feeding the chooks'. The police were still optimistic that the roadblocks would produce a suspect. They hoped that the culprit had gone to ground somewhere in the Territory to wait out the surveillance. On Monday they issued a new release seeking assistance from anyone travelling past the crime scene between 5 pm on Saturday and 3 am on Sunday. The media release repeated the description of the gunman and his dog, which, as several reporters pointed out, matched about half the men and dogs in the Territory.

Meanwhile, traffic was banking up at the roadblocks. For the first two days, no one was allowed through, and little campsites sprang up along the road. Armed officers from the Tactical Response Group (TRG) searched every vehicle, and police showed drivers identikit pictures of the gunman. Police were advising people to avoid unnecessary travel, not to travel alone and to take an alternative route if possible, but the only alternative routes were rugged off-road tracks, not suitable for most travellers.

At Tennant Creek, Constable Tony Peterson stopped a group of Israelis travelling south to Adelaide. They were impatient to proceed because they had a plane to catch.

'We must get past,' the driver pleaded. 'We'll miss our connection. What is the cause of all this trouble?'

'Sorry, sir,' Tony told him. 'We have an armed gunman on the loose.'

'Only one?' the driver snorted incredulously. 'All this trouble for one gunman?'

Families pulled out cricket sets, folding chairs and umbrellas, portable stoves and billy cans. People who'd never met before exchanged tea and gossip. Others became impatient. But the police were determined to avoid any criticism of their handling of the case.

Police media releases reassured the public that a 'fully resourced task force' was being put together; that they were 'not sitting on their hands'; the commissioner would leave 'no stone unturned' to find the gunman, and although the search was 'like looking for a needle in a haystack', according to Commander Bob Fields, they would 'never give up the hunt'. These clichés did nothing to assuage the media's hunger for features, and especially for an interview with Joanne Lees. So far, she'd been kept out of sight, and many photographers didn't know what she looked like.

Late on Monday afternoon, Mark Wilton attended a police media conference. Commander Bob Fields was the man on the spot.

'Is there any truth to the story that video footage has been handed to police showing a man and truck matching the description given by Joanne Lees?' Mark called out, sparking a hubbub in the media crowd.

'No,' Fields said confidently. 'I have no knowledge of that at all.' Mark Wilton was insistent, and Fields lost his cool. 'If such a video does exist, I suggest you use all the resources of your organisation to find it,' he snapped. 'But I don't believe that's accurate at all.' Though Fields did not know it, the tape was sitting right inside the police headquarters.

Media frustration was developing into distrust of the police. Why wouldn't they produce Joanne Lees? Why didn't she make the usual televised plea for public assistance to find her missing boyfriend?

Why had she been locked in with the police for hours on end? Was she a suspect?

That night, Mark Wilton was working late at the *Advocate*, fashioning his first story since the big event, although he had little new information to give it an edge. At about 11 pm, his phone rang. It was Helen Jones.

Helen had worked as a booking clerk at the *Advocate* before moving out to Barrow Creek. She knew Mark and trusted him.

'I'm hiding with Joanne Lees,' she said.

Mark was surprised. He'd known Joanne must have been hiding with someone in town, but had not thought of Helen.

'We're just talking about the story,' Helen told him. 'Does it need a kick along, do you think? She's worried about talking to the media, but I told her she could trust you.'

Mark's heart raced. Here he was, in his little cubbyhole at his small-town paper, with the world's media slavering to get an interview with Joanne Lees, and she might be willing to talk to him. It would be the biggest break of his career.

'Why don't you put her on?' he suggested, as casually as he could. 'Hullo, Mark,' came a hesitant voice with a Yorkshire accent. 'Look, I'm not sure about this. I know it's a big story and all that, but out of respect to Peter and his family I'm not sure if I should say anything.'

'If you want to talk, I'll talk,' he told her, without pushing.

'I'll discuss it a bit more with Helen. I might call back.'

'Damn!' he swore as he hung up, but he sat tight. Around 1.30 am, she rang back.

They spoke for a while about the behaviour of the police. Joanne was tired and tearful after another marathon interview. She resented the length of the sessions and the repetitiveness of the questions.

'Do you think I need a lawyer?' she asked. 'Are you a suspect?' he asked her.

She told him that she felt as if that was being treated as one and that she was quite angry and wanted to move from Judy and Bill's place. 'They're coming for me again in the morning,' she told him.

'I need a break. Can you come and get us and take us to Helen's son's house?'

'What, now?' he asked, checking his watch. 'Yes. As soon as possible. And I'll talk to you.'

Despite the time, Mark rang a lawyer friend to assess Joanne's status. His friend told him that if she hadn't been cautioned it was unlikely the police were treating her as a suspect. He also told Mark to tape the interview and to make it clear to her she was being interviewed by a journalist for a story.

Mark put fresh batteries in his tape recorder and set off. When he arrived at the house, Helen and Joanne ran out and jumped into his car.

'Thank you for coming, Mark,' Helen said.

'It's all getting to me,' Joanne told him. 'I can't face being picked up in the morning by the police. Sorry,' she gulped tearfully. 'It's just that I'm a bit worried about it …'

At first Mark felt that she was making a play for his sympathy, but he soon changed his mind. 'From the time I actually interviewed her, I never, ever doubted that this had happened to that girl,' he told me later.

But he was not getting his interview that night. Joanne wanted to sleep. The next day, two female friends from Dymocks were arriving to support her. She wanted to escape the police and go to meet them. But she promised she'd do the interview the following afternoon.

'I didn't have far to go home,' Mark told me. 'Helen's son David, it turned out, lived two doors down from my place.' Mark fell into bed, fervently hoping Joanne would keep her appointment the next day.

David was about to turn in at the unit he shared with his girlfriend and their new baby when he heard his mother calling out to him from the front door.

'What the …?' he said as he opened the door. 'Mum, what are you doing here at this hour?'

Helen explained who Joanne was and told him she was trying to get respite from the police questioning.

'They've been at her for hours. Her friends are arriving tomorrow and she needs to go shopping, get some clothes. Everything is in her Kombi. She needs her phone, her shoes – she has nothing!'

David was curious to hear Joanne's story. He made tea and they talked.

'You could make a lot of money if you wanted to sell your story to the reporters,' he suggested. 'I bet they'd pay for it.'

For the first time, Joanne seemed really animated.

'I'd never do that! I'd never, ever sell my story to anyone!' She became a bit tearful as she spoke. David finally made up a bed for Joanne and Helen on the lounge-room floor and went to bed about 3 am.

'What have you been doing out there, talking to that girl?' his girlfriend whispered angrily as he slid in beside her. 'You could get in trouble, you know. You realise she's a suspect, don't you?'

As luck would have it, soon after they had settled down, police were called to a disturbance at one of the other units in the complex. Helen went to the door to see what was going on, and the police spotted her. An officer told her that Joanne would still be needed later that morning for further questioning.

Helen was cross. 'She'll come in when she's good and ready,' she told him and shut the door firmly.

◆ ◆ ◆

A friend of Helen's drove them to the airport about 11 am, and Joanne had a tearful reunion with her friends over lunch at Bojangles. Although the town was swarming with journalists, none of them realised she was there.

At about 2.45 pm, Joanne phoned Mark from Judy and Bill's. She said she intended to stay there for a while longer, and that Mark could come and do his interview. Helen sat in, for moral support and to put Joanne at ease. But Joanne was far from relaxed.

Mark reminded Joanne that he was a reporter and would be taping the interview for his paper. She said she would do the interview because she wanted to correct inaccuracies in other newspaper reports. Mark could hardly believe his luck as the tape rolled. Even after the tape ran out, he continued scribbling while she spoke.

Afterwards, he returned to the *Advocate* clutching his prize. His chief of staff, Jason Scott, was sitting in his big blue office, thinking about how he and his small team were going to hold their own on the story. They had two subeditors off sick just as the 'story of the decade' had broken.

Mark Wilton poked his head in. 'Got a minute?'

'Sure, Mark. What's up?'

'We've got Lees,' Mark said matter-of-factly. Jason didn't move. Then he said, 'What?'

Mark waved his tape recorder. 'We've got Lees. I've just done a one-on-one with her.'

'You little bewdy!' Jason yelled. He picked up the phone and called the chief of staff at the *Daily Telegraph* in Sydney.

'I don't care if he's talking to God,' Mark heard Jason say. 'Put him on. It's urgent.'

After a short wait, Jason got through. 'We've got Lees! Mark Wilton, our man, got Lees.'

When Jason hung up, he grinned. 'Good work, mate! I could almost hear him salivating.'

The atmosphere at the *Advocate* became frantic. Once Murdoch's British papers learnt of the interview, the phones began to ring. Every News Limited paper was waiting for Mark to finish his story. In Sydney, the *Daily Telegraph* was also deluged with calls. The editor delayed the page one conference and offered to fly a subeditor to Alice Springs to help out.

The first 200 words or so were faxed to the *Daily Telegraph* at

8.05 pm in the eastern States, and the rest arrived ten minutes later. The *Northern Territory News* in Darwin had to act as a group distributor because the *Centralian* had an inadequate email system.

A *Telegraph* insider told Martin Chulov of the Australian, 'It was quite a funny night. Here we were all waiting breathlessly while some bloke in the middle of nowhere got the interview and sent it down.' Chulov observed that journalists from the rival Fairfax group and Fleet Street reporters were 'staring forlornly into their beers, some cursing the collective weight and reach of News Limited'.

As Jason Scott told me later, there was a certain satisfaction in knowing that all those highly paid journalists had 'had their girl pinched from under their noses by a hick newspaper in a hick town'. Mark's story was on front pages all over Europe, and was the lead article in London's *The Sunday Times* World Page that week.

But his own paper would not appear until Friday. For just a few minutes, Mark and Jason discussed holding the story over until then. But it wasn't really an option. 'Sydney wouldn't have let us, and we had to get it out there.'

Rival newspapers began to phone them, trying to buy the story. *The Daily Mirror* rang Jason from London, saying, 'Send us this story, no by-lines, no questions asked. We'll put any cheque you want in the mail.' Someone from the London *Sun* phoned at midnight, wanting to offer Mark big money. Most of them pinched the story anyway, some artfully running it as if Joanne had spoken directly to them.

In the interview, Joanne had criticised the police, and some papers played that angle for all it was worth. They also began asking if she was a suspect.

Then Joanne denied everything she'd said to Mark. She also denied that her mother, whom Mark had contacted for comment, had said that the police had been 'very nasty' to her.

'The journalists also became very nasty,' Jason Scott told me later. 'Mark Wilton was defamed left, right and centre by rabid journos – the Australians were as bad as the Poms.'

Mark's colleague Glenn Morrison told me Mark was under a lot of pressure. 'The other journos were calling him "Mr Falconio" – as in "Let's see what Mr Falconio has to say about this or that".' At one point, an Australian Associated Press journalist even questioned whether Mark's tape existed.

Mark became the butt of a lot of accusations from police and journalists. It was claimed he'd fooled Joanne into giving the interview by saying he was a lawyer. In fact, as he put it, he'd made it 'painfully clear' he was a journalist. But he didn't play the tape to anyone outside the paper until he lent it to me in 2003. Why should he? He knew what was on it. And so did Joanne Lees.

He says the police dragged Joanne in and told her off for talking to him. 'They were really pissed off with her.' About five days after the story hit the headlines, he started getting calls from media unit head Denise Hurley and Assistant Commissioner John Daulby. They wanted a copy of his tape. When he refused, they made 'veiled threats' about bringing charges against him.

'They indicated that I misrepresented myself. Daulby said that the interview was obtained under false pretences. Then I got really pissed off. I said, "You pack of pricks can think what you f--king well like. You can shove it up your arse. And you know about protecting sources."

'Our lawyers told them to shove it up their arse too. Told them to go through the proper channels if they wanted a copy. "Rupert owns it," they told me. "We can make sure they don't get it for three or four years." After everyone simmered down, Daulby came down and had a coffee and I gave him a transcript, but not the tape.'

The fight was on now to get a story. But apart from the interview with Mark Wilton, the sole witness and survivor of this remarkable attack was steadfastly refusing to face the media and enlist them in the effort to discover what had become of Peter Falconio.

Chapter Seven

PUT TO THE TEST

Every case has the potential to blow up in your face.

Dr Peter Thatcher, Head of Forensics, Darwin

In Darwin, forensic testing was conducted in a tiny lab with very limited bench space at the Peter McAulay Police Complex until October 2001, when a new forensics centre was opened nearby. One of the service's senior scientists was Joy Kuhl, known Australia-wide for a mistake that could have blighted her career – the erroneous identification of foetal blood under the dashboard of Lindy and Michael Chamberlain's car. While working with the New South Wales Health Commission, she was asked to examine the impounded car, which had been taken to New South Wales because the Territory did not have appropriate forensic facilities. Much of her evidence was criticised by other scientists, including Professor Barry Boettcher of Newcastle University. The court, however, believed Joy Kuhl, the hands-on practitioner, rather than Boettcher, whom the prosecution portrayed as an ivory-tower academic. In November 1982 Lindy Chamberlain went to jail to start a life sentence, and in December 1983 Joy Kuhl accepted a job as a forensic scientist in the Northern Territory.

◆ ◆ ◆

Early on Sunday 15 July 2001, Joy Kuhl received a phone call asking her to get a forensic scientist to Barrow Creek as soon as possible to examine a crime scene. She elected to send Carmen Eckhoff, one of her most experienced people. 'We don't go to every case,' Joy told me later, 'but this one sounded like a biggie.'

The first batch of items Carmen had collected at Barrow Creek arrived in Darwin the next day. The police wanted these tested as quickly as possible. On Tuesday, Carmen herself returned with more samples from Barrow Creek and material from the Kombi van.

'The van was very clean and tidy, with nothing out of place.' Carmen said later. The items from the van included passports, a wallet, photos, fuel receipts held together by a bulldog clip, keys, email addresses, Peter and Joanne's CVs, a Ventolin puffer that was used as a control for checking Peter's DNA, CDs, sewing gear and the contents of the ashtray.

There were also samples of the blood from the highway, swabs from the truckies, swabs from the back of the Kombi near the rear window and numerous items picked up beside the road. The trick was to isolate anything that matched what they already had. Saliva from a drink can or cigarette butt, an empty cigarette packet that might reveal fingerprints or a favourite brand – any little clue would help. Eventually the sample tally rose to almost 400 items – enough to keep everyone busy for months.

Joy Kuhl had already examined Joanne's clothes. She later recalled, 'We'd been told that Joanne Lees wasn't badly injured, and this was already causing some suspicion. Her clothes had no dirt, no twigs, no grass stains, no burrs – nothing that made you feel, "Oh this poor girl!" Her clothing was quite unremarkable forensically.'

Brian Bates made the same point. 'Her clothes did not show what she had been through. They totally bemused forensics – it was very confusing. That's why the forensic tests were so important.'

But the T-shirt did carry a few smears and spots of blood. 'It was not heavily bloodstained,' Joy said, 'and most of the marks were small. Quite often in forensic testing, where you have a group of blood spatters or spots, you don't sample every single one, just a random sample in the cluster. But in this case, because there were relatively few marks, we ran them all.'

One tiny spot produced a different profile. 'They were printing out, one after the other – all Joanne's – when this one came out different. We did get a bit excited. It didn't match Peter's DNA, but it was male. So it seemed someone else might have been at the scene after all.' The spot looked like a small smear, or maybe something from a pimple or sore.

Much later, Superintendent Kate Vanderlaan told a journalist from Scottish TV that the spot was 'a good lead. It's certainly conceivable that the person who committed the crime left that DNA on her T-shirt.'

The investigators speculated that Joanne might have bitten her attacker during the struggle. It seemed the mark was deposited by 'more than a casual touch'. Unfortunately, Joanne had washed twice before police arrived at Barrow Creek, so no other useful forensic material was obtained from her mouth, under her fingernails or anywhere else on her person. The male DNA on her T-shirt was kept secret in the early days of the investigation.

The blood from underneath the Kombi was tested and found to be of animal origin – probably roadkill. The scientists also tested the manacles Joanne had been wearing. Joy Kuhl described them as having 'a very intricate design'; they were made from a porous material, 'like black, sticky duct tape'.

On 31 July the forensic team received a memo from Commander Colin Hardman, requesting further tests. He asked that the interior of the Kombi be tested for blood because of the 'absence of complementary blood at the actual scene'. There were no drag marks, trails of blood or pools or spots. 'If we can confirm blood in the vehicle, it may be something extra we can put to the suspect at interview. It may discount some versions of events that are alleged to have taken place outside the vehicle'.

He also wanted the whole steering wheel examined for DNA and the rear of the Kombi tested for gunshot residue. He thought it was 'worth a try' to test Joanne's clothing for gunshot residue as well. The handgun she had described would have had an open cylinder, which would be likely to disperse residue on the attacker's hands, and she had said that the gunman pushed her forward when he put the ties on her wrists. 'I know this is a long shot, but it may confirm, in conjunction with the testing of the vehicle, that a gunshot actually took place.'

Hardman paid particular attention to the manacles. Examination of the manacles could 'hold the key as to who actually constructed them'; it could 'redirect the investigation'. Officers attempting to construct similar manacles had taken over an hour and had found it very difficult, 'especially the covering of the links with tape. The tape constantly stuck to the members' fingers.' He was therefore keen for the tape to be tested for DNA and fingerprints.

Did these questions indicate that police had doubts about Joanne's story? Was she the 'suspect' Hardman mentioned? Why was he considering discounting 'some versions of events' when the only versions the police had, came from Joanne? Was he looking for an accomplice?

After the manacles had been tested, Peter Thatcher, the head of the Territory's forensic services, took them to a Command briefing, where Assistant Commissioner Daulby and Commissioner Brian Bates both tried them on. This caused some consternation, as the manacles could now be contaminated. Command scoffed at this possibility, and the two officers subsequently refused to supply the forensic lab with their DNA. At first, the handcuffs were described as being made from 'zip ties' or 'cable ties'. It was only when the media expressed doubt about whether Joanne could have brought her hands to the front that police mentioned the links made of 'porous, sticky tape'. A set of similar manacles, mocked up by the police, was eventually shown to a media conference on 21 March 2002, almost nine months after the incident.

◆ ◆ ◆

Back in Alice Springs on the Wednesday afternoon, Luciano and Paul Falconio had arrived and had agreed to meet the press.

Luciano looked small and crushed by anxiety. His voice faltered when he spoke. He said he was still hopeful his son had survived the ordeal. 'Otherwise I would not be here.'

His tall, handsome son, Paul, told the journalists that the family didn't know anything other than what was on the news. 'The details from everywhere – the police, Australia, everyone – are very, very sketchy.' He said that he had spoken to Joanne on the phone and she had been 'very distraught'. He told the information-starved media, 'Yeah, she's obviously very upset. I think she needs some help.' He said that Peter had kept in touch with his family during the trip, phoning and emailing them. 'We spoke to them on Friday,' Paul said, seeming surprised at how little time had passed since then. 'They were both very happy.'

Sympathy for the Falconio men ran high among the journalists, but it was Joanne they wanted to talk to. Her continued refusal to front the media was beginning to raise questions. Phillip Cornford, senior journalist with the *Sydney Morning Herald*, said, 'The sooner people in these sorts of situations confront the media and cameras, the sooner the heat is off. Why doesn't she just get it over with?' Others were saying that the police were 'allowing her to call the shots'.

Denise Hurley told the dissatisfied media that Joanne was quite firm about not wanting to appear. What she didn't say was that Joanne didn't want to see the Falconios, either.

Journalists hate being thwarted, especially when their editors are screaming for a story. Could Joanne Lees have something to hide? Was she afraid to face questions in case she couldn't handle the heat? An insidious change began. There were inevitable comparisons with the Chamberlain case twenty-one years before – the lack of a body or any substantial forensic evidence; an 'unidentified culprit'; a young, dark-haired woman who appeared to lack any emotion about the death of a loved one. The difference was that Lindy had talked, and it had destroyed her. Joanne wasn't talking, and that could destroy her.

Neither young woman met expectations. Neither had any experience of dealing with a media frenzy, with reporters ready to feast on their every word, nuance or expression. As Colin Evans said in his book *A Question of Evidence*, 'Every country has its "Crime of the Century". Not many get to stage that crime in the shadow of an undeniable national treasure.' He was referring to Azaria's disappearance in 1980 at Uluru. Now there was a new case, early in the new century, just up the road, in Territory terms – and with some of the same key players.

The pro-Joanne and anti-Joanne camps began to polarise. Already, British editors who didn't understand how easily the gunman could have disappeared were demanding features on how Joanne must be guilty of something. Even the Australian media were taking sides. Joanne did herself no favours by lying low.

Inaccurate reports were also sneaking through. One reporter wrote: 'Cold rain had muddied the footprints Ms Lees left as she stumbled away, bound and gagged by the madman, but they still told their story of terror.' This was impossible; no rain had fallen in the area for several days.

The papers also quoted medical opinions suggesting that Joanne should have exhibited signs of frostbite. Yet on 14 July the temperature at Ali Curung was 16.4 degrees Celsius at 9 pm and 13.2 degrees Celsius at 3 am. Normally, July nights are cold in the outback, with minimum temperatures averaging 4 degrees Celsius. That particular week, however, a low cloud band in the area created milder conditions. This also undermined the story that Joanne had crouched, shivering, in freezing temperatures for hours. She might have been shivering with fear, but not with cold.

Meanwhile, the *Centralian Advocate* had managed to contact Joanne's stepfather in England. Vincent James told them that he had spoken 'briefly' to Joanne and that she was 'traumatised and shocked'. He couldn't rush to her side because he did not have a passport, but the Foreign Office was helping to expedite his application so that he could join Joanne as soon as possible. Her mother was too frail to travel. Vince James had not been told that Joanne had said she didn't want to see her stepfather when he arrived.

The police travel warnings were beginning to take effect. Some cars were travelling in small convoys; others were staying put in major centres until the hue and cry died down.

The head nurse at Ali Curung was John Turahui, a big, expressive New Zealander with a highly developed sense of humour. He told me about the response to the incident in this remote Aboriginal community. 'We received one of the emails from a massive government mail-out, telling us a gunman was on the loose and to look out for a white ute or Landcruiser. We all fell about laughing. We drive one ourselves, and so does half the Territory. There was a hand-sketched truck picture attached to the email, but it didn't look anything like the photo from the Shell stop they released three weeks later. So if you'd been looking out for the sketched truck you would have missed the other one.

'It was quite eerie out here for a couple of weeks after it happened. We have six or seven hundred people in this community, and usually we're run off our feet every day. Bashings, car accidents, babies arriving unexpectedly, people wanting Band-Aids for a blister – from the sublime to the ridiculous, you name it, we get it. All day long. All night long too. We're always on call.

'Anyway, the community didn't need to get an email – the bush telegraph was working overtime, and everyone had barricaded themselves into their houses. We didn't have any patients for days on end. It was quite relaxing, actually – I caught up with my paperwork for once.'

The community bus, which was used to run patients down to Alice or up to Tennant if they need more specialised medical care, stopped picking people up on the highway. 'They usually pick up all the bunny-hoppers – that's what we call the mad hitchhikers who go out along the highway in the heat, expecting a lift.' John locked up the clinic as well. 'We kept the clinic locked all day, just put up a sign to say "Ring the bell", but it hardly rang for three weeks. People were terrified.'

A woman who lived on the Plenty Highway phoned ABC radio in Alice Springs and said she was so scared that she'd installed a lock on the inside of her walk-in wardrobe door so that her children could lock themselves in if an unfamiliar white four-wheel drive came in from the highway. She kept a loaded shotgun close to her, night and day.

At Willowra, an Aboriginal community north-west of Ti Tree, everyone left their homes and went bush. Similar things happened at Harts Range, 140 kilometres north-east of Alice Springs, and Ngukurr, 280 kilometres east of Katherine. The front-page headline of the 17 July edition of the *Centralian Advocate* announced:

'Gunman could strike again,' Commander Bob Fields had told reporters, 'We believe the nature of the crime is such that we may have a person who is not thinking particularly rationally. It is not unknown for such a person to then become involved in another incident in a short space of time.'

◆ ◆ ◆

Leads from the public were coming in steadily, giving the police plenty to follow up. One passer-by claimed to have seen the Kombi and a white four-wheel drive parked together on the side of the road around 7.30 pm. Others had seen one or other of the cars, but not both. Two definite sightings of orange Kombis a long way apart confused things for a while, until the second Kombi was located. Police put out a call for Izabelle Jetee, who had travelled with Peter and Joanne to Alice Springs.

The police asked Joanne Lees if she'd be willing to participate in a re-enactment of the event. This seemed to signal that they didn't believe her. Otherwise, why would they put her through something so traumatic? They seemed to want to see if she would trip up.

She agreed to the re-enactment, even though it must have been difficult. Commander Max Pope, who'd been sent down from Darwin to 'handle the media', explained that she had agreed to do it in case returning to the site jogged her memory. He also said: 'We know that we'll be criticised if we don't do it.'

Before Joanne left Alice Springs, police sent out a decoy car, hoping to put the media off the scent, but they were not fooled and followed her to the scene of the attack. As they neared the spot they moved into a small convoy with police, travelling on the wrong side of the road. Long lines of cars were waiting at barriers set up on either side of the location, leaving the road between bare, apart from a small huddle of police and cars in the middle of the open stretch. The media were stopped and held back at the roadblock, much to their disappointment.

Police huddled around the place where Peter's blood had been found beside the road. Crime scene people had outlined the spot with their distinctive pink fluorescent paint. Other pink lines on the road showed where the two vehicles had parked. Joanne looked away from the marks. A white Landcruiser with a canvas canopy had been borrowed from the Toyota dealership in Alice Springs and trucked to the scene by Outback Vehicle Recovery.

The Kombi was still under police guard in the Alice Springs workshop and could not be used. It was reported that the police forgot all about needing a Kombi until they arrived at the scene. *The Sunday Times* said that the police were forced to flag down some tourists in an orange Kombi. Other stories claimed that the police offered to hire an orange Kombi that was caught up in the road closure. Stung by these criticisms, police issued a statement four days later saying that they had brought a Kombi up from Alice Springs for the re-enactment. Tempers were becoming frayed on both sides.

The police waited until dark so that the re-enactment would be as close as possible to the 'real thing', but they did not ask Joanne to re-enter the bush. A policewoman played Joanne's part, following her directions. The police believed the lip-balm lid showed where she'd hidden. A police officer told me later that Joanne had said she'd tried to use the lip balm to lubricate her wrists and get out of her manacles. She had also tried to chew them off.

Media representatives were huddled together about two kilometres from the re-enactment site. Channel Nine's Fleur Bitcon said later that the conditions made her feel sympathy for Joanne.

'It made us realise how dark and cold it was and how cold and scared Joanne Lees must have been.' But as the journalists vied for the campfire's warmth, more questions arose. Why didn't the man and his dog find her? Where was any physical evidence of their presence? How did Peter Falconio's body disappear so completely? How did Joanne get the sack off her head? How did she manage to bring her hands to the front?

Fleur Bitcon returned to the Barrow Creek Hotel to join the long queue for the payphone. The police had taken over the pool room, and with it Les's phone and fax lines. For most of those present, the pay phone was the only link to the outside world, and it was never on the hook.

Eventually, Fleur gained access to a mobile satellite dish. She was filing a report for *Nightline* when she heard the police returning from the re-enactment.

'I was told that the CIB head wanted to see me in the pool room – now! "What's he want?" I asked. "I'm busy. Tell him I'll be there shortly." Anyway, the messenger came back and said I had to come right away. I thought maybe there was a break in the case, so in I went and this guy who didn't even introduce himself started dressing me down and accusing me of breaching the police cordon around the re-enactment scene with a secret, hidden camera. He said I had compromised the integrity of the operation and could have interfered with a crime scene.

'I was furious. I told him the only pictures we had we'd used on TV already, so he should have a look at those to see where I was. It was so ridiculous. The crime scene had been open for a couple of days, and anyone could walk around there, so how could the crime scene security be compromised?'

The 'crime scene' was not very secure anyway. People waiting at the roadblocks were wandering off into the bush to go to the toilet. Anyone could have walked a few hundred metres in the bush to get a closer look, or even taken photos with a long lens. But Fleur Bitcon was not one of them.

The police were full of praise for Joanne's co-operation, and insisted that the re-enactment had been a success. Kate Vanderlaan said later, 'The re-enactment proved the crime was physically possible.' Joanne's account had been demonstrated to be 'factually correct'. They confirmed that she had been tied up and placed in the front seat of a four-wheel drive, then had crawled or been pushed through a gap between the seats to the back tray and escaped while the gunman was distracted.

Asked if there was any physical evidence of the offender, Commander Pope looked very uncomfortable, pursed his lips and said, 'I'm not going to comment on that.' His face and the agitated movement of his Adam's apple indicated he had something to say – but what?

Mark Wilton told me, 'At that time journalists made the assumption that there were no other footprints, so no one else had been there.' These doubts were shared by about half of those who read about the case.

Out on the highway, communications between media and police remained terse, with the police refusing several requests for photo opportunities.

After the re-enactment, Joanne was taken to meet the Falconios and moved into a safe place, accompanied by two police 'chaperones', Helen Braam and Libby Andrew. Exactly one week after the incident had taken place, Detective Braam was sitting with Joanne in her hotel room. It was late in the evening, and Joanne was becoming agitated. She got up and looked at the clock. Turning to Helen Braam, she said, 'You know, it was at this time that it happened.'

Judy Pilton hadn't been too sorry to see Joanne leave. 'I ran my legs off making cups of tea for her. Every five minutes she'd ask for another one,' she said. 'And she was very rude. Just sat on the floor, watching the TV to see what the media were saying about her.

'Never a please or thank you. Not even when she left. She just walked out with her girlfriends. They said thank you for looking after her, and she didn't say a word.'

Judy was cleaning up when she found the track pants Helen had lent Joanne.

'I'd better wash these and get them back to Helen,' Judy said to Bill, who was sitting in his chair as usual. Judy often chatted away to her husband, not really expecting a reply. She plunged her hand into the pockets and pulled out some bits of paper.

'Well I never!' she told Bill. 'She's left a letter in the pocket of Helen's pants. How am I going to get that back to her?'

Unable to contain her curiosity, Judy smoothed out the sheets of paper, found her glasses and started reading.

'My goodness, Bill! You'll never believe …' She stopped. Bill got a bit confused these days. You never knew what he remembered. And what he might say to people.

Judy went to her handbag and pulled out a business card left by Paula Dooley-McDonnell, the detective who had collected Joanne from the house. With shaking fingers, Judy dialled Paula's mobile number.

'Paula,' she quavered. 'I've just found a letter Joanne wrote.' She read it aloud to the police officer. 'Do you think that might be important?'

Paula said she'd come right over.

Police were at pains to remind the media that Joanne was a victim. Max Pope said, 'She is not a suspect. We believe her story.' In fact, they did have doubts about Joanne's account of events.

About six months later, Assistant Commissioner Daulby said on Scottish TV, 'I find it remarkable that only the shoe print of Joanne Lees was there. There was no physical evidence to identify her attacker. Where are the footprints? Where is the dog?'

Though investigators did not publicly voice these doubts at the time, they asked for permission to tap Joanne Lees's phone conversations. 'We decided to pursue Joanne and what she said to the nth degree,' Brian Bates told me. 'We made sure we got to know the person by having someone with her whenever she went out. We figured if she was involved, she'd want to contact someone at some stage. She was very keen to get her mobile phone back, but we weren't in a hurry to give it to her until we had it covered.'

Another officer on the case, Detective Senior Sergeant Jeanette Kerr, later told me that neither she nor the chaperones were informed that any listening devices were operating. As far as she knew, Joanne was provided with chaperones because she was 'alone, vulnerable, frightened and traumatised', as she subsequently told the court.

'We had to keep an open mind,' Brian Bates said to me. 'All we could go on was what we were told. But how much of what she was telling us was truthful? How much had trauma blotted out? She is a particularly difficult person – very closed, very uncommunicative. She seemed very off-hand about it all, which was difficult to understand, and she was less than convincing when she was put under any sort of pressure.'

It was hard to reconcile the person he was describing with the one her Dymocks boss had known – an 'attractive and popular' young woman who was 'almost like the social organiser for all the staff'. The 'trials of Joanne Lees', as one media outlet called them, had barely begun.

Chapter Eight

DODGING THE MEDIA

*I think she thought we'd all go away ... and that was never
going to happen.*

Fleur Bitcon, Channel Nine News

In the week after Peter Falconio disappeared, the media personnel
congregated in Alice Springs were frustrated at every turn. Police
spokespeople faced constant criticism for not forcing Joanne to tell
her story, and Joanne herself became the butt of cynical and sceptical
remarks.

Some journalists offered Joanne huge sums for an exclusive, using
Denise Hurley of the police media unit as a go-between.

'One British journalist got off the plane, found his way straight to me
and said, "We'll pay more than anybody else",' Denise said. Sums of
up to half a million dollars were mentioned. 'I think Joanne didn't want
the media to make her look weak, and she was afraid she'd be filmed
and photographed if she broke down. The Falconios were excellent –
they did quite a few press conferences and would have done more –
but Joanne remained quite strong about not doing anything.'

Kate Vanderlaan also tried to persuade Joanne to do at least
one press conference for the sake of the investigation. She told the
anxious media, 'We'd like her to put a face to what's happened out
here, but at the same time she's a victim. I can't stand and yell and
shout and say, "Joanne, you have to do this!" Obviously, we'd like her
to co-operate, but we can't force her.'

Media representatives were not impressed. Some also felt that the
police were deliberately obstructing them. 'Almost every day a media

conference was called and we were told to meet police spokespeople on such and such a street corner at say, eleven o'clock,' Fleur Bitcon recalled. 'Then we'd stand around, waiting, waiting, sometimes for two hours or more. Sometimes they'd ring one of us out on the street and tell us to reassemble again at 2 pm, because they weren't ready. Sometimes we'd be given some miserable bit of information right on filing deadline. After a while we didn't all bother to go to the street-corner assemblies. We'd get one person to hang around and ring us when something was actually happening.' It was also difficult to contact police spokespeople. 'There was only one phone line to police media in Alice Springs for days after the incident, and it was always busy,' Fleur said. 'There was no clear chain of command, either in the investigating police or the media unit. We didn't care that we were getting different police fronting media conferences every day, but we did expect to hear from someone who could tell us what was going on.' Denise Hurley knew journalists were upset with police media management, but there was not much she could do to improve things. Some police spokespeople were doing themselves no favours. On the Monday after the incident, Commander Bob Fields had denied the existence of the truck-stop video. Then, two days later, Max Pope contradicted him and said that a video from a truck stop had been made available to police, but there was nothing of any use on the footage. The media were not allowed to see it.

There appeared to be a plethora of senior police 'in charge' of the investigation. But Sergeant Gert Johnson from Ali Curung told me later, 'There was no sense of confusion on our part about who was involved.' Crime management in the Territory is divided into Northern and Southern Commands, each reporting to an assistant commissioner in Darwin. 'In Southern Command, we had Bob Fields, who reported to Max Pope, who reported to John Daulby, who was Assistant Commissioner, Crime. It's a typical thing – an investigation is never static. You can't have a commander tied up for months on one investigation, so you put more staff in so he can go back to his overall responsibilities.'

Brian Bates agreed. 'Daulby had overall commission to oversee the investigation, but it may have appeared to outsiders that a number of different people were in charge. I'm also aware that there may have been some friction internally. I know some of my staff in Alice Springs, Kate Vanderlaan in particular, may have been upset when I sent down additional staff to assist or review the investigation at some stages. Likewise, the local forensic people. Later in the investigation, Kate Vanderlaan transferred to Katherine, but that was a promotion and was always on the cards.

'As commissioner, I was once removed from the investigation, but I was regularly appraised of developments. We had many meetings to discuss the case, and I kept asking for the facts. There was so much speculation, even amongst our members, but all we could go on were facts.

'The media were very quick to condemn Joanne Lees – they wanted us to assassinate her – but she had been very traumatised. I always felt we had to believe her – he was found tied up – but of course you sit thinking about the motive. I've sat for hours thinking Why? Why? Why? This is the sort of question you're confronted with here, and based upon my experience, there are no answers.

'Maybe the man saw the couple and stalked them. He could have already been a predator, done other crimes of this nature and not been caught. He must have been carrying those handcuffs, because they could not have been made at the roadside in the timeframe of Joanne's story. Of course we discussed whether the incident could have been somehow contrived between her and her boyfriend.

'Was she ever a suspect? We had to keep an open mind. All we could do was go on what we'd been told by her, but there was evidence of someone else at the scene ...'

The evidence to which he was referring was the male DNA profile identified on Joanne's T-shirt. Although police could not be certain that the spot of DNA they had found had been deposited during the incident, it was sent to all states for checking against their forensic databases. Within a couple of days, a partial match was obtained with the DNA of an Irish-born man who had been suspected of a crime in another state. The lab staff became quite excited about this result, as sixteen out of the eighteen markers matched the sample.

This man's DNA had remained on the interstate database illegally; he had been released without charge, and at that point his DNA should have been removed. But the case was too important to allow that to become a problem. It seemed possible that the DNA on Joanne's T-shirt might have come from him or one of his five brothers, some of whom were in Australia. On the advice of Dr Peter Thatcher, the Northern Territory police sent a team to Ireland to obtain DNA samples from the man's parents and attempt to rule their family members in or out of the frame.

By Wednesday 18 July, police had received more than 500 calls offering information. The search of the crime scene was scaled back, only to be renewed after the report came in about the Kombi and the four-wheel drive being seen parked together. Police took the informant to Barrow Creek to go over his information, then examined a campsite about sixty metres from where they found Peter's blood. Police were not sure if the site was significant. How recently had it been occupied? Had the camper been involved in the incident? Had he been waiting for an accomplice to pull Peter and Joanne to the side of the road? The campfire ashes provided no clues.

Meanwhile, Luciano and Paul Falconio asked to visit the place where Peter was last seen. On Thursday 19 July, after giving blood samples, they were driven to the site, followed by scores of media representatives. At the site, the Falconios walked around quietly, trying to visualise what might have happened to Peter. Paul Falconio plucked a bunch of gum leaves from a stunted tree and put them in his pocket, while his father looked around slowly, lost in his sorrow.

Denise Hurley was still trying to convince Joanne Lees to speak to the media. When Joanne refused, Denise suggested taping an interview or even a short account in her own words for the TV stations.

Eventually, Joanne agreed to a staged walk across the courtyard of the police station on her way to sit with Paul and Luciano Falconio while they spoke to the media. The appearance was planned for the afternoon of Friday 20 July.

Then, at the last minute, Joanne baulked. Denise Hurley pleaded with her, explaining how important it was to help with the investigation and to quell the rumours that her story had been fabricated. Joanne was unmoved. 'Here's a photo of me and Pete,' she said mutinously. 'If what they want is a photo, they can use this.' She handed over a snap of the young couple looking back over their shoulders in their Kombi van, setting off on the adventure of a lifetime. 'And I've written something for Paul to read. I'm not doing it! And that's that.' She flicked her hair defiantly and refused to budge.

The assembled media had to be satisfied with a sombre Paul Falconio reading Joanne's statement. She said she was not prepared to sell her story to the media. She had been 'very lucky to have escaped and to be OK'. Her statement continued, 'I don't want to lessen the severity of what happened, but I believe there has been speculation that I was sexually assaulted, but this did not occur.' (The speculation had arisen because journalists had been told 'off the record' that Joanne had refused to be examined for signs of sexual assault.)

She asked people to 'concentrate their efforts on finding Pete' and on 'finding the man'. She asked that journalists respect her privacy and let her get on with her life.

There was fat chance of that. She had let the media down, and the reaction was vicious. A BBC correspondent said, 'We've had enough of this messing around! We'll go after her – and we'll get her!' The Australian correspondent for *The Sunday Times* threatened to 'knock on every door in town'.

The British press were under even more pressure than their Australian counterparts. Only months before, a girl called Tracy Andrews had told a similar story. She said she had been travelling in England with her boyfriend when they were stopped by a man who stabbed and killed the boyfriend. There had been extensive sympathy from the British media. Then the bombshell exploded. Tracy had done it herself. She had stabbed her boyfriend in a murderous frenzy. Headlines told the tale of the 'cold, calculating killer', the 'lying murderess'. Whispers had already begun that Joanne Lees had hoodwinked the Northern Territory police. Many UK editors were telling their reporters 'Lees must be guilty. Go get her!'

Australian journalists were also muttering their suspicions over cold beers and empty notebooks. The prevailing opinion in the streets of Alice Springs was that Joanne Lees was involved somehow. If she wasn't, why didn't she come out and say so?

On Saturday 21 July, police held a press conference with two Aboriginal trackers in attendance to demonstrate their skills. One of the trackers arrived a bit worse for wear. He drew a squiggle in the dust and informed the rapt overseas correspondents it was a 'Nake'. Then he drew three little splayed-out lines and said seriously, 'Bird'. Everyone nodded.

The trackers followed Denise Hurley across the lawn in front of Belvedere House, where the conference was being held. Peering at the holes made by her high heels, one of them sagely announced that a woman had recently passed that way. Fleur Bitcon, Mark Wilton and other Australian journalists were propping each other up, trying to contain their hilarity.

Police announced that a website dedicated to the Falconio investigation was receiving more than a thousand hits per day. Daily updates were being posted as they came to hand.

A fairly ambiguous hand-drawn sketch of the gunman's vehicle was handed out to the assembled media – perhaps a bit lean on detail to encourage responses from the public. The information-starved crews looked around the surrounding streets. In all directions were four-wheel drives that resembled the sketch.

'Could you take us to a car yard so we can film something that actually looks like the real truck?' a TV journalist asked, without success.

After their display in town, the two trackers were taken to the crime scene to look for any tracks or other clues. One of them was Teddy Egan, a well-respected tracker who had assisted many past police investigations. (Teddy had grown up at Yuendumu and had adopted the name of Ted Egan, the manager of the community, as a mark of respect.) Teddy told his mates later, 'Waste of time, that search. All I find is hundreds of bloody big police boot prints.'

The roadblocks were lifted on 23 July. Max Pope explained, 'While we feel that we moved very quickly to put the roadblocks in place, we have never discounted the possibility that the offender may have left the Northern Territory. Alternatively, since the roadblocks were established, he may have found a way to get around them using his four-wheel drive.' He thanked the travelling public for their patience, and warned them to avoid travelling at night or alone. He concluded: 'It is always a possibility that the offender continues to lie low in the Northern Territory and will make his move once the roadblocks are down. Therefore, it is vitally important that the travelling public continue to keep their eyes and ears open for any sighting of the offender or his vehicle, particularly at fuel stops and roadside rests.'

By this time, police had searched approximately 320,000 square kilometres around the incident site and taken about a thousand calls. One of these came from Luke Campbell, who had been competing in the Camel Cup on 14 July and had won the Honeymoon Derby. He and his parents stayed in Alice Springs overnight, celebrating his win, then headed south from Alice Springs early in the morning. They missed the early announcements of the hold-up and did not encounter any roadblocks.

At Stuart Wells, ninety kilometres from Alice Springs, they decided to have brunch at Bob's, a local truck stop. There, Luke's parents walked past a white four-wheel drive and saw a strange-looking man get out. He was tall and limping, leaning on a stick as he made his way to the pumps. 'He had a shifty look,' Luke's father later told police. 'He kept glancing over his shoulder.'

Luke's car was parked nearer the passenger side of the four-wheel drive. There was a man sitting bolt upright in the passenger seat, staring straight ahead, unblinking. 'I went inside,' Luke told me later, 'and said to Mum and Dad, "Did you see that bloke in the truck? I wonder what he was on." Dad thought the other bloke looked really suss as well.

'We thought the pair might have been a couple of dealers or something. The four-wheel drive was heading south, and we didn't think anything more about it until we heard the news of the hold-up later on. The big bloke could have been the gunman and the guy I saw, well, he was youngish, with very short hair – I actually thought he was bald when I first saw him, but he could have had short hair. He had that round, girlish sort of face like Peter Falconio. They rang the cops as soon as they heard of the incident. Many months later, Luke still wondered, 'What if that had been him, propped up dead, to look like a passenger? We never heard back from them, though.'

Reports came from all directions. Many were unlikely. There was a fleeting sighting of Peter Falconio at the Darwin night markets; a fat guy who looked like Angry Anderson driving around Tennant Creek boasting that he 'knew stuff'; a mysterious flask found west of Barrow Creek; spot fires seen on the road near Katherine. Among hundreds of rumours and good leads, the trick was to identify which was which.

An itinerant worker from the Hunter Valley in New South Wales phoned the Channel Nine newsroom in Sydney saying he knew the killer – same four-wheel drive, silent red cattle dog, same description, and he was in the Northern Territory at the same time. Peter Harvey from Channel Nine flew in the network chopper to collect him. Harvey filmed the interview, informed the police and waited for the scoop. But he never heard back from the police, and his interview stayed in the can. Later, when a different informant rang from Perth with a similar story, naming the same man, Harvey didn't bother to follow it up.

All this gave the media something to write about and discuss. Even though it was coming up to the Territory election, Mark Wilton recalled, 'not one journo was interested in the election stunts. I reckon it got the least amount of coverage ever for any election. A story needed to be an absolute cracker to get anything but a left-hand page. But we were all getting pissed off waiting for Joanne Lees. We were talking at the *Advocate* of pulling the story from the front page until the cops gave us something.'

What they all wanted on their front pages was Joanne Lees. But she remained in hiding.

Chapter Nine

NO TEARS, NO ANSWERS

I've got a problem with all press that doubt my story,
misquote me and make false accusations …

Joanne Lees, 25 July 2001

In an effort to put an end to the stalemate, Commissioner Bates flew to
Alice Springs to persuade Joanne to face the press. He also wanted
to meet Luciano and Paul Falconio, to reassure them that everything
possible was being done to find Peter.

Glenn Morrison, a reporter with the *Centralian Advocate*, was
doing his shopping when he spotted Joanne Lees, Brian Bates, Libby
Andrew and Kate Vanderlaan making for a secluded booth at the back
of a cafe. Glenn couldn't believe his luck; he sidled up to the adjoining
booth and sat with his ears tuned to their conversation.

'I thought I was on to a major scoop,' he told me later, 'and strained
my ears to overhear. All they talked about was their favourite books
and music, travelling in the Northern Territory and sport. Joanne's
minder said she was a Stephen King fan and Joanne revealed she
was a soccer fanatic.'

Then Glenn's ears began to burn as the discussion turned to the
behaviour of the media and Joanne's reluctance to speak out. Libby
Andrew and Brian Bates were urging her to face the media. Bates
assured her he wouldn't force her, but also explained that it was
something he would 'like her to do'. Soon afterwards, without Glenn
hearing an agreement, Joanne was spirited out through the lunch-
hour crowd, back to her hotel.

Later, Bates addressed the media. He said the police were working 'across Australia' to 'bring this person to justice'. Things became a little heated when a reporter vigorously questioned the commissioner about a potential suspect who had been detained by the New South Wales police.

'I already knew it was more than likely not the person,' Brian Bates told me later. 'But one reporter was very rude and called out "Has the offender been caught in New South Wales?" When I said "No", the reporter said, "Mr Commissioner, you are lying to us." I was not impressed. I told them if I had the slightest belief that was our man, I would have had police on a plane to New South Wales immediately.'

Commissioner Bates finally prevailed. Joanne Lees agreed to attend a media conference, supported by Paul Falconio. But the arrangements for this event were almost farcical.

Once it was announced a press conference would take place, negotiations with Joanne Lees began. She wanted to speak to a video camera in an empty room. The media said 'No way!' Then she said she'd speak to just one journalist; the question was who? She didn't want a print journalist, and she didn't want TV. No photographers, either. The police media people shuttled between the journalists and Joanne, each time returning to the fray with new conditions from her. Exasperation reigned.

Finally, the arrangements were settled. There would be no print journalists, one radio journalist (Penny Doust from ABC Darwin was chosen) and one TV camera. All questions were to be provided in advance, in writing. Members of the media went into a huddle.

'We prepared about thirteen questions,' Fleur Bitcon told me. 'The usual sort of things – what actually happened on the night, what do you think happened to your boyfriend, what did the man look like, why weren't there any footprints … you know, just basic, normal stuff. Then we all congregated outside the room where this staged event – please don't call it a press conference! – was going on, waiting for the answers.'

Holding tightly to Paul Falconio, Joanne made her first official appearance. After all the hype, the media were tense, and so was she. She seemed to be controlling her anxiety by taking deep, slow breaths, hauling in courage with the oxygen. There was a rumour she'd insisted that a hairdresser open up early to do her hair, which was immaculately groomed. She was also expertly made up, with thick mascara and a fine aqua line of eyeliner under her bottom eyelid, emphasising her large, distant eyes. Her eyebrows were plucked into an expression of frail astonishment.

She sat between Paul Falconio and Commander Max Pope, clinging tightly to Paul's hand below the desktop. Pope, also looking tense, told the silent audience that Joanne had decided to answer only three of the prepared questions, all of them about her relationship (or lack of it) with the media. Joanne stared straight in front, her only movement a small but defiant toss of her head as Pope announced her decision.

The camera crew and Penny Doust held their breath, waiting to hear her voice for the first time. At a signal from Pope, Penny Doust called out the first question: 'What is your reaction to the doubt expressed about your story?'

'Anyone who has spoken to me or has been in contact with me – no one doubts me,' Joanne replied. 'Only media doubts my stories.'

'Why have you been reluctant to meet the press?' 'Because I find it all so overwhelming and intimidating.'

'Do you have a particular problem with the British press, and why is that?'

Joanne licked her lips, took a deep breath and replied, 'I've got a problem with all press that distort the truth … and doubt my story, misquote me and make false accusations.' Her anger was barely disguised.

Without much more ado, Max Pope said, 'Joanne has a statement she will read out to the press.'

Joanne hauled in another breath and began reading from a single sheet of paper in a flat, quavering little voice. 'I hope that people will respect now my privacy and allow me to get on with my life.' She said she was certain Peter was still alive, and she hoped the public would continue to support the search for him and the gunman. She also assured the media that she had not been sexually assaulted.

Joanne lowered the paper, looked at Paul Falconio and squeezed his hand, mouthing, 'Thanks, Paul.' Then the three of them trooped out in silence.

Assistant Commissioner Daulby told media representatives later, 'If I was in charge, I would have said it would do more damage if she only answered three questions.' He was probably right – and he was in charge. But by then Joanne probably couldn't have got it right, no matter what she did. If she remained composed, she would be accused of being cold and uncaring. If she cried, she risked being accused of bunging it on and trying to conceal some involvement in Peter's disappearance.

Fleur Bitcon had been nosing around her other contacts and discovered that the police minister had approved a huge reward. Fleur phoned Denise Hurley and asked her if it was true.

'You can't use that,' Denise told her crossly. 'It hasn't been announced yet.'

'But it is true, isn't it?' Fleur persisted.

Denise refused to comment. Fleur took out the local phone book, looked up Bob Fields, and rang him at home. He was not amused.

'How did you get my home phone number?' he exploded. Fleur felt mischievous. She mumbled something about a contact; she didn't remind him that his number was listed in the phone book. He agreed that the reward would be offered and she phoned Denise back, saying, 'I have confirmation of the reward and I'm going to use it on *Nine News* tonight.'

The official announcement was made next day from the office of the police minister, Mike Reed. The Northern Territory government was offering $250,000 – the biggest reward in Australian history – for information leading to the apprehension and conviction of the person or persons responsible for Peter Falconio's abduction. Any accomplice who came forward would be recommended for immunity from prosecution.

The reward had been in the pipeline for a few days. Police had planned a media conference in Darwin so that Reed and the commissioner could make the announcement, but they were pipped at the post by *Nine News*.

Mike Reed told me later, 'We always leave it to the commissioner to set the amount of the reward, and then it's approved by cabinet. It doesn't come out of the police budget, because that may inhibit the police in their decision about how much to offer. In this case, the commissioner decided that, as they were not making much progress, a big reward might flush someone out.'

Although the police had the truck-stop video, the number plates were partially obscured, and they were too late to catch up with the driver. As Mike Reed put it, 'They were in danger of hitting a brick wall.'

After the reward was announced, the media were notified of a 'photo opportunity' at 2.15 that afternoon. This consisted of trailing around after 'some uniformed cop, who was putting up reward posters', Fleur Bitcon recalled. 'I suppose it was better than nothing.' The uniformed cop was Sergeant Colleen Gwynne, who was later to be promoted to superintendent and take command of the operation.

Mandy Taylor, presenter of the ABC *Drive* program in Alice Springs, was also critical of the police handling of the case, although she stressed that the police learnt from their mistakes.

'They were churning out releases, but not giving any of the information people wanted to know. Because that information was so thin, if you weren't familiar with the place, you'd interview any freak to get a story.'

She added, 'People talk in a small town. We all knew about the truck-stop video, for example, and police were denying it even existed. There seemed to be so many police heads involved. Daulby came down himself and so did the commissioner. It made you think: what sort of a grip do they have on this? Daulby looks good on TV, but they never told us anything. They should have had a strategy. It was so obvious they didn't.'

Mandy spoke off the record to several police she knew, and most of them said they believed Joanne's story. Mandy did too, and told me later she was concerned about the initial police handling of Joanne. 'She'd been tied up by a gunman, and the man she loved had been killed. She should have been treated the same way as a rape victim. You should always treat victims as if a rape had taken place – it may not have, but she should have had the counselling. Sometimes the rape story comes out later.

'There were a few details of her story that seemed to change later on. I always thought there was more to it, really. She struck me as a woman who was pretty much balanced on the edge.' So why was she allowed to stay with the Piltons rather than being offered counselling? 'I think it was pretty professionally off,' Mandy said.

'In hindsight, the guy would have buggered off straight away. The police didn't have a clue. They were acting like he was still in the area – roadblocks, choppers full of TRG people flying over Alice Springs – but they hadn't a clue where he'd gone. They had no answer when I asked publicly, "What makes you think he's still here?"'

For his part, Mike Reed was critical of the media. 'They are dreadful creatures! They barely saw the flames, never felt the heat and still tried to tell everybody else about the fire. They should have a look at their own approach. They are not the police, and the police are not there to make the media happy. The location was shocking, the case was very strange, we had difficulty getting police there – resources from the city had to be thrown at a case that was in the middle of nowhere. Of course we sent more and more senior police over the following few days, and the level of criticism would have been huge if we hadn't.'

After the reward was announced, Aboriginal residents of outlying communities began emerging from their houses, hoping to find the gunman.

'It was a hoot,' John Turahui recalled. 'There were these three old ladies – one was blind, another deaf and the third one far too infirm to be wandering around in the scrub. They all set off to Jara Jara to find the gunman. The whole community's attitude turned from fear to greed overnight.'

On 1 August, another senior police officer became involved in the case when Commander Col Hardman took over from Bob Fields and Max Pope. The police media unit explained that Fields and Pope had 'taken up new positions in Darwin and Katherine, which had been planned before the incident'. And the investigation was now a CIB operation. This meant the uniforms were out of the picture, though they were still doing the legwork.

The next day, Assistant Commissioner Daulby released the news of the unidentified DNA. He told a packed room, 'We have found and have established a DNA profile of a male person on the clothing of Joanne Lees. All that can be said in relation to this is that it could be the offender and I can't speculate any more on that.'

In answer to a barrage of questions, he said the DNA was not Peter Falconio's and that databases were being searched in Australia, New Zealand and elsewhere. The discovery was a 'significant breakthrough', but the investigation was still primarily focused on finding Peter Falconio.

Daulby headed most media conferences from then on. It was rumoured that he wanted every conference on police records, so all his pronouncements were captured – for the record – by police video cameras.

On 3 August, new 'portraits' of the alleged offender were handed out. He'd had a haircut and lost his moustache, to allow for the possibility that the fugitive might have changed his appearance. Police also indicated that he might have ditched his dog and swapped his vehicle. The needle in the haystack was burrowing deeper and deeper.

Mr Daulby announced that Peter's father had left Alice Springs, not because he had lost faith in finding his son, but because his wife was faring badly at home. Ever since the awful morning of 14 July, when she'd collapsed on hearing the news of Peter's disappearance, Joan Falconio had been distraught. She and Luciano were well known in New Mill, where they ran the general store. They had already planned to retire on 1 August, but the events of 14 July changed that. They hadn't been back at work since.

'Because of what's happened to Peter,' she told people, 'we came out. We're just ... at a loss.'

Chapter Ten

IN THE FRAME

*Physical evidence cannot be wrong, it cannot perjure itself
... only its interpretation can err.*

Paul L. Kirk

On 5 August, sixty kilometres south of Alice Springs, a group of tourists who'd stopped at a rest stop to stretch their legs found a rental car and a white man's body. Police would not confirm or deny that the body might be Peter Falconio, but the body seemed too close to the road to have escaped notice for almost three weeks. A call went in to the Forensic Science Centre in Darwin, and Joy Kuhl decided to fly down to help out. She travelled to the rest stop with Sergeant Bill Towers, the senior forensic examiner at the local Crime Scene Unit, and an Aboriginal tracker. The tracker looked around and told her a man had stood on a nearby tussock of grass. At first, Joy was sceptical, but her scepticism turned to admiration when he showed her how he had arrived at this conclusion. After gathering as much information as possible from the crime scene, Joy accompanied the body back to Alice Springs for an autopsy.

Later in the day, Commander Hardman told the media that early investigations did not indicate the remains were those of Peter Falconio. The body was identified within a couple of days as that of 39-year-old Stuart Rhode, a local identity who had recently returned from Adelaide to Alice Springs.

Mr Rhode did not remain the focus of attention for long. On Monday 6 August, the day after his body was discovered, police finally released two images from the elusive truck-stop video. The police media release said the photos were taken in the early hours of Sunday 15 July. 'The man, driving a white four-wheel-drive Toyota utility with a canvas back, parked in the truck area and purchased diesel fuel. He entered the shop and bought ice and water. Police have enhanced the images from the security video and are now seeking public assistance to identify the man and the vehicle.' One of the photos showed a canvas-canopied white four-wheel drive parked at a diesel pump; the other captured a tall man entering the Shell shop. He wore a black baseball cap with a barely decipherable motif, jeans, runners and a windcheater. He was wearing glasses. The time shown on the still was 0:45:50 – a quarter to one on the morning of 15 July.

In the sunshine outside the Alice Springs police station, Commander Hardman fielded hostile questions about the police decision to withhold the video for three weeks. Mark Wilton, wearing a black baseball cap not unlike the one in the photo, was standing right beside Commander Hardman, and his anger was clearly visible on several TV cameras. He audibly sighed 'F--k!' when Hardman made his opening remarks. 'Why was that tape ruled out so early in the investigation?' he asked loudly.

Hardman replied that it was just one of the vehicles and lines of inquiry that were being followed up. He held up a photo of the vehicle and then produced a torn photo of the man, saying that the images would be distributed to all media outlets. Hardman added that there was nothing to link the man with the investigation.

Mark Wilton told me later, 'They danced all around it. I think Hardman had come onto the job and said, "We've got to get this video out there." My feeling was that they knew who the bloke was all along and were hoping he'd return to his normal life and then they'd grab him. I asked Hardman some questions about the motif on the guy's hat, and Hardman was sarcastic – "If the cap fits, Mark, you wear it." Not a good attitude after they'd withheld vital information for so long.'

Daulby too was non-committal. He said the man 'may be an innocent traveller' and called on him to make himself known to police as soon as possible, to rule himself out of the investigation.

Mark Wilton claimed that the video had sat in someone's in-tray for days. Other rumours did the rounds: Joanne had identified the man, or she hadn't; her stepfather had told someone she'd said it was 'the best likeness of anyone she'd seen'.

Mandy Taylor, Fleur Bitcon and many other journalists distinctly remembered being told that the images had been recorded on 'old VHS tapes' and had to be sent away for enhancement. But Val Prior, the security supervisor at the truck stop, was adamant that their images were the best you could get.

'We installed new CCTV equipment only a couple of weeks before,' she told journalists. 'The cameras were not new, but the other equipment was. There were absolutely no old tapes. Our equipment does not use tapes. The police brought someone to download those images directly from our equipment. And they walked in with brand-new VHS tapes.' This naturally increased the media's scepticism about the official reasons for the delay.

Shane Ride, who downloaded the images, later told me, 'I don't believe any enhancement was done. An officer came to my place on the Sunday night to collect me to download the images. Our company had installed the CCTV unit not long before. The police supplied ten new VHS tapes, still in their wrapping. The police manpower was very stretched, so I don't think any cops stayed with me while I did it.

'I was working on it for a few hours, and then we went over to the police station to view the VHS tapes to make sure they had recorded properly. I could have enhanced them a bit when I was downloading them – changed the pixels or the grey-scale a bit – but I didn't, because when you're dealing with a police case, you have to have the original footage. Otherwise you can add a moustache or cut someone's hair – you can do anything these days. So it has to be the original. That's why I downloaded all those little boxes along the bottom, to demonstrate it was straight from the tape. The picture that made the papers was the one I recorded. No enhancement.'

The police were stung by the media's disbelief. Acting Commissioner John Valentin issued a statement that said, 'The delay in releasing the images was necessary to ensure that the images were sufficiently clear to be useful to the victim of the incident, Ms Joanne Lees, and the public ... The timing of the release of the service station images is a matter for the investigators ... The criticism by some sections of the media is something of their making, not mine, and such criticism does nothing to help our inquiry.'

◆ ◆ ◆

Former Senior Constable Wayne Hartley from Alice Springs police told me later that an effort was made to enhance the visuals. If he'd had his way, police would have simply obtained a warrant and taken possession of the CCTV, over Val Prior's protests if necessary. He had sent copies off to Darwin and Brisbane, but got no better result. The police actually had six digital stills, but they chose only to release two shots from the VHS tape, which was much less distinct.

The footage from the truck stop became the focal point of the investigation. Police identified more than 16,000 four-wheel drives similar to the one in the video. Oddly, the truck in the video bore little resemblance to the earlier sketch made from Joanne Lees's description of the gunman's vehicle.

◆ ◆ ◆

Another video was about to play a role in the case as well. At the Alice Springs Crime Scene Unit, where the orange Kombi was held, Joy Kuhl was under pressure to do another examination of the van. Carmen Eckhoff had already used ortho-toluidine to test the van for blood, but Towers informed Joy that Detective Sergeant John Nixon wanted it tested with luminol, which reacts with blood and sweat to produce a glowing luminescence that lasts for about thirty seconds.

Joy was not happy about this. 'Luminol is very good for outside crime scenes or even a room,' she told me later, 'but in a car or confined space it's not so effective, because it picks up all sorts of contamination on various surfaces that may show a similar reaction to blood.' Luminol has largely been superseded by ortho-toluidine for these kinds of tests.

But Towers insisted. 'I want to film it,' he said, 'because we need to get some proper video equipment that can film in the dark.' A private filmmaker, Chris Tangey of Xplor Media, had agreed to come in and do some filming after dark with his own 'you-beaut gear'. Towers hoped that the film would show how useful the equipment was and help him lobby for new kit.

'There's no point,' Joy replied. 'Carmen has done the van all over. There's nothing there. If we use luminol, we won't get any blood, but we're likely to get all these non-specific reactions.'

'I've bought some meat in a Cryovac pack,' Bill told her. 'I want to dribble some across the floor and outside so we can film the reaction as well. Look, Nikko wants it done, OK?'

Reluctantly, she agreed. She spent the rest of the afternoon going over the van with ortho-toluidine 'just in case', but found no bloodstains.

After dark, Chris Tangey arrived with his 'you-beaut gear'. He had agreed to donate his time in return for exclusive use of the master tape after six months.

The van was brightly lit. On the rear, around the engine hatch and the right-hand rear wing, examiners had drawn a grid of six-inch squares, hoping to pinpoint any brain matter or blood spatters. Bill Towers asked Chris to take some footage before the lights went out. While filming the interior, Chris noticed that the front seats were bucket seats, with a gearstick between them. It crossed his mind that it would be difficult to grapple with someone across those seats, especially for a large man.

Next, Towers turned off the lights. 'Are you getting this, Chris?' he asked.

'Yeah, no worries,' Chris replied.

'I'm going to spray the light fitting first, because I know I'll get a reaction,' Joy said. Sure enough, a faint blue luminescence appeared.

'I'm doing the door,' Joy said. 'Can you come around to the door?'

Chris tried to manoeuvre between Joy and the open driver's door. 'It's a bit awkward,' he told them. Then he asked, 'What are those marks?' He had four marks in his viewfinder, glowing in the shape of three fingers and a thumb of a right hand, on the vinyl lining of the driver's door. His camera was pointing downward at roughly forty-five degrees, quite close to the door.

'I don't know what it is. It can't be blood,' said Joy Kuhl, sounding a bit anxious. 'I went over this whole thing this afternoon. It's a good thing Nikko can't see this. He'd be convinced it was a bloodbath!' Chris pulled back and panned to the right to capture the image from a slightly truer perspective before the marks faded.

Towers asked Chris if the sound recorder was on. Chris said it was, and Towers suggested turning it off, which Chris did. The testing moved to the dashboard and other parts of the van, but no other reactions were obtained.

A few days later, Chris made a digital copy of the tape and gave it to Bill Towers. Chris was keen to find out whether the 'handprint' would be followed up. From time to time, he'd play the film. Not being a forensic biologist, he wondered how the scientists could rule out the presence of blood without conducting further tests. He also wondered why Joy Kuhl had swabbed that area earlier. Had she found something with ortho-toluidine and taken swabs to follow up?

◆ ◆ ◆

The police, for their part, were wondering about some aspects of Joanne Lees's story. There seemed to be large gaps in her version of events. Experts analysed her statements and came back with the opinion that 'vital information' was missing. Aboriginal trackers who had been shown the place where Joanne said she'd crouched for five hours all said that nobody had stayed in that spot for that long.

They also thought the footprints suggested she'd been running, but there were 'no other footprints in pursuit'. Various medical authorities suggested she lacked the injuries you'd expect from such an assault.

On 7 August, Joanne was called back to the Alice Springs police station and interviewed by Detective Senior Sergeant Jeanette Kerr, who was trained in negotiation and interrogation, and Detective Sergeant Tony Henrys. Joanne was told that the interview was to 'raise concerns and inconsistencies that had arisen from investigations made so far'. She was challenged on almost every aspect of her story.

Detective Kerr told Joanne that they had not found 'a single vehicle' matching her description, especially one with a crawl through behind the seats. If such a vehicle existed, it was very well hidden. Also, a firearms and ballistics check had turned up nothing to match the gun. Kerr pointed out that the Kombi door had 'scrolling' similar to that she'd described on the gun. Could Joanne have mixed them up?

Joanne refused to budge.

'What about being able to hear Peter and the man talking with the engine running?' Detective Kerr asked her. 'We don't think you could see or hear anything the way you've described.'

Joanne insisted she had.

Joanne was asked about the tape found around her ankle. 'It was only seventy centimetres long,' Detective Kerr told her. 'It's not long enough to have gone around your ankles.'

Joanne had not been able to see the man while he was attempting to tie her legs, so she was unable to shed any light on this.

'And the dog. It's a big coincidence that the dog you saw just happened to resemble the one you saw soon after at Barrow Creek Hotel? And the mailbag that was near the door at the hotel. Could that have triggered the idea of a canvas bag being placed over your head?'

Joanne was tearful, tired and angry, but she stuck to her story.

Chapter Eleven

THE 'LINDYFICATION' OF JOANNE LEES

I won't have you treat the victim like a suspect. I don't want another Chamberlain on my hands.

Assistant Commissioner John Daulby

Joanne Lees was now staying at the same hotel as Paul Falconio. The room staff told their friends and relatives that she was never alone. 'She either has one of those police with her during the day,' said David Jones's flatmate, who was a chambermaid, 'or Paul Falconio watching over her at night.'

It became known in some circles that the police had discovered that Joanne had made hundreds of dollars' worth of phone calls. She often made overseas calls and kept in touch with friends and family by email. A senior police officer told her to keep the costs under control or her access would be cut off. It also emerged that she had two separate email accounts.

◆ ◆ ◆

As Joanne maintained her silence, questions were bandied around at every gathering of journalists playing the waiting game in Alice Springs. How did she get a bag off her head with her hands tied behind her back? And how was it that she was found with her hands tied in front? What was the dog doing? It seemed remarkable that the only physical evidence found at the scene – other than Peter's blood – belonged to Joanne. Three of her shoeprints, her lip-balm lid, but nothing to help identify her attacker. Why were there no useful footprints around the Kombi, when it was abandoned in soft ground?

Why didn't Joanne see Peter's body on the road? How was she able to evade an experienced bushman, with or without a dog, in pretty skimpy scrub? Why did she remain in the bush for so long? Why did the man drive away, leaving her there to tell her story?

Loose lips in the police force produced more rumours, which swirled around the pubs. There was talk that Joanne's diary suggested her relationship with Peter was rocky; there were whispers that police had found the descriptions of aspects of their private lives quite diverting. It was said there was an air ticket to Thailand in Peter Falconio's name, but none for Joanne, leading to speculation that Peter had planned to go his own way in Darwin.

Media anger simmered. Here was a girl who'd starred in a story of international interest, and she was avoiding them. What was she hiding?

Kate Vanderlaan made it obvious that she was frustrated at Joanne's reluctance to enlist public support. She told media representatives, 'I can't understand her logic. I think she feels very intimidated.' Commander Bob Fields tried to hose down the speculation, saying, 'I find it offensive that anyone would question this young woman's story. We have no doubts about what she has told us.' Assistant Commissioner Daulby told the media Joanne was 'free to go any time'.

Commissioner Brian Bates spent hours pondering the imponderable. 'It was a peculiar type of incident that had occurred. Was it contrived between herself and her boyfriend? Is he alive somewhere? Why did she say the man's interior light was on so she had such a clear view of the man and his dog? Why was he driving with the inside light on along a dark highway at speed? You just don't do that, do you? Why did her clothes not forensically reflect what she'd been through? Investigators were quite taken aback by her description of the revolver. These are some of the things that make this case one of the most puzzling ever.'

From England, stringers were being asked, 'Do you think she did it?' Her version of what happened was not as commercial as the story of the smart, devious backpacker who'd killed her boyfriend and outwitted a provincial police force – a force still haunted by the spectre of Lindy Chamberlain.

Paul Toohey from the *Australian* described this as 'the Lindyfication of Joanne Lees': the Lindyfication of Joanne Lees has begun. For the first time yesterday, journalists began asking hard questions: whether police still believe her story ...

Police did what they did not do in the case of Lindy Chamberlain – they stood firm behind the woman in the middle.

Lindy Chamberlain's name was mentioned almost as often as Joanne's during the weeks following 14 July 2001.

Lindy Chamberlain now lives in a secluded nook of the Hunter Valley with her second husband, Rick. When we spoke, she was mourning for her beloved father, who had died during preparations for daughter Kahlia's twenty-first birthday. 'An ending and a continuation of life,' Lindy told me. Kahlia was born inside the high-security prison in Berrimah and was taken from Lindy only a few days later.

Lindy sympathised with Joanne Lees. She told me, 'Joanne went through a terrible ordeal, but she was smart and kept her head and saved her life. But afterwards she was in a terrible position. Because the police couldn't find the gunman quickly, it was certain the media would turn on her. If you don't talk at all, the press gets mad at you because they want a story and they think you've got something to hide.'

Lindy is not angry at the way she was treated. 'Anger is self-destructive,' she said. But the bad memories linger. She and Michael Chamberlain were advised by the police to give interviews, which were later used against them. 'In Joanne's position, you're damned if you do say anything and damned if you don't. I believe her. I would've liked to help her if she had needed me. There's nothing worse than being accused of murdering a loved one. All her reactions were typical of shock, stress, trauma and the long interrogation she went through.

'She's been compared to me, but I don't think that's true. Everyone is an individual and no two cases are the same. She was right to keep quiet. A lot of the media hype is all about selling papers. Newspapers are a business, you know, not a source of accurate information. Murdoch's worldwide networks in particular employ 'swing' reporters – specialists in writing good stories about you one day, bad the next. "Did she, or didn't she?" What would they know? Anyway, at least they won't be able to throw her comments back in her face. The less you say, the less it can be misreported.

'She knows what happened. Knowledge sets the heart at rest. What you don't know is what you fear.'

Unable to interview Joanne, the media began interviewing one another. Speaking on Scottish TV, Richard Shears from the London *Daily Mail* commented on the similarities between the Chamberlain and Falconio cases. 'There was no body in either case, only a bloodstained jumpsuit/a large pool of blood. In both cases, how the woman performed on TV affected the public perception; everyone believed Lindy did it/people believe Joanne did it; the media contact in both cases seemed stage-managed and unspontaneous.'

Polls about Joanne Lees were done in city streets: 'Do you think she did it?' Public opinion swung away from admiration for a plucky tourist to scepticism and borderline scorn.

Scottish reporters interviewed John Bryson, the award-winning writer of *Evil Angels*, a book about Azaria Chamberlain's disappearance. He said, 'If we were not looking at a dingo in the Chamberlain case, we were looking at a woman. If we're not looking at a male assailant in the Falconio case, we're looking at a woman.'

Bryson pointed to the wider context of the Chamberlain case.

'The English-speaking world had been saturated with supernatural movies like *The Exorcist*.' In another interview, he said, 'There were these very strong figures of evil priests, and people at first believed that Michael Chamberlain, a Seventh Day Adventist pastor, had taken Azaria to sacrifice her on Ayers Rock.'

Fears of the occult were kindled by rumours that Michael Chamberlain had used a child-sized coffin in his services and that Azaria had often been dressed in black. Both stories were true, but taken out of context. The 'coffin' was for cigarette smokers to throw in their packets of smokes. Azaria did have a frilly black outfit. Her mother has donated it to the National Museum of Australia; along with Azaria's yellow matinee jacket, it has become a powerful symbol of her story.

That both cases occurred in the dead centre of outback Australia contributed to the myth. Neville Dawson, an artist who has painted more than sixty works about the Chamberlain case, believes that fears were fuelled by Australians' uneasy relationship with the outback. The Chamberlain case was 'the first time in Australian history when we were confronted with the way we think about the land,' he said in an interview. 'We see it as both a threat and a comfort, and when this happened with Lindy Chamberlain, she became a sort of substitute for that view of the land, the hostile mother. If this had happened in a suburban backyard, it would never have gripped the nation as it did.' The same was true of the Falconio case.

Away from the media scrutiny, ordinary cops were getting on with their jobs. Detective Wayne Hartley and his sidekick, Aaron Haselman, were assigned to the vehicle search. This meant following up hundreds of leads.

Hartley, who had only been a detective for about a year, was keen to work on the case. 'It was pretty much mayhem at the start,' he told me later. 'We were all getting a hundred different directions from higher up. Everyone wanted to work on it, so I just put my hand up.' He went to see his boss, Detective Sergeant David Chalker, and said, 'Give me another guy and I'll take all the car enquiries. I'll send the crap around to the States and keep the really good ones to follow up ourselves.'

He approached the job systematically. 'I drew up a pro forma and set up a system – low, medium and high priority – and within two weeks it was working sweet. My first priority was any vehicle with a crawl-through from the cabin to the rear tray. Of course, I was relying on what Joanne Lees had told the guys taking her statement. A front-to-rear access is so unusual in the outback, because of the dust and lack of cabin security, that I did hope I wasn't wasting my time.

'It was a big thing in terms of a lead – but a bad thing if it wasn't right. It was going to destroy anything I did if her description wasn't correct. Dozens of leads came in every day. We'd sort by number plate and send them out to traffic divisions in the right States for elimination. It was a huge operation.'

The vehicle photographed at the truck stop was his personal priority. Although 'Truck Stop', as it was now called, bore little resemblance to the vehicle Joanne had described, and the man in the pictures did not have a moustache or long hair, Hartley told Haselman, 'We've got to find that bloke, even if it's only to eliminate him from the inquiry.' He sent a copy of the video to the Police Technical Unit and another to the Queensland police lab to see if it could be enhanced.

A different video went to RMIT in Melbourne. It had been shot by a tourist, and showed a car travelling on the Tanami Track.

'It was pretty fuzzy because they were moving and so was the four-wheel drive, but I thought if RMIT could get a number plate off that then I'd let him look at Truck Stop. I didn't want to send Truck Stop out to a whole lot of civilians at that time, because we were keeping it pretty much under wraps.'

Each day after work, Hartley spent four hours in the security centre at the Alice Springs casino, where he could run the VHS tape from the truck stop and freeze every frame. At the end of this, he had hundreds of frames from which he could isolate aerials, hubcaps, canopy ties – fine details that might give him a lead. 'No number plates, though,' he recalled ruefully.

He was 'pretty fixated on that truck-stop video. But at work it was put first into the low-priority pile because Daulby had shown the photos to Joanne the day after we got them and she didn't ID him. Nothing like him. Too old. So we thought if this bloke wasn't him, we could use up a lot of resources trying to find him when it's a waste of time. We could only go by what she said. If she wasn't telling us the truth, then we were f--ked.'

Chapter Twelve

OFFICIAL SECRETS

I'm a little concerned about your line of questioning.

Commander Col Hardman

Four weeks after Peter Falconio's disappearance, the case seemed to be sliding into limbo. None of the thousands of leads had proved fruitful. Apart from odd sightings in town, Joanne had hardly been seen since 25 July. Her friends had returned to Sydney, and her only companions were the police 'minders' and Paul Falconio – apart from the ever-present surveillance operators, of whom she was unaware. Then, in a bid to revive public interest and elicit more useful information, Joanne agreed to make another media appearance.

To the horror of police, she arrived for the media conference wearing a pale pink singlet with the silver words 'Cheeky Monkey' across her well-developed chest. 'I begged her to change her top,' Denise Hurley said later. 'It was far too tight and not the right look for a grieving girlfriend.' As always, Joanne's resolve remained firm.

The top was instantly the focus of every camera in the room. Penny Doust said she was certain that many cameras were readjusted to a wide lens. There were whispers and sniggers from female journalists. Accompanied by Assistant Commissioner John Daulby and gripping Paul Falconio's hand, Joanne made her way to a table bristling with microphones and stared defiantly at the assembled media who were craning to see and hear her.

Mr Daulby announced that Joanne did not intend to say anything. Paul then spoke for Joanne and his family.

'Anybody in Australia, if you see anything or know of any information, if you could come forward. This is from myself, Joanne and both our families. We both want the same result and that's to find Peter and find out what's happened.'

'Do you believe your brother is still alive?' someone called out.

'Yes, we both do, and the families do as well. Both families are under a lot of stress and are very worried.'

'Are you happy with the investigation so far?'

'Yes, we can't give any complaints. Obviously, we don't know exactly the ins and outs of it all, but they do seem pretty forthcoming with information.'

'How long will you both stay in Alice Springs?' a journalist asked.

'We're just taking everything day by day,' Paul replied.

He was asked about the release of the images from the truck stop. 'We think there is a very good possibility that it was the gunman,' Paul said – although Joanne had told police the man was too old.

'Are you happy with the quality of the images?'

'We're happy with them. Yes, we're pleased about that. As I understand it, it took a while to get the best images.'

When asked about how the media had treated them, Paul answered carefully. 'Scepticism from the press has made things harder – compounded our grief, if you like. It doesn't help, and anything that detracts from what we are all about, and what we want to achieve, doesn't help anything.'

'Do you have any message for Peter? What would you say to him now, if he could hear you?'

'I'd say, "Just hang in there, just, if you can hear us, just wait. You know, we'll see you soon."'

Paul became a little emotional, and Daulby brought the conference to a close. Joanne's only movement had been a small nod as Paul spoke. Now they all stood and filed out. Some reporters took particular notice of the body language between Joanne and Paul, especially the way she held his hand as they left the room.

A few days later, Joanne and Paul left Alice Springs for Sydney. Their departure was the signal for many overseas stringers to go home.

On Friday 17 August, during an uncomfortable doorstop interview outside the Alice Springs police station, Col Hardman had said, 'With the information that we are gathering, we expect to be able to identify this person. We are making slow progress, day by day.' Sources were claiming that the police had already identified the gunman but were withholding his identity because they didn't want him to know they were on his trail. Hardman said, 'We have a [DNA] profile. But it has not been identified.' He also said it was possible that more than one offender had been involved.

Journalists asked Hardman which way the truck-stop suspect was travelling; why trackers had not been called in at the beginning; whether Hardman thought Peter Falconio could still be alive; whether the police had found anything useful in the Kombi; and, most insistently, why the police were 'withholding information' about the investigation.

Hardman's appearance fitted his name. Stung by the tone of the questions, he replied, 'We are certainly not withholding information that we believe the public could assist us with. Naturally, there are parts of our inquiries that we retain for investigation and which we do not want the suspect to know.'

He turned back on the steps and said as a parting shot, 'I'm a little concerned about your line of questioning.'

The *Adelaide Advertiser* retorted: 'The fact is that there are people out there that are more than a little concerned about the Northern Territory police "line of questioning". Or not questioning.'

Some police were also concerned about the direction the investigation was going – or not going.

The Northern Territory police force was small, and many of its members were disgruntled about funding cuts and lack of advancement opportunities. Some said the force had a culture ruled by fear and intimidation, with too many chiefs and not enough Indians. A small 'clique' at the top seemed to be dominating the hierarchy and the investigation policy.

Political changes were also afoot in the Territory. Soon a new Labor government would be elected, replacing the long-entrenched Country Liberal Party, and a new police commissioner would be appointed from South Australia, dashing local applicants' hopes of filling Brian Bates's shoes.

The people at the pointy end of the investigation were frustrated and angry with the people at the top. Rumours about the personal lives of senior officers circulated freely. There was paranoia about a media snitch in their midst, and conflict over the handling of the early interviews with Joanne Lees, which were done before detectives arrived on the scene. Some officers were worried that the description of the crawl-through was wrong, and criticised the roadblock teams for failing to obtain number plates and names on the Sunday while 'sitting beside the road getting double pay'.

Then there was the vetoing of a warrant to seize the truck stop's CCTV hard drive before the clear images were taped over; the failure to prioritise essential tasks; the possible contamination of the manacles by senior officers who refused to provide DNA. The frustration of having the eyes of the world on the investigation and knowing it was not a copybook exercise contributed to poor morale and rumour-mongering among the investigators on the job.

◆ ◆ ◆

Press speculation persisted. As part of an article on 18 August, reporting Hardman's terse press conference, the *Adelaide Advertiser* ran a long list of unanswered questions:

- Have the police identified the man on the Alice Springs roadhouse security videotape?
- Why did it take police three weeks to release the roadhouse video images of the man described as a 'person of interest'?
- Why would a roadhouse security camera designed to catch petrol thieves not reveal the registration number of the vehicle in question?
- Whose fingerprints were found on or in the Kombi van in which Ms Lees and Mr Falconio were travelling?
- Why was a large team of police sent in to the crime scene on foot before the Aboriginal trackers, making it virtually impossible for the trackers to isolate the attacker's footprints and movements?
- Why are the NT police withholding information?
- Is it really possible someone has not identified the mystery gunman whose image has been displayed in every corner of the country?
- If he has nothing to hide, why has that person not come forward?

The paper also published an interview with Aboriginal tracker Teddy Egan, who told journalist Peter Hackett, 'It would have been a lot easier for me if the police had not gone in there. I saw the blood on the road. And I found signs that someone had dragged something from the roadside.'

Hackett added that the police 'didn't exactly go into combat mode, full alert' when Les Pilton and Vince Millar phoned them. He suggested that they might have thought the late-night call was a hoax. And it was much later, too late in fact, when they finally called in the real experts, the traditional owners of the land.

Teddy could not help the police, because too much time had elapsed and too many people had stomped over the site. He was able to identify Joanne's footprints, but after half a day there he figured there was no point staying any longer, because too much damage had been done. On the other hand, he was sure that a man had been shot at the scene and that the gunman had left the area. 'I found the tyre tracks,' he told Hackett. 'He didn't drive into the bush. He went back on to the highway, and south towards Alice ... There are places out there where he could have got rid of the body. There is a mining area out there near Barrow Creek. I don't believe the man who shot him is out there in the bush. He went down the highway.'

The Northern Territory police were furious about Hackett's article and released a rebuttal later the same day. This only gave the media more ammunition. (Experienced media managers usually advise against entering into slanging matches with journalists.)

The police rebuttal, labelled 'Barrow Creek Update No. 52', said that the police did not think more than one person was involved at the scene (in spite of the fact that Hardman had said the opposite the day before). They defended the placement of roadblocks within an hour of Joanne's report (but did not mention that they had not taken the number plates and names of people passing through the roadblocks); and they claimed that the crime scene at Barrow Creek was preserved, 'with only forensic scientists permitted to enter until they had conducted their initial investigation of the scene'. This last assertion was clearly not the case. Vince Millar had witnessed a line search of the scrub, and Senior Sergeant Geoff Sullivan later told Scottish TV that his men had immediately done line searches.

The document went on to criticise the 'tone' of Hackett's article and defend the policy of withholding information. From the tone of Update No. 52, it was clear the relationship between police and media was on the rocks.

Joanne Lees was welcomed back to Sydney by her former manager, Gary Sullivan, and her friends at Dymocks. She was given her old job back, and Gary's brother, who was overseas, offered to let Joanne and Paul Falconio house-sit his lovely home at Beauty Point. Joanne returned to Dymocks, most days running the gauntlet of the media.

Her colleagues were very protective of her, refusing interviews and clustering around her when they took coffee breaks at Earl's Café at the rear of the shop. This did not deter the photographers camped out in front of Dymocks and in Earl's.

Joanne's friends were taken with Paul Falconio's quiet manner, good looks and gentle voice, and he was a big hit on the outings he attended with Joanne. He told her friends that he was just trying to do his best to get through the long wait for news of Peter.

'We're helping each other,' he said. 'She finds it hard to talk to me about Peter and what happened, so I think she found it really, really hard to speak to strangers in front of cameras.'

One of Joanne's friends put her in touch with a grief counsellor named John, who specialised in dealing with people who had experienced sudden or violent bereavement. But as soon as Joanne and Paul visited him at his office, John knew that the session would not be a success. Joanne had hardly sat down when she asked him what he knew of 'her case'.

'Not that much, Jo,' he replied.

She seemed put out. 'How can you expect to help me if you don't know anything about my case? It's very important – one of the most important cases of all time.'

John told me he tried to offer some advice, but he found the process tedious. Joanne seemed 'vacuous' and not very smart. At the same time, he was certain 'she knew more than she let on.' Paul seemed pleasant enough, but when they left together, he knew they would not be back.

DPP Rex Wild said later in an interview with News Limited that throughout the trial, his team had been worried that Lees presented an aura of superiority and defiance that wasn't playing well. They'd wanted less of that from her.

'But she wasn't going to give it. It was all explained to her: be yourself; let it all hang out; the jury will want to see your raw emotions. But no. Stiff upper lip. It was not as though she was an upper-class girl – she was middle class. But she was not going to let these people get at her.'

Lees knew best.

Joanne's friends told her that police from the Territory had questioned them and obtained fingerprints and DNA samples. The police had wanted to know whether she or Peter had made any enemies, and had also asked questions about their relationship.

Peter's friends had been asked similar questions and had also given DNA samples. Among them was Peter's friend Paul Dale, who had been following the case since he saw the report of a missing backpacker on the TV news the first night. 'I was stunned,' he told me later. 'I guessed straight away that it was Peter. He was heading that way and it all fitted. I rang the police, who were cagey at first, but eventually they admitted it was him.'

Paul Dale was questioned by Territory police; then Paula Dooley-McDonnell came back and asked him about Peter's relationship with Joanne. She also asked whether Peter had worked at another furniture factory before January Design. But if Peter had worked elsewhere, he had never mentioned it to Paul.

Paul felt Joanne and Peter's relationship was in good shape.

'I told her I didn't think they had any real relationship problems and that, as far as I knew, they planned to get married when they got home to England. Peter had said to me he was a bit worried about Jo being interested in some bloke who worked at Dymocks, but I told him I didn't think he needed to have any worries on that front.'

For months afterwards, Paul couldn't believe that Peter was dead. 'I kept hoping he'd been kidnapped and one day he'd just turn up.'

After a few weeks, Paul Falconio returned to England. Joanne stayed until the end of November before deciding to fly home.

She later told Gary Sullivan that a strange thing had happened at the airport. When she reached the front of the passport queue, she was quietly asked to accompany an immigration officer to an interview room.

She was very upset about this delay. She said she was held there for quite some time and missed her plane. The officials were all smiles and apologies, but gave no explanations. She finally left on the next flight. Had she, as Daulby said, been 'free to leave' at any time? Had her name been added to the immigration watch list in the early days of the investigation and inadvertently left there? Or did the police just want to know when she was leaving? Whatever the reason, it takes quite a bit of paperwork to get someone's name on the watch list. Joanne couldn't have been on it accidentally.

Chapter Thirteen

THE SEARCH WIDENS

No one doubts me. Only media doubts my stories.

Joanne Lees

By September 2001, Assistant Commissioner Daulby was admitting that police were stumped. 'We've run out of clues and we've run out of ideas,' he told the die-hard journalists still following the case. The investigation had been scaled down, although a huge amount of work had already been done.

Police had logged more than 5600 jobs, following their own lines of inquiry and leads supplied by the public. There were still about twenty calls from the public each day. Wayne Hartley and his crew had ruled out about 350 vehicles, and more than 800 calls had been received about vehicles similar to the one Joanne had described. In response to a public appeal, twenty-four amateur videos of the Camel Cup had been handed over to police, but only two showed glimpses of Joanne and Peter. There was no sign of the picture the police hoped for, of a man stalking Joanne – a man with straight, grey-streaked shoulder-length hair, a long thin face and a droopy grey moustache.

The police commissioner quietly approached cabinet for more money. Former Treasurer and Police Minister Mike Reed told me, 'The investigation ran into several million. There were aircraft searches, specialised forensics, overseas trips – all essential elements of the investigation, and all costing money.' He believed that, when it came to the police doing their job, 'financial considerations should not be an impediment'.

The coffers were duly topped up, but funds remained tight in Alice Springs, where fourteen members were still engaged in the investigation. The regional officer in charge set out to limit spending on travel, overtime and replacement of officers on sick leave. To demonstrate the effect this had on morale, someone leaked the memo to the media.

Police in other States had also been busy. One man in particular had received more than his fair share of scrutiny. In the weeks after Peter's disappearance, Chris Malouf, a carpenter in Broome, Western Australia, began to feel his life had become 'a living nightmare'. Police repeatedly pulled him over; they had saliva samples taken and held him in lock-ups in the Northern Territory and Western Australia.

Of medium height with a droopy moustache and long hair, Chris had passed through Barrow Creek and camped about fifty-five metres from where the incident took place – on the same night. The photo at the Shell truck stop looked like him. 'It's me, I reckon – that's the same thongs, black hat and jacket as I wear,' he told Genine Johnson of the *Broome Advertiser*.

Genine had goose bumps as she took her notes. Chris said he was being driven to desperation. 'I got nowhere to go. They just won't leave me alone. I'm no angel, but I'm no criminal, neither. It's doin' me head in. I'm scared some twisted bastard is gunna send me to jail.'

Chris Malouf could have camped at Barrow Creek that night and been at the truck stop, but he wouldn't have had much sleep. The Shell photo was taken at 12.45 am, and the trip to Barrow Creek would have taken at least two hours. He wouldn't have got to sleep before about 3 am.

Chris claimed he had been stopped on several occasions by armed police, stared at and catcalled by members of the public, and taken to the Northern Territory to confront Joanne Lees, 'who was forced to feel his hair and inspect his car'. (This claim seems far-fetched.) Chris also said he'd participated in a 'fashion parade', being photographed by police in various items of clothing. Was Joanne Lees watching behind a two-way mirror? Police said no.

Territory police said that Chris was just one 'person of interest' among several. Several people had been pulled over more than once, and various DNA samples had been volunteered and classified.

Chris desperately wanted police to catch the gunman. 'I just don't have the words for it,' he said. 'I've even written "IT'S NOT ME" in the dust on the back of me truck, shaved off me mo and changed the colour of me canopy.' He had gone into hiding on the outskirts of Broome, praying that Peter would be found pretty damn quick.

One of the reasons police were interested in Chris Malouf was that they believed he ran drugs in and out of Western Australia and the Northern Territory. He had an ex-girlfriend in Darwin, and some said a child as well. To keep in touch with them, they suspected he ran drugs up and down the Stuart Highway, often stopping at Aboriginal communities to help out with carpentry jobs in exchange for cash, a feed and bed for the night. The police did not believe he was the gunman, but there was a chance he knew who was.

Another Broome resident had come under scrutiny from the police, but had also persuaded them that he was not the man they were after. Bradley John Murdoch, a former truck driver, bush mechanic and all-round fixer, owned a white four-wheel drive with a canvas canopy. In October 2001, the police visited him at home. They checked his vehicle and asked him some questions from the pro forma devised by Wayne Hartley's team.

Chris Malouf has claimed that Murdoch told him, 'I was on that road that night, but don't tell the cops.' Whether this was true or not, Murdoch had a partial alibi. Several of his friends placed him in Broome in the early hours of Monday morning. If he had been at the Shell stop, he would have had to drive 1200 kilometres, mostly on rough tracks, in about twenty-seven hours. It was possible for an experienced rough-rider like Murdoch. But the Northern Territory police passed him over as being of no further interest.

With progress stalled, the profilers were called in. While some police are sceptical of profiling, it can help to identify character traits from certain kinds of behaviour, including how offenders relate to the victim and the crime scene, their choice of weapon and their use of language.

Forensic criminologist Wayne Petherick from Bond University believes that profiling is of most use in cases where 'the offender displays evidence of psychopathology, such as rape, murder, torture and mutilation'. The characteristics of the crime scene can be used to distinguish between psychopathic (organised) and psychotic (disorganised) offenders. In a paper on 'Criminal Profiling', Petherick reproduced a table developed by the FBI:

ORGANISED	DISORGANISED
Offence planned	Spontaneous offence
Victim is targeted stranger	Victim or location known
Personalises victim	Depersonalises victim
Controlled conversation	Minimal conversation
Crime scene reflects control	Crime scene random and sloppy
Demands submissive victim	Sudden violence to victim
Restraints used	Minimal use of restraints
Aggressive acts prior to death	Sexual acts after death
Body hidden	Body left in view
Weapons/ evidence absent	Evidence/ weapon often present
Transports victim	Body left at death scene

John Daulby would have been familiar with this methodology, as he had been trained at the FBI Centre in Quantico, Virginia. He had faith in the use of profilers, although he qualified this by saying that profiles could also be limiting. Videos of the interviews with Joanne Lees were given to other profilers in Australia for review. One almost immediately expressed the opinion that Joanne Lees had suffered or was suffering from a personality disorder or other mental illness.

Somehow, this was leaked to the media. At Daulby's next media conference, Paul Toohey from the *Australian* shouted the question everyone wanted to ask. 'Does Joanne Lees have any history of mental illness?'

Taken aback by the unexpected question, or cross because it had hit a nerve, Daulby picked up his papers, snapped, 'I can't answer that!' and virtually stormed out.

The police had also engaged a hypnotherapist to elicit any detail Joanne might have overlooked in her statement. Many trained people were left with the impression that there was something missing from her telling of the story.

Those working on the gunman's profile came up with pretty much what you'd expect: a loner, maybe a bit obsessive, possibly with a troubled childhood, strong likelihood of failed personal relationships, very well prepared for the outback, possibly a repeat offender. That description would probably fit half the men in the outback. Rank-and-file police grumbled that engaging profilers was a waste of time and money.

A police officer who was in daily contact with Joanne Lees at that time told me later, 'I don't take much notice of those profilers. Ninety-nine per cent of what they come up with is straight common sense. She just wasn't smart enough to kill him – simple as that. They'd only been in the Territory for a few days. How would she organise it?

'Her personality was her problem. She was a real princess – very narcissistic and quite introverted as well. Borderline personality disorder, I'd say. Very self-focused. She loved the attention. For four or five mornings running I'd collect her from where she was staying and never once, did she ask, "Do you have any news?" She was only interested in how she looked, what people would think of her. Joanne thinks she's a nine out of ten. I'd give her about a two myself.'

This widely held opinion of Joanne Lees was borne out many times during the long-drawn-out process to follow. In a later interview prosecutor DPP Rex Wild gave to News Limited, he said that Joanne's attitude was widely concerning to all the investigators and his legal team and at times put the trial in jeopardy. He said he could 'never quite fathom Lees' and for that reason considered her a risky witness. He said he never doubted her story, but that she was difficult. He said she 'insisted on absolute control of her image'.

Chapter Fourteen

A TERRIFYING STORY

I would never, ever sell my story to anyone.

Joanne Lees, 17 July 2001

In February 2002, when 'Falconio stories' had almost petered out, a new development made headlines. Joanne Lees returned to Australia. At first it was thought that she might be back for the big announcement that the gunman had been found. But the real reason was almost as sensational. She was going to re-enact her ordeal once more – not for the police, but for money. It was reported that she'd accepted £50,000 (around AU$120,000) to appear on ITV's *Tonight* with Trevor McDonald, with interviewer Martin Bashir.

In Sydney, the TV station put her up at the Ramada Inn, not far from Dymocks. She went out for drinks with all the Dymocks staff a couple of times during the week she stayed in Sydney. She told them that she had been mistaken in thinking it would 'all go away' when she returned to England. In fact, she had been 'pestered' by media outlets wanting exclusive rights to her story. She said she'd chosen Martin Bashir because she trusted him to 'do a good job and treat her well'. Bashir was famous for his dramatic 1996 interview with Diana, Princess of Wales, in which she confessed her adultery with James Hewitt.

Joanne denied any suggestion that she missed the spotlight. She said she was expecting to be well treated and well paid, and hoped that by doing this program, she'd get the media off her back.

Police were caught off balance. Out of the blue, Joanne phoned saying she was in Alice Springs and asked if the film crew could interview Kate Vanderlaan (to which they agreed). They were amazed she'd returned to Australia without telling them, let alone to make a TV program. John Daulby decided the crew should also interview him in Darwin before they left.

The broadcast version of the program opened against the panoramic backdrop of Sydney Harbour Bridge, then moved dramatically to the 'red heart'. Bashir began by saying, 'The Australian outback is desolate and mysterious, and the setting for a terrifying story.' He highlighted the fact that Peter and Joanne had set out on their trek into this dangerous country from 'Adelaide – the murder capital of the world'.

On camera, Joanne seemed poised and immaculately made up; her hair had grown to her shoulders.

Before Peter's disappearance, she said, 'Our relationship was stronger than ever. We hadn't spent so much time together for a while – it was probably what I was looking forward to. We never felt claustrophobic. We did still do our own thing on the trip, took time out to do things separately.'

Bashir asked her if they had argued along the way.

'Me and Pete never argued,' she replied. 'There is no truth whatsoever in the story we'd had a row in Alice Springs.'

Then she began to recite the now familiar story in a sing-song way. Martin Bashir listened quietly, not interrupting the flow.

Graphic re-enacted footage accompanied the story, with images of a tall, ugly-looking brute wrestling with the girl playing Joanne's part. The camera returned to Joanne when she described how she cowered in fear in her 'little hiding place'. She looked beseechingly at Bashir, lifting her voice a little.

Vince Millar and Les Pilton both endorsed Joanne's story. Then the scene switched to Alice Springs, with Joanne running from cameras, dodging reporters and shopping in the mall.

She said, 'I couldn't go out anywhere in Alice Springs. I went out with my stepdad to get some fresh air one day and a young girl stopped me and said, "Do you know there are ten cameras behind that pillar?" Another day a camera crew cut me off in a car across the pavement. They chased me down the street.'

The scene returned to the studio, with Bashir and Joanne seated facing one another.

Bashir reminded his viewers that Joanne did speak to the press but refused to answer any questions related to the crime; instead, she had turned on the media.

Joanne said, 'I found the media overwhelming and intimidating. I've got a problem with all press, they doubt the truth, they doubt my story, misquote me and are making up false accusations and stories.' Bashir pointed out that the only questions she answered were three out of fifteen, all about the press.

Joanne described the others as 'ridiculous questions, such as "What were you arguing about with Pete on July 14?" Things like that, implying that we'd had an argument. "Where is Pete?" Things like that.'

When Bashir asked why she didn't answer the other questions, she said, 'I guess in hindsight I could have, but I had no experience. I was just thrown into that. I didn't realise how people were going to analyse every answer that I'd give, or criticise me for every question I didn't answer, let alone those I did. To me, they were ridiculous questions. Couldn't people just focus on Pete and finding Pete?'

'Don't you think it might have been useful to use the media?' Bashir asked.

'Looking back, it may well have been, but at the time it was in every newspaper in every news bulletin. For thirty days in a row it was on the front page of the local paper and the *Advocate*. I probably would have been willing to do more to raise public awareness without having had such bad treatment from the press. Yeah, I did become withdrawn – I didn't feel strong enough at the time. I didn't understand then. I do now.'

Then the mood of the interview changed. Bashir said, 'Parts of the story didn't add up. Your hands being tied behind. That was an inconsistency focused upon by the media.'

'I told the police the truth – hands behind back, hands in front. While I was in the bush and I heard the man drive off in the vehicle the first time, I brought my hands to the front of my body.'

Bashir pointed out that a police officer had said this would require 'the flexibility of a contortionist'.

'Yeah, well we read that, me and Paul Falconio. "A trained ballet dancer of twelve years could not possibly carry out that act", and me and Paul just performed that. We did that.'

Bashir asked about footprints. 'The trackers say, "We only found Joanne's."'

'They only found two in my hiding place in the whole crime scene, under the bush where I hid. The ground was branches, it wasn't hard, solid ground at all. I'm not particularly heavy. I have no idea why they didn't find tracks. If it wasn't for the fact that I'd left a lip balm they might never have located my hiding place. So that was a marker for where I was hidden. So maybe they're not looking in the right place, or not looking thoroughly.'

Bashir said, 'There was no blood on the van, only on the ground. Wouldn't it be reasonable to find bits?'

'I guess so, but I'm no expert on bullet wounds and gunshots. I wouldn't have a clue.'

Next, Bashir asked about the dog.

'I'm not sure if the gunman had the dog with him,' Joanne replied. 'He was yards away. I don't know about the dog's temperament or about the different … apparently those type of dogs, are working dogs, to round up the cattle, they're silent dogs so they don't scare the cattle. Much as I'd like to think my dogs would be able to sniff me out, unless they're trained sniffer dogs it's not the case.'

Bashir continued to probe. 'He didn't have to travel far. Within a forty-metre area he would probably have stumbled across you if he was determined to find you? Surely you can understand that?'

'Mmm, yeah. Pitch black, absolutely – or maybe – I've no idea.' She shook her head, defeated by the logic of the question.

'Was the DNA on your clothing blood?' Bashir asked.

'Mmm, I don't know for sure how it came to be on my clothing. It could have been when I was kicking out at him. Didn't see any blood whatsoever on his clothing – saw none at all when he grabbed and assaulted me.'

Bashir pressed the point home. 'There's no weapon, no body, no footprints except yours, Peter's blood on the ground – what do you say to people who say you killed Peter Falconio?'

Joanne looked at him and giggled nervously. 'Totally untrue. No. No idea who did.'

She also spoke of her present feelings about the incident. 'I feel guilty. I feel the man didn't want Pete at all, it was just me he was after, and if I hadn't been there, he probably never would have stopped Pete.' 'What do you say to people who say Joanne Lees did it, or knows who did it?'

'I just keep thinking if Pete was here, if he was found tomorrow alive, he'd be just so mad at the treatment that I've got – had. He knows the truth and I know the truth and I guess it's hard for people to believe, but that's how it happened.'

Bashir asked, 'What about Peter?'

Joanne spoke for the last time: 'It's really difficult to talk about Pete. Before I start crying ...' She lowered her head for a few seconds, looked up again, and delicately used her forefingers to wipe tears from under her lower lashes before continuing. 'I can live the rest of my life without Peter, I can, but I don't want to. What happened to me ... I nearly lost my life and it's made me appreciate every single day and I do love life and I'm going to get on with it. I'd prefer it if Pete was by my side doing that, but I think that would be a miracle for that to happen.'

◆ ◆ ◆

The interview with Bashir was not shown in Australia until late 2003, but it still created quite a stir when the program was completed in March 2002. The producers supplied an audio of the unedited version to a 'sister' radio station, which picked up on some unflattering remarks Joanne had made about the Northern Territory police. One of the Murdoch newspapers in London ran the story, which duly came over the wire to Australia.

On the day the show was aired in England, the Territory police put out a media release emphasising their support for Joanne's story and indicating that there were still fourteen investigators full-time on the case, with a $250,000 reward for information leading to a conviction. But later they heard that Joanne had criticised them, claiming they had dismissed the first phone call as a hoax, that they had treated her 'insensitively' and that they had asked her to talk to the media in a way that 'more or less implied that I was the murderer'.

On the unedited tape, Joanne also suggested that Helen Jones had exploited the attack by taking money for talking to the media, and that the hotel had made a lot of money because Helen had made sure everyone knew she was involved. The media quoted Joanne as saying, 'I'm quite disgusted that she can get off on someone else's tragedy.' As a result, Helen faced a barrage of phone calls. Asked whether she and Les had exploited Joanne, she said, 'No, absolutely not. If that's how Joanne feels, well, those four days didn't mean much, did they? … I am very surprised. I honestly thought I was helping. I have always held the highest regard for Jo, and I have not exploited her by talking to the media. I thought I was doing a good thing. But I can live with it.'

Les had no comment. He wanted to wait and see the program before he'd believe Joanne had said those things.

Police investigators were puzzled that Joanne had not visited them while she was in Alice Springs – especially when they found out that she had made time to consult a lawyer there and commence proceedings against the Northern Territory Solicitor General and an unnamed 'second respondent' (the gunman) for compensation as the 'secondary victim of an act of violence'. Under Territory law, she could claim that she should have expected safe passage on the Stuart Highway. She sought compensation of up to $50,000, and the case was unlikely to be contested if police confirmed to the court that a crime had been committed.

In any event, by the time the TV story ran in the UK on 19 March 2002, all negative references to Les and Helen had been removed, and little remained of Joanne's criticism of the police, other than the claim that they had initially treated the call as a hoax. Not knowing exactly what would go to air, Channel Nine's *A Current Affair* wanted to record the reactions of Les, Helen, Vince Millar and Mark Wilton. Chris Tangey of Xplor Media wangled an invitation as well. A satellite relay was arranged to a room at the Territory Motel, set up to broadcast live as the show went to air in England.

Chris Tangey recalled the tension in the room. 'While the tape rolled, Vince looked pretty uncomfortable. He shifted a few times in his seat and seemed quite disturbed about what she'd said in places. Helen was in a terrible situation, because she'd already heard what Joanne had said about her trying to make money out of the tragedy and she'd already begun privately expressing doubts about some of Joanne's story.

'Les watched intently, refusing to say anything until it was over, but then while ACA were setting up, he was wandering round the room expressing a few doubts. Helen told him he should trust his doubts, if he had any. Les seemed surprised that for the first time he was doubting what he always believed, and was getting upset with himself for doing it. Vince was confused. He said, "When I found her, her hands were in front of her. She said they'd been tied behind her head and she'd brought them over her head." Mark Wilton didn't say much. He believed her absolutely. Still does, I think.

'I wasn't sure what to think. A lot of her story doesn't add up. I know the bush pretty well. Five hours in that scrub? I'm not so sure ...'

ACA filmed the reactions and did the interviews, but the show was canned by Channel Nine's legal advisers.

Chapter Fifteen

A SLAP IN THE FACE

*Christopher bloody Tangey! Every time Daulby hears your
name, his BP goes through the roof!*

Overheard at Overlanders restaurant, Alice Springs, April 2002

Another videotape was about to create its own sensation – the tape of the luminol testing that Chris Tangey had made back in August 2001. He had been given exclusive rights to the footage after six months. No doubt the police had thought the whole thing would be wrapped up by then.

Chris had been uneasy about the tape ever since he had seen Joy Kuhl's reaction to the marks inside the driver's door. He did not think any additional testing had been done on the Kombi. His dilemma was whether to sit on the tape or go public to stimulate some action. In February 2002, with the six months up and Joanne Lees back in Australia generating renewed interest in the case, Chris decided to give the video to Paul Toohey of the *Australian* to ensure maximum coverage by the News Limited network.

Before the story appeared, the police seem to have heard it was on the way. On 13 February, John Daulby issued a media release addressed personally to Paul Toohey, saying that Chris Tangey was 'not qualified to comment' on the testing of the van. Daulby was confident that the forensic examination had been thorough. He closed by announcing, 'Mr Tangey does not have permission to release the police video footage of the testing and had agreed not to record sound. It is disappointing that he appears to have breached police trust.' Police also suggested that Chris had recorded the audio without their knowledge or permission.

It is extremely unusual for police to address a media release to an individual journalist, criticising both him and his source, and then put it on the official website. If it was meant to embarrass Toohey, it didn't. The public rap over the knuckles only reinforced the importance of his story and made him laugh. More stories and accusations followed, linking Joy Kuhl with mistakes made in the Chamberlain investigation. The UK media carried comments from Joanne's family about their concerns that there should be a proper investigation, and other journalists began searching for an angle to extend the story further.

At 2 pm that day, Chris Tangey received a call from Kate Vanderlaan.

'I understand you have a tape belonging to us.'

'It's my tape,' Chris replied. 'I've given you a copy, as I agreed.'

'It's our property. It's possible it's police evidence under the Listening Devices Act.'

'I was asked to make the tape by your officers,' he told her. 'I was there filming in the dark at their request and at no fee.'

'You must have made a fair bit of money out of releasing the tape?' she continued.

'No, I haven't,' Chris told her. 'I've made nothing.'

'Well, if it's a question of money, just send us an invoice.'

Chris told her it wasn't a question of money and that he wouldn't surrender the tape. He became convinced the police were trying to buy his silence.

Next, he received a phone message from John Daulby, who'd been trying to get through from Darwin while Kate Vanderlaan was on the line. Chris rang back. Daulby told him that Commander Hardman and Dr Peter Thatcher (Joy Kuhl's boss) would sit in on their 'little chat'. He asked Chris if he was recording the call, 'because we are not. This is a confidential matter.' For forty minutes or so, they discussed the handprint and the ownership of the tape. Chris said that only an idiot would have ignored what he had seen. Daulby told him he was not qualified to interpret the luminol marks.

'No, maybe not,' Chris replied, 'but what I'm saying is that someone saw something and ignored it.'

At the end of the conversation, Daulby assured Chris he would not be charged with any offence if he released the tape to other members of the media.

When he hung up, another message was blinking on his recorder. This proved to be a playback of his own mobile voicemail message, which suggested that someone was taping his calls. He sat down and sent a long, angry email to Kate Vanderlaan, copying it to Paul Toohey. He summarised the conversation with Daulby and asked her to confirm Daulby's assurance in writing.

He finished, 'As a final comment, you may not be aware that presumably, subordinates of yours called me on my message bank home number today at 3.19 pm playing back my mobile phone answering message to apparently demonstrate to me that they were apparently capable of, if not actively involved in, intercepting and taping my calls. I would request that you instruct them to cease this immediately, as our dealings are not a criminal investigation. I am sure we all have the best interests of a successful investigation in mind.'

Vanderlaan replied the following day saying that if the others who had been parties to Chris's filming and recording were aware of being recorded, there did not seem to be a legal problem after all. She also apologised for any 'confusion about a gentleman's agreement', but stressed that the police on the spot had no authority to make such an agreement. 'As such we will have to leave it at that.' But Chris was spooked. He documented all the police calls and emails and on Friday 15 February sent the lot to the Northern Territory Ombudsman. He did not ask the Ombudsman to act on the information, just to hold it for safekeeping.

The following Monday, Daulby phoned again. He said Hardman was there, although he did not speak. Daulby wanted to know if Chris had decided to release the tape to the media. He said that the police needed the original because there was no audio on the copy. Chris objected, saying that his copying would have locked the audio to the vision. Daulby also told Chris that the commissioner was going to announce a major review of the case by external consultants, and they would need the original. Chris capitulated and said they could 'have the bloody tape if they wanted it'. He'd get it to them over the next couple of days.

◆ ◆ ◆

Rightly or wrongly, Chris linked Daulby's insistence on obtaining the master tape with the possibility that the testing of the Kombi might look bad under review. He obtained some legal advice from Stuart Littlemore, QC, a man renowned for not mincing words.

Littlemore wrote to the police commissioner on 21 February 2002, the day the external review was announced. His letter was couched as a 'formal complaint'. After summarising the phone calls and demands made by various police, Littlemore wrote, 'My client and I can only infer that the extraordinary and overbearing conduct of your officers is the product of their anxiousness to conceal from the Review process potentially embarrassing audio recordings on the tape. May I make this absolutely clear to you: the master tape is the property of Mr Tangey.'

He went on to say that whatever verbal undertakings Chris may have given, he would not provide the master. Chris had already made several copies and distributed them widely to lawyers and the media, so 'any attempt to seize the tape would not only be a criminal offence, but also futile. No doctored tape, with audio track erased, would conceal the truth.'

Littlemore concluded by asking that a copy of his letter be provided to both the review team and the person responsible for receiving complaints about police. And just to make sure, he sent a copy to the police minister.

On 22 February, Toohey ran an exclusive feature with photos. Other media picked it up, and it created its own sensation.

On 26 February, Bruce Wernham, the acting commissioner, wrote to say that police would not seize the tape after all; a copy would be useful (thank you); and if Chris wanted to proceed with a 'formal complaint', he would have to be prepared to make himself available for interview by the Ombudsman. Could he please advise?

If the police had left the matter there, that might have been the end of it. But they again used their media unit and website to personalise and extend the debate. From New Zealand, where Daulby was visiting his children, came another public shot at a journalist who had run a story on the issue.

COMMENT BY ASSISTANT COMMISSIONER JOHN DAULBY
27 February 2002

Att: Michael Coggan 7.30 Report

I am confident that the NT Police have done a thorough and professional forensic examination of the Kombi belonging to Joanne Lees and Paul Falconio.

We acknowledge that we enlisted the assistance of a civilian cameraman for the use of his camera for a short period about three weeks after extensive forensic examinations had been carried out.

However, the result of his filming did not indicate that there was any forensic evidence on the Kombi other than that which police had already obtained in July.

Chris Tangey immediately pointed out that the final comment was contradicted by the tape, which showed the forensic scientists' surprise at the reaction to the luminol.

The next day brought another media release, not directed at any particular media person:

STATEMENT BY COMMANDER TERRITORY CRIME – COL HARDMAN

1. *The luminol testing of the Kombi van belonging to Joanne Lees and Paul Falconio was carried out by a highly experienced forensic biologist to see if any further biological evidence could be found that had not previously been identified. However, given the extent of the previous examinations, we did not expect to find any. The result was that there was nothing further located.*

   During the procedure, a low-light camera was tested to see if video under such circumstances was a viable option for providing footage of such a procedure to a court in the future. As can be seen by the video, the presentation was not useful.

2. *While recording, the biologist, who has high expertise in forensic examinations, expresses interest in the way certain parts of the car illuminate during the procedure. She was fully aware that a more specific biological examination had already been conducted and she was aware of the results. When an area on the door illuminates, she points out that she has already swabbed that area. That area had been examined on two occasions by biologists and by a fingerprint expert and had not produced any evidence. The forensic scientists did not interpret any stains or other deposits that could have been interpreted as a handprint.*

3. *During the procedure, the forensic biologist was also well aware and expected that metals and other objects would illuminate in this process, as did occur. While she knew that the illumination seen during the filming was not new forensic evidence, she commented that others who don't fully understand the procedure might think the luminescence were signs of a 'bloodbath'.*

   In fact, the luminol test did not identify anything of additional forensic value.

   Reports to the contrary by persons outside the investigation have no substance and any interpretation of any results from this testing could only be made by a trained forensic biologist.

Police remain confident that they will solve this case and that forensic science will continue to play an important role in the investigation.

Chris was hopping mad. He sent a critique of this document to Stuart Littlemore. He pointed out that Hardman had admitted that the test had a real forensic purpose, 'when they were earlier trying to convince the media that my filming was entirely to test the camera (yes, in the middle of a major crime investigation with a key exhibit!)'. Chris went on:

If Kuhl was already aware of the results, why does she express surprise at the luminol reaction on the door? Importantly too, why didn't she then immediately mark the sample area that reacted? After all, wasn't this the purpose of the test in the first place – to find such a reaction? (According to an independent forensic scientist from the University of New South Wales interviewed on the ABC, this would be correct procedure.) ...

[During] Daulby's second phone call to me on 18 February Hardman heard him state that the reason the police needed the master tape was that their copy had 'no audio'. However, they quote the 'bloodbath' line from the VT audio on their copy. Further, the 'bloodbath' comment refers to a totally different part of the test, not the handprint section, where they clearly discover something new and then ignore it.

In a later release, on 1 March, Hardman reiterated all his earlier points, but deleted any reference to a 'bloodbath' and inserted a sentence saying he 'had full confidence in Ms Kuhl's expertise as a forensic biologist'.

Meanwhile, Littlemore had replied to Acting Commissioner Wenham to tell him Chris's 'formal complaint' still stood and that further investigations should be carried out by the Ombudsman's office.

But all the correspondence overlooked the main question. Was it a handprint or not? And if so, whose print was it?

Chapter Sixteen

THE INDEPENDENT REVIEW

*Nothing major came out of the review. It was purely
procedural stuff.*

Superintendent Colleen Gwynne

The independent review was announced on Thursday 21 February
by Commissioner Paul White, who held a media conference later
the same day. He said the review would bring a 'fresh set of eyes' to
the investigation and provide 'an independent assessment that will
help the investigation team solve this case'.

He expected the two-member review team to report in four
to six weeks. The members of the review panel were named as
Superintendent George Owen, who was in charge of road safety in
the Territory, and retired Assistant Commissioner Jim Litster from
South Australia.

The announcement brought a sigh of relief in some quarters
and hoots of derision in others. Jim Litster was an old colleague of
Commissioner White, who had recently been appointed from South
Australia, and White was also believed to be friendly with George
Owen, who had no detective training. But it didn't seem an onerous
task. They were being asked to do a strategic and organisational
review of an opportunistic crime with little concrete evidence. Their
job was not to cast blame, but to highlight any avenues of investigation
that had been overlooked.

When Litster arrived in Darwin, he and George Owens met the
senior members of the investigation team and began to review the
case. They viewed the videos of the interviews with Joanne Lees. Jim

Litster found her story quite convincing. 'Whilst there might have been the odd irregularity, she always told the truth. You can get around the fact that she never saw Mr Falconio's body because it was on the road. The Northern Territory police believe her story, although there was some doubt early in the piece. The motives for a crook story are usually domestic problems or insurance. There was no question of those issues.'

They had a look at the truck-stop video and stills. 'When they showed her the photos, she said he was too old, but they still released it. That night when the bloke pulled into the truck stop, the girl on duty was seconds away from writing down his number plate and then the man working with her said he'd do it instead.'

They watched the tape of the re-enactment and drove to Barrow Creek to view the site. 'She was telling the truth, but accuracy might have left something to be desired. If you were manhandled as she was, you might not be accurate because you were subjected to trauma.'

While they were in Alice Springs, they visited Chris Tangey's studio, at his request. He had already sent them a detailed email outlining the story so far, and had made a high-quality copy of the tape to give to them. Owens and Litster came, had a cup of tea and viewed the video in absolute silence. Afterwards, they declined the offer of a tape to take away and left.

Owens and Litster saw the Kombi at the vehicle lock-up and pored over items police had bagged and tagged. An air ticket in Falconio's name, Joanne's diary, a bong, some dope – nothing provided any revelations. 'The tests were all finished on everything by then – we could have danced on the exhibits,' Litster told me. 'But we didn't,' he hastened to add. 'We kept our hands in our pockets.' The review took about six weeks and produced a report of about fifty pages. 'We covered everything,' Litster said.

'You should have a good media strategy – that was certainly a recommendation. I've had [the media] go skew on me. You should keep back some exhibits, dole them out week by week, keep the press happy. If you can't give them anything, the media will make things up.

'There was so much speculation. The trouble is, if the general public believe that a murder hasn't happened, they may not report things. They tend to dismiss it, and that's quite dangerous.'

The review's recommendations about doling out the exhibits must have had an effect, because on 21 March, almost nine months after the incident, John Daulby produced replicas of the 'handcuffs' used to restrain Joanne Lees. He said his aim was to reveal the composition of the ties and to counter any inaccurate details depicted in the British TV documentary (even though it had not been shown in Australia). The police also wanted to show that Joanne could have brought her hands to the front, as she claimed. A policewoman of Joanne's weight and height demonstrated how this could be done.

Police also explained that the gunman's car 'could have been a Landcruiser or other similar four-wheel drive', not necessarily the Jeep depicted in the docudrama, and that the 'gunman' in the TV story had incorrectly been shown wearing a cap with a drink logo.

The handcuffs were made of four looped black cable ties held together by three smaller loops, like a paper streamer. The small loops were covered in a black porous tape known in the outback as 'hundred-mile-an-hour tape'.

Daulby said, 'The makeup of these restraints is quite intricate, and the effort in making them demonstrates that the offender was very organised. We used replica ties because the original ones were pulled apart for forensic testing. We have made quite a few of them and it took us about half-an-hour to an hour to construct each one.' Three different tapes had been used on Joanne – silver insulation tape for her face, duct tape for her legs, and hundred-mile-an-hour tape for the handcuffs. Police had investigated thousands of outlets where these items might be sold. 'Such tapes and the cable ties are used in all sorts of trades and skills, including builders, electricians, miners and many other tradesmen.' In fact, most blokes in the outback wouldn't leave home without them.

Just before the first anniversary of the Barrow Creek incident, the police released part of the review report. They said the review had found that Northern Territory police had followed appropriate procedures, and that they were on track to solve the case. The review provided strong evidence to support Joanne's story.

After reading more than a hundred statements, appraising nearly 23,000 pieces of information and interviewing police, witnesses and forensic specialists, the review team described the early response to the incident as timely and appropriate. There had been initial difficulties in coping with the huge volume of information, but these were quickly rectified. Any inaccuracies in Joanne Lees's statements could be attributed to the extreme trauma she had experienced. The management of the crime scene was in line with accepted practices. The police made the right decision to enter and search for Peter Falconio, even though this search contaminated the scene.

The establishment of roadblocks was as timely as it could have been. There had been no need to carry out additional tests on the Kombi after the luminol testing, as it had already been tested with ortho-toluidine, which is more effective. The forensic personnel had performed professionally. And the investigators had shown great dedication.

Daulby continued to assure the public that the police believed Joanne Lees's story. 'Not only does the evidence we have at the crime scene support her statement, but so too do the witness accounts of those who drove past the incident as it occurred.' He then revealed for the first time that six witnesses had provided accounts of having seen one or both of the vehicles.

'This is an extremely difficult case. It occurred in the black of night in a remote part of Australia in harsh, unyielding terrain where witnesses were scarce. But the review has shown that police have carried out the right procedures in a timely manner and I remain confident that we will catch the offender. As with any investigation there is always room for improvement. Much of that which we will change is in administrative and reporting procedures, and we are spending considerable money updating our police information system.'

A couple of days later, Daulby announced that five members were being withdrawn from the investigation and that two experienced detectives would do an investigative audit of the case. This would mean putting the whole approach to the investigation under scrutiny, looking over evidence and checking out leads that may have been overlooked. But while the case was being put under the microscope, the gunman remained as elusive as ever.

Chapter Seventeen

THE BROOME CONNECTION

If I knew where half my patrons came from and
what they'd done, I'd have to close my pub. I'd be too
scared to come to work each day.

Publican in Broome, July 2003

Broome is a town where people go to lose themselves for all sorts of reasons. It's also a town where big money is made and lost. The locals have an adage: 'If you want to leave Broome with a small fortune, go there with a big one.'

In 2001, Brad Murdoch had been living in the north-west for about fifteen years. He'd worked as a farm labourer, rouseabout, long-haul truck driver and seat-of-the-pants mechanic. He knew a lot of people along the highway from Fitzroy Crossing to Broome, and down to Perth, where his elderly parents lived.

Murdoch was born at Northampton, north of Geraldton in Western Australia. His grandfather was a butcher who had walked all the way from Port Pirie in South Australia to the Coolgardie goldfields – about 2000 kilometres the coast way or a bit less trudging over the Nullarbor Plain. Later, his grandfather moved to Donnybrook, where the timber industry was thriving and real men ate lots of meat. He opened a butcher's shop and settled the family on a dairy farm. Brad's father, Colin, enlisted in the army for the duration of the Second World War and married Nancy, his sweetheart, while he was on leave in Perth. After the War, Colin became an engineer and moved his wife and two sons to Northampton to establish an engineering business. Nancy, a hairdresser, ran a small business from home.

When Brad was born on 6 October 1958, his parents were middle-aged. His two older brothers, Robert, aged fourteen, and Gary, aged thirteen, led separate lives. Young Brad grew up almost as an only child, feeling isolated from his brothers and his parents. He attended the local primary school and ran pretty free and wild, although he always treated his parents respectfully. He has said that when he was six, he was badly beaten up several times by some Aboriginal residents of Northampton, who were angered because his father had reported their lawbreaking to the police.

Brad's parents are very fond of him. 'He has great PR,' Colin Murdoch told me. 'That stands for Personal Relationships. From a little kid, he could walk into a crowd and talk to anyone, and in minutes you'd think he'd known them all his life.'

His older brothers did itinerant work. Robert worked in bulk handling of wheat, and Gary learnt the shearing trade. Tragedy overtook the family when Robert contracted Hodgkin's disease and died at twenty-three. They moved back to Perth, where Brad went to Canning Vale Primary School, then shifted south to Busselton to be closer to Nancy's family. Brad attended the local high school.

After Brad left school, he and Gary spent several years driving big rigs along endless stretches of highway, with nothing but the radio and widely spaced roadhouse stops to ease the lonely hours. Like many truckies, they took speed (amphetamines or 'benzos') to stay awake. At twenty-one, he married a girl he had met through his family. His wife bore him a son, but Brad left by the time his son was eleven. Soon his wife and son became part of a gentler past that he had left behind. He headed for the Kimberley in search of 'independence and freedom'.

Brad inherited his father's mechanical ability and his grandfather's stamina and self-reliance. Unlike his forebears, though, he often travelled armed, and was not afraid to let people know he had firepower if he needed it. In the outback, where police stations are few and far between, authority defaults to a person with a gun. Some people called him 'Brad Eastwood' because he always carried a pistol, a rifle or both. In 1977 and 1978 he had run-ins with the police for failing to register his firearms; in 1991 he was in trouble again, although the unlicensed weapon was inoperable.

But Murdoch had no record of anti-social behaviour. A lot of the time, he kept to himself. He was well regarded among the tough men and women of the Kimberley, and was never short of work. He had a reputation as a hard worker and an all-round good bloke.

At one stage, he and a mate decided to open a roadhouse on the Northern Highway between Fitzroy Crossing and Broome. Most of the plans were in place when the local Aboriginal community objected, saying the area was a sacred site. This rankled with Murdoch, but he reluctantly shelved his plans and went to work as a station hand at nearby Brooking Station. He still had good friends in the area, in particular a mate called Paul Jackson*. They were both members of the Pannawonica Riders motorbike club – one of the oldest in Western Australia – and Murdoch would often stay with Jackson and his family when he was driving trucks along the Northern Highway.

The 'Brad Eastwood' nickname gained wider currency after an incident on 20 August 1995, while Murdoch was employed at Brooking Station. He'd been drinking heavily at the Fitzroy Lodge in Fitzroy Crossing – beer followed by rum and coke. When he set out for home in his four-wheel drive, he found the bridge over the Fitzroy River blocked by a number of parked cars belonging to the local Aboriginal football team and its supporters, who had been celebrating a grand final win.

The football crowd swore at him and harassed him, he later said in court. They refused to make way, forcing him to take the long way round to Brooking Station, a distance of several kilometres. Fuelled with alcohol and anger, he collected a .22 magnum lever-action rifle and a .308 bolt-action rifle and returned to the river crossing. He fired at the cars on the bridge, putting out a headlight.

Thinking no one was inside the cars, he shot another round, which grazed the shoulder of a woman who was taking a break from the party. In all, he let go up to ten rounds from each rifle.

The gunshots had the desired effect, and the revellers ran for cover. Murdoch took off in his truck and spent the rest of the night and most of the next day hiding out by the river. Finally, he gave himself up to police and admitted the offences, saying the combination of alcohol and the confrontation at the crossing had made him lose his temper.

A prison psychologist who evaluated Murdoch said he had a 'fairly rigid character structure', which might have influenced his admitted prejudice on the night in question. In the Perth District Court, Murdoch pleaded guilty to charges of 'causing terror to various subjects of the Queen', being intoxicated in charge of a firearm and possessing two stolen, unlicensed rifles, which he had knowingly bought from whoever had pinched them.

His lawyer tendered seven references on his behalf, saying that Murdoch had been 'extremely diligent' in employment and had shown 'no outward signs of extremist behaviour … Mr Murdoch is a person who is well respected in the community, generally liked and obviously his behaviour has surprised and shocked his peers and his employers.'

He got fifteen months for discharging the firearm and six months for possession. He also had to surrender his rifles. Brad Murdoch had entered the criminal justice system for the first time.

After doing his time, Murdoch headed for Broome, about as far away from jail as he could get. His reputation preceded him. In a region where there is little love lost between cultures, the white community welcomed him as something of a hero. He'd done what many of his mates would like to do – 'shoved it right up those black buggers' arses'. He was hailed as 'The Big Fella', 'Brad Eastwood', 'Brad the Spannerman', and was spoken about as a bloke you didn't cross lightly. Murdoch presented a formidable figure. He was tall, with a muscular body and long, thin legs. He wore his salt-and-pepper hair in a number two buzz cut and was usually clean shaven, although he occasionally allowed a moustache or a bit of stubble to grow. In prison he'd acquired quite extensive tattoos of wizards, Ku Klux Klan logos and Yosemite Sam, applied like a sleeve along both arms, ending at the wrists. When applying for jobs, he wore long-sleeved shirts, in spite of the heat, to hide his prison souvenirs. 'Once people got to know me, it was OK,' he told me later. 'But a lot of employers are nervous about heavy tattoos.'

For the next couple of years, he drove long-distance cattle trains to Wyndham, hauling steers cramped in mobile crates, moaning as if they anticipated their fate. He was also entrusted with carrying explosives to the Argyle diamond mines. This involved pushing his truck to the limit over 2000 kilometres in a thirty-six-hour round trip. When he tired of that, he changed over to hauling heavy equipment – snail's-pace bumping along unmade outback tracks in huge, ungainly machines.

On the highways and byways, Murdoch, his brother Gary and other knights of the long-distance haul crossed paths at roadhouses over steak sandwiches, sank tinnies at pubs, snorted speed and popped pills. Murdoch, however, cut right back on his drinking. In a night at the pub, he'd nurse one can of Carlton mid-strength to others' six. He did not enjoy the memory of being locked up.

Sick of the road, Murdoch took on a job in the mines – heavy work, but he didn't mind the physical grind, until he got a hernia. While he was off work, in late 1999 or early 2000, he had a fit of guilt and asked a friend who was a former tax inspector to help him file his tax returns for the previous twelve years. From that tax year he realised $5000 return, and from the previous years he netted another $13,000 – a nice golden egg looking for a nest.

Sometime in 2000, Murdoch became friendly with another Broome personality, a Maori man by the name of James Tahi Hepi. A former bouncer in Sydney in the 1980s, Hepi had been very well connected in the Sydney underworld and then headed for Broome to dive for the Paspaley Pearls company. He had to abandon diving after he developed a severe case of the bends. His wife took their two children to live in Perth, but Hepi stayed on in Broome.

For a time, Hepi drove for Chinatown Taxis, using his taxi as a mobile sales outlet for cannabis. He drank at the Divers Tavern and used his compensation money to buy an interest in the West Kimberley Slashing Company, which was widely known to be a front for cannabis, speed and pills. The illicit income from these sales was ploughed back into the legitimate company.

Around June 1999, Hepi and his business partner fell out, and Hepi left town. He moved to South Australia, where he bought an isolated property near Sedan, north-east of Adelaide. He returned to Broome around May or June 2000 and rented a house in Forrest Street with Brad Murdoch. They lived there with Murdoch's pets, a male dog called Jack and a female cat called Tom. By this time, Hepi had gone into business running hydroponically grown cannabis from Sedan up to Broome. He was looking for a driver, and Murdoch was looking for a profitable return on his tax refunds, so Murdoch put up some money to join Hepi in the 'hydro' business.

They had a few associates. When Murdoch was in South Australia, he would often catch up with a friend called Dags* and a couple called Susan* and George*, who lived up in the hills outside Adelaide. In Perth, there was Billy Gibbs, another Pannawonica Riders member, who ran the Boorong Trucking Company as a partial front for getting speed from Perth into Broome. (Hepi and Murdoch rarely carried speed.)

Another member of the group was a girl known as Jazz*, who had worked behind the bar at the Divers Tavern when Hepi was in town the year before. Jazz would often call in at Forrest Street to buy dope and stay for a chat. She had left the Divers Tavern and was working for Paspaley Pearls – a fortnight at sea and a week off at home. Murdoch and Hepi were doing well out of the South Australian run. Murdoch told me later that between mid-2000 and mid-2001, more than $1.2 million went through his hands.

Broome was a perfect market, with a permanent population of

about 13,000 swelling to 35,000 during peak tourist season. The hydro money was good, but competition was fierce. The Coffin Cheaters, a very active bikie club, were also alleged to be dealing, and Murdoch and Hepi also believed there was competition from an outwardly law-abiding source.

The key to successful drug-running is not to get caught. Among other things, this means taking care of your vehicles. No one wants to break down on the road in a truck full of illegal drugs. Hepi and Murdoch had their four-wheel-drive trucks meticulously maintained by an experienced mechanic called Brett, who owned West Kimberley Diesel. Brett had hired Murdoch as a mechanic on and off, and Murdoch was good mates with Brett, his wife and his young children.

Two trucks were used for the drug runs. Hepi's vehicle was a white 1994 Toyota Landcruiser trayback with Western Australian registration plates. The tray was aluminium, without a fixed canopy. Under the back of the vehicle was a 200-litre long-range petrol tank about thirty centimetres (twelve inches) square, running the full width of the tray. A removable plate inside the tank divided it into two compartments – one for legitimate use and one for drugs, weapons and money. The vehicle had a black bull-bar and a reversible tarp.

Murdoch drove a similar white Toyota Landcruiser trayback, probably a 1996 model, with Western Australian registration plates. Instead of a canvas canopy, it apparently had a fixed cage of diamond-shaped aluminium mesh with a solid top. It also had removable green plastic dust covers that fitted around the cage. The sides of the cage were hinged, so they could be opened out to provide shade or shelter during stops, or to provide access to tools or camping gear. The back was fully enclosed by the cage. The bull-bar was black, and there was a Perspex rain-shield fitted to the right-hand door. Murdoch's vehicle had been modified to take the extra fuel tank when it was his turn to do a run.

Murdoch and Hepi did about two runs a month, one each. One would usually stay at Forrest Street while the other did a run; they would overlap for three or four days to sell the gear, get the vehicles serviced and change over. They drove hard, fast and usually alone, although Murdoch's dog Jack was always at his side.

One route involved driving non-stop to a small town called Menzies, stopping there for the night and then going through to Sedan the next day, arriving about 10 pm — more than 3000 kilometres in a forty-hour trip over two-and-a-half days. One of the return routes ran up the Oodnadatta Track (suitable only for four-wheel drives) through Marla to Alice Springs, then a hard slog up the Tanami Track to the Western Australian border and on to the Buchanan Highway, then linking with the Northern Highway and straight through to Broome. When the weather was dry, Murdoch preferred this second route. He was a harder, tougher driver than Hepi, he enjoyed the solitude of the Tanami Track, and he knew he was less likely to come under scrutiny. If he did break down, he could fix his vehicle himself.

Sometimes they took a third route, straight up the Stuart Highway, west onto the Buchanan Highway 340 kilometres north of Tennant Creek, then along the Northern Highway to Broome. The routes were pretty similar in length, but the difficulty of driving varied. Outback tracks kept the drivers alert, whereas long runs on straight highways could cause 'white line fever', where the driver enters a trance-like state and risks running off the road.

Occasionally Murdoch would detour across the Nullarbor to the west coast so that he could visit his parents, with whom he maintained strong ties. To avoid police tracking their mobiles, he and Hepi maintained silence during the journeys; the runner would phone to say he was leaving Sedan, then there would be no further contact until he arrived in Broome, unless Murdoch rang from a public phone in Perth.

In September 2001, while Jazz was on holidays from her Paspaley Pearls job, Hepi invited her to accompany him on a run. He and Murdoch were thinking of getting out of Broome for a while. They were starting to be of interest to the Broome police, and they were having trouble with the Coffin Cheaters. Hepi also thought Billy Gibbs was creaming off the Broome profits. Hepi wanted to extend the business into Victoria and New South Wales, using his old contacts, while Jazz ran the Broome distribution. They still planned to supply Broome, but wanted to live in Sedan until the scrutiny had diminished a bit.

Hepi would live on his own property at Sedan, and Murdoch planned to stay in a granny flat on a neighbouring farm occupied by some of Hepi's friends – Frankie*, a former brothel operator who was chronically ill, Lurline*, one of his former staff, and Lurline's twelve-year-old daughter. They had become quite fond of Murdoch, and the girl was attached to Jack. Hepi and Murdoch planned to continue renting the Broome property as their distribution base. In October, on her return from the run, Jazz was invited to move into Forrest Street, with Tom the cat to keep her company.

By November, Jazz had handled distribution of several deliveries from Sedan. Then disaster struck. Billy Gibbs was caught red-handed with a truck laden with speed and trippy pills. He ended up in Casuarina Prison doing a long stretch. Word was that only three other people had known of Billy's movements – Jazz, Murdoch and Hepi. Around the same time, Murdoch's nephew in Perth was pinched for cannabis dealing – his first offence.

Hepi left Sedan soon after on a hydro run via Perth, saying he wanted to pick up a friend on the way. When the days passed in Broome with no sign of Hepi, Jazz became frightened. Had he been dobbed in, too?

Murdoch phoned her from Sedan. 'What's going on?' he asked. 'Is anything weird happening up there?'

'James is four days late,' she told him. 'What will I do?'

'Sit tight. Did you hear about Billy?'

'Of course I heard about him. The whole town's been waiting for that run.'

Hepi eventually arrived in a foul mood, accompanied by a female friend and claiming he'd broken down on the highway.

Then he accused Jazz of shopping Billy. He said everyone knew it must have been her and she'd never be trusted again. He ordered her to leave Forrest Street immediately.

Jazz packed a few belongings and ran, hoping Hepi's girlfriend would look after Murdoch's cat. She spent the next few months hiding out at the Roebuck Bay caravan park, afraid to show her face in town, with Murdoch silent and Hepi leaving death threats on her mobile. She decided to leave as soon as possible.

Chapter Eighteen

A SUSPECT AT LAST

I know who did Falconio.

James Hepi, May 2002

In early March 2002, Jazz heard that Hepi had gone to Sedan and Murdoch was back in town, so she went to Forrest Street, where she found Murdoch packing up and cleaning. Some of her belongings were still in the house, and she gave him a hand. Murdoch reassured her that he didn't think she was to blame for Billy Gibbs being caught – rather, he blamed Hepi. He also thought Hepi had shopped his nephew. It was obvious to Jazz that the two men had fallen out. Murdoch told her he was not doing any more runs, but planned to go south to visit his parents. He was furious that Tom's collar had been pulled so tight that she could barely swallow and had nearly starved to death. Tom was nursed back to health while Murdoch made his farewells around Broome.

One of Murdoch's close friends, Julie*, was unhappy to hear that he planned to leave so soon. She had hoped he would stay in Broome, but it looked as if he wouldn't be back for a long time. When he came to say goodbye, he was carrying everything he owned. His four-wheel drive was crammed full, and he was towing a piled-up trailer, covered by a tarp weighted down with a spare wheel. She asked where he was going but, on this subject, he was even more taciturn than usual. With his bush savvy and driving skills, Murdoch could live rough for as long as he wished. He left town with Jack and Tom soon afterwards and pretty much dropped out of sight.

◆ ◆ ◆

On 14 May 2002, James Hepi drove quietly into Broome with another delivery of hydro. The arrival routine was to split the load. Some of the gear would be unloaded at Twelve Mile or Blue Haze outside Broome, and the rest was stashed behind false panels and other hiding places in the vehicle for the trip into town. If that delivery was successful, the driver would return to collect the rest, welded into a forty-litre gas tank. That way, only part of the load would be found if they were caught. And they figured it would be a brave cop who took a blowtorch to a gas tank on the off-chance of finding a stash.

The next day, Hepi picked up the second part of the load and headed into Broome. He had nearly four kilos of hydro in the tank and a small amount in the cabin for personal use. He passed a service station about thirty kilometres outside Broome and waved to a member of the Coffin Cheaters, who was filling up. The bikie pulled out his mobile, smiling, and spoke briefly into the phone. Ten kilometres down the road, Hepi saw the flashing lights of a patrol car heading straight for him. The detectives knew what he was up to and they knew where to look.

Hepi was charged with possession of cannabis with intent to sell or supply and possession of a smoking implement. Probably tongue in cheek, he gave his profession as 'gardener'. He was bailed on $45,000 surety, about the same as the street value of the confiscated drugs, and ordered to return for trial at the beginning of August. But Hepi had information to trade. He told his lawyer, 'I know about a regular run from Perth to Broome – and I also know who did Falconio. It was Brad Murdoch.'

Given the spectacular lack of progress in the Falconio manhunt, Hepi's claims were manna from heaven for the police. Paula Dooley-McDonnell and two other police flew into Broome to begin piecing together Murdoch's movements in mid-July the year before. They were particularly interested in Hepi's account of events on Sunday 15 July 2001. That night, Hepi claimed, Murdoch had returned from a run, but on his way home he had left his Landcruiser at Tropic Upholstery, a body-works business in town, to have the canopy remodelled. Murdoch had walked in and denied having anything to do with the Falconio incident before Hepi had time to say hello.

Hepi also identified Murdoch as the man in the truck-stop video. He claimed the man's cap carried the logo of West Kimberley Diesel, and said he had recognised Murdoch when the video was released the previous year, but had kept his suspicions to himself. Now, faced with confiscation of his assets for running drugs, he was eager to share his hypotheses with the police.

After Hepi's revelations, police began hunting for Murdoch in the Northern Territory, South Australia and Western Australia. In an effort to establish whether the DNA on Joanne Lees's T-shirt belonged to him, they approached Murdoch's brother, Gary, to ask him to supply his DNA. The sample revealed common alleles to the 'Unknown Male' police were seeking. The net was tightening around Murdoch.

Gary warned Brad by phone that the police were on his trail and that Hepi was to blame. Gary had also heard that one of the Coffin Cheaters had put out a contract on his brother.

Police visited Murdoch's former house in Forrest Street and interviewed his friends: Brett at West Kimberley Diesel; Paul Jackson, his mate at Fitzroy Crossing, who had now moved to Broome; and Julie at the Chinatown Bakery. They spent hours asking questions and searching premises and seeking confirmation that Murdoch was in Broome on that Sunday night or the following Monday morning. Julie was questioned about her knowledge of Murdoch, his likely whereabouts, his associates and his sexual preferences. Various items were confiscated from the Kimberley Diesel workshop.

Loi O'Dore, the manager of Tropic Upholstery, was shown a still of the truck-stop video and said the canopy could be the one he'd fitted to Murdoch's four-wheel drive about a year before.

O'Dore said that after police released the truck-stop video, Murdoch had said he was the man in the video, but added that he had nothing to do with the Falconio matter. 'I'm no killer,' Murdoch had said. O'Dore said he'd passed that information on to police at the time and did not know if they'd followed it up. He agreed that Murdoch had asked him to replace his canopy in about July 2001, at a cost of some $6000, to prevent police hassling him. Murdoch had returned about a month later to get curtains fitted to the new canopy.

The Broome police made room for their colleagues at the police station, but only accompanied them to execute search warrants at Forrest Street and West Kimberley Diesel, where Murdoch had lived in a caravan for a short time. Although some local police had been suspicious of Hepi's associates, a sergeant close to the case told me later that he'd never known about Murdoch until October 2001, when he had gone to question Murdoch about his four-wheel drive as a routine inquiry for Northern Territory police. He also said that Murdoch had always had a number two buzz cut, and was clean shaven. But rumours flew that Murdoch had shaved off a Mexican-style moustache, grown a full beard to disguise it, cut his long hair short and so on. His friends and colleagues insisted he'd never had long hair or any kind of moustache. Photos that might verify any of these claims seemed to be in short supply.

Some of Murdoch's associates said, 'He had it in him, all right. He wouldn't take shit from no one.' Others said they had seen him carrying weapons, or had bought stolen or illegal weapons from him. A former girlfriend claimed he had 'acted strangely after a trip he'd done in mid-July 2001. He said there'd been roadblocks out, and he had to get home the long way.'

But another woman who was friendly with him from June 2001 to March 2002 told the police, 'I have never seen Brad with a weapon in the entire time I have known him. I assume he did have a weapon of some description, but I have never seen one.' On the other hand, she had seen James Hepi with 'a stainless-steel .357 pistol with a rotating barrel'. She said he used to keep it at Forrest Street, but took it with him when he travelled, although the weapon was not among the items police found in Hepi's vehicle when they arrested him.

She also told police, 'Brad and James had been talking about getting a pair of night-vision goggles with long-distance laser sights from the Douglas air force base.' This base was on their route from South Australia to Broome; she thought they planned to trade some dope for the goggles, but she did not know if the deal had taken place.

Murdoch's associates in Broome could not work out why the police were interested in him until James Hepi went on trial on 5 August 2002. During the trial, Hepi's lawyer revealed that his client had been co-operating with the police in providing 'information about a major crime in another State'. Local journalist Narelle Hine covered the trial for the *Broome Advertiser*, and on 8 August she reported the verdict:

> *Judge Antoinette Kennedy said people had to realise that if they dealt in drugs there were now wide powers to seize their property. While it was the case that cannabis use was widespread in the [Broome] community, its increasing potency, combined with high rates of suicide and depression, meant Hepi would normally face a prison sentence for trafficking and possession. But Hepi's co-operation with the police, his good record and glowing references meant he would get a one-off chance with an eighteen-month suspended prison sentence, suspended for twelve months.*

Once Hepi's deal became known, he left town, and Murdoch's friends clammed up completely.

Unknown to all his associates except his mate Dags, Murdoch had been moving between various hideouts in South Australia: a shed he had fitted out near the Bolivar Gardens Caravan Park, the caravan park itself, and Frankie and Lurline's property at Sedan. Fearing that something might happen to him, he'd left over one hundred thousand dollars in cash with a trusted friend to mind, to help get his parents into a retirement home. The week before Gary phoned to say the police were after him, the money had been taken – Murdoch believed, by police. The only other person who knew his friend had the money was Frankie, and Murdoch was furious with him and Lurline for not keeping their mouths shut. He was in a fighting mood. He decided he was going to deal with Hepi, possibly permanently. He thought he was going to die himself, and had decided he 'might as well go out being a martyr', as he told a friend later.

Frankie was ill in hospital in Adelaide, and Lurline and her daughter had seen no sign of Hepi at Sedan. Murdoch thought Hepi must have returned to Broome, and planned to head north to have it out with him. He took about $20,000 in cash and packed all his gear into his four-wheel drive and trailer. He stashed his money and papers, including his 'paperwork on Hepi' – records of transactions and deals in one hidden compartment, and piled his weapons into the back of the truck. The arsenal included a 9 mm Glock, a 38 mm Beretta, several rifles and his prize possession, an army crossbow with a visioscope that could be removed and held to one eye for night vision. 'It was just like a TV screen,' he told me later, 'clear as clear for 150 feet.' He had thirty-six arrows and about 8000 rounds of ammunition. He was ready to fight it out with Hepi or face down the whole Coffin Cheaters club.

He left Sedan and went to stay in his hideout near Bolivar for a few days. He visited Dags a couple of times to say goodbye, but Dags was not home. Murdoch had given Dags a Glock and a few thousand dollars to buy himself a new car, and had also asked him to look after Jack and Tom. He was planning to travel fast and rough, and didn't want the responsibility of his pets.

Around dawn on Thursday 28 August, Murdoch went for a final visit to Dags. This time, he went inside. The place was deserted. There was a half-eaten plate of dog food on the floor in the TV room. No sign of Jack. The kitchen dishes hadn't been done.

Murdoch's neck prickled. *That's not Dags*, he thought; he always washes up. He made his way to the garage, where he found a huge bowl of cat food left out for Tom, who was nowhere in sight.

When he'd found out about Hepi dobbing him in, Murdoch had told Dags, 'If you feel something is not right, pack up and f--k off quick.' Now it looked as if he'd done just that. Murdoch knew that Dags had heard about the Coffin Cheaters' contract, and he was sure the Coffin Cheaters knew that Dags was his friend. It was probably just as well he'd made himself scarce, and Murdoch decided to do the same thing.

He drove to the service station next to the Bolivar caravan park, filled up with fuel and had a big breakfast. Then he wheeled into a little-used truck bay where he occasionally met people during his stays at the caravan park. He lifted his truck bonnet to make it look as if he was doing something legitimate, unscrewed his Western Australian plates and substituted a set of South Australian plates that he used during long drug hauls.

Thinking he hadn't been observed, he set off for Port Augusta in South Australia. To prepare for the long haul, he had two new rear tyres fitted to his four-wheel drive, then went to Port Lincoln to collect $5000 he was owed. After a 700-kilometre round trip, he returned to Port Augusta at about 4.30 pm. He decided to stock up on food at the supermarket. Then, as he was walking out of the supermarket, his radar told him something was wrong.

'What's going on?' he said out loud. There were no cars anywhere near his, and no people. A moment later, he saw a squad of armed police with their guns trained directly at him. His arms full of shopping, he couldn't move.

Murdoch later told me what happened next. 'They made me lay face down while I was handcuffed. The c--t that did that used the middle of my back with his knee to get up, and I felt something crack.'

The police arrested him and took him away. He claims he was mistreated in custody. 'From the time I was arrested – five pm Thursday to four pm Friday – I had no clothes on, just a light bleached piece of canvas they call a rug.' In the dead of night, at 3 am on Friday, the police took him to Whyalla, about a hundred kilometres away, for a DNA sample. He was freezing. 'I remember the temperature being around three or four degrees. I was made to stand in a cell for half an hour, barefoot, waiting for the doctor. F--k, I was so cold. And then back just on daylight, coldest time. Clean coppers don't do that sort of shit.'

On Saturday 30 August, the police claimed he was threatening officers who came to his cell, so they decided to transfer him to Adelaide. 'They handcuffed me the same way and used their knee the same way. F--k, I don't think I need to describe what the pain felt like.'

He was put in G Division at Yatala maximum-security prison. It was a harsh place. 'No bullshit, they still have bread and water for the first five days' regime. I was on bread and water, breakfast, dinner and tea.'

He was given statements to read, and lawyers came to see him while he pondered his future. He had been arrested by the South Australian police on a charge that was not remotely connected with the disappearance of Peter Falconio. He was charged with two counts of abduction, two counts of false imprisonment and two counts of rape. The alleged victims were Lurline and her twelve-year-old daughter from Sedan. He vigorously protested that he had been set up, but no one took him seriously.

On 30 August 2002, Northern Territory police put out a media release:

> *Acting Deputy Commissioner of Northern Territory Police John Daulby said today that South Australian Police have notified Northern Territory Police about a man arrested and charged in Port Augusta for the rape and unlawful imprisonment of two females.*

'As with other persons that have been brought to our attention in respect to the disappearance of Peter Falconio, this person is, at this stage, no more than a person of interest,' Mr Daulby said.

That 'person of interest' was Bradley John Murdoch. In fact, police believed he was their quarry, the man in the truck-stop video. Game over. Or was it?

Part Two

FOLLOWING
THE TRACK

*This case is one of the most puzzling ever ... what the truth
is, I'm damned if I know.*

Former Northern Territory Police Commissioner Brian Bates

Chapter Nineteen

THE DNA DEBATE

Nothing done by the NT police apprehended that man – he was master of his own destiny.

Northern Territory police investigator

ike everybody else, I had followed the Falconio saga in the media
and wrestled with the strangeness of it all. It seemed like a complex
jigsaw with impatient players trying to push bits in where they didn't
quite fit. But what really galvanised my interest in the case was the
vigorous public debate that followed Murdoch's arrest. Many issues
were canvassed – the alleged rape victims' rights to a speedy trial; the
issue of whether the South Australian police had violated Murdoch's
civil rights by forcing him to give DNA samples; and whether these
samples could then be made available to the Northern Territory police
for their investigation of the Falconio case.

The South Australian police had compelled Murdoch to provide
a sample of blood, pubic combings, a sample of pubic hair and a
penile swab. This was lawful under Section 26 of the South Australian
Criminal Law (Forensic Procedures) Act of 1988, which allows a
forensic procedure to be carried out on someone without consent
if there are reasonable grounds to suspect that the person has
committed a criminal offence.

There are several other provisos. The authorities must be satisfied
that the public interest in obtaining the evidence outweighs the
need to protect individuals from unwanted interference, and should
also consider whether there is a less intrusive way of obtaining the
evidence. The decision must take into account the seriousness of the

suspected offence, the 'extent to which the procedure is necessary for the investigation', and the likely effects on the prisoner's welfare.

While the South Australian police were within their rights to take DNA samples from Murdoch, because they believed he had committed abduction and rape in their jurisdiction, this did not give the Northern Territory police the right to put their hands up and ask for a bit to compare with their forensic samples in the Falconio investigation. Murdoch had not been charged with any offence in the Northern Territory, and any other evidence against him on the Falconio matter was purely circumstantial.

Murdoch's lawyer quickly lodged an objection to sharing any DNA results with the Northern Territory investigation. As a result, all the samples obtained in Whyalla were stored without being tested until the matter could be heard in the magistrates' court.

At this hearing, which was held on 6 September, the police presented their case against Murdoch on the charges of abduction and rape. They alleged that on Wednesday 21 August, he had digitally raped a young girl in a guest house on her mother's property. The girl knew Murdoch and had gone to visit him in the guest house, which was some distance from the main dwelling. He was smoking marijuana and drinking alcohol. At first his attitude to the girl was friendly, but then his demeanour changed. 'He grabbed her and placed handcuffs on her wrists, and a blindfold over her eyes and something in her ears. He pushed her onto a bed and put tape over her mouth and around to the back of her head. He removed part of her clothing, threatened her and then raped her, which according to the girl, caused her to bleed. He then put a shackle on her ankles and connected it to the handcuffs with a chain.'

The police claimed that Murdoch put some of the girl's clothes back on, but left the handcuffs and shackles in place, and forced her into the back of his Landcruiser. He then went to the main house and abducted the girl's mother, also handcuffed and blindfolded. He was wearing a handgun in a shoulder holster, and made threats to both of them. He set off in the vehicle with both of them in the back.

He drove them along country roads to a tyre dump out of sight of the road, and kept them there for some time. Here, he assaulted the mother. He was still smoking cannabis, and also took some amphetamines. He told them that he had been taking amphetamines for about fifteen years.

Eventually, on the night of Thursday 22 August, he drove his captives to Port Augusta and released them at about 11 pm. He gave them a thousand dollars, but 'in effect ... threatened to shoot them if they went to the police'. After they were released, they hired a taxi and travelled to Adelaide, where the mother's de facto husband was a patient at the Royal Adelaide Hospital. They arrived at about 3 am. The next morning, they returned to the mother's home, and then came back to a place near Adelaide. The girl had a shower, and the mother disposed of the clothes the girl had been wearing when she was abducted.

The mother was afraid of Murdoch, and did not contact the police until Wednesday 28 August. That afternoon, a crime-scene examiner went to the guest house on the mother's property. He found a cigarette butt and an open carton of flavoured milk, which he forwarded to the State Forensic Science Unit on 3 September 2002, along with the pillowcase, the mattress and a mouth swab taken from the girl. The police did not disclose if any forensic tests had been undertaken on these items.

Murdoch's lawyers argued that the magistrate who had ordered the DNA testing in Whyalla had made a mistake. They pointed out that no bloodstains were found on the mattress or pillow, and there was no evidence of any DNA on the cigarette butt or the milk carton. They also claimed that none of their client's pubic hair had been found 'on the girl, the bed, pillow or otherwise in the guest house'. And even if pubic hair had been found on or in the bed, it would mean nothing, because Murdoch did not deny he'd been staying at the guest house.

The lawyers said the material found at the guest house should have been properly tested before any DNA was forcibly taken from their client. Now that the police had taken Murdoch's DNA, it should not be tested until a prima facie case of rape had been established through tests on the DNA at the scene.

The magistrate, Gary Gumpl, rejected these arguments and ordered that the testing proceed, but Murdoch's lawyers immediately lodged an appeal to the South Australian Supreme Court. The testing of the samples was delayed until the appeal was heard. The following Monday, 9 September, the Supreme Court confirmed that the testing would not proceed until it had dealt with the appeal. Evidence was taken within a few days, but the court reserved its decision. The waiting game was on again.

South Australian Attorney General Michael Atkinson and Northern Territory Police Minister Syd Stirling took advantage of the delay to sign an agreement allowing the DNA samples to be sent to Darwin, provided that the court allowed the testing to proceed.

On 2 October, Senior Judge Ted Mullighan finally handed down the Supreme Court decision. After reviewing all the evidence, he concluded that there were reasonable grounds for suspicion on the charges of abduction and rape. And, according to the girl's story, she had had body-to-body contact with her attacker. It was possible that pubic hair and body fluids might be found, in spite of the three-day delay after the attack and the fact that the girl had showered and her clothes had been destroyed. The judge raised the possibility that Murdoch might not have washed before his arrest, so the girl's cells might still have been present on his person. Furthermore, if an ejaculation had occurred on the bed, this could provide a DNA match.

There was also the issue of Murdoch's alleged drug use. Mr Mullighan pointed out that a blood sample could be used to test the women's claim that Murdoch had been taking amphetamines and cannabis. 'The analysis could establish that he was a consumer of drugs ... a piece of circumstantial evidence, not necessarily of great weight, but nevertheless of some weight, tending to establish that the appellant was the attacker.'

Mr Mullighan conceded that there had been a 'serious invasion of the appellant's privacy, particularly by the forensic procedures involving his pubic hair and penis', but said that no less intrusive procedure was available. He pointed out that the charges against Murdoch were very serious. After balancing all the competing considerations, he found that none of the grounds of the appeal was established. The appeal was therefore dismissed.

Murdoch's lawyers initially sought leave to appeal this decision before the full Supreme Court, but on 8 October they announced they were dropping the second appeal. Tests were immediately conducted on the samples, and it was agreed the results would be sent to the Forensic Centre in Darwin as soon as possible. The media were on tenterhooks waiting for the results. Would there be a match with Joanne's T-shirt?

◆ ◆ ◆

While the court battles were raging, several other diverting stories kept the case alive. Police received an anonymous letter from England claiming that before his departure, Peter had investigated ways in which someone could fake their disappearance and claim on an insurance policy. The police discounted this letter, saying the insurance angle had been investigated early in the case. Peter's mother described the claim as 'absolutely disgusting'. How could anyone think that Peter would put his family through such pain?

'My son is not here to defend himself, is he? No one has ever had a bad word to say about him.'

As if to add credibility to the insurance scam theory, William Smith, a retired British commando living near Terrigal on the coast of New South Wales, told police he had seen Peter alive and well, in the company of a gruff-looking fellow in a white four-wheel drive. He had followed the man and taken photos, and gave the police an address. He contacted the Northern Territory police so often he was given a log number, so that police not familiar with his claims could check him out on the database.

Mr Smith felt so strongly about his sighting that a few weeks later, when he and his wife went to England for a holiday, he visited the Huddersfield police and provided them with a copy of his dossier. The Yorkshire family liaison officers for the investigation listened to him for two hours and walked out shaking their heads.

'Better send it on to the Aussie police, just in case,' one said. Mr Smith was plausible, but hard to take seriously.

Another person who said he knew Peter claimed he'd been seen in Western Australia, giving police there a wild goose to go out and chase. A couple from Bourke in New South Wales, Melissa and Robert Brown, were convinced they'd sold Peter Falconio a Mars Bar and a Coke eight days after he disappeared. They said he'd arrived at their roadhouse just on dark in a white Toyota or Hi-Lux, accompanied by a thickset man, a small woman and a dog. Police showed Mr Brown a photo of Peter that had not been publicly circulated, and he identified it immediately. 'That's him! That's the one I seen.' When asked about the man's demeanour, Mr Brown told police: 'He wasn't anxious or upset. He was good as gold.' Mr Brown had been studying Peter's photo in a newspaper minutes before his double walked into the store. He was so certain the man was Peter that he went outside and pretended to call his dog so that he could get a better look.

Police asked if he'd managed to get the vehicle number plate. 'That would've been too easy!' he said. He told police the three people stood around casually beside their vehicle, 'talking amongst themselves, like three people going on a holiday.'

Then there was the argument between the Northern Territory police and Chris Tangey about the alleged handprint on the Kombi. Chris was still seeking an investigation by the Ombudsman. Dr Adam McCluskey, an independent DNA expert at Newcastle University, viewed a copy of Chris's video and emailed him, saying that although it was 'virtually impossible to draw any hard and fast conclusions, if a positive luminol reaction is observed … it is generally accepted as prudent to conduct further biological tests to confirm or rule out the presence of blood'.

The videotape was subsequently forwarded to Professor Barry Boettcher, the forensic expert who'd disagreed with Joy Kuhl during the Chamberlain trial. Boettcher told Chris and the media 'It looks like blood to me.' The announcement made front pages around the nation. Boettcher said he was 'baffled' that Joy Kuhl did not conduct further tests on what appeared to be 'a clear, strong, positive, unambiguous response in an area that looks very much like a left hand.'

Once more using the media as a forum, Acting Police Commissioner Wernham wrote a disparaging letter to the editor of the *Centralian Advocate* saying that he was concerned about the welfare of his forensic personnel, one of whom had taken stress leave over the incident. He dismissed Chris Tangey as a 'camera technician' who had no forensic expertise, and described Professor Boettcher as a 'retired academic, not a forensic scientist'.

Tangey responded in kind, saying Wernham's letter was a 'thinly disguised attack on my credibility' and he was not a 'camera technician'. He also supported Boettcher and accused Wernham of conveniently ignoring Dr McCluskey's opinion altogether.

The Falconio story grew legs again.

◆ ◆ ◆

On 9 October, John Daulby announced that police were 'unable to exclude' Murdoch from the investigation into Peter Falconio's death. The media realised what this meant. Police rarely say they have a DNA match, because such an announcement could jeopardise a trial. Unconstrained by these niceties, newspapers around Australia trumpeted 'The DNA matched'. It looked as if Murdoch would be done like a dinner.

Daulby said the Northern Territory police would be concentrating on establishing Murdoch's movements after 14 July 2001. The following day he told the press that Northern Territory police had already gone to Western Australia and South Australia. Paula Dooley McDonnell and John White had returned to Broome to obtain more details from Murdoch's associates there, while Superintendent Colleen Gwynne and Detective David Chalker were trying to interview Murdoch in prison. When they visited him at Yatala on Thursday 10 October 2002, he exercised his right to remain silent.

Chalker turned off the tape recorder and tried to get Murdoch to speak to them 'off the record'. Murdoch just swore at him and pointedly asked his lawyer to have him taken back to his cell.

Joanne Lees and the Falconios were advised of Murdoch's arrest and the matching DNA. They all expressed relief and hoped that Peter might still be found – alive or dead.

A few days later, Joan Falconio told the ABC's *Australian Story*, 'One minute this horror happens. And it is a horror. Basically, Peter's vanished, and that's the worst thing. I mean, Joanne is still here. We've got Joanne, and her parents have got Joanne. And it must be terrible for Joanne, like it is for us. But it's not knowing exactly what happened and why this man took Peter. If he shot him, why didn't he leave him there? Why did he take him?'

Tales had begun filtering through to Alice Springs of a spirit woman who said she knew where Peter was buried. The *Advocate* ran a story about Anna Martin*, a woman of Aboriginal descent who now lived in Perth, but had previously lived in the Territory with her former husband. On 27 September 1998, Anna's sixteen-year-old son had died in a car accident near Aileron, about halfway between Alice Springs and Barrow Creek. Anna had not been to the accident site to put his spirit to rest. Now she was plagued by visions of her son, who appeared to her as a magpie, accompanied by a kookaburra – another restless spirit who she believed was begging her to help set him free to return to his own country. Eventually, Anna realised the kookaburra was the spirit of Peter Falconio. The two spirits told her what had happened to

Peter, and she decided to go to Alice Springs to put her son's spirit to rest and help Peter to go home.

In December 2002, Anna quietly took off for Alice Springs. During the flight, she had another vision. She felt she would have to undergo a test before Peter's location was revealed to her. In Alice Springs, she sought out another spirit woman, Kathleen*. Kathleen's family was Kaytetye, which meant their country was around Barrow Creek. Anna sought Kathleen's help (and her family's permission) to look in their country for Peter's body. Kathleen said she would help, but first she wanted help from Anna. This was the test Anna had envisaged.

For almost a year, Kathleen's family had been in mourning for a family member, a young man called Thomas Braun, who had gone missing after leaving his girlfriend's house. After spending some time alone, Anna told Kathleen she could see the place where Thomas lay. She made a drawing of the location, although she had never been there.

Anna, Kathleen, and Kathleen's uncle set out for a location twenty kilometres west of Alice Springs to see if Anna was correct. Kathleen had implored the police to go with them, but the police refused. Less than two hours after arriving at the place Anna had identified, on a high ridge on top of a mountain, they found a skeleton. It was later identified as Thomas Braun's.

Next, Anna visited the site of her son's death. After she arrived, she became anxious about the messages she felt she was receiving from Peter. She thought the killer might still be in the vicinity, working or living nearby, and she feared for her safety. She was sure there had been more than one perpetrator. She told Kathleen that she saw three men, one of whom might have been Aboriginal. They had stopped the van to look for a wallet bulging with money. Peter had been enticed from the Kombi and had a hessian bag placed over his head. He was then taken to a nearby house and bashed to death.

She could clearly see in her mind the place where he was buried. She described a location with a huge gum tree beside a creek bed.

Kathleen thought it sounded like an old tree where she had played as a child, and she arranged for Anna to visit the site. When she approached, Anna became very afraid. She feared the killer might hear that she knew how Peter died and where he was buried. She returned to Alice Springs the same day and took the next flight to Perth, leaving Kathleen to persuade the police to go and dig.

The police were not enthusiastic, especially when they learnt that Kathleen could not leave her job during the week, so they would have to go out the following Saturday, the Alice Springs police picnic day. But they could not ignore the fact that Anna had found Thomas Braun, so two police were sent with Kathleen to the place Anna had picked out, on Neutral Junction station, about a kilometre north of Barrow Creek and seven kilometres off the highway.

The region was in drought. Normally the creek would have been in full flood during the December wet season, but its sandy pathway had not seen a current for a couple of years. The owner of the station, Charlie Frith, brought his bulldozer down and pushed aside a great swathe of red dirt beside the ancient tree. With its roots exposed and torn, the huge gum fell over, crashing down on top of the pile of newly shifted dirt.

Back at home in Perth, Anna was sitting in her lounge room, reading, when she felt an unbearable weight crushing her chest, squeezing breath from her body. She fell to the floor. Her family rushed her to hospital, where she was admitted, covered in dark purple bruises. At Neutral Junction, however, the search proved fruitless.

Eventually the men packed up, watched by a tearful Kathleen. She was certain they had not dug in exactly the spot Anna had shown her, but she did not have the courage or the desire to ask them to keep digging. They all headed back to Alice Springs, Kathleen sitting silently between the two police.

Chapter Twenty

DOING SERIOUS LAG

I did not kill Peter Falconio. And how do you know
he's even dead?

Brad Murdoch, March 2003

By now, I had decided to mount my own investigation into Peter Falconio's disappearance, so I contacted Murdoch's solicitor, Mark Twiggs, and asked him to sound Murdoch out to see if he would let me visit him in prison. Much to my surprise, Murdoch agreed. The message did not come through his solicitors, but through a phone call from his Broome friend, Julie, who said he'd sussed me out and was willing to let me visit. Carrying a long list of questions and feeling a bit nervous about venturing into Yatala, I flew to Adelaide in March 2003.

I was soon told the rules. My visits would be short (forty minutes each, early on Saturday and Sunday mornings) and no writing implements were permitted. That was a bit of a blow. My memory would really be tested. Years of jotting down notes after meetings have helped me to develop a retentive recall, but I wanted to know so much, and the details were important. I hoped I was up to it.

On a crisp, sunny autumn morning, I pulled my hire car in to the visitor parking lot at Yatala. I'd arrived about twenty minutes early to make sure I wouldn't have to sacrifice any visiting time. I sat sipping a takeaway coffee, alternating between skimming the Saturday newspaper headlines and watching a couple of magpies fighting over some treasure they'd found in the car park. A rather battered Japanese sedan pulled in beside me. The driver, a young woman, alighted and came around to open the passenger door. Inside was a toddler in a fairy dress.

'Stand there,' the woman said to the fairy, 'while Mummy changes Billy.' Billy was a baby, about six months old. His mother took him from his rear car seat, laid him flat on the passenger seat and changed his nappy, watched with equal attention by the fairy and me. I wondered who they were visiting. More cars were arriving. The young woman gathered her kids around her, locked her car and began walking along the path to the gates. I followed and caught up. Behind us, a small crowd of people, mostly women, were beating a path to the prison gatehouse.

'Hi, are you visiting a relative?' I asked brightly.

'Their dad,' she replied, nodding at the boy on her hip and the little skipping fairy. 'He's in remand.'

'So's my friend,' I told her. 'What's he in for, your bloke?' 'Rape.'

'Oh, so is my friend,' I told her, as if it was quite a normal thing to have in common.

'My old man did it, but,' the young woman announced. 'He's guilty. He'll do time. I only bring the kids on Saturdays now because they deserve to see their father. But when he's sentenced ...' Her voice trailed away into the crunching sounds of our feet on the gravel.

'Will he be inside for long?' I asked her.

'Dunno. Dunno if I'll wait for him, anyway. He's a bit of a bastard.'

Keen to change the subject, I confided, 'I haven't been to visit before. What happens?'

'You go in the office, get a key that's got a number on it for a locker and put all your stuff in there, then you go through the gates and sit at the table inside with the same number on it and they'll call your friend and he'll sit there.' She looked sideways at me. 'They'll make you take off all that jewellery,' she said. 'Looks like you should've got here a bit earlier, with all that clobber you're wearin'.'

We both laughed. I do tend to wear a lot of bits and pieces. Sure enough, the guards told me I could take in $10 in change, but nothing else. After struggling with some rings I've worn continuously since my twenties, I did a deal with the guard. Extending my reddened fingers, I pleaded, 'If you can get these four off you can keep them.' He gave me a dispensation and let me through.

The first gate was a simple barred door between the reception area and the rest of the prison. Once through here, I collected my $10 in change from the guard, who'd passed it through from the front desk. No metal can pass through the first door, or the supersensitive monitors will screech a warning. Swept along by visitors anxious to spend time with their loved ones, I had little time to look around, though I noted the high cement walls topped with steely grey coils of razor wire and a sort of no-man's-land between the front wall and the grey concrete paving leading across the yard to the grey steel front door. Everything was grey. The visitors' coats and jumpers stood out in a multicoloured blur as they almost ran to the front door, which magically swung open at their approach.

Then small groups of us were filtered into a kind of submarine lock, a few at a time. A heavy door swung tightly shut, and we were trapped in the confined space until a warder in a glass box above us released a second door ahead, which spilled us into the cavernous visiting area. The second door closed swiftly behind us. I found Table 22, which was bolted to the floor, and sat in nervous anticipation, trying to assemble all the questions I wanted to ask. I'd promised the lawyers that I would not discuss the rape case with Murdoch; I'd assured them I was only interested in the Falconio matter, which they had not yet been briefed on. A few tables away, I saw the fairy joyously leap into her father's arms, and then Brad Murdoch was making his way straight towards me.

I was amazed at how huge he looked. I never would have picked him from Joanne Lees's description – 'dark, straight hair to the shoulder with grey streaks, long thin face, droopy grey moustache with corners tapering down below mouth, heavy bags under his eyes, medium build, deep voice, Australian accent'. He was over 190 centimetres tall, with a thickset body in the regulation sky-blue sweatshirt and long, thin legs in jeans. His hair was clipped and stubbly; he was clean shaven, and when he enveloped my smallish hand in his roughened paw, his smile revealed a large gap created by four missing top front teeth. I offered him an iced coffee, as Julie had told me he was fond of it. When he said yes, I bought two from the small cafeteria, so I wouldn't have to interrupt the visit by getting up again.

I was surprised at how open he was. He freely admitted his nefarious activities running hydro, even though he had not been charged with this offence. He told me, 'I used to buy for $2500 a kilo and sell for $4500 a kilo, mainly to the blacks around Broome. The cops know it goes on, but they turn a blind eye. They'd rather see the blacks stoned than drunk.' He told me how much money had passed through his hands, and I wondered what had become of it.

He spoke quickly and softly, leaning forward with his elbows on his knees as if he wanted to give me as much information as possible. His voice was quite well modulated and less rough than I had expected. The other conversations in the room provided plenty of camouflage for the allegations he was making. I really wished I had a pen and paper.

He even alleged that some police were selling hydro in Broome at $5000 a kilo and were upset that he had been undercutting them. He also claimed that there was a healthy business in smuggled exotic birds and eggs, brought in through Derby from Indonesia, and that some people in authority had very rare collections of birds, about half of them illegal. He was not part of that operation, but knew of it – and so did everyone in Broome.

'What about the bikies?' I asked. 'I've heard the Coffin Cheaters are pretty active all through Western Australia.'

'Yeah, they do a few deals,' he agreed. 'I've never been a member of their gang, so I don't have first-hand knowledge. I belonged to the Gypsy Jokers for a while, but I left when the young guys started mainlining and dealing speed. I've never dealt speed and never used the needle. It's a mug's game. I don't agree with it. I did use speed to keep alert on long-distance trips, but never shot up.'

'Tell me about when you were arrested,' I asked.

'They treat you like an animal,' he told me in a low mutter. 'When I was in prison in G Division, I didn't see the sun for weeks. Then they put me in this exercise yard, six metres by six metres, with mesh roof and walls six metres high. They left me there for about two hours and I got rained on three times and caught a cold. I was already trying to see a doctor about my back, from when the cops who arrested me kneed me, but the first week I handed in the form on the wrong day, because the doctor only came once a week. Then he called in sick. It was agony with a bad back, and I couldn't read because the bastards broke my glasses …'

The big hand on the wall clock was nearly where I didn't want it to be. 'The police from Northern Territory came to see you on the Falconio matter, I believe?' I interrupted.

'Yeah. I told them to get stuffed. Wouldn't talk to them.'

'But they have interviewed you as a suspect at some stage, haven't they? The papers say you were interviewed and let go.'

'Never. They've never interviewed me as a suspect. Some Broome cops did come to my house around Christmas last year, asking about my truck and where was I when that bloke disappeared, and I told them. Haven't said anything to them since, other than that I've been set up for this rape.

'It's a f--kin' joke, if it wasn't so serious. With this set-up and the other shit that Mr Hepi has done to me, I'll probably get twenty years and have to do at least fifteen. Still, I might finish my schooling and end up with a ticket or a degree, who knows?

'Frankie and Lurline, who's the cow I'm supposed to have rooted, are mates of Hepi, you know. That's how I met them. Frankie knew a lot about what I had planned, and he was the only one.'

'What was your plan?' I interrupted. Just then, a warder began walking through the seated crowd, saying 'Time's up' in a voice that left no leeway for lingering farewells. 'Oh damn,' I said loudly, then leaned over to him. 'Do you want to keep the rest of the $10 for cigarettes, or more coffee?'

'You're kidding! No, thank you. Nice of you to offer, but they strip-search us after every visit, into every orifice. Lovely way to pass the time.'

Grateful that I was heading outside and not in his direction, I rushed to the locker, collected my belongings and hurried to my car, where I sat writing down everything I could remember. I looked up just in time to wave goodbye to the fairy as her mother drove off.

Next day was a repeat of the gatehouse routine, only this time I left my jewellery at the hotel. I'd written a list of questions on my hand in black Pentel, in case I forgot something. I bought two iced coffees while I waited for him to appear, with a sinking anxiety that he wouldn't show. But he had just been delayed, and when he appeared, we got right into it.

'What was your plan?' I asked again.

'I heard that Hepi had made up some crap to the cops about that Falconio deal, and I was sure he'd set me up on the rapes, to get me in jail so the cops could get my DNA.

'Anyway, there were a few people up north I had to settle some scores with, so I loaded up my truck and decided to go and have it out with all of them. I was ready, don't you worry. I had a bloody arsenal in the back – you realise if I'd shot that Falconio there would've been stuff all over the road? I reckon I'll have some serious lag coming for that arsenal, probably three to five years.'

I drew a deep breath. 'Bradley, did you kill Peter Falconio?'

'No, I did not kill Peter Falconio. And how do you even know he's dead?' He looked me in the eye. I wasn't prepared for the straight denial – or the tacked-on question – so I did not reply.

He continued, 'Police did the rounds of all my friends three times after my arrest, trying to get dirt on me. They missed one guy, Ted*, who actually knows the guy who owned the property where it happened, Neutral Junction. What a coincidence! But they did send over one of the Northern Territory Drug Squad detectives to ask questions. Why, if they were investigating a murder? I saw an article in the paper saying Falconio might have faked his death. Have they investigated that properly?'

'What about Joanne Lees?' I asked. 'Have you ever met her, or bumped into her?'

'Never set eyes on her in my life.'

'How about the DNA they say is yours on her T-shirt, though? That's going to need some explaining.'

'If it exists, it was planted,' he replied earnestly. 'Hepi must have given them some of my clothes with blood on them, where I'd cut myself. A lot of my clothes had my blood on them. I was always injuring myself in my work, and my cat was very playful as a kitten and often scratched me.'

'What about the dog? Have you got a dog?'

'Yes, I have, or did have. Jack used to travel everywhere with me, but guess where he is at the moment?'

'In the police pound? Not on a laboratory slide, I hope!'

'No, they never got him. I gave Jack to a friend called Dags to look after, but now I've heard he's living with Lurline and her daughter. I got a letter from some people up at Sedan who told me the mother takes Jack in the car every day, driving the girl to school. She hasn't missed a day, by the way – no counselling, nothing. I would think the last thing you would want to do is play with a dog whose owner is supposed to have raped you.

'They went and took him from my shed, where Dags had him. Pinched a vehicle as well. You'd think they'd be too scared to go near the place, in case I got bail. Maybe they were certain I wouldn't.' He looked knowingly at me, and I got a feeling I was missing something.

'What sort of dog is Jack?' I asked, looking for safer ground.

'Yeah, put this in your book. He's a friggin' Dalmatian.'

'What, a white-with-black-spots Dalmatian?'

'Yeah, a pure-bred, four years old. I've got a photo of him in my cell. I asked a friend to try to get him back, but Lurline saw her and called the police. She bumped into Lurline later on at a weighbridge, and

Lurline gave her a hiding. Told her to stay away from her dog. Poor old Jack!'

I was stunned by this news. Joanne Lees had described a blue heeler. What did this mean?

'Do the police know? If your dog travelled everywhere with you, his hairs would be all through your car. Lees would have got hairs from your dog on her if she'd been in your truck. They could try for a DNA match, surely?'

'I haven't told them about Jack, because I haven't spoken to the bastards. They probably know from talking to my friends, though.' Our time was suddenly up and half my questions remained as blurs on my sweaty palm. The Dalmatian was a surprise. The murder denial wasn't, but it did sound genuine.

There are no guilty people in prison, I told myself on the way to the car. If he's half smart he'd know I was going to ask that question. He'd probably been rehearsing his guileless reply for hours.

◆ ◆ ◆

Murdoch had told me that James Hepi's hideout was past Sedan, about a hundred kilometres north-east of Adelaide, on a dirt road off the main highway. I'd said I might drive out and have a look, but he'd warned me against it.

'You'll never get in,' he said. 'The entrance driveway is deliberately blocked with tree trunks. Anyway, he's dangerous. You should be careful of poking around out there. People have secrets to protect – and they have guns.'

But Sunday alone in Adelaide stretched out before me. Flicking through a booklet listing the local attractions, I saw I could combine my research with a trip through the Barossa Valley. That clinched it.

The valley was very pretty, and the names of familiar wines flashed past my windows. Moist clouds had turned the day a dull pewter, and it began to rain. I turned off the Stuart Highway and passed through Angaston and Tanunda, promising myself a Devonshire tea on the way back. As I followed the signs to Sedan and Swan Reach, the vegetation began changing from grapevines to scrubby pasture. The road was climbing a bit towards distant hills, which meant I was getting close to my destination.

I came upon the dirt road Murdoch had described and turned off, keeping an eye out for any Maoris driving Toyotas. I could just glimpse a weatherboard house, set back about a hundred metres off the road, almost invisible behind the trees. I wondered if it was Lurline's place. It looked deserted and unkempt, the hallmark of small holdings with few prospects. I could make out some buildings at the back. Maybe Murdoch's granny flat was one of them. If so, he would have had a good view of anyone coming. For all I knew, I might be being watched as I drove past at a crawl.

Hepi's property was supposed to be about a kilometre further on. I took the next dirt road to the left and almost immediately spotted a driveway off to the right. The gate was padlocked and looked as if no one had passed through it for some time. I got out and peered through the trees, looking for any sign of habitation. I'd heard Murdoch always kept his guns handy when he was there – taped underneath the kitchen table in easy reach, just in case a stranger called by. Although Murdoch was locked up in Yatala, Hepi could be anywhere.

The air felt washed clean by the rain, and the long grass trailed wetness along my legs. The silence was fractured occasionally by the carking of crows. It felt spooky. The lush Barossa seemed a long way away, and so did anyone who could help me if I found myself staring down a gun barrel. Suddenly I felt an urgent need for that Devonshire tea. Abandoning my expedition, I hightailed it back to the security of cobbled footpaths and milling tourists.

Chapter Twenty-One

THE MURDER CAPITAL
OF AUSTRALIA

It's a circumstantial case, but it's getting stronger.

Jim Litster, March 2003

I had a few other people to see while I was in Adelaide. In particular, I wanted to interview Vince Millar and Jim Litster. The following morning, I set out to find them. Neither was listed in the phone book, so I wandered down to try my luck with the electoral roll in the State Library. Vince Millar was not listed; I'd heard he'd left town, so maybe he had. But there was an entry for J. Litster, and his house was on the way to Bull's transport depot, where Vince Millar used to work, so I swung past to check it out. Lacy double-fronted Victorian weatherboard, neat front cottage garden, car in the driveway. I was tempted to stop right then, but Bull's depot closed at 4 pm and I wanted to interview Vince's former boss, John Lewis, before he left for the day.

I would never have picked John Lewis as a truckie. He was charming and courteous in his soft green silk shirt, tailored trousers and expensive brogues. We couldn't get any privacy in his 'office', a desk in the thick of the open-plan action at the depot – drivers coming in for their assignments, others reporting back after completing a haul, customers on the phone chasing deliveries – so we retired to a small meeting room.

John was happy to retell the story of the sensational rescue involving two of his drivers, and he also filled me in on the Barrow Creek pub. 'All the guys stop there – it's a natural place for Vince to have taken Joanne. Les is a good bloke. What you see is what you get.

Helen is a bit proper at times, but can get stuck into you if the freight goes missing. I know her better than some clients, because her mum lives in Adelaide and sometimes drops in a little something for us to take to Helen on our way through.

'Helen was very good to Joanne. We were all shocked when Joanne started saying Helen was using the media to cash in. The media were like treacle – you just couldn't escape them. They were all over us here, and Rod Adams, in particular, just couldn't take it.

'A funny thing happened quite separate to Falconio. We got a call from a fifteen-year-old girl claiming that Rod Adams was her father. Said he'd been working for a bus company that went broke when she was very young, and he'd left her and her mother and gone drifting. She wanted his phone number, which we didn't provide, of course. Later the same day, the child support crowd rang us, chasing him for back payments. He got on the road on the next truck, and then the tax department called him on his mobile, saying they wanted a little chat. He was mightily pissed off, I can tell you. He rang me from Coober Pedy and said, "I've had enough. I'm getting out!" He was quitting, there and then. Left his co-driver and the load, and I haven't seen him since.'

I asked John if he still had any phone numbers for Adams, and he went off to his desk to get his 'little black book'. It was indeed a black book, small and dog-eared, filled with cramped entries in different-coloured inks. 'I have everyone in here,' he said, thumbing the fraying pages.

I believed him. 'My God, what would you do if you lost it? Do you have it on computer?'

'Nah. Don't use those things myself. I leave them to the girls. But I look after it. Every so often I transfer some of the material to a new book, but I keep coming back to this one. I know where to find things in here. Ah, here it is!' he pounced. 'Don't know if these numbers will help, but there was a new missus, I think, so she might still be around.'

I copied down the numbers, and he took up the story again.

'About the same time as all the Falconio drama was going on, I had reports from along the route that the police were investigating drugs allegedly being carried on our trucks. One of my drivers came back one day and said when he pulled in to the truck stop, at Alice, an Aboriginal bloke came out of the shadows looking for his twenty dollars' worth. That driver told him that all our trucks look the same, but it took a while to convince the guy he had the wrong driver.

'I also had a call from an officer in a small town up past Tennant Creek, who told me he'd stopped and searched Vince's truck. Found nothing, but he called to say, "If your fellows are running drugs, we'll stop them and unload them if we have to." That's a real inconvenience for a trucking company trying to meet schedules. It's not as if we're a bikie gang running trucks full of empty cardboard boxes with secret compartments stuffed with drugs,' he told me a bit indignantly.

I didn't know how to reply, so I kept my eyes on my notes. We ordinary citizens are unaware of so many things that go on.

'Anyway, I asked Vince about the police search when he got back and he got pretty upset, especially since his truck was clean. He said, "I need a bit of a rest and I'll be back in a week or two," but I haven't seen him since either. It affected a lot of lives, that Falconio business.'

'So do you know what became of Vince?' I asked hopefully.

'I heard he went to Sydney and nearly killed himself.'

'Killed himself? What on earth for?'

'It was some kind of accident, I believe, although he was a very careful bloke. His judgement may have been affected by all the goings-on – I couldn't really say. He did have a girlfriend, and I think she was pregnant when Falconio happened. I'll give you their number.'

We chatted generally while he looked through his book again. 'Do you think they've got the right bloke?' he asked me.

'They say his DNA matches the mark on the T-shirt,' I replied.

'That's hard to talk your way out of. But it doesn't necessarily place him at the scene. He could've brushed up against her at the Camel Cup, for example. I don't know exactly where the DNA was found on her shirt, so who knows? And even if it was Murdoch at the Shell truck stop, it doesn't put him 300 kilometres north with a gun at Peter Falconio's head, does it? He might have just been on one of his regular runs. It's a likely spot to fuel up for a run along the Tanami Track.'

'Yes, anything's possible,' he said.

John told me his wife was a lawyer who had spent years working to clear a man who had been convicted in a celebrated South Australian murder case.

No guilty people in prison, I thought again. I took down the numbers and let John Lewis return to directing operations.

◆ ◆ ◆

Murdoch's lawyer, Mark Twiggs, had an office not far from Bull's; it was also quite near the prison, which probably saved him time on house calls. When I'd first contacted him to arrange a visit to Murdoch, he told me he'd been receiving a lot of material from William Smith, the former British commando who was convinced Peter Falconio was still alive.

I'd phoned William Smith, who said he'd met Peter and Joanne outside a real estate office in Terrigal in early January 2001, before they set off on their trip. He had noticed their English accents and said hullo. They told him they loved Australia; Peter mentioned the possibility of migration, saying that if they sold their unit in the UK, they could buy a mansion in Australia. William liked them both and was moved to give them a print of one of his paintings, a selection of which he keeps in the car – *Giants of the Flinders Ranges*.

'It was quite a big print,' he told me, 'rolled up in a tube and with my signature. I've always said to the police they should tell me if it was found in their van, or posted home. That would demonstrate I'm not making this up.'

'Do they think you are making it up?' I asked him.

'How can you tell?' he snapped back. 'I've given them pages of proof of my sighting of Peter after he disappeared, but they don't seem to have acted on it at all – either in Australia or in England. I wanted to contact the Falconio family while I was in the UK, to tell them Peter was still alive, but the UK police were not at all helpful.' He told me he'd sent Mark Twiggs a file with all his documents about the case, and he was happy for me to have a copy. I'd arranged to call in and collect it from Mark, who had kindly photocopied it for me. I picked it up and put it away safely, thinking it should make interesting reading in my hotel that night.

◆ ◆ ◆

At about 7 pm, I pulled up outside Jim Litster's house again, hoping he'd finished dinner. A lady answered the door, and when I asked for Jim, she showed me through a delightful entry hall and dining area to the back veranda, where her husband was enjoying a cigarette with his beer. I introduced myself, and he said I could join him, so I did. Fortunately, I'd brought my pen and notebook.

He told me his appointment to the review had nothing to do with his friendship with the police commissioner, Paul White. Rather, Paul White came from a 'culture of review'.

'A review is not designed to say, "You blokes have messed it up and we're here to tell you how",' Litster said. 'I've been subject to reviews myself. You have to be diplomatic. A good review will suggest options – you don't want to be hard. It's a nice way of saying you've done OK, but if you do it this way next time you might get a better result. You also aim to get the glory hunters, people who get good information and keep it to themselves. Police should work as a team.' The reviewers had been given a contract with a detailed charter.

He said John Daulby too was very keen to get the review done in case they'd missed anything. He wanted to show that the force had done everything it could.

'Was that part of your brief?' I asked.

'Not at all. We were not there to investigate the Northern Territory police. We were there to support or enhance what they'd already done. Our job was to look at what had been done, look at future staffing, general investigations strategies and future directions.' He described Daulby as 'a man's man. Straight from the shoulder.

'A good cop. Chamberlain had a nasty influence on Daulby,' he added. 'They wanted no repeat performance.'

He and Owen had concluded that Peter was probably shot in the chest or head and died instantly.

'What evidence did you rely on to come to that conclusion?'

'There was quite a bit of blood on the road, covered by dirt,' he told me. 'The killer probably used a .22 or .32. A heavier calibre would be likely to leave bullet fragments or even the bullet as it exited the wound. The killer was coldly efficient – probably put the body in the ute and took it south, then dumped it fifty or sixty kilometres on.'

'How do you think it happened?'

'Well, there were the two cars stopped beside the road, the body was on the road and the girl escaped,' he explained.

I felt I should raise a question that had been puzzling me. 'I've thought a lot about why Joanne Lees has always been adamant that she did not see Peter's body at any time,' I said. 'She said she didn't believe he was dead, and got upset with people who said publicly that he was. If she was there, dragged from the Kombi to the four-wheel drive, she must have been dragged straight past his body – especially if he died instantly and just dropped where he stood. How could she not have seen Peter's body?'

'Oh, that's simple,' Litster said. 'The cars were parked on a shoulder. There was a dip away from the highway. He could have dropped when he was shot and then rolled. And anyway, she would have been looking directly into the headlights of the four-wheel drive. They could have blinded her. And she was traumatised.'

'Dead weights don't roll easily, especially if the incline isn't steep,' I replied, unconvinced. 'He'd be unlikely to have bled on the highway if he'd rolled immediately into the gravel dip. And how was she able to describe a chrome bull-bar on the gunman's car, right beside where

Peter must have been lying, and not see his body?'

'Look, she was very traumatised. She could have mixed up a few details. Like when she described the gunman as "average height and build", for example. Everybody is average height and build to a witness. You have to be very careful of descriptions.'

Just then, I didn't want to say that I knew how big Murdoch was. Litster was dismissive about the 'luminol incident'. 'We spoke to Joy Kuhl. There was a bit of a carry-on at one stage. A guy with a camera reckoned he'd found some marks. It was a storm in a teacup, really. She'd done a pretty good job. There was not much there. The scene was wide open.'

As for the criticism of the way the site had been managed, he said, 'The police were four hours away. Given what they were faced with, the first members on the scene were OK. It was the early hours of the morning. They had to find out if he was in the scrub injured. They looked. They couldn't wait for black trackers.'

'Did you look at all the evidence, the exhibits?' I asked, hoping for some clues about exactly what the police had on Murdoch.

'We saw everything. Went everywhere. Interviewed everyone. There were not many exhibits, really.'

'The handcuffs, what were they like?'

'Quite unique. The way he'd made them, there would have been room for her to bring them to the front, as she said.'

'But why would someone make restraints with so much free play in them? And how was she so easily able to untie her feet before she ran into the bush?'

'I can't answer that. Unfortunately, we had no feedback from the public about those restraints once the investigators released their picture and the mock-ups. But maybe they found similar ties in Murdoch's vehicle when he was arrested. They might have provided more information.'

'What about the dog? Was there any dog hair in the exhibits? Any on her clothes?'

'I'm not sure if there was dog hair on her clothes. Not sure about any dog hair – or the dog. I don't remember any evidence of a dog.'

He changed the topic. 'We did look at the VW and all its contents and found that Peter put in his income-tax return before they left Alice Springs. That's not exactly the act of someone who's about to disappear voluntarily, is it?'

The evening sun had disappeared, and the mozzies were big enough to carry us off. But I didn't want to suggest a light or some mozzie spray in case he stood up and showed me the door. So I soldiered on, my writing becoming less and less legible as I scribbled in the advancing darkness.

'Why do you think Peter pulled over when he already knew his van was backfiring and had been told by Rod Smith that he'd be mad to try to get to Darwin in it?'

'It was an old Kombi, and they have a tendency to catch fire. The oil builds up and they get too hot on long trips. If the man just pointed at the back and they couldn't hear what he was saying, I think it's quite natural that they pulled over. Especially when they'd had problems before.'

'Did you see the air tickets found in the Kombi?' I asked, flying a kite. 'The ones in Peter's name only?'

'Yes, there were some tickets. I think they were to Papua New Guinea. I can't really remember.'

I wasn't sure if he couldn't or wouldn't, so I asked if he was happy with the documentation of the custody of the exhibits.

'Yes, quite happy. And by the time we saw them, all the tests were completed. There were witnesses who saw people at the scene, you know. One witness saw a vehicle turn and go south at about nine o'clock. He could have made it to the Shell stop in three hours – it's only 311 kilometres. I don't know if the police went to interview that fellow in Broome or not. It doesn't matter if it's him in the picture, anyway. They've got the gunman's DNA.'

'Did you interview forensic people about the exhibits?'

'Some. We didn't see Bill Towers – I think he was on leave. And so was David Chalker, I believe. One of them was on stress leave, but I can't remember who. We did speak to Joy Kuhl, though. She's all right,' he volunteered.

'I've heard she resigned part way into this investigation. Did you hear why she might have left so suddenly?'

'She might have gone to a better job. I don't know. There was so much speculation about everything in this case.'

I was being eaten alive, and I didn't think I'd get much further. I stood up to leave, and he walked me down the hall. A row of ancestral photos lined the walls; when I asked about them, he told me his wife's family had occupied the home for more than a century. It was a very attractive house, and I said so.

'Do you think they've got the right man?' I asked him at the front door.

'It's a circumstantial case, but it's getting stronger. Personally, I'd like to be as sure of winning Tattslotto as I am of his guilt. He'll get life if he's guilty – and life is life in Darwin, in the toughest prison in the State. I suspect this guy will try to do a deal.'

As I walked to my car, I reflected that Murdoch didn't have too many aces to do a deal with.

◆ ◆ ◆

By next morning I'd tried all the numbers John Lewis had given me for Vince Millar, with no luck. Two rang out, and one of the mobiles was disconnected. I had three hours before my plane, so I decided I'd get to the airport early and go over my notes. But on spec, I tried the mobile number one more time.

'Yeah? Vince here.'

'Vince! Vince Millar, is that you?'

'Yeah. Who's this?'

I explained in a rush who I was. He didn't sound too keen to meet me. He'd had enough of the Falconio story to last him a lifetime. And he wasn't very well. 'Do you live in Adelaide?' I asked. 'Are you anywhere near the airport?'

'Yeah, not far from the airport, about twenty minutes,' he drawled. It was building up to be a hot day. I persuaded him to let me bring over a beer – 'Hahn Premium, not that light stuff,' he instructed me. I checked the map and stepped on the accelerator.

He was near the airport, but about forty minutes' drive from where I was. I figured aloud as I drove, 'Forty minutes to get there, arrive at the airport forty minutes early, twenty minutes to drive from his place, that's one hour and forty, leaves just over one hour to meet him, reassure him and interview him. If I don't get lost.' Squeezy! And Vince didn't sound like the kind of bloke you could rush.

Luckily, my car seemed to know the way. I arrived at a modern house in a sprawling new subdivision, tight-roped along a builder's plank through a garden of rocks and clay, and was met at the door by Vince's partner, Naomi. She told me she was hoping Backyard Blitz might take on the landscaping, because Vince had virtually come back from the dead and couldn't do it himself.

'Yeah, I had a bad accident,' he told me from his seat at the kitchen table. 'Nearly killed meself.'

They'd only recently moved in; hence his absence from the electoral roll. They had a little son and a big dog.

I accepted one of the beers and listened. Vince said he'd been driving in Queensland for a while after he left Bull's, but gave it up because 32,000 kilometres a month was too much, even for him. He took a delivery job in Sydney and was unloading pallets of doors when he found himself flattened under one of the pallets, which someone had loaded incorrectly.

'He was really flattened,' Naomi said. 'He had what they called an open-book fracture of his pelvis – like it was open pages.' She gulped. 'They told me he might die, and our baby was only a few months old. It was terrible.'

'I was in a coma for three months. I've lost nearly half me bodyweight,' he added. 'I only got home from New South last week.

We musta been at physio when you rang yesterday.' He did look frail and couldn't walk without a frame. He told me he'd just graduated from a wheelchair.

At first, he wasn't inclined to say much about the Falconio case, other than that he'd 'had it up to there'. After the news got out, he had more than fifty calls from journalists in Australia and England, wanting to hear his story.

He sipped his beer, feigning memory loss as he hedged around, not wanting to go over it all again. He was obviously torn, feeling a bit ungracious because he'd agreed I could come. I was watching the kitchen clock, feeling pressured, but not wanting to pressure him.

Naomi saved the day. Making conversation, she asked me what it was like being a journalist, and I said no, I was a book writer – different species. She wanted to know what else I'd written. Thinking she'd know the story of Jaidyn Leskie, a toddler who'd been murdered in Victoria in 1999, I started with that.

She squealed and said she'd gone to school with Jaidyn's mother. She'd followed the case very closely and knew about me. After that, it all turned out fine. We talked non-stop for an hour, and Vince told me the whole story again, this time from his perspective.

He told me that when he drove the Stuart Highway at night, he could see other cars' headlights about twenty kilometres away. At about 12.30 am on the night he found Joanne, he noticed some very bright headlights in the distance. They seemed to be stationary – or, if they were moving, they weren't coming towards him. It looked as if a car was reversing across the highway or doing a U-turn.

Vince's truck was doing about eighty-five kilometres an hour, and it took about fourteen minutes to reach the spot where he'd seen the lights. That was where he saw Joanne jump out in front of his truck.

'I don't think I told this to the cops, but I remember a small Japanese-type sedan driving fast towards me, and passin' me before I reached Joanne.'

He immediately noticed Joanne's distress. 'She was shakin' like I've never seen anyone before. She looked like absolute crap.

'I also forgot to mention to the cops that when I put my arms around her, she was warm. I remember thinkin' that was a bit strange – her in a skimpy little T-shirt. I even thought for a minute that she might have just got out of the car I'd seen.

'The other thing was, she wasn't dirty. Her clothing all looked pretty intact, and there were only a few little blood smears on her shirt, like they might have come from her elbows.

'Ya know, I've done a lot of thinkin' about that car since then, because she wasn't cold, like you'd expect. What if that car took off with the evidence – the body even – and she stalled me by gettin' me to look for her Kombi? But on the night, we got caught up in lookin' for the boyfriend – he might have still been alive at that time until she told me the bloke had a gun. Then we took off, quick bloody smart!'

'If he was still alive, what about the blood on the road? How do you think that could have got there?'

'Easy, mate. You could bring it in a bottle or a plastic bag, and just pour it on the road. Looked very like it could have been poured, just in a small puddle like that. If you wanted to carry it hidden, you could put it in a thick plastic bag and suspend it in the petrol tank. People hide all sorts of stuff in their tanks.'

'Really? I'll keep that in mind,' I laughed.

I asked him if he'd noticed any cuts or bruises on Joanne or any dog hairs on her clothes.

'Her wrists were a bit red when I found her, but not bleedin' and she had a sort of whisker of dried blood on her nose, like she'd wiped her arm on it. There were some grazes on her elbows and knees. She probably did have dog hairs on her later on, because I gave her me big blue Sloppy Joe to put on. I thought there might be a few hairs on it, because I leave me work bag next to Hartly's bed when we're at home, and he sometimes sleeps on me jumper when he comes on the road with me. I said, "Don't mind the dog hairs, it's clean and it's nice and warm." It's me favourite jumper,' he assured me, 'and I never got the f--ken' thing back. I think the cops still have it.'

I looked at his dog. Hartly was a blue heeler, with mixed blue and red hairs. 'He's got a white heart shape on his back,' Vince pointed out, 'so he's called Hartly. Get it?'

I did. What I didn't get was the lack of dog hairs on Joanne's clothes. She said she'd been thrown in next to a cattle dog and then wriggled awkwardly out across the tray – an area that should have been coated with loose dog hairs. Now Vince was telling me about more dog hairs – cattle-dog hairs – that would have come from his jumper. And Murdoch had told me he travelled everywhere with a Dalmatian. I'm no scientist, but I would have thought Dalmatian hairs would be significantly different from cattle-dog hairs.

'I wonder if the police realised that the hairs on the jumper she was wearing were from your dog?' I asked him.

'Ah, just what I asked meself on the way down to Adelaide. I had to get going as soon as possible the next day – we were running late. After I did the Keystone Cops trip out to find the van and gave me DNA samples, we left. So I forgot to say it was my jumper.'

He went on, 'So on me next trip to Alice, about ten days later, I stopped in and made a second statement, and added in the jumper. I didn't want them to think they were finding the man's dog hair when it was my jumper and my dog's hair. In the end, I made three statements, about sixteen pages altogether. The last one was made to a lady cop in Alice Springs, Paula someone, on 18 March, about eight months later. In that one I told her more about the jumper, said I'd seen the sedan heading north and I also mentioned a truck I'd seen at Marla just before Christmas.'

'What truck?' I asked with one eye on the clock.

'I pulled in to Marla, just where the Oodnadatta Track joins the Stuart Highway, and I saw a vehicle parked out the front of the garage like the one the police were lookin' for. It was a white four-wheel drive with a green canvas canopy with rounded edges at the corners. The back-driver's side wheel was hangin' down – that's why he must've pulled in. There was no one around, so I walked over and undid the driver's side zip and looked in the back tray. It was all very sorted out and covered up – everythin' in its place, you know. And you could walk through from the front to the back.

'Just then the owner came back. He was a big bloke, about 110 kilos and taller than me.'

'How tall are you?' I asked. I hadn't seen him on his feet.

'About 1.8 metres,' he told me. 'Or I used to be, before me accident. I'm all bent up now, like an old man.' He pulled a wry face.

'Anyway, I told him I was lookin' at his vehicle because it looked like the Barrow Creek truck. He said he'd already been pulled over and searched, and I just left it.'

'Have you seen the photos of Murdoch in the papers?' I asked. 'Did he look like him?'

'He had short brownish hair, white skin, not tanned and no beard or moustache. I don't think he looked much like the bloke in the truck-stop video, though, if that was him.'

'I guess as you were the one who found Joanne Lees, you must believe her story of what happened out there?'

'Well, I did, completely. Tell me how a couple of backpackers could meet their destiny at Barrow Creek? It's maiden country, out in the bush, it's so unreal, it's almost gotta be true. And she was scared – of somethin'.

'But I wonder about her bein' warm. And another thing she said on the British TV video has me curious. She said he put her in the front of the car, then he took her out and put her in the back. The story she told the cops at Barrow Creek was that she crawled through between the seats across the tray and wriggled down.

'But when I picked her up, she was quite clear. She said, "He tied me up in my car and then dragged me to his car and threw me in the back." Now, I'm not that clever, but I reckon she'd say what really happened the first time she told it, before all those cops and microphones were hasslin' her later on.

'I dunno, really. Maybe somethin' different happened and she saw a bloke somewhere else that looked like that description she gave and got it in her head. And she told me he tied her hands behind her head, not at the back. It's a mystery, all right.'

'Have you spoken to her since that night?'

'Not once. I even bought her a little present, 'cause I felt really close to her. I've tried to get in touch with her through the media, see if she's OK, but I just hear she wants to put it all behind her. I dunno how you can put somethin' like that behind you until it's all settled. I'll see her at the trial, I suppose.'

Naomi chimed in.

'You'd think she'd at least say thank you to Vince. It's changed our whole lives, because of him finding her. It'll never be the same again.'

'Murder tends to have that effect on people,' I agreed.

I left in a rush, not sure if I'd catch my plane. But the detour had been worth a missed flight. In the departure lounge I stared at a photo of Hartly they'd lent me, thinking scrambled thoughts of outback yarns and shaggy dog stories. That dog factor kept nipping at my heels.

Chapter Twenty-Two

THE TRUTH IS OUT THERE

There's only one way to test your theories, Rob – go and find out for yourself.

Clive Bowles

When I returned from Adelaide, speculation about the case was rife – especially at our house. So my husband, Clive, and I decided to visit all the key locations, looking for people and clues that could help us understand how an English city girl could outwit an armed bushman and his dog.

Unfortunately, my little dog, which usually accompanies me on my research trips, could not come this time. Clive wasn't keen. It was one of those 'it's him or me' situations, and I thought Clive would be more help under the circumstances. Probably better company too. So the dog missed out.

It was just as well, because by the time our medium-sized hatchback was packed, there wasn't room for the dog. I was placed under strict instructions not to buy a single thing on the way, because we wouldn't get it in with a shoehorn. We had bed linen, my sharp kitchen knife, teabags, a first-aid kit, insect repellent, hot rollers, books and other essentials. Without these, we would really be roughing it.

The main bone of contention, though, was two outsize folding armchairs I'd bought for the journey: a leopard-patterned velour number for me, and a plain one for Clive. He said we'd never use them, but I insisted; most caravan parks don't have comfy chairs. After some fairly heated negotiation, I prevailed. (As it turned out, we were glad to collapse into them at the end of a long day, although I refrained from gloating.)

We battened down the hatches at home and set off on 4 July 2003. Clive's detailed schedule – the overnight stops, what we'd do and who we'd see in each location – was tucked into the door pocket, the only vacant space.

Our first stop was Renmark, where we rented a demountable cabin beside the Murray River and entertained pelicans at dinner and breakfast. One was so keen to join us that he wouldn't take 'piss off' at face value. We finally had to close the glass sliding door to keep him out, but he beat the glass with his beak for hours, demanding to share our dinner.

In the morning he brought his family to meet us, and we forgave him. They seaplaned across the river on origami wings, braking with their feet and settling into water still golden from the sunrise. They waddled ashore to check out the provisions, but we were almost ready to leave.

We spent the next night at Port Augusta – 'Port Aggutta', as the locals call it – then renewed our acquaintance with Coober Pedy, which we'd visited in 1997. This time we were on a mission, so we didn't look up any of our previous contacts. We wanted to get to Alice Springs in time for the second anniversary of Peter Falconio's disappearance.

Our arrival in Alice Springs coincided with the Alice Springs Show and the Camel Cup, two of the biggest tourist drawcards in the Centre. The town was teeming with people from all over the world. Conversations in German, Japanese, Canadian and English (as spoken in England) swirled around us.

The first person we met in Alice was Chris Tangey. I had been talking to him for some time by email, and was expecting him to be a big, rugged bushwhacker. He turned out to be a smaller version of my expectations, but an action package nevertheless.

As we sat on his spacious back veranda, surrounded by scrubby bush, Chris and I discovered that we'd both lived in Tasmania during the 1970s. While I was nursing in Hobart, Chris had been searching for the elusive Tasmanian Tiger. He'd given himself three years to try to prove or disprove its existence. To keep himself in walking boots, he worked as night-time presenter at 7EX, a commercial radio station in the north of the State.

I said I had a hazy memory of some nutter up north looking for the tiger. 'Well, it was worth a try,' he said, grinning ruefully.

'Never really came close, though.'

In Alice, he makes documentaries, ads and corporate videos, and occasionally shoots news footage for the TV channels, but he also follows a new passion. He is gradually mapping all the campsites of the Burke and Wills expedition in the hope of discovering Wills's brass astronomy instruments, which were abandoned on Burke's orders during the trek. On Chris's lounge-room wall was a huge map of northern Australia covered in intertwining black lines, each line representing a trip – in all, more than 250,000 kilometres of hard outback driving.

'Some notes and diaries were found with them where they died in 1861,' he told us. 'But I'm sure there's more stuff out there. What a find that would be!'

Chris's wife, Annie, heaved a little sigh, but there was a smile lurking around the corners of her mouth. We all sipped tea and discussed our theories, smart and silly, about what could have happened to Peter Falconio.

Chris did not believe Joanne Lees's version of her escape. We had our doubts too.

'That bush out there is mulga and spinifex, mainly,' Chris explained. 'Like this stuff around here. See,' he said, pointing to the mulga trees around his veranda, 'mulga has a thin trunk with branches that fan out from it, but most of the leaves are at the ends of the branches. Also, you can see the branches all point skywards, so that rain is channelled direct to the roots. So if you hid behind one in the dark and someone shone a torch at you, you'd be seen clear as day, because there's no cover. Especially in pale-coloured clothing.

'Under the mulga you've got spinifex grass, which is nasty stuff. It's bloody sharp pointed long grass, and slippery too. If you're running and your foot lands on the middle of a clump, you can slide off and turn your ankle. And it scratches bare legs to pieces. That's why bushies always wear leggings, even when they're in shorts.

'Also, when a mulga branch dries out and falls off, it stays there on the ground – a nice little obstacle to get tangled in, if you're running full pelt in the dark. Noisy too, dragging along behind you while you try and extricate yourself. And there are lots of quite sharp rocks lying around – granite, mostly. If she was only wearing sandals, she'd be pretty cut up.'

I said, 'Police media releases say they found her sandal prints at the scene, which helped them pinpoint the location of her flight into the bush.'

Clive cut in. 'Didn't Vince tell you it took him about a kilometre to stop after he saw her? Then she ran along the road and crawled under his trailer?'

'That's interesting,' said Chris. 'That road is very sharp blue metal, and the gravel on the shoulders is no Persian rug either.'

'I've just thought of something,' I piped up. 'You know how Vince said she crawled on her elbows and knees under his trailer? What if that was when she got the grazes everyone keeps talking about? By the next day, when the police took photos and the hospital staff examined her, they wouldn't have known if the injuries were twelve or twenty-four hours old. I've seen the TV photos of the grazes on her arms, and they are under her forearm, in front of her elbow, not on her elbow itself. And her clothes weren't messed up. "Unremarkable forensically", "all pretty intact", "no dirt or bad stains" – that's how they've been described.'

Chris looked thoughtful. 'You'd think she'd have a bit of stuff from the bush stuck to her clothes and hair if she'd been in there five hours. With her hands tied, she wouldn't be able to tidy herself up.' We decided to re-enact Joanne's escape into the bush, with me tied up and Chris using his bush skills to hunt for me. Same place, same day of the year, same time at night, same cable ties, as close as we could get. We sat for another hour planning our excursion, then Chris said, 'Righto, that's enough. I'm taking you to meet Ted Egan. He said he's got a bit of info for you.'

◆ ◆ ◆

Ted Egan is a legend throughout Australia – a singer, writer, songwriter, teacher, and all-round larger-than-life good guy. He has taken a keen interest in Aboriginal culture and speaks several Aboriginal languages. He also wrote a fascinating book on the Caledon Bay and Woodah Island massacres of 1932–33 in Arnhem Land. He's a big man in every way.

We met him outside Alice Springs, in the sprawling mud-brick house he built on his property, Sinkatinnie Downs. His Welsh-born wife, Neris, offered us tea, and we sat in a vaulted lounge room, discussing the case. Ted recalled his experiences with the roadblocks on the weekend of 14 July 2001.

He went on to say that when he'd seen the truck-stop video he was convinced that the man in the photo was a person he knew as Dave the Ringer. Dave was a drifter who had married an Aboriginal woman and had knocked out one of his front teeth to become accepted by her family, for whom this was part of the traditional initiation. Ted had also seen this fellow in town around that time.

'He can be the life of the party one minute and really bad the next,' Ted told us. 'I wondered if it might have been him. I phoned the police and suggested they ask Joanne Lees if the man had anything wrong with his front tooth.'

I sat up straighter, remembering the large gap in Murdoch's upper teeth.

'One missing, or more?' I asked.

'Just one,' he replied. 'The cop was very patronising, said that lots of people have false teeth these days. I'm sure he didn't understand what I was telling him.

'The police were terribly touchy over this case,' Ted went on. 'There was a great sense of "Not again, we'll all be made to look like country bumpkins". Nevertheless, I believe Joanne.'

Ted had spoken to his namesake, the tracker Teddy Egan.

'Teddy found her tracks from her shoes, and he says she ran and then crouched behind something. They'll never find the body – eagles can clean up a whole kangaroo on the road in no time.

'I did hear a story from the trackers that Teddy looked at the blood on the road and followed a few signs that indicated the car had a flat tyre. He said later that the car went west on a bush track, then east. It stopped at a bore at a small community and the driver threatened the Aborigines [sic] with a gun and said, "Fill up my car". I don't know if that happened or if it was just gossip. I do know that Dave the Ringer wasn't questioned, and that he has disappeared.' The bush telegraph is still buzzing, I thought as we waved goodbye. But I need more than rumours. I have to talk to the police – if they'll agree.

◆ ◆ ◆

I got lucky. After a few phone calls, Colleen Gwynne, now a superintendent and in charge of the case, kindly agreed to see me at police headquarters that afternoon. It was my first official interview with the police. The two of us sat in a big meeting room, surrounded by empty chairs. She agreed to let me take notes. Because I didn't know how long she'd give me, I'd made a little list of need-to-know questions. I didn't expect her to share any investigation information with me, so I kept the questions pretty general:

- Could I have a copy of the drawing of the four-wheel drive that was released before the truck-stop pics?
- Could I have copies of police media releases?
- Could she tell me the exact location of the incident?
- What happened at the police re-enactment?
- Have police interviewed Murdoch? Charged him?

- How does she respond to criticism of the police?
- Who else should I see in Alice or Darwin?

Colleen was tall, trim and tailored – a contrast to me in my tank top and army surplus cut-offs. She looked like a runner; definitely not a couch potato. Although the air-conditioned room was cold, she was friendly and efficient and a little curious about me and my writing. I promised her one of my books as a thank-you for seeing me.

She told me she still had detectives working on Operation Regulus, the police name for the Falconio investigation, but now their main task was preparing the brief for the Director of Public Prosecutions, Rex Wild. She'd had a number of meetings with Wild, and they were both convinced: Murdoch was the man.

'Have you interviewed him? Has he actually been charged?' I asked.

'We made an attempt to interview him,' she told me. 'I travelled to South Australia with Detective Sergeant Chalker of the Major Crime Squad, but he refused to speak with us. As to charging him, there is an arrest warrant, but we can't charge him until he is in the Northern Territory. We expect to transfer him by ministerial agreement as soon as the other matter has been dealt with in South Australia.'

'What do you think of the chances of a conviction in South Australia?' I asked. 'He says he's been set up.'

She smiled slightly. 'I've seen the statements. I think the two females make excellent witnesses, and I think he's guilty.'

'Will the Falconio case be heard quickly after the South Australian trial ends?'

'I hope so. Our main consideration is the family. We're very mindful of their pain and worry. I expect the brief will be ready to go to the DPP in a few months' time.'

Colleen struck me as the kind of person who could develop a comforting and counselling role with bereaved families.

'Did you take Murdoch's photo to Joanne Lees when you last went to the UK?' I asked. 'Did she identify him?'

'I can't disclose that information, but I will say that last November we went to England to follow up with the family. It was a courtesy visit, to let them know how things were going. Victims are a priority for our police force. We provide compensation, focus on the victims' needs, help with debriefing and counselling. So our visit contained some of those elements.'

'Did you find the Canadian girl you were looking for? Did she shed any light on Peter and Joanne's relationship?'

'I can't remember everyone's names, but we did have more than thirty witnesses and I can tell you there is no one outstanding on the list of people we were looking for.'

'How do you respond to media criticism of the police handling of this investigation?'

'I think it is without foundation. We responded very quickly. Roadblocks were on within a couple of hours of our being informed, and I think the initial response was very good. There were a few small management things – like who's in charge, detectives or uniform? – but considering my officers went straight into this and were working twenty-four to forty-eight hours straight organising roadblocks, helicopters and so on, I think things were handled pretty well. Everyone has an opinion, and the media will portray people the way they want.

'It's frustrating at times. It's really hard to deal with the doubters,' she said earnestly. 'Often you get negative yourself, don't know what to say or do to cope. But in many ways, I had it easy. I had more concern for the people who work for me. The pressure on staff was enormous. I had to help to formulate the release of media information to the best advantage of the investigation.'

'Drip-feeding the chooks?'

She smiled. 'You might say that.'

'What about the review? Did you or your staff take that personally?'

'Not at all. We saw it as a sort of self-auditing debrief. Nothing major came out of the review anyway; it was purely procedural stuff.'

This seemed like a good note to finish on. I'd love to read that report, I thought, as we exchanged goodbyes, but there wasn't much chance. Jim Litster had told me in March, 'It's not a very big report, only about fifty pages, but a lot of people would like to get their hands on it.'

I was one of them.

Chapter Twenty-Three

SNIFFING AROUND ALICE

The bush telegraph still operates. You don't need the
TV to tell you stuff.

Les Pilton, publican, Barrow Creek Hotel

Alice Springs is not a very pretty town. The windows and doorways of shops and private houses are covered with aluminium mesh grilles or cyclone-wire fencing, and even Coca Cola dispensers are wrapped in metal mesh. I hoped the people didn't put up similar barriers.

That night, I consulted my list of the people I still had to see in Alice. They included Rod Smith, the mechanic; Helen Jones's son; the staff at the Shell Truck Stop and Melanka Lodge; journalists at the *Centralian Advocate*; Bill Towers, the forensic police officer; tracker Teddy Egan; and Bill and Judy Pilton. I also wanted to gauge local reaction to the events of that weekend by doing 'grass-roots' survey in the mall.

Next day I put my skates on and headed for 1 Railway Terrace, where Peter had left the Kombi at Alice Auto Craft. Damn and blast! Bulldozers had just finished levelling the block. Rod Smith certainly didn't work there any more – and, being called Smith, he would be hard to track down.

I asked a girl painting some veranda railings nearby. My luck was in. Rod was her mechanic, and he'd moved to the Toyota dealership a couple of blocks away. Small towns are good for researchers.

Rod was a big bloke, older than I'd expected, and not very keen to talk. I told him I'd come a long way and I wouldn't take much time. I'd already waited about half an hour for him to come back from a job, and that, plus my Victorian number plates, helped to persuade him to chat for a few minutes. He told me about the work he'd done on the van, and said it was in pretty poor shape. He said its problems 'could've caused it to misfire and show sparks in the dark. I told them they'd be lucky to get to Darwin.'

He said, 'I never spoke to her, only him, but it was quite obvious they'd had a big row when they came back to collect the van.'

'Why obvious?' I asked.

He grinned. 'I'm married, aren't I? She stomped off to the car and slammed the door when she got in, and he was very surly and cross. Whinged about the bill. Typical whingeing Pom. I told the police that.'

He went on, 'I thought no more about it until I heard the news on the radio and I thought, I know that bloke. They're the ones with the crook Kombi.

'I thought her story was very fishy. Funny thing, just after they left the Kombi with me, one of my regulars turned up – a bloke who's a dead ringer for the bloke she says pulled her over, like half the men in the Territory. Those two walked right past him.

'And also, I don't believe a blue heeler couldn't find her – I've got one, and he could find anything. I did an experiment later on with my wife and the dog. We were out camping and I wandered off quietly while my wife kept the dog. After a while, when I'd hidden a long way from the camp, she let him go and he was beside my leg in minutes.'

Not quite the same situation, I thought. Even my Pekinese could probably sniff me out in similar circumstances.

He said he'd been besieged by journalists, and they'd written rubbish. 'One made up this bloody silly story my son is supposed to have said about my dog snapping at Joanne Lees. What a lot of rot! He'd never snap at anyone. Another woman – a Pommie – came to Auto Craft and asked me why the police couldn't find the body. I told her to drive out to where it happened, walk off the road, leaving someone there to guide her back, get into the scrub, close her eyes and spin around a couple of times – see if she could find her way back. Damn stupid questions!'

I was keen to tap his knowledge of four-wheel drives. 'If the Landcruiser is the one in the truck-stop video, could the man have later modified it and remove a crawl-through that was there before?' I asked.

'Very, very difficult, almost impossible, for that to be done and not detected by forensic testing. But the original drawing done by Joanne Lees is almost a dead ringer for a CJ6 or CJ10 model Jeep, which does have a crawl-through as standard.'

Rod said the description of the vehicle had changed after the police released the truck-stop photos. 'Before that, it was a different-looking man and a different type of truck, according to her description.'

'That's right,' I agreed. 'That truck in the photo, how far could it go on $115 worth of diesel?'

'Depends on the cost per litre. But I can tell you that a 75 series Landcruiser would get about a thousand kilometres from 140 to 180 litres of fuel, depending on the driver and the terrain. Some people add long-range tanks too.'

He was looking anxiously at the workshop, so I thanked him and said goodbye.

◆ ◆ ◆

My next stop was the office of the *Centralian Advocate*. Before leaving Melbourne, I'd had a chat by phone to Mark Wilton, the journo who'd interviewed Joanne Lees. He was now working in Cairns, but he'd advised me to call in and see his colleagues, Jason Scott and Glenn Morrison. When I arrived, Glenn was on holidays and Jason was surrounded by cardboard boxes in the chief of staff's office.

'This is my last day here,' he told me. 'I'm off to Townsville, but I can share a few minutes with you.'

He enumerated what made the story different from others he'd covered.

'One: The media circus that followed. All the London tabloids sent out their guns to get the story. We've never seen that before. I got the impression they were so keen to get an angle they'd run with anything, even make stuff up.

'Two: Many reporters didn't believe it was true. Ask anyone in Alice Springs and they'll still tell you they don't believe the dingo took Lindy's baby. There's a stigma attached to unexplained murders. I believe Joanne. There's nothing forensic on her. I believed Vince absolutely – the way he explained her fear, how he explained her demeanour.

'Three: There was a lot of flak thrown at the police by outsiders about why they couldn't catch the guy. Our local journos had to make a conscious effort not to stitch up the police on this. Foreigners can come here, slag off on the police and go home. But you don't have to be a Philadelphia lawyer to know you won't get any local co-operation if you mess your own patch.'

He looked thoughtful. 'I think the reasons they stuffed up were the same as Azaria. Too many chiefs running the show – four officers in charge in four months, all jockeying for media attention but providing no direction; trackers in too late and only finding police boot prints; roadblocks on too late – not their fault. It was a mess.' He chuckled when he remembered beating the world to the Joanne Lees scoop. 'Before that, Mark had been dogged with a double handicap – he was an Australian journalist.'

He agreed to make the *Centralian*'s photo library available to me and then advised, 'You should talk to Mark.'

'I'm going to. He said if I come to Cairns, he'll let me listen to the tape of the interview, so I'm going there on the way home.'

◆ ◆ ◆

I thought I'd get an early sandwich, then do my little survey during lunchtime in the Mall. In the Yeperenye Centre, I popped into a Dymocks bookshop to see if Joanne Lees had done the same.

Bev, the manageress, said Joanne had not come in, but that I should talk to Justin Heath at the cafe across the arcade.

'He's Helen Jones's son. Lovely boy, and the best lunch chef in town.'

Helen's son! How lucky was that?

Justin was hunky and charming. I thought I'd try his lunch and ask a few questions. He was very accommodating on both counts.

He said his mother had brought Joanne for breakfast the first morning in Alice. 'Monday, it must have been, on their way to the police station. Mum wanted her to have breakfast before going through the mill again.

'She didn't say much,' Justin recalled. 'No one noticed her at that early hour, because the story was just coming out into the public and not many reporters were in town by then. They were all going to Barrow Creek.

'Jo was very quiet, no tears. I suppose she might have been in shock. I didn't see any injuries on her at all, which I thought was a bit odd. She really wanted to go shopping to get something to wear. All her stuff was in the Kombi, but Mum had promised to take her to the police station, so I think that's where they went next.'

'Was it your place she stayed at after leaving Les's parents' house?'

'No, that's my brother, David. I'll give you his phone number. You should go and talk to him.'

I intend to, I thought. This is my lucky day.

At lunchtime, I surveyed fifty people – not a big sample, but an interesting snapshot. After making sure each person I stopped was a local who was in town at the time of Peter's disappearance, I asked three questions: What do you think was the effect on Alice Springs? What do you think happened to Peter Falconio? Did you believe Joanne Lees's story?

Most people were resentful that the drama had been played out in their backyard. 'Still getting over the Chamberlain thing', not wanting to be seen as ridiculous (or a dangerous place to visit) were high on their list of concerns. They felt tourism might suffer. They resented the media invasion. Most people thought Peter was dead. About half believed Joanne; the rest either didn't or were unsure. Several had theories about Peter's present whereabouts and Joanne's story. No one refused to participate. They all seemed keen to have their say.

◆ ◆ ◆

Bill and Judy Pilton were easy to find, because they were in the phone book. I wanted to see where Joanne had spent her first two days in Alice and ask the Piltons if she'd confided in them at all. To reach their front door, I had to squeeze past an ancient single-decker bus that occupied most of the front garden. It was covered in location stickers from all around Australia, but it looked as if its travelling days were over.

I knocked, and a small dog inside went berserk. Slowly the front door opened a few centimetres and a little round-faced woman peered out through the narrow opening.

'Yes?'

'Hullo, Mrs Pilton?' I smiled. 'Yes.'

This was the critical moment. 'Um, my name is Robin, I'm a writer and I wondered if you could spare me a few minutes?'

'Writing about what?'

'Actually, I'm doing a book on Peter Falconio ...'

'Ooh, we're not meant to talk to reporters.' She pulled back a little.

'No, it's OK. I'm not a reporter, I'm a writer. I'm doing a book.'

'Not one of those journalists?'

Without thinking, I replied, 'Shit, no!' Oh dear.

But she laughed. 'Shit, no, eh? Well, you'd better come in.' She led me into a small, crowded lounge where a big snowy-bearded man sat in an armchair in the corner.

'Look, Bill,' she shouted. 'This lady's writing a book. It must be a lot of work, doing a book?' she said to me. 'Do you want a cuppa?'

'A cuppa would be good, Mum,' Bill replied for us both, as I looked for a seat without something on it.

I was introduced to the dog, which jumped onto my knees, and we chatted about Les and Barrow Creek and how kind Helen had been to Joanne. Judy was a bit indignant about Joanne's 'rude and unfair' comments about Helen and, the final insult, failing to call in and see Helen and Les during the making of the TV special, when she'd been 'just down the road'.

I told her we planned to go to the Camel Cup and then stay a couple of nights at the Barrow Creek Hotel. She said it was shaping up to be a busy weekend at Barrow Creek, with all the other rooms booked out to the ABC.

'What are they doing there?' I asked.

'Some kind of film about Joanne and Peter, I think,' she replied. 'I don't think Helen's looking forward to it. She probably won't talk to you about it. She's too upset by what Joanne said.'

As I got up to leave, she mentioned a couple of letters she'd received from a clairvoyant in Melbourne.

'I gave them to the police, but I made copies,' she told me. 'Would you like to have them?'

She scurried into the depths of the house and returned with several pages of scrawled information purporting to be the location of Peter Falconio's body, signed by someone called Adam*. I thanked her.

Then she said quietly, 'There was another letter. She wrote it. It was in Helen's track pants. Well, I couldn't help noticing ... I mean, in the letter it says, about Peter, you know ... it says, "I haven't killed him yet, but I'm going to." Do you think that means anything?'

'Probably not,' I told her, although I was surprised. 'Young people say that sort of thing all the time. I say it myself sometimes, about one or other of my grown-up sons – "I'm gunna kill that boy!" What did you do with it?' I asked hopefully.

'I gave it to Paula Dooley. Straight away, when I found it.'

'Don't suppose you made a copy?'

She looked crestfallen. 'No, I should've. But I wanted to get it to the police as quick as possible.'

'That's fine,' I told her. 'You did the right thing.'

◆ ◆ ◆

Even for a seasoned op-shopper, pickings are a bit lean in Alice Springs, but I needed a pale T-shirt for my re-enactment plan. I didn't want to risk ruining any of my clothes. I eventually found a pale pink number in Vinnie's Boutique. Although Joanne's had been pale blue, I didn't think it would matter much in the dark. Either shade would stand out in torchlight.

When I got back to my car, I phoned Bill Towers, the forensic examiner, hoping that he might agree to talk. He was not happy to hear from me. He said he couldn't discuss the case at all – ongoing inquiry, not worth his job, not interested.

Oh, well; you don't ask, you don't get.

I was almost peopled out. Clive had spent the day with Chris Tangey, and I had arranged to meet them at the Shell truck stop on the outskirts of town, so I decided to make that my last call for the day. While I had my phone out, I had a quick chat to Val Prior, who had been head of security at the truck stop.

Val told me there were problems with the quality of the pictures at the truck stop, although the equipment was brand new. 'I've always had a niggle of misunderstanding why they told everyone the images had to be sent away for enhancement. The only thing I can think of is that the pictures themselves were never very clear in the first place, because we didn't replace the cameras. And you can't enhance a poor picture – if it's fuzzy, it's not going to improve much, no matter what you do to it. We often complained to management that the camera quality was poor. It makes it difficult to be certain of number plates, which is why some staff make a practice of jotting down number plates when a sale reaches a certain figure.'

Before leaving Melbourne, I'd been in touch with Gale Spring of RMIT University. After seeing how tall Brad Murdoch was, I wanted to see if we could definitely find out if it was him at the truck stop. If the guy was 1.8 metres, for example, it couldn't be Murdoch. Gale said he could measure the man's height to within about a centimetre, but he needed to know the height of the marker on the doorjamb beside the man's figure, the distance from the doorway to the camera, the height of the camera lens from the ground, and the focal length of the camera lens.

'How do I get the focal length?' I asked.

'There's usually a plaque on the camera,' he said. 'Use your telephoto lens and get a shot of that, and we should be able to work it out.'

I'd emailed Chris Tangey to ask if he could take these measurements, but the people at the truck stop were unwilling to let him measure anything.

'You didn't ask permission, did you?' I teased him. Now that they knew what he looked like, I'd have to do it myself.

I did a recce. The truck stop was packed. Every pump was in constant demand. The video camera was behind the counter, where about thirty people were queued up. To get a good shot, I'd have to stand behind the girl at the counter, slightly to her left. The whole queue would be facing me. The only benefit was that she was so busy she probably wouldn't have noticed if I'd stood beside her and taken off all my clothes. But someone in the queue might want to know what I was doing, or another staff member might suddenly appear to help her.

I decided to get the measurements in descending order of risk. Photo first, because the flash would go off almost at her elbow; then I'd try to measure the camera height; and then, if I hadn't been arrested, I'd measure the marker at the door, in full view of the camera. Must remember to keep my back to the damn thing, I thought as I went outside to prepare for my sortie.

Peter Falconio photographed in Huddersfield, England. Peter disappeared on the Stuart Highway near Barrow Creek in the Northern Territory on 14 July 2001

Jayne Russell / Alamy Stock Photo

A younger Joanne Lees pictured in Spain, not long before she met Peter
Jayne Russell / Alamy Stock Photo

Peter and Joanne, in a restaurant in Brighton in mid-2000
Jayne Russell / Alamy Stock Photo

British tourists Joanne and Peter inside their Kombi van, date unknown
PA Images / Alamy Stock Photo

The Kombi van in which Joanne Lees and Peter Falconio were travelling
down the Stuart Highway on 14 July 2001, when they were flagged down
by a man with a four-wheel drive
Newspix

The Ti Tree Roadhouse where Joanne and Peter stopped for petrol, and then sat and watched the sun go down, before heading north towards Barrow Creek (90 km away) and Tennant Creek (a further 225 km away)
Photo reproduced from author's collection

The rig photographed at the Alice Springs truck stop
Photo reproduced from author's collection

The Barrow Creek Hotel, where Vince Millar and co-driver
Rod Adams first took Joanne Lees after she waved them down for
help on 14 July 2001
Photo reproduced from author's collection

Les Pilton, the genial publican at Barrow Creek Hotel. Les helped Joanne Lees on the night Peter went missing after she was brought in to the pub
Photo reproduced from author's collection

Helen Jones at Barrow Creek Hotel. Helen looked after Joanne Lees on the night Peter went missing, and for several days afterwards
Photo reproduced from author's collection

Northern Territory Assistant Commissioner John Daulby at a news conference called by police in Alice Springs. During this conference, Daulby said that there were significant differences between the man in the truck stop security video footage and Joanne Lees's description of Mr Falconio's suspected attacker. Daulby made a fresh appeal for the man in the video to come forward so that he could be eliminated from the investigation

PA Images / Alamy Stock Photo

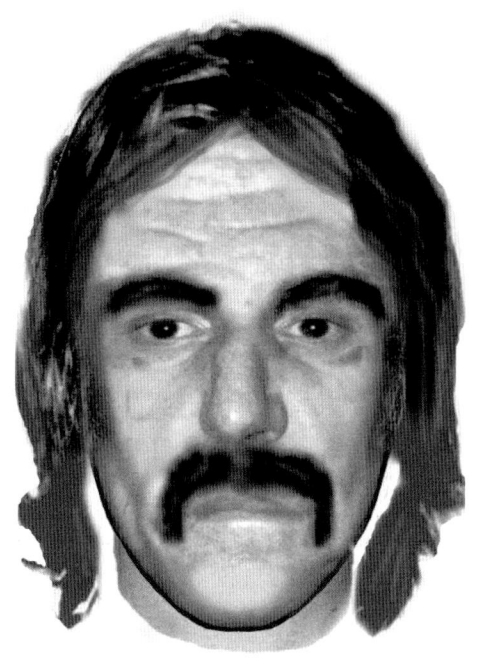

Phone: *89223112*		*NT POLICE*		**Fax:** *89223570*	

INVESTIGATOR STATION	SGT. IAN KESBY ALICE SPRINGS POLICE	**COMFIT DATE**	15.7.01
OFFENCE LOCATION	AGGRAVATED ASSAULT BARROW CREEK	**OFF. DATE**	14.7.01

AGE	45 + YRS	**HAIR**	GREY/BLK SHLDR LE
HEIGHT	ABOVE 5'11"	**COMPLEX.**	FAIR TO MEDIUM
BUILD	STOCKY	**OPERATOR**	CUMMINS
WITNESS	JOANNE LEES	**DRAFT**	9

An e-fit composition from the Alice Springs Police following Joanne's description of her alleged attacker, which was made available to the public

PA Images / Alamy Stock Photo

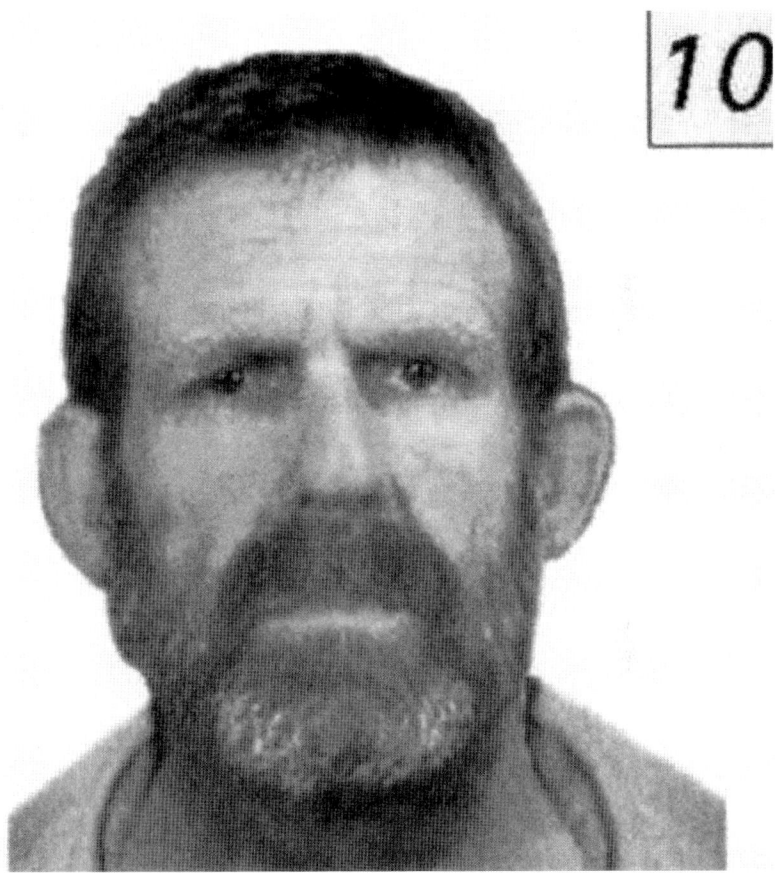

Police mug shot of Bradley John Murdoch from his arrest in 2002
Media Liaison Office, Northern Territory Supreme Court

The five-dollar note left at the Barrow Creek Hotel by Paul Falconio in case Peter ever turns up for a drink. A note by former barmaid Cathy Curly is pinned beside it
Photo reproduced from author's collection

Anne defies her cultural taboos to help Clive dig in search of Peter's remains
Photo reproduced from author's collection

James Hepi after giving evidence on his former business partner,
Bradley Murdoch
Photo reproduced from author's collection

Joanne Lees leaving court in Darwin on 17 October 2005, after giving evidence in the trial of Bradley Murdoch

PA Images / Alamy Stock Photo

Peter's parents, Joan and Luciano Falconio, arriving at the NT Supreme Court in Darwin on 31 October 2005. On this day, the court heard that the forensic laboratories where samples from Peter's suspected murder case were tested were not officially accredited

PA Images / Alamy Stock Photo

Director of Public Prosecutors Rex Wild QC arriving at the NT Supreme Court in Darwin on 2 November 2005. On this day, the court heard that samples of DNA from the pools of blood at the desert crime scene matched a sample taken from Peter Falconio's inhaler
PA Images / Alamy Stock Photo

Dr Jonathan Whitaker, UK forensics expert on 'low copy number' DNA, arriving at NT Supreme Court in Darwin on 3 November 2005
Wesley Johnson / PA Images / Alamy Stock Photo

Peter Falconio's brother, Paul (left) and Nick (right), leaving the NT Supreme Court in Darwin on 11 December 2005. On this day, the judge had told jurors to disregard Joanne's belief that her attacker was caught on security footage near the scene of her ambush and alleged attack
Wesley Johnson / PA Images / Alamy Stock Photo

Chief Justice Brian Martin in the NT Supreme Court in Darwin on 15 December 2005, after ordering Bradley Murdoch to serve at least twenty-eight years in prison for the murder of Peter Falconio before being considered for parole
Northern Territory News / PA Images / Alamy Stock Photo

Joanne Lees leaving NT Supreme Court 15 December 2005, after Bradley Murdoch was sentenced to twenty-eight years in prison for the murder of her boyfriend, Peter Falconio. Behind her are Peter's brother Nick, father and mother
Wesley Johnson / PA Images / Alamy Stock Photo

I realised I was now on their tape, and I didn't want to be recognised taking measurements, because I was already 'known to the police', or at least to Superintendent Gwynne. Fortunately, I had a collapsible sunhat, big glasses and a lightweight cardigan. I could put all this clobber on, then walk in again, head down, do the deed, keep back to camera on way out and put all the gear away as soon as I got outside. But that's not going to work, I thought.

The way to get away with doing something outrageous is to look as if you're meant to be doing it. Taking photos and measurements inside a building in a floppy hat and Jackie O sunnies is not being inconspicuous. Someone might giggle; the girl might turn around; the police might be called. I'd just have to do it without props. I hoped my khaki cut-offs might look a bit like a uniform, so I took out the camera, put it on maximum telescope, walked in, stood about a metre from the girl and aimed at the camera above my head. Flash!

The queue kept moving; the girl kept serving. What if it's out of focus? I always take two shots if it's important. So I took another one. No reaction.

Next, I swapped the camera for a builder's tape. I felt quite vulnerable as the tape rose almost three metres into the air, like some charmer's calibrated snake. It could have been hard to explain if I was caught, but no one batted an eyelid. Perhaps they're used to kooks in the Territory. I walked outside, triumphantly reciting the measurement to myself.

Clive and Chris Tangey arrived at that very minute. I was a bit sorry they'd missed my bravura performance. 'I got it!' I told them.

'All I need is the marker height and the distance to the camera. I'll use the tiles to work out the distance – they're thirty centimetres square, so that's easy enough.' Keeping my shoulder to the camera, I unwound the tape measure again, measured the doorjamb marker, then counted the floor tiles and made myself scarce.

I sat at a big, round outdoor table for a minute to write down all the measurements and regain my equilibrium. There were three women sitting at the same table, finishing cigarettes.

'S'pose we'd better get back,' one said. 'Kaylene* looks run off her feet in there.'

I pricked up my ears. 'Excuse me, do you work here?' I asked. They did; they'd been on their break while I was photographing their security system. Whew!

'I'm writing a book about the Falconio case. I don't suppose any of you were on duty the night the truck-stop video was taken?'

'Nah, none of us. We're not supposed to talk about it, anyway,' one replied.

'Who says, police or management?'

'Police and management,' she replied.

'Can you please tell me who was working that night?' I persisted. 'Won't do you any good,' another woman said as she got up to leave. 'Doesn't work here now. His name's Andrew Head, and he's working on a community just near the South Australian border. Dunno the name of the place.'

But Chris Tangey did, and I wrote it down for later on.

Chapter Twenty-Four

JIGSAW PIECES

The more you stir, the worse it stinks.

Sixteenth-century proverb

Chris Tangey and I spent most of the next morning looking for Teddy Egan, the tracker man. Big Ted Egan had told us the best place to find Teddy would be in one of the Aboriginal communities near Alice Springs, and Chris felt it would be unwise for me to venture out there alone.

'For a start, unless you know someone or they know you, you need a pass, or permission to enter,' Chris told me. 'And secondly, it's just not the Territory way, a white woman wandering around on her own out there.'

I was shocked at the poverty confronting me as we drove around several communities asking for Teddy Egan. Whole families seemed to be living in the open, under rough tarpaulins, sleeping on mattresses on the dirt. Roughly erected houses looked as lifeless as cardboard cut-outs against the bleached-out sky. Little kids chased us or hung back shyly in the shade of scrubby trees, ignoring swarms of flies clustered around their runny noses.

Chris speaks a bit of Arrernte, the language spoken by most of the families near Alice, and he climbed in and out of his truck several times to speak to men sitting in small groups on the ground, asking them about Teddy.

'Bad news,' he told me. 'Yesterday was pension day, and most of the men are in town. They think he might be visiting some family. I know the house they mentioned, so we'll try there. If we strike out, that'll be it, I reckon. These guys can stay out of sight for months if they want to. He'll know by now you're looking for him. Bush telegraph.'

The house was about half a block from where we'd set off two hours earlier. Chris told me to wait in the car while he went to check it out. He was gone for about ten minutes, then walked back shaking his head.

'He's there, but he won't talk to you,' Chris said. 'He's got some nasty minder who's guarding the gate. Teddy's sitting there on the lawn saying, "I'll talk to her", but this guy was adamant he wasn't going to.'

'That's infuriating!' I squawked. 'Let me talk to the minder.'

'Won't do any good,' Chris said, sounding peeved. 'If I couldn't change his mind, you won't.'

Putting on my friendly middle-aged writer smile, I walked to the gate, which was guarded by a tall, skinny streak of a man in an ankle-length partly buttoned Drizabone and an Akubra that looked as if it had melted to his head. A thin rollie hung from a corner of his mouth, emitting wispy smoke. He put a bony hand on top of the waist-high gate as I approached. His wrist was adorned with several strands of beads and I could see a few more at the neck of his dark blue T-shirt.

I told him who I was and why I wanted to speak to Teddy Egan. He rubbed his thumb against his two first fingers in the universal sign meaning money.

'I'm sorry. I don't pay for interviews,' I told him. 'I could get him some beer, though?' I said hopefully. I could see Teddy sitting on the grass. He waved at me. How frustrating, I thought. Who is this bloody man?

'Not interested,' he replied, tightening his grip on the gate. 'He has a contract with the ABC. They pay. He's not talking to anyone else.'

'OK. Thanks anyway,' I told him.

I made a strategic retreat. 'Sorry, Chris, you were right. Who is that guy?' I asked as I climbed back into the truck.

'Just some minder. What was that about the ABC, anyway?'

'Not sure what they're up to. Something to do with the case, though. They're booked in at Barrow Creek tomorrow night as well, so maybe we can ask them.'

'They'll be pleased to see you,' he chuckled. 'Do they know we'll be there?'

'I doubt it. I booked after them.'

Before Chris left, I gave him Judy's letters from the clairvoyant, which contained detailed map references. I asked if he could check them out to see if the clairvoyant could be right about Peter's resting place.

Helen's other son, David Jones, had agreed to see me at his unit that night. He was big, warm and friendly, with a winning smile. A keen amateur photographer, he had several professional-looking shots displayed around his lounge room, including some of Barrow Creek at sunset. We settled down with more tea (the Territory seems to float on the stuff), and he chatted away quite openly about the night he saw Joanne.

'Joanne was pretty antsy, but she might have been upset by the police. She'd had a day of it.

'She seemed to be more concerned about getting her mobile back than talking about Peter. She really wanted that phone, and the cops were holding on to everything. She was worried about the police finding her diary too – said it was personal – and her pipe and stash. She thought she might get in trouble for having the drugs on board. I told her, "Look, Jo, they're investigating a murder. They won't worry about a bit of hash."'

I was interested, though. It was the first confirmation I'd had that Joanne, and maybe Peter, were regular users of marijuana – and not just rollies.

'They kept a log of all their purchases and the mileage and so on. Peter did that, I think. Anyway, they recorded the exact speedo reading each time they filled up. A friend who lives with one of the police told me the speedo was fourteen kilometres out when they measured the distance from Ti Tree to where it was found and compared it with the Ti Tree entry.'

'Over or under?'

'Over. They couldn't account for an extra fourteen kilometres the van must have done.'

'I wonder if they did a side trip. Did she tell you anything about the gunman?' I asked him.

'She said he was slimmer than me, but fairly stocky and shorter. I'm about 100 kilos and 185 centimetres.' Joanne also said the gunman was wearing a thick long-sleeved checked shirt.

David said he was very confused by Joanne's description of the gunman's vehicle. 'At first the vehicle she described seemed to have a twin cab – that's like a ute with a special compartment behind the driver's seat, or even a four-door ute – but then it sounded more like a Toyota Landcruiser. But I couldn't understand why you'd have a crawl-through, letting in dust and thieves and what have you. She said that night at my place that he'd thrown her in the back and she'd crawled through to the front to escape.

'A lot of her stories have changed since that night,' David added. 'She said her hands were tied tightly with the wrists crossed over behind her back with cable ties. I thought at the time the ties would've cut into her, but her wrists only looked a bit bruised. The restraints they showed on TV later didn't look anything like the ones she described.

'Look, I don't know if this interests you, but I've since heard stories that Peter had travelled to Thailand and back a couple of times from Sydney. What if someone heard a rumour he was carrying drugs in the van, without Joanne's knowledge and followed them and it all went wrong? I mean, I'm not saying he was carrying drugs, but what if someone thought he was?'

It did interest me – especially since I knew air tickets had been found in the Kombi – but I had no proof. Only that Joanne admitted having grass and a bong in her van. So what? Lots of people smoke dope, and I said so.

He laughed. 'That's true. There was other talk later on about an insurance scam, or whether she was in cahoots with the guy that did it. Lots of gossip.'

'Did the police question you about anything Joanne had told you?' I asked.

David laughed. 'Well, yeah, they did. But about six or eight months later. Someone called Paula rang and asked me to make a statement, and this stocky bloke collected me. Some of the information they'd found conflicted with what Jo had said on the night. Even he had his doubts, that cop, asking questions about the drugs.'

'I'm spending the weekend at Barrow Creek,' I told him. 'Can I take anything up for your mum? Or any message?'

'No, thanks. We keep in pretty close touch. She probably won't talk to you about any of this, though. She was pretty pissed off when Joanne spat in her face about Mum making money out of the media and then went and sold her story herself, so Mum talks to no one now.'

David told me that Outback Vehicle Recovery had brought the Kombi in from Barrow Creek. I gave them a ring the next day. A girl called Tammy answered the phone, and I asked to speak to Russ, the proprietor. I told her why I was calling.

'You don't want to speak to him – it's me you want,' she told me. 'And I know who you are. I've read all your books.'

Tammy was thrilled and scared about being involved in one of the crimes of the century. 'I wanted Russ to do the job, actually, but he had another job further up the highway, so I was it.' She told me about how they had loaded the Kombi from the rear, so as not to mess up the surrounding ground.

'There'd been a fire there recently and they were hoping to get some prints from the ash, so we had to bush-bash in further on. Luckily the scrub wasn't very thick at that point,' Tammy recalled.

'Nothing really seemed wrong. My first impression was that the van had been beautifully reversed in. Not hurriedly parked at all.

It was dark by then, so I couldn't see much around the van, but I could see straight in the windows by the tow-truck lights and it was just like you'd expect of a couple of travellers. A few cardboard boxes piled up, outdoor chairs and so on. No mess, no blood – nothing we could see.'

She said a police officer rode back with her and she dropped the Kombi at the lock-up, where she overheard police speculating about the fight at Melanka Lodge the previous night. 'I was so stirred up that when I got home, I couldn't sleep. I went to a twenty-four-hour servo where I used to work, and hung out there for a while. Then, when it was nearly dawn, I went home.

'I had just got to sleep when I heard my truck start up in the front yard. I was shitting myself, but I was not going to let any bastard pinch my truck. So I kind of forgot about being scared and ran outside to stop whoever it was.'

It turned out to be one of the drivers, who needed to swap his truck for hers. Unlikely to get back to sleep, she went into work to bring Russ up to date with the latest gossip when he got in.

Later that day, Clive and I met Glenn Morrison from the *Centralian Advocate*. He was still on holidays, but he'd rung me when he found out I was looking for him. Glenn was taking over from Jason Scott as the new chief of staff. He also worked casually as a singer at various local nightspots. He was a 'Peace, brother' kind of guy, not at all like most journalists I'd met. He told us more about the crazy period following the incident, the dramas with the roadblocks (and lack of them), the media and police antics.

'On that night I was camping near Tennant Creek with my daughter. It was a starry night and you get a lot of light from the stars up here. The next day we were driving along and heard the news. We passed the time playing "Spot the Gunman", but only passed one roadblock in 1200 kilometres, at a side road that went off to Borroloola.'

'Did the clairvoyant woman I read about ever get close to finding Peter's body?' I asked him.

'I had quite a bit to do with her,' he said. 'She seemed genuine. She believes there were three men involved and that two of them still live in this district. One of them is an Aboriginal man from the Barrow Creek mob, with long skinny legs.'

We all laughed. 'That's a pretty generic description,' I said.

'Yeah. Well, her version is that Peter and Joanne stopped for Joanne to use the toilet at Barrow Creek. Peter did not go in. Joanne got the key from the bar, because the public toilets are out the back, and walked right past these three men, who were drinking outside because Aborigines are not allowed to drink in the bar. On her way back, she stumbles on a wallet bulging with money. A huge roll. She jumps back in the Kombi and they take off. Minutes later, one of the men realises he's dropped his wad on his way out from the toilets, looks for it, realises Joanne must have found it, and they follow the Kombi, waiting for an opportunity to pull them over. Peter resists, doesn't tell them Joanne has the money and they shoot him, but he is not dead. They take him to a nearby property and beat him to death, then bury him under the tree that Kathleen showed the police. Meanwhile they tie Joanne up to make it look like an attack on her, shoo her into the bush and tell her she'd better give them a good head start, or they'll find her and kill her too.'

'That makes more sense than some of the theories we've heard,' Clive said. 'This idea of an opportunistic attack on Joanne, or a killer hunting the highways in search of prey, is a bit far-fetched, especially if it's supposed to be Murdoch. Did Rob tell you she's met Murdoch? He doesn't seem right to her. But he was running drugs from South Australia to Broome, using different routes. Maybe it was his money? Maybe he was the third man, but not the only perpetrator? Where is the alleged burial spot, do you know?'

'Beside a creek-bed on Neutral Junction station, just north of Barrow Creek. But if Murdoch wasn't there that night, what about his DNA on her shirt?'

'That only places him near her T-shirt, not at the scene,' I said. 'Not even necessarily near her, if you want to be pedantic, only near the shirt. And the defence barrister will be pedantic, you can bet on that.'

We stayed on after Glenn left, and I ordered a seafood salad. Big mistake. Within two hours I was writhing in pain, and within three hours Clive was rushing me to casualty. I had never felt so sick. Dying was looking like a positive outcome.

Cool air embraced me like winter as we staggered into reception. Competent hands took charge of me, and Clive was sent off to the visitors' room to watch some dreadful late-night movie on Imparja TV. I lay all night with an IV line in my arm, although I think I must have already forcibly ejected all but the tiniest speck of whatever had made me ill.

'Seafood salad?' one nurse exclaimed. 'Oh dear. Prince Charles had the same problem when he was here.'

'Nice of him to warn us,' I mumbled, before falling into a fitful sleep.

Chapter Twenty-Five

ANNIVERSARY AT BARROW CREEK

Joanne Lees – did she, or didn't she?

Graffiti on the Stuart Highway near Barrow Creek

They let me out next morning and told me to rest. Fat chance. It was Saturday, the second anniversary of Peter's disappearance, and we had a big day ahead. Packing up the motel room left me weak and sweaty. I was dreading the Camel Cup. The plan was to go to the racetrack, leave in time to get to Ti Tree, fill up with petrol, watch the sunset and then do the re-enactment. Annie Tangey would use an infra-red video to get the whole drama on tape. The rest of our crew would count passing cars.

Feeling wobbly, I mingled with the crowd at the Camel Cup. The racetrack was hot and dusty, milling with people of every walk of life from miles around Alice, and hundreds of tourists. Akubras, tight jeans and cowboy boots seemed to be de rigueur. I tried to wangle my way into the VIP tent, but missed out because I wasn't a member – of what was not clear. Anyway, the enclosure was only a big bit of tarp slung between steel poles. The shade, which was what I was after, and a metal sheep-race fence around the circumference were all that set it apart from the madding crowd.

We left after watching the Honeymoon Derby, a fiercely contested event, where tuxedo-clad men in double saddles rode hell-for-leather round the track, screeched to a halt halfway, scooped up their waiting 'brides' and raced to the finish line. Someone told me the men used to wear top hats, but crash helmets were introduced after a few blokes fell on their heads while grabbing their brides.

It was very entertaining, but we had a schedule to keep and I was still feeling queasy. I slept on the way to Ti Tree, where we filled up with petrol. I asked the staff at the roadhouse if anyone remembered serving Peter, but they became very secretive. I left my mobile number, in case they had a change of heart.

While we were parked in a lay-by waiting for the sun to go down, we noticed another convoy arriving – the ABC. With them was a tracker who looked suspiciously like Teddy Egan. Luckily, they hadn't seen us.

'Abandon the sunset!' I decreed. 'Let's roll! I want to bag the spot first.' So as darkness descended, we raced up the road another ninety kilometres. After lots of to-ing and fro-ing in the dark, we found the spot where we thought the incident had occurred.

The excitement acted like an adrenalin hit and I began to feel better. I put on my Vinnie's T-shirt, extended my arms behind my back, and Chris tightened the black cable ties he'd brought for the occasion. Unlike Joanne, I was wearing long pants and shoes. I didn't want to be crippled as well as sick. They said they'd give me a five-minute start.

Clive said, 'Be careful, Rob' as I took off into the scrub in the dark, looking frantically for a place to hide. Any place. Boy, was that scrub devoid of decent cover! Even allowing for the fact that Joanne Lees is a lot smaller than I am, there was bugger all to hide in.

Almost as soon as I left the gravel shoulder of the road, I ran between two head-high mulga trees and straight into a big cobweb. By spitting hard, I cleared my mouth, but for a few seconds I felt as if I had a fine gauze bag over my head, with no hands to wipe it off. As if that wasn't bad enough, minutes later I was stung on the neck. If that's a poisonous spider whose home I've just wrecked, I thought, I'm a goner. The bite was right over my carotid artery. Sometimes it's a not a good thing to know anatomy.

I struggled on and finally crouched in a clump of grass between two thickish trees. This will have to do, I thought. Every sound seemed magnified. Even moving my foot a little bit, set off crackles that sounded like Tom Thumbs exploding in the silence. Although I was about thirty metres from the road, I could hear Clive and the others talking. I strained my ears and became acutely aware of the sounds of the bush. Rustles, twigs rubbing together, the irregular swish or rumble of a car or truck on the road, my own breathing.

Chris had set off in the opposite direction to me, on the right-hand arm of a fan shape rather than the left. I was already getting cramps in my legs from crouching, and my pale T-shirt was a too easy target. Since I still couldn't hear Chris coming towards me I figured he couldn't hear me either, so I risked a bit of noise and knelt down, then lay on my side, arms still behind me and knees curled up in the foetal position. The disadvantage was that I soon lost all sensation in my arms. My face was about an inch off the cold sand, my hair was in the spinifex and my ear was hard to the bush floor, picking up all sorts of buzzes, rustles and tickles. I hoped that nothing nasty would discover a nice warm burrow.

For about an hour I stayed there, motionless, while Chris searched the area in a tight grid pattern. We'd talked about bringing one of his dogs, but decided it wasn't necessary. Gradually I began to hear his progress as he crunched through the bush, coming closer and closer. My heart beat faster; I could imagine how Joanne might have felt, lying silently in her dark space of fear. If Chris had started at the end where I'd run off, I'd be in the nice warm car by now, I was certain. Suddenly, I was illuminated by a glare of light.

'Gotcha!' Chris yelled. He was still about ten metres away, but his roving torch beam had easily caught the pale blob of my T-shirt. Annie came running to film the 'discovery', and Clive called out to make sure I was OK. I was very pleased to be found, and manoeuvred myself into an upright position. I was shivering. My arms were numb, my face was sandy, and I was covered in bush bits and scratches. I was hanging out for a medicinal Scotch or two.

Cold and hungry, we all retreated to the Barrow Creek Hotel, where Saturday night was in full swing. It was late, and the kitchen was shut.

Rick, the chief cook and bottle washer, got the others a meat pie and sauce, but I couldn't even drink the Scotch I'd been craving. After saying a brief hullo to Helen and Les, I started feeling ill again and took to my lumpy little single iron bed, just as the ABC team walked in from whatever they'd been doing.

In the true spirit of his role as research assistant, Clive stayed up till the early hours sharing most of a bottle of whisky with Les, interspersed with memories of That Night, while I lay dreaming of spiders.

◆ ◆ ◆

Around dawn I staggered out into the bar, looking for a cup of tea. Rick was already up, cleaning down the bar, sweeping the floor, and occasionally wandering out to fill up a petrol tank for a passing tourist. (There's no self-service at Barrow Creek. The bowsers are kept padlocked.)

I watched people come in to get the keys for the public toilets. From opening to closing, there's heavy traffic at Barrow Creek, outside and in.

When Rick came back, I asked him about that night. 'Were you here?'

'No comment,' he said with pursed lips. 'I have nothing to say.'

Oh, be like that then, I thought crossly. I helped myself to free tea from the urn, which is kept boiling for travellers, and went back to bed.

I woke again at noon. I was horrified. How could Clive have let me sleep so long when we had so much to do? Although if Helen won't talk and Rick won't talk, that just leaves Les, and the ABC has probably wrung him dry. Grrr!

I found Clive on the front porch, doing his crossword. The others had gone back to Alice, as planned.

'You look just like part of the scenery,' I told Clive.

'I feel like it. I've been directing traffic to the loos, the tea and coffee urn and so on, all morning.' He lowered his voice. 'I've also shared several smoko breaks with Rick. You'll never believe this, Rob, but he used to work with Carlotta.'

'Carlotta! Our Carlotta?' I knew Carlotta in Sydney, where she became a female impersonator dancing at Les Girls.

'The very same. I told him you knew her, and he's dying for a chat.'

A former Les Girls dancer working as a barman at Barrow Creek? What a hoot, as Carlotta would say. 'You're kidding! What on earth is he doing here in the middle of nowhere?'

'He's looking forward to telling you.'

So Rick and I became mates. Over several cups of tea, we reminisced about those hazy, crazy days of our youth in Kings Cross in the 1960s, and he shared lots of information with me about that night at Barrow Creek. He had been on deck almost the whole day. He saw Joanne sitting alone and offered her something to eat and a little something for her nervous shock. 'She was icy cool,' he told me. 'Didn't want anything to calm her down. Just sipped her tea and sat there waiting to tell her story to the police. I didn't feel very welcome, so I left her alone, looking at the arsenal piled on the pool table.

'The police and media totally occupied this place for days. It was absolute bedlam. Journalists sleeping in bedrolls all down the hallway.

'In my opinion, it was a very fishy story. I saw you come in last night, covered in grass and twigs. She had no mess on her at all – after five hours? Not likely. Did you wear shoes while you were hiding?' he asked pointedly.

'Yes, I must confess I did.'

'Well, you ask Helen about Joanne's feet.'

If she'll talk to me, I thought. I hadn't seen her since I surfaced.

'Do you know anything about Neutral Junction station?' I asked him.

'What do you want to know? I worked there for a few months as a station hand. Hell on my fingernails,' he joked.

'I want to check out the place a clairvoyant says Peter could be buried.'

'Hmph! Not very likely, in my view. Charlie, the owner, is here for the muster at the moment, so I suggest you ask him or Mick, the manager.'

'Thanks, Rick.'

Clive and I headed off to check out the incident scene in daylight. We wanted look at the 'burial site' too, if we were allowed on the property. On the way, Clive told me the vehicle count from the previous night.

'From Ti Tree to Barrow Creek, there were six cars and four trucks on the road. From Barrow Creek to the re-enactment spot, another two cars and three trucks. In the hour you were in the bush, we saw nine cars and four trucks. Same time at night, same time of year. How come only one person driving by saw the two cars together, when they must have been parked for at least an hour? No one slowed down while we were parked there, by the way. Just flew by at 150 kilometres an hour.'

Clive seemed to be thinking aloud. 'Unless they weren't parked there for all that time – or at all. What if a pre-arranged meeting was taking place off the road? What if Peter slowed down for that fire outside Ti Tree because he was expecting a signal, but didn't stop because it was too soon? What about that man Chris Malouf, who's a dead ringer for the Joanne Lees description, camping so near that night? I can hardly believe in that coincidence. Maybe he lit a fire and they drove off the road somewhere? Don't forget the fourteen kilometres on the speedo that the police couldn't account for.

'It really has been bugging me, that question of why they set out so late from Alice in a dilapidated old van,' Clive went on. 'It doesn't make sense. But it could, if they had arranged to meet someone.'

I chipped in, 'Murdoch told me that a friend of his knew the owner of Neutral Junction. Could there be any connection? That clairvoyant said Peter was taken to a nearby building. What other buildings are around here?'

We arrived at the Neutral Junction turn-off just as a ute emerged from a cloud of dust and flew out through the gate. We pulled up side by side in the driveway, and I jumped out. So did the driver, a huge smiling fellow with outdoor eyes crinkled at the corners and cheeks scorched as red as his shirt.

'Hi. I'm looking for Charlie or Mick.'

'I'm Charlie. Who's looking?'

I told him who I was and what we'd like to do. He said it was fine for us to go in. The site was at the second creek along the road. Then he checked his watch and cast a long look at our city sedan.

'Look, I'm in a bit of a hurry, but I'd better show you. I'm not sure you'll find it on your own.'

He spun his wheels in a wide U-turn and took off back down the corrugated dirt track at about a hundred kilometres an hour. We didn't even try to keep up. After a bone-jarring ride, we spotted him parked beside a sandy dip, next to a fallen blue gum.

'This is it,' he told us. 'I drove the dozer when the police came out here. Stayed on a while and poked around a bit more after they left. There's nothing there, though.' He shook his head. 'All a lot of rubbish, if you ask me. You'd never find a body out here. This place is a million acres. It's thirty-five kilometres from east to west.'

He said he had to get away and set some cattle traps. (During a muster, the cattle are lured in from the scrub by strategically placing water inside fenced areas.) He took off at the same pace as before, and we got back in our car.

'Just as well he showed us,' I said. 'I'd never have picked this as a creek. It's hard to imagine it running at all, but it must be quite a torrent in the Wet by the look of all that dried grass and twigs up there in the trees.'

Clive was looking hard at the speedo. He's good at noting those things. 'Rob, this spot is exactly seven kilometres from the highway – a return trip of fourteen kilometres.'

I prickled with goosebumps. 'The missing fourteen kilometres? Could Anna be right? How spooky.'

Before Chris had left that morning, he had told Clive that Adam's idea of the location placed it much further north than Anna's, but the fourteen kilometres might give more weight to Anna's story.

We drove back to the highway to look at the hold-up site in the daylight. There were still faint police marks outlining the pool of Peter Falconio's blood on the bitumen, and a few other smaller marks as well. I wondered if they signified bloodspots. It looked as if a big puddle had formed, and then smaller drops had surrounded it.

The scrub started about twenty metres in from the road. It looked dense from the bitumen, but became very sparse once we started walking through it. It was just mulga and spinifex, with a few rocks strewn around. The ground was quite hard, and I wondered if trackers would be able to tell if we'd been there. Probably. I went back to the road and picked up a few bits of detritus, including some very weathered bits of an iced-coffee container.

'Look at this shoulder,' Clive pointed. 'Right beside the bloodstain. There's virtually no slope at all. I can't see how Peter could have rolled out of sight into a dip. There isn't a dip.'

He was right.

About 400 metres further north, we found the track where the Kombi was abandoned. There was a gate about 250 metres in from the road, and a fence where the van had been parked. On the side of the fence toward the road were quite thick clumps of mulga. The Kombi would have been well hidden. Vince had said only the white top was visible.

'Why hide the Kombi so carefully? Why not leave Peter's body there as well? It was crazy to take it – unless he wasn't dead,' I said. Even if a bullet remained in his body, it would be easy to get rid of the gun. It was a huge risk driving off with a body in your car, especially if you had drugs on board.

'And why didn't Joanne make a move when she heard the Kombi drive off? She says there was only one man, so if he was out of hearing in the van, why not make a run for it?'

'He would've been gone for about fifteen minutes by the time he drove here, hid the van and walked back,' Clive said. 'She could have run further away – or even crossed the road to make it harder for him to look for her.'

'Maybe she did. Maybe the action took place here, and she ran to where she was found. But that doesn't explain the blood.'

Had the van been driven in before the incident and carefully parked off the road so it wouldn't be seen? Did the altercation then take place on the highway, beside the four-wheel drive?

More puzzled than enlightened, we headed back to Barrow Creek.

Helen had made an appearance. I said hullo and ordered a beer. I told her I'd seen her sons in Alice. She seemed surprised and delighted; she is proud of them both and wanted to make sure I'd been impressed. I assured her I was.

'Look, Helen, I told you I wouldn't bother you about my book,' I said tentatively, 'and I'll honour that promise. But could I ask you one question?'

'Maybe,' she said warily.

'When Joanne came here, that night when you first saw her, was she wearing shoes?'

'I wasn't up when she first came in,' Helen said, 'but I helped her get dressed in some clothes we loaned her after the police took all her clothes. She had bare feet then.'

'So did you see her feet? Like, what condition were they in?' Helen's eyes locked onto mine. She knew exactly why I was asking.

'I helped her put on some white sports socks. Put them on her myself. There wasn't a mark on her feet.'

She turned away and busied herself at the bar, knowing I'd got the answer I was expecting. But it still didn't solve the puzzle.

Next morning, we were due to head north to Darwin. Before we left, we had a last coffee with Rick. He pointed out two pieces of memorabilia hanging over our heads. 'Look up there on the pillar, next to that big hunk of dried Northern Territory bullshit,' he directed.

The first item to catch our eye was a five-dollar note, with 'Peter + Paul Falconio' written on it in black pen. 'Paul and his father came in here,' Rick told us. 'Poor men, they were so distressed.

Paul left the money for us to buy Peter a drink, if he ever turned up. It was very sad.'

The other piece of paper held a little note from Cathy Curly, the barmaid.

1-8-02
Dear Peter,
May you always know the truth and see the LIGHT surrounding you?? May GOD bless you.
Love, Catherine xxx

Later that morning, as Clive drove past the ghostly marks on the road, I turned to him with a hint of frustration. 'It's two years since Peter vanished, but I can't seem to get any sense of him – of the real person before that. All we have is this kind of frozen image of Peter always smiling, having fun, constantly at Joanne's side, never an individual. Who is Peter Falconio?

'People seem to be wary of talking because of the media saturation and police nervousness. And all the attention has focused on Joanne Lees. There has been so much published about who she is, what a victim she's become, how difficult it'll be for her to resume a normal life, but almost nothing about Peter. What about him? It's as if the real victim has faded to a shadow, just an excuse for continuing the investigation. And if we don't know the victim, how can anyone figure out why he was killed?

'People don't just wave down a complete stranger, shoot him, remove the body and leave behind the only eyewitness. I reckon the police should be figuring out what happened here first, not who did it.'

Chapter Twenty-Six

ACROSS THE TOP END

Strangers in Broome stand out like Mt Fuji on a clear day.

Local saying

Our next stop was Darwin, which in July is a magnet for tourists from all over the world. Hotels are expensive, and rooms in short supply. The ten-day Darwin Cup Carnival is a big draw card, and the town was overflowing with punters, along with the usual backpackers and other travellers. Fortunately, we found a room at the Cherry Blossom Motel, which was cheap, clean, handy to town and opposite the beach.

We expected to stay in Darwin for nine days, with a three-day side trip to Broome for me. I had a short but critical list of prospects, headed by Assistant Commissioner Daulby, who had agreed to an interview some weeks earlier. But at the last moment, his secretary phoned to say he was leaving for Papua New Guinea on secondment. Unavailable as of immediately.

I was cranky and let my feelings be known to the secretary, who suggested trying Commander George Owen, the other half of the review team. That was some consolation. I phoned him, explained the last-minute hitch with Daulby and made a time for the following week.

'You'd think Daulby would speak to me,' I grumbled as I hung up. 'He's known about my appointment for weeks, and he's not leaving town for a few days, only finishing up at the office. It's not as if he's camera-shy.'

'I don't know, Rob. I reckon some people would do anything to get out of an interview with you,' Clive said, jollying me along. 'You should know by now how difficult it is to penetrate the barriers the police put up when they don't want to talk to you.'

I moved along to my next name, Joy Kuhl. She was on her way to the beach with her grandchildren, but she agreed to meet me at her local pub after 5.30 pm.

To fill in the day, Clive and I did some touristy things around Darwin, including a long, hot walk down to the wharf, where we stopped at the historic Seamen's Mission for a drink. A burly bloke with a droopy moustache asked me where we came from and why we'd come to Darwin. When I told him about my research, he said he'd been pulled over by police three times because he drove a white Toyota 75 series.

'The cops were full-on about that case,' he said. 'Gave me the irrits bein' pulled over, but I s'pose they were just doin' their job.'

The Northern Territory had recently passed Freedom of Information legislation, and I resolved to test it out by applying for the Litster–Owen review document, hoping I'd get a copy through some bureaucrat who didn't realise its importance. The office only had two staff, both of whom were at the Darwin Show touting the new legislation. The Act was so new that the other staff in the building had never heard of it. 'It's probably on one of those interminable in-house memos we keep getting,' said a man in a brown cardigan. 'Never read them myself.'

After ringing the FOI man on his mobile, Brown Cardigan found a form and issued instructions. I noticed I'd be the thirteenth FOI applicant since the legislation was passed. That did not augur well.

Later in the day, I managed to meet the Director of Public Prosecutions, Rex Wild QC, and prosecutor Tony Elliott just before Mr Wild took off on leave. They spent half an hour with me, explaining what was involved in getting the case to court. They were expecting the police brief from Alice Springs fairly soon; then they had to await the outcome of the trial in South Australia. There had been some discussion about hearing the Falconio case first, but the Northern Territory police were not ready, and the South Australian police were keen to proceed because a minor was involved.

I asked, 'If Murdoch's found not guilty of the rape and abduction, what then?'

'In that unlikely event, he'll be arrested as he walks from the court, and we will extradite him to Darwin,' Rex Wild said. 'A warrant is ready. It just hasn't been served. If he's found guilty in South Australia, he'll be transferred here and begin serving his sentence in the Northern Territory.'

'What if he appeals the South Australian conviction?'

'His lawyers in South Australia can mount an appeal in his absence, providing they have grounds, of course.'

The prosecutors were polite and friendly and I risked a big question.

'Apart from the DNA on the T-shirt, what else have you got? It all seems pretty circumstantial to me.'

'Circumstantial cases get up,' Rex Wild said. 'There's a good case, in my view – circumstantial and otherwise. I'd like a body, though. If you could bring me a body, I'd be very happy.' He laughed. He'd dodged my question like a true QC.

'I'll see what I can do,' I replied. 'You'll be the first person I'll call if I stumble across one.'

With a very flimsy motive (in my view), no murder weapon, no cause of death, no body and no reliable witnesses, I thought the prosecution was pushing the proverbial uphill. Until my next meeting.

Joy Kuhl had obviously been home and spruced herself up for our meeting. I felt a bit grubby in my old shorts and singlet, ratty hair and no make-up.

Joy is a nice lady – small, dark-haired and over sixty, which is why she'd retired. It seemed there was nothing sinister about her resignation part-way through the Falconio investigation. It was simply that the time had come to cover up her microscope and play grandma.

We settled in for a couple of drinks, and she told me about her career. She graduated from Sydney University with a Bachelor of Science and Master's degree in biochemistry, then worked as a biochemist and a forensic biologist before taking ten years off to have her family. She went back to work at the New South Wales Health Commission – 'Then Chamberlain happened,' she said a bit defiantly. I had expected Chamberlain to rear its Gorgon head, but we didn't dwell on it. Instead, I raised Chris Tangey's story about the luminol test on the Kombi.

'Oh, that filmmaker is a crazy man!' she said in an exasperated tone. 'He's complained to the Ombudsman, you know. I had to go in and answer a heap of questions, after I'd left my job. The filming was purely an experiment. Nikko [Sergeant John Nixon] wanted it done, so Bill Towers put the hard word on me to get them out of his hair. I told him we wouldn't get any blood – both Carmen and I had already been over it, and so had other qualified crime scene analysts – but I said we might get other reactions.

'To show him what I meant, I sprayed the light bulb and the side of the fridge. They glowed, but not like blood – that comes up brightly, lasts for about thirty seconds and disappears. I think I did make some comment that Nikko would be convinced the whole van was covered in blood. The Ombudsman did show me some glowing thing he had on film, but it looked like a footprint to me.'

'Was any gunshot residue found on the back of the van?' I asked her.

'I don't think so. Carmen did blood spatter analysis and there was no spatter, no pooling – nothing on the van that I can recall.

'We knew it was serious by the time Carmen arrived back,' Joy went on. 'A few things had already come back – Joanne's clothes, the manacles, the Ventolin puffer from the van that Joanne had said was

Peter's. We used this as a control to isolate DNA reactions from the small spots of blood on her T-shirt and later on, from blood samples from the road.'

She told me about the tests they had done on the porous black tape that had formed the links of the manacles. 'The police were very insistent that we test and re-test these. They thought the offender must have left some skin cells or other material – hairs, for example – on them when they were being made, since they were so sticky. But all we got were a few of Joanne Lees's skin cells on one of the bits of tape. We re-tested them when Carmen brought back the DNA swabs from the truck drivers, but Lees's DNA was all we got.' I told her how I'd emerged from our re-enactment covered in bits of scrub and spider-web, and she said everyone had been a bit puzzled about the lack of any twigs or dirt on Joanne's T-shirt. Joy added, 'She obviously hadn't been injured, which didn't quite fit her story.'

Joy went on to describe where they found the male DNA on Joanne's T-shirt. She held up her little finger. 'The spot where the DNA came from was about half the size of this fingernail,' she said. 'At the back of her T-shirt, in the area where she said he'd tied her up. It was haemoserous, a weepy sort of stain, rather than actual blood.'

'At the back?' I exclaimed. 'Are you sure?' The police had always held up the T-shirt facing the cameras, and I'd assumed the marks were on the front.

'Yes. Definitely the back.'

'But that is a gift for the defence,' I said. 'If it's Murdoch's DNA, he could have brushed up against her anywhere – at the Camel Cup, for instance – and she wouldn't have known. I bet I had half-a-dozen strange DNAs on my T-shirt after spending the afternoon there. It was packed.'

'Maybe. But we did find the same DNA on the steering wheel of the Kombi. Carmen swabbed the wheel and we got a match. So he must have been at the scene – probably drove the van – but certainly touched the steering wheel.'

Her words slammed into me. Wow! I thought. How's Murdoch going to explain that? Suddenly reasonable doubt was getting a bit less likely, even in my own mind. Had Murdoch lied to me?

Joy must have read the look on my face and realised this was news to me. She leaned forward across the dark wood table and said quietly, 'I'm not sure how widely known that is. I probably shouldn't have told you. But it was there, and that's why the police think he was there too.'

'I won't tell anyone except my husband,' I promised. Her news was a bombshell. It made things look pretty bad for Murdoch. He would find out about it once the defence received the brief. But that could be months away.

We ordered another drink, and she told me about the Territory law on keeping DNA. 'We have more legislation to back keeping people's DNA on databases than anywhere else in Australia, thanks largely to Mike Reed, who wanted all Northern Territory babies DNAed at birth,' she laughed. 'He didn't get that through, but we do keep DNA longer than any other State.'

I could hardly contain my excitement as I drove back to tell Clive. The fact that the DNA was on the back of the T-shirt could have got Murdoch off the hook. But the DNA on the steering wheel put him firmly back on it again.

I've always wanted to go to Broome, but I wouldn't hurry back. It's definitely a 'destination', not somewhere you drop in on the way to anywhere else. People go there for all sorts of reasons – many for a holiday, but many others to disappear. The rule of the day is casual dress, casual attitude and not too many questions. But I had lots of questions, and only three days to get the answers. Although I was dressed like a local in shorts and singlet, everyone knows when someone new is in town. Hence the local saying: 'Strangers in Broome stand out like Mt Fuji on a clear day'.

To get there, I'd endured a three-hour flight in a tiny plane with my knees under my armpits. Fortunately, we'd stopped over at Kununurra ('Gateway to the Last Frontier', as the sign said at the airport), which had alleviated the risk of permanent muscle impairment. Around Kununurra, the farms looked amazingly civilised after weeks of looking at scrubby red dirt. Huge swathes of different greens stretched for miles in every direction, thanks to the Ord River Irrigation Scheme, which waters the market gardens that supply most of Western Australia. No such views surrounded Broome. I craned my neck to see the fabled Cable Beach, the booming resort town, the hub of the pearl industry I'd heard so much about, but saw only a shanty town clinging to the edge of the Indian Ocean. I was reminded of that song – 'Is this all there is?'

Murdoch's friend Julie had arranged a bed for me at her boss's house, and she met me at the airport to show me the way. We sized each other up and decided we liked each other enough to share some information. Thanks to Julie, my first night in Broome was spent visiting two of Murdoch's friends – Brett, who owns West Kimberley Diesel, and Paul Jackson, formerly from Fitzroy Crossing – at Brett's home. Their wives were there too, contributing from time to time, but mostly the men did the talking – it's the way in the far north.

Brett pointed out a Toyota truck parked in the driveway. 'That was Brad's old car,' he said. 'He changed cars and canopies quite often. There's nothing suss about it. When you more or less live in your vehicle, you look after it. He was meticulous about his stuff. He's a great spanner man. Can fix anything. That's why he'd work for me sometimes. I'd give him a job any time.'

'Yeah, he kept his gear in prime condition,' Paul chipped in.

'Brad was really pissed off with Hepi once when he drove Brad's vehicle into a sand dune and bent the chassis.

'Look,' Paul went on, 'this stuff they've got him on in South Australia, that's just rubbish. I've known Brad for years. I've left him alone with my wife and daughter. Do you think I'd do that if he was likely to hurt them? It's a set-up.'

'So's the Falconio shit,' Brett went on. 'He was here at dawn on Monday morning. I know he was. How could he be here in Broome, at the Shell stop, and killing that bloke all at once? It doesn't stack up.'

Paul agreed. 'He was at my roadhouse at eight o'clock on the Sunday night, fuelling up. How could he do that and have driven all the way from Alice Springs? It's total bullshit.'

'What about the new canopy he's supposed to have ordered from Tropic Upholstery?' I asked.

'I'd like to know when he was supposed to be getting all that work done on his truck,' Paul said. 'Brad and me and my son and father-in-law all went away fishing to Barred Creek on 25 and 26 July. I'm certain of the dates, because the old man keeps detailed diaries. I've even got photos of the four-wheel drive that show Brad had a solid rear piece on the back. If Joanne Lees says she crawled out of the back of that vehicle, she's lying.'

I wondered if Paul would lend me those photos.

'Yeah, that's just some crap Hepi's come up with. Look, Tropic is in Hunter Street, quite a few blocks from Forrest Street. Do you really think Brad would arrive here at night from driving over 3000 kilometres, park his truck in the front yard of Tropic on a Sunday night when it's deserted, leave his gear in it and then walk to his place, and the first thing he says is "I didn't kill that bloke"? It's just f---en bullshit.'

'It does seem odd,' I agreed. 'The whole Hepi business seems very strange to me. He knows those women Brad is supposed to have raped, doesn't he?'

'Of course he does. Brad met them through Hepi. They're Hepi's neighbours. I reckon they've been put up to it.'

'But what would be the benefit to anyone to do that?' I asked. 'Easy. They get him in jail, they can take his DNA, especially on a rape charge. He's got no say. Then the Northern Territory cops can get some and tie him to the Falconio job. It's a set-up – part of Hepi's deal with the cops.'

'But why would those people put themselves through that?'

'Who knows? Compensation money if he gets convicted? Maybe they owe Hepi, or he might have something on them. Frankie used to run brothels before he got sick, and Lurline … well, least said about her the better.'

I found it difficult to accept that anyone would subject a twelve-year-old girl to such an ordeal if it was concocted, but I guess anything's possible.

'Brad's DNA on the T-shirt is going to be hard to explain,' I suggested.

'Why? It's probably been planted. Anyway, you know about the f--k-ups they're famous for. What about Lindy Chamberlain?' Everyone nodded, and Brett went to get us another drink.

'Did the police visit you when they came to Broome?' I asked when he returned.

The question provoked guffaws of cynical laughter.

'They were here for hours on end – all through the f--ken night. That Paula sheila, did not let up for one minute,' Brett told me. 'My statement was seventy-four pages long. Then they wanted me to sign it on the spot, without even a read through. No bloody way. I made quite a lot of alterations before I signed it, I can tell you.'

'They had a search warrant,' his wife said. 'Went through everything in the workshop.'

'Did they take anything with them?' I asked.

'Yeah, a few things. They wanted the baseball caps I used to have to promote Kimberley Diesel, to check the logos. Someone had told them the man in the truck-stop photo was wearing a Kimberley Diesel cap. What rubbish!'

'They wanted my business cap too,' Paul added. 'Wanted to look at the logo on the back of the cap. Some of them have two logos,' he explained.

I figured this must mean that the police have photos showing a logo on the back of the cap, which is not that common.

'But it was cable ties and duct tapes they were mostly after,' Brett said.

'Any hundred-mile-an-hour tape?' I asked.

'Yeah, they did take samples of that too. Why? I've had half-a-dozen rolls of that stuff for years. Don't use it that often, but everyone carries it out here.'

'What is it exactly?'

'It's black and very strong and sticky. The idea is that you can use it for fixing bits that fall off your car and then drive at a hundred miles an hour to the nearest garage and the bits won't fall off. Almost every truck in the outback would have some in the back, so what's so important about that?'

'What I want to know,' Paul interrupted, 'is how this bloke who climbed in her Kombi managed all the f--ken stuff he was supposed to be carrying – pistol, sack, duct tape to tie her legs up, some other tape to gag her, cable ties, then he turns off the ignition, grabs hold of her, puts handcuffs on – he musta been a f--ken octopus. With her struggling and kicking, he manages all that gear in just two hands?'

'Maybe he was a juggler?' someone else suggested.

He left out the hundred-mile-an-hour tape, I thought. But I joined in the mirth around the table. It was a bit hard to visualise.

For three days and nights, I did my rounds in Broome, visiting the police, who had refined their media responses to 'I can't tell you and I can't tell you why I can't tell you', while still looking serious and on top of it all. I caught up with Julie between interviews, during her breaks outside the busy cafe where she worked. I spent my nights trying to find Murdoch's truckie mates and spending my diminishing research fund on bourbon and coke – for them.

Loi O'Dore's workshop was in a side street on the outskirts of the residential area. It had a big front yard behind a high cyclone fence, but the gate did not look as if it was ever closed. Not very secure, as Brett had said. Loi O'Dore, a small, dark-complexioned man, was obviously uncomfortable with my arrival, which I'd timed for just after hours so that he could not plead pressure of work to end our conversation. He lives behind the workshop, and he chatted for a short time while his wife cooked dinner for the kids.

'Brad seemed like a good bloke,' he told me. 'He never caused us any problems. Always paid cash, on the dot. Rarely complained. I remember we did a boat canopy for him one time, and we did it standard height, forgetting he was such a big bloke. When he came to collect it, he was banging his head on it when he stood up, so we offered to re-do it and raise it. Some people might have whinged or got a bit nasty, but he was jake about it.'

I tried to get Loi to differentiate between the vehicles associated with the incident: the sketch prepared on Joanne Lee's information, the still from the truck-stop video, and the fully packed rig Murdoch was driving when he was arrested.

'The canopy in that truck-stop photo looks like one that we do,' he said. 'I can't be a hundred per cent sure. I told the police I'd need the clips enhanced, because we use a special way of tying the canopy on.'

'I thought you told the police that was your canopy?'

'No. What I said was, "We do those canopies, but it wasn't necessarily the one we do." I told them I needed better pictures of the clips to be sure.'

'So did you tell the police that Brad had said he was the man in the truck-stop video?'

'Well, Brad did say something like that. He brought in his truck to have the canopy changed over, and I queried it with him, because he'd spent six thousand dollars on a new one not that long before – less than a couple of years, if I remember rightly. He said the cops were "bloody hassling" him. He also said, "I possibly did stop there, I was there at the time." So I did tell that to the police.'

'What was his truck like before you changed the canopy over?'

'It was an HJ75 ute. He had done quite a big job on that car before he brought it here to get the first canopy on it. Changed the whole car, really. Bigger wheels, bigger motor, aluminium tray, long-range tanks. We only do upholstery and canopies, so we changed the regular canopy to fit an aluminium frame with a solid back and front, and mesh sides that you could lift up. There was green PVC on each side and a solid top. That was about eighteen months or two years before the Falconio thing and it was still in good nick, so I wondered why he wanted to replace it.'

'Hang on. So the rear of the canopy on Murdoch's truck, before you put on a new one, was solid aluminium? Above the tailgate, I mean?' Although Murdoch's mates had told me about the solid rear panel during our talk the night before, this seemed to be independent confirmation.

'Yep. Only opened at the sides. And not into the cabin, either.'

'So it was that canopy he asked you to change after 15 July?'

'Yeah, he said the cops were hassling him and that's why he wanted it changed over.'

'Do you know what the date was?'

'No, I don't. The police asked me that. I keep a log on the work we've done, but I often don't put any dates. It was two years ago, you know. I do a lot of work here – it seems like we're flat out twenty-four/ seven.'

He said the police had taken his logs on the jobs he'd done for Murdoch.

Very interesting, I thought as I drove back to town. No access from the tailgate. How did Joanne drop herself over the tailgate? Whose car was Murdoch driving on 14 July 2001? Or was he even there?

The Roebuck Bar, known as 'Roey's', was already packed. Elbows on every inch of damp bar towel, drinks lined up and patrons in various states of relaxation after the long, hot day.

I struck up a conversation with the publican, who knew Murdoch as a patron. 'He's not a bad bloke,' he told me. 'Came to the rescue of a lady in my pub once when she was in trouble with a drunk – not here, up at Fitzroy. I was a bit worried about taking the bloke on, but

Murdoch told him to leave her alone and get out of the pub. He's not a big drinker. Like a gentle giant – if you're on the right side of him, that is.'

The publican was leaving Broome soon to go to the Whitsunday Islands, where the crowds were a bit more predictable.

'If I knew where some of my patrons in Broome came from and what they'd done, I'd have to close my pub,' he confided. 'I'd be too scared to come to work each day.'

I asked him to point out any locals who drove trucks, and soon I was sidling up to some likely prospects with my business card on the bar and the offer of a free drink on my lips. About the only thing I discovered was that those northerners can drink. Truckies are a clannish lot and no one was saying much about Big Brad, except that he was a champion bloke.

One guy said cryptically, 'You're looking in the wrong place.

Don't spend time with the truckies, look at the boats.'

I tried to get more out of him, but soon afterwards he passed out and was carried off by his mates.

Chapter Twenty-Seven

MEDIA BITES

Crime doesn't pay.

FBI slogan

Next day I wasted a lot of time looking for a bloke with a dodgy boat business, which I thought might tie in with Murdoch's comments about exotic bird smuggling. But the only likely prospect was at sea for the next week, so I decided to get back to the more pressing business of interviewing Narelle Hine, the journalist who exposed Murdoch to the world as the 'prime suspect' in the disappearance of Peter Falconio.

The historic Broome boardwalk is largely taken up with tourist shell-and-pearl shops, but one small shopfront houses the *Broome Advertiser* office. Narelle Hine was a small, pert young woman, full of enthusiasm and pleased with my interest in her big scoop. She was very helpful, burrowing through her files to come up with reams of information.

'I knew James Hepi,' she confided as we raided the files. 'I knew about him being picked up with the hydro on board. A few months later, in late July or early August, I called in to see a girlfriend, and James was visiting her too. We were watching some stupid show on TV when James turned to me and said, "If you want a good story, I'll tell you one."'

Hepi told Narelle why he was not in prison. The conversation led her to a story that was picked up across Australia and around the world. She had a good relationship with Broome police, and had checked her story thoroughly before going into print.

If Murdoch was Peter Falconio's killer, she figured Hepi had done the community a service. She thought the South Australian case might demonstrate a pattern of abducting and hurting helpless women.

'Which won't do the police case in the Northern Territory any harm,' I commented. 'They'll probably argue he's done this kind of thing several times and not been caught.'

'Don't you think he's the killer?' she persisted.

'I'm not convinced. But it's possible. They don't all foam at the mouth, I guess.'

But I couldn't find anyone in Broome who'd ever seen Murdoch with a beard or long hair.

I spoke by phone with Genine Johnson, who had written the story on Chris Malouf, the Broome drifter who said he had camped near Barrow Creek on 14 July. She said Chris had pleaded with her to run a story so that police would stop harassing him.

'That's me on the video,' he told her. 'It's my hat and my thongs. I'm so freaked out by all this. The police are pulling me over day and night.'

'I think he was into a bit of a drama,' Genine told me. 'Maybe he just wanted his face in the paper. But it was a huge coincidence, him looking so much like the alleged gunman, camped nearby on the same night, being from Broome, possibly even knowing Murdoch. One of the local police, Bill Black, had a look at Chris and said, "It's not him in the truck-stop picture." So that was it.

'I did hear a rumour that Joanne Lees had known Chris somehow. The police told me that they thought he was expecting a parcel from her. That's why they kept pulling him over. You could get anything in through Broome Airport back then – the security was non-existent.' I guess all that changed after the attack on the World Trade Center – even in sleepy, isolated Broome.

But not much else had changed in Broome. Whatever I might have unearthed there seemed to have vanished when Murdoch and Hepi left town.

Before catching my plane, I received a call on my mobile. It was Commander George Owen, cancelling our meeting. He was unfortunately unavailable.

'I can re-schedule,' I assured him. 'I will be in Darwin for a few more days after that date.'

'Not possible, I'm afraid.'

'When will it be possible?'

'After the trial.'

'Oh, come on, Mr Owen,' I said. 'Who's leaned on you?'

He wouldn't say – and he wouldn't meet me. Why were the police suddenly being so cagey? I resolved to get in another way.

◆ ◆ ◆

Back in Darwin, I met a journalist who had some background on the case. She had been living at a police station on a community near Katherine at the time of the incident, and she had attended most of the media briefings during the early days of the investigation.

We chatted at a sunny outdoor cafe. She wasn't surprised that Owen and Daulby had dodged their interviews with me. They were very sensitive about the case.

She said, 'I once asked Daulby, "Is this another Lindy Chamberlain?" and he got really pissed off and picked up all his papers and stormed out. I also heard that the "happy couple" story was not true. They were having screaming matches the whole way, and only travelling together as a convenience until they got to Darwin.' She'd been told that a witness statement said that during one fight, Peter got out of the van and walked away, and she followed him and hit him.

She had also heard that the vehicle at the truck stop had no rear exit. 'Lots of cops on the ground were saying Joanne's story was bullshit. They blew up the truck-stop photos and checked every detail, and the back did not look as if it would open. There are so many of those Toyotas up here.'

I phoned a senior police officer, Detective Superintendent Bert Hofer, whose name I'd been given by a police friend in Melbourne. He agreed to see me, although I told him I'd been given the brushoff by Daulby and Owen. If I came in to police HQ late on Friday afternoon, he'd have a chat before going to collect his kids from sport.

'I just want to talk about procedures,' I told him.

'That's all I can discuss,' he agreed. He was on leave when the case began.

It turned out he had recently sat on a working group examining national investigative powers. This was relevant to the Falconio case, which had involved police from all States. Superintendent Hofer explained that currently the law is different in each jurisdiction. Large operations can suffer from lost time, lost evidence and lost momentum while agencies grapple with the complexities of the legislation. For example, warrants or authorisations issued in one jurisdiction are not automatically valid in another. Investigations can also lose steam when overworked police are asked to assist colleagues, interstate. The State and Territory police ministers and attorneys general had established a National Working Group to identify the problems and offer some solutions.

Bert Hofer and I were immersed in this discussion when a smallish man in civvies appeared in the doorway.

'I'm off for the weekend now,' he told Hofer. 'OK, sir,' Hofer replied.

Whoops! There were not many people senior to Hofer at that complex, but Commander George Owen was one of them. Sure enough, the man in the doorway was staring at me suspiciously.

'Have you met Robin Bowles, sir?' Bert asked. I stood up and extended my hand. I wanted to say something cheeky, but kept my mouth shut. I was worried that Hofer would catch it on Monday.

'Mr Hofer and I are talking about interstate policing and the command structure in the Northern Territory,' I reassured Mr Owen. 'Nothing about Falconio,' I added hastily. I even read him back a few lines of my notes. But I suspect Hofer did catch it on Monday.

◆ ◆ ◆

By the time we left Darwin to cross back to the east coast, I was beginning to feel the need for some retail therapy, but room in the car was tighter than ever. I'd sneaked in a few small purchases while Clive was in the shower.

Our next research stop was Cairns, where we had arranged to meet Mark Wilton, now working at the Cairns Post, and listen to his tape of the interview with Joanne Lees.

Cairns was sunny, thriving and full of tourists. We lashed out on a decent hotel room. Mark proved to be quite a character; he was a former teacher of Design Technology and English Literature who'd grown up in New Norfolk, Tasmania. He'd been a cricket umpire in his spare time, and was invited to write a sports column for the local newspaper. Before he knew it, he was a full-blown journo. What is it about this story that attracts Tasmanians, I wondered?

I sat and listened to his tales of the craziness that followed Peter's disappearance. He was not very complimentary about the police handling of the case.

'For example,' he said, 'they put a lot of store on her description of the dog. She wouldn't have seen the dog for more than a split second, across Peter while he was driving, but they put out the blue heeler description anyway – accurate or not.'

He said Joanne was pale and tense when he arrived for the interview. 'She'd had about forty hours of grilling from the police up until then and she really looked as if she didn't want to do this. She was very upset about things she'd read. Her eye was bruised, and she looked fragile.' Before she began to speak, she was hyperventilating, as if to psych herself up.

Mark knew Joanne had received no counselling or medical attention other than her initial physical examination, because his wife, who was the police psychologist on call that weekend, had not been called.

After sussing me out, he trusted me with his tape overnight. I took it back to our hotel room and played it several times. I heard him introduce himself as a journalist. Then Joanne took over, reciting the chronology of the events.

She launched into a singsong monologue. 'We stop at Ti Tree. We did set off – the police have gone through our mileage and recorded our receipts. We keep petrol receipts ... we see a suspicious fire on the side of the road. We do not stop at the fire.'

She described how the other driver had pulled them over and engaged Peter in conversation. Then she had heard a loud noise, and the man had appeared at the Kombi's window with a gun.

Mark interrupted, asking her to describe the man and what happened next.

'I don't know if I can give any details,' she told him, suddenly seeming to realise the tape was rolling. 'When I speak to Pete's family ... I have to tell them first.'

Peter's father and brother had not arrived in Alice Springs at that point.

'But they got it wrong in the papers,' Joanne said firmly. Some reports had said the gunman had dragged Pete out of the vehicle.

'The man did seem amicable,' she continued. 'I became more at ease. But whether Pete had stopped or not, I believe now he would have shot our tyres.'

'Did you notice him following you?' Mark asked.

She told him she had not seen anyone near the fire or on the road behind them until he came alongside.

'Did he move the Kombi, do you know?' Mark asked.

'I don't know the facts. The timescale seems like an eternity. It might not have been. I can't give the facts.'

Joanne seemed to be wrestling with herself, wanting to tell her story, wanting to be believed, but nervous in case she blew it by giving away something that the police had told her not to reveal.

Mark looked for another angle, asking about Joanne's friends who had arrived from Sydney, but Joanne begged him not to mention them.

'Are your family coming out?' he asked.

'I'm unsure of whether my family has been told,' she said a bit distantly.

Mark was surprised. Surely Joanne had spoken to them? 'Officially been told?' he clarified.

'Yes. I don't know. I think my stepfather ... Pete's family has been told,' she said wearily.

Then she seemed to get a second wind. 'I've had no updates from the police,' she said firmly. 'I'm still angry with the way I've been treated. I feel like I'm left in the dark, but perhaps they're doing that so the man ... to make him feel like they have no leads. Which they have. Before, I was doing things for them, but now I'm doing things for myself,' she finished firmly.

In the background, Helen said quietly, 'On Sunday morning, at Barrow Creek, I asked if anything like this had happened along the road. Then Jo asked. They said it hadn't, but later on we overheard a conversation that "a lot of things have been going down".' Helen took this to mean that similar incidents had occurred before.

Joanne returned to the theme of her treatment by the police. 'During interviews, if I started to cry, they gave me some water and gave me a rest,' she said a bit crossly. 'I'm in shock and trauma and don't know which boss I'm dealing with – Alice Springs or what.'

'You haven't been told who's in charge?'

'It is that way, Mark. I'm pissed off and mad with them, but they might have good reason.'

She seemed to realise she'd said too much, but Mark reassured her that he wouldn't be testing her claims with the police at this stage.

Just before Mark turned the tape off, Joanne said, 'One comment you could put – thank you for everyone's thoughts, for people who are out there and thinking of me in Sydney and England. I really appreciate it.'

After we'd played the tape for the third time, Clive and I both shook our heads. Why had she done the interview? Far from reviving interest in the search for Peter, as Helen seemed to have hoped, it had relentlessly focused attention on Joanne. In any case, by the time the tape was recorded, she'd probably gone over things so many times with the police that it seemed like something she'd learnt by heart.

The next morning, I returned the precious tape and thanked Mark for his help. Over a couple of coffees, we continued discussing Joanne's story. Mark felt she had been poorly treated by the police. 'The police questioning her rotated – they never let up on her,' he told me. 'Although she was questioned for hours at a time without a rest, they took regular breaks. She felt she was being interrogated as a suspect, rather than supported as a victim.'

He also felt Joanne had been unfairly portrayed by his media colleagues. 'People build up in their own minds how a victim should behave,' he said. 'If the victim doesn't fit that image, they attack her.'

Clive and I had planned to spend a couple of months in Airlie Beach, on the sparkling edge of the Whitsunday Islands, while I assembled my research and Clive went sailing. I had a joyous reunion with my little dog and placed advertisements in the Alice Springs and Darwin papers asking for information about Peter Falconio. Replies poured in, including one from a clairvoyant in Darwin who faxed me detailed directions about where to find Peter's body, not far from where Anna had indicated. Most of the other replies were pretty useless, apart from a phone call from Rita, who'd been working at Barrow Creek Hotel on the night.

Rita told me she and Cathy Curly had had difficulty coming to terms with the reality of what had happened to Joanne, especially in view of her apparent calm – and all the guns on the pool table.

Rita said one of the few times Joanne seemed ruffled was when the police wanted all her clothes and would not allow her to have anything from the Kombi. Rita felt sorry for her, and offered some of her own new underwear and a T-shirt. When Joanne was getting dressed, Rita noticed she was wearing an anklet and a bracelet, which she thought the police allowed Joanne to keep. 'She said something about the anklet being a friendship bracelet from Pete,' Rita recalled.

Rita also put me in touch with Cathy Curly, who was now working as a barmaid at Heartbreak Hotel in Cape Crawford, east of Katherine. Clive and I had stopped there to get petrol and have lunch a couple of weeks before, and had unknowingly sat next to Cathy on the veranda while she was taking her lunch break, as Cathy and I figured out when I rang her.

Cathy told me about what had happened after Vince woke her that morning at Barrow Creek. She also commented on Joanne's impassiveness – but she did say that after Joanne bent to pat her dog outside the bathroom, Cathy thought she saw a tear in her eye as she straightened up. 'It was the only time I ever saw her show any emotion, after what was supposed to have happened,' Cathy said.

Then Rick phoned from Barrow Creek and said a letter had arrived there for me. Intrigued, I asked him to forward it. When it arrived a few days later, I turned it over, checking for a return address, but all that was written on the back was 'THE AVENGING ANGEL'.

Feeling rather wobbly, I bought some fine rubber gloves from the chemist, took it home and opened it carefully at our dining table. There were pages and pages. They were from Adam, the kooky Melbourne clairvoyant. He'd been ringing me ever since we left Alice Springs, and he now said he'd elicited 'new and more accurate information' at a special 'brainstorm' he'd organised with some like-minded friends.

'Let's see what the brains trust has come up with,' Clive said as he took the pages.

Later that night, while we sat on our balcony watching the yachts at anchor, Clive said quietly, 'He's pretty close to the other two, you know. Perhaps we should have had a better look at that Neutral Junction site when we had the opportunity.'

About two weeks later, Glenn Morrison rang from the *Centralian Advocate* in Alice Springs. He said that Anna, the Aboriginal spirit woman, had phoned him from Perth saying a Sydney newspaper wanted her to fly to Alice Springs and help them look for Peter's body. She wanted his advice. She was wary of city journalists and fearful because she believed she knew who the killer was and thought he was still in the neighbourhood.

'Why don't we fly her in?' Clive said after I told him about the call. 'It really is strange that one person in Darwin, one in Melbourne and one in Perth are all saying he's in almost the same location. And they don't know what we know. One: Murdoch told you he has an intermediate link with the previous owner of Neutral Junction. And two: what about the fourteen kilometres?'

'But how can we organise a dig from here?' I protested.

'We can't. We'll have to go back.'

'Go back!'

'What if he's there, Rob? You'll never forgive yourself.'

'But the round trip is five thousand kilometres.'

'Never mind. We'll have another opportunity to stay at Barrow Creek.'

We made the necessary arrangements with Anna, boarded out our bewildered dog, packed up the car and headed back to Alice Springs.

'I hope Chris Tangey will help us,' I said to Clive as we set off. 'We need someone as crazy as we are on this expedition.'

Chapter Twenty-Eight

THE DIG

If you could bring me a body, I'd be very happy.

Rex Wild QC, Director of Public Prosecutions, Darwin

Before we left, I obtained a faxed copy of the Victorian regulations on how to conduct a forensic retrieval of a body. We wanted to follow the procedures as best we could.

We timed our arrival in Alice to coincide with Anna's flight from Perth and found her at the airport. She was accompanied by a big middle-aged bloke, whom she introduced only as Max* and described as a 'good friend' who lived in Alice Springs.

Max is a cop, I thought. Probably retired. 'Why would she feel she needs a bodyguard?' I asked Clive as we followed them into town. Max had Victorian plates on his sedan, which made me suspicious.

In the motel bar, we prepared our plan of action with Chris Tangey and Kathleen, the Barrow Creek spirit woman who had become close to Anna. My job next day was to buy fluoro tape and stakes for cordoning the dig area, an extra shovel, film, water containers and food for a picnic lunch. Meanwhile, Chris would prepare his site-search equipment, metal detectors, satellite phone, ropes, shovels, buckets and all the other bits. I gave everyone written instructions on the procedures we needed to follow.

Glenn Morrison wanted to come along. I was anxious about this, but I could hardly refuse. I trusted Glenn; it was his 'membership' of News Limited that bothered me. If we did find anything, I wanted to make sure the police found out before it hit the media. But Glenn gave his word, and I accepted it.

Kathleen had to work on Friday, so we could not leave until dawn on Saturday. I phoned Barrow Creek to book rooms for us all on Saturday night. I wanted to make sure that the two Aboriginal women would be made welcome. Rick was pleased to hear from us and told us it would be fine.

On Friday, I made enough sandwiches to feed an army, using the motel dressing table as a bench. Kathleen had said she'd bring along a few men from her family to help with the digging. We bought big drums for water and made sure everything was easily accessible in the car. Anna and Kathleen obviously shared a strong bond, and both were nervous. Anna had elected to stay with Kathleen, and we thought they were probably preparing themselves for the dig. Max was coming too. I wondered if he had a gun. Chris Tangey was bringing a rifle 'just in case'.

Charlie had already given us permission to dig, but Kathleen still had to seek permission from the Kaytetye elders at Barrow Creek. There are protocols that need to be followed when intruding on traditional land, and we'd be in trouble if the elders refused. I was counting on their support for their tradition that people take their spiritual power from the land, so that after death their spirits need to be returned to their own country.

While the women talked with the elders, the rest of us assembled at the gate to Neutral Junction. I made my first note in my log:

'Conditions windy, overcast, temp. about 16 degrees Celsius.'

We made quite a party: Clive, Chris and me; Glenn and a cadet journalist who had begged to come; Kathleen's son and daughter, and a friend of the son. Max was with the two women.

When they joined us, Anna was sweating and shaking. Clive treated her with great consideration. For a confirmed cynic, he was amazingly respectful of the tradition and culture that had led us this far. Everyone was a bit antsy, each for our own reasons. What if we found Peter?

After shuddering slowly along the corrugations, Max's car in the lead stopped just out of sight of the creek bed. He ambled back to us, second in line, and said the women had to perform a little ceremony.

Kathleen and Anna approached the fallen tree beside the main creek bed, which was just out of sight beyond a bend. Kathleen sat quietly. She told me later that she was communicating with her ancestors – 'the aunties' – telling them that we were about to disturb the land, looking for a body. It was permissible to do this because, if Peter was there, he needed to be returned to his own country. But the aunties had to be kept informed anyway.

Anna had a different mission. She was a stranger like Peter, far from her own country. But we would be disturbing the area beside the creek bed, and in Aboriginal culture, every waterway has its own spirit. She picked up some sand and threw it into the empty creek-bed to attract the attention of the river spirit. Then she and Kathleen held hands while Anna asked the spirit's permission for us to disturb his country.

Once the women were satisfied, the rest of us moved in and set up the dig. Based on Anna's directions, Clive and Chris pegged out a site ten metres square with hot-pink tape and garden stakes. In the middle was the huge fallen blue gum. The men eyed the tree and their shovels with some dismay, but no digging could be done until Chris ran his metal detector over the site and I took photos.

My job was to record the scene, itemise the time and location of any discoveries and keep a log. Because of a shoulder injury, I couldn't dig – and I wasn't sorry. The other women were afraid to dig because of their fear of the dead, so they set themselves up in the shady creek bed in our folding chairs. Kathleen's son and his mate took a rifle and went off in search of kangaroos, and Max mumbled something about an old back injury. So that left Clive, Chris and Glenn to move tonnes of hardened red dirt – and the remains of a twenty-metre blue gum.

We marked all the metal finds with tent pegs and more pink tape, and then the men began digging. Anna had a strong feeling that Peter had first been taken to a building in the vicinity, so she and I decided to drive along to the Neutral Junction 'farm house' and see if anything struck a chord with her. On the way, we passed the track that led to the Aboriginal outstation.

'Kathleen's mob,' Anna told me, nodding at the track. 'They'll be down later, to check us out, no worries.'

I asked how they would know we were there. 'They'll know. Bush telegraph.'

As we approached a bend, she said, 'Stop here! When we go round this corner there will be big machines, earthmovers or really big machinery over there on the right. I can feel it. I'm sure this is the place.'

Sure enough, as we rounded the bend, there was a huge shed on our right, filled with heavy earthmoving machinery. We could use some of that down the road, I thought, but I couldn't help feeling a frisson of something, knowing Anna had got it right. Ahead of us was a miniature village with about twelve buildings – houses, work sheds, a little schoolhouse, huge water tanks, a tall bell-tower to warn of fire or call the hands for meals, a clinic (identified by a faded red cross on the door) and a lawn like a village green. We couldn't see anyone about, so we parked and began going from house to house. The place was deserted. Most of the buildings were wide open. Either there was nothing worth stealing or they'd already been ransacked.

'I'll bang on each door and call out,' I told Anna, 'and if no one answers, you can duck inside and see if you can feel anything.' Anna was nervous, but keen to test her theory.

'Cooee!' I yelled at each door. 'Anyone home?' When there was no reply, Anna slipped inside, testing her senses, seeking some indication that we might be in the right place, while I kept lookout at the front.

We visited all the buildings except the clinic and a large house near the school, fenced and protected by a huge Rottweiler. 'That might be the boss's place, I reckon,' I told Anna. 'I don't fancy taking on the dog – what do you think? Do you have any special powers with dogs?' Anna was scared of dogs, so we wandered over to the heavy equipment shed. There, almost hidden in the darkened recesses of the interior, were two men fiddling with a truck chassis. They told us they were fencing contractors who'd come to fence the property off from the new Adelaide–Darwin railroad, which ran through Neutral Junction. Their post-hole digger had broken down, so they were filling in time helping out at the homestead. I asked if their dozer still worked. It did. I filed away that information, in case.

No wiser about where Peter might have been held captive, we rejoined the others. The three diggers were hot, sweaty and making a surprising impression on the site. The young Aboriginal men returned from their hunt. To them, the dig was our project, so they did not join in. Lunch came and went, and the hot sun poured down from a cloudless sky. Clive requested first aid for his blistered hands, and they soldiered on. Anna hovered, pointing or suggesting, conferring with Clive, or sitting in the sandy creek-bed, trying to get closer to Peter. No kookaburras made an appearance, although a few magpies watched from branches nearby.

By 4 pm, the men were talking of calling it quits for the day. Chris and Glenn were a good twenty years younger than Clive, and even they were whacked. 'I vote we get the men with the dozer,' I suggested. The niceties of the procedure manual were being overcome by necessity. Although we planned to stay overnight at Barrow Creek, most of our party had to leave by lunchtime next day. At this rate, we'd need two weeks – and lots more manpower.

So I was delegated to go and persuade the manager, Mick, to abandon his Saturday-afternoon footy game on TV – before the final siren – to come and help a bunch of crazy city slickers dig for a body that he was certain was not there. I took a couple of chicken sandwiches for the dog and a six-pack for Mick, and headed back up the corrugations. The dog was a pussycat once he smelled the sandwiches, and he licked me all the way to the front door.

Mick was a good sport and pulled on his boots. Said he'd be there shortly, and he was. In no time, he scraped the old tree out of our way and levelled the dirt down to match the creek bank on the other side.

'That's more like it,' Chris said. 'Now we're starting from where whoever buried him would have started.' In spite of his labours, he was still confident. Every expedition needs an optimist.

I passed beers around and we sat on stumps and dirt piles, looking at the big red hundred-square-metre scar awaiting our efforts. I sat beside Kathleen's son, who had been educated interstate at boarding school and had been a rising football star before stress fractures wrecked his feet.

'It's going to get dark soon,' I said, making conversation. 'We'll have to watch out for the Kadaitcha man' (the spirit-person who avenges dead souls).

'He's over there in that bush,' the young man said, motioning to the far creek bank. 'He's been watching us all day. He followed us when we went hunting – that's why we didn't get kangaroos. He's out there, man. Don't mention his name after dark.'

I stared hard at the bush he'd indicated. Try as I could, I saw nothing. But I felt prickly. I didn't believe, but I wasn't brave enough to scoff.

By contrast, the dining room of the Barrow Creek Hotel was a brash, white, Ocker environment. Rick had prepared meals fit for dishing up at the Ritz, and we were all starving. Then, halfway through our meal, a big fierce-looking Aboriginal man came to the doorway and motioned to Kathleen to follow him outside. Anna made to go too, but Clive restrained her. He knew from our previous visit that this man was a big shot in the local mob. It was better not to argue, but if any arguing needed doing, he'd do it, since Kathleen's son had gone home to Alice.

We all watched Kathleen's dinner get cold while we strained to hear the dressing-down she was getting outside. Eventually, chastened but defiant, she returned and finished her meal. She later told me she'd 'copped it' because she was in a whitefella's hotel eating with all of

us when her family was outside, not allowed to eat in the dining room
or drink in the pub. She'd explained it would have been rude to knock
back our hospitality. Besides, she was hungry after a hard day at the
creek.

Next day we were all up at daybreak. We arrived at the site too early
even for bird chatter, and the air felt cool and damp on our exposed
skin. Chris, Glenn and Clive were soon being watched by a delegation
of about ten people from the community up near Neutral Junction. The
three of them kept at it for a couple of hours, looking for a 'forked root'
that Anna said would lead us to Peter. Just when they were flagging,
a forked root appeared. They dug down to a big damp patch in the
ground, isolated from the surrounding soil and of a different texture.
Had Peter's body been here and then been moved? The damp patch
was hard to explain. I did not think of taking any samples, and cursed
myself later for the oversight.

Chris and Glenn left about 11 am, and we were joined by a pair of
travelling lady yodellers we'd met in the Barrow Creek bar the night
before. The site took on an atmosphere of its own, with the Aboriginal
family group changing and feeding babies, kids playing around and
the men watching Clive labour on alone. Kathleen had moved away
down the creek bed, because one of the men present was someone
her culture did not allow her to speak to, and Max and I entertained
the lady yodellers while Anna directed Clive's shovel.

Then Anna picked up the shovel Chris had left and began digging.
She dug almost desperately, convinced Peter was there and afraid
Clive would throw in the towel. Although they uncovered a network of
roots from the mighty fallen tree, Peter's body did not appear.

By 3 pm, Clive could dig no longer. 'What a hero you are,' I said as
he mopped rivulets of sweat from his reddened face with a towel.

'Such a gentleman too. Poor Anna. She's going to be devastated.'
She was. She would not leave the site with us, or even with Max, who
had to return for an appointment in Alice. Setting aside her fears for
her own safety, she told Max to phone Kathleen's son from Barrow

Creek to come and collect her and Kathleen; they would stay on for three hours or so until the young people got there.

The watchers from the community had disappeared, and we reluctantly left the two women alone, with two shovels and our remaining water. We were heading back towards the coast the next day, but planned to stay one more night at our favourite pub. At sunset, a dusty car pulled in carrying Kathleen, Anna and a few young people. They joined us on the veranda for a cup of tea and a sandwich. Anna was subdued and sad. Kathleen was pragmatic.

'We might come back next weekend, have another look,' she told me. 'He must go back home. If he's there, we'll get him back to his mother.'

She took my arm and gently pulled me aside. 'That book you're writing. Will you put this in? We don't want to find Peter for a big story, or for any gain to us, you know. Our family here is very angry that someone done this terrible thing to him, on our land, in our country. We have responsibility to get him home, if we can. He won't rest here. This is not his country. All we want is for his spirit to rest in peace.'

I nodded. I already knew why they were there.

Clive and I waved them off into the spectacular sunset, black arms and white grins flashing as they pulled away. The two days we'd spent together might have been fruitless, but were definitely not a waste of time.

Chapter Twenty-Nine

THE DOG FACTOR

Where are the footprints? Where is the dog?

Assistant Commissioner John Daulby

After a brief sojourn at Airlie Beach, we drove back to Melbourne by way of several planned stops: Terrigal on the central coast of New South Wales, to check out the 'sighting' of Peter at the beach; Newcastle, to see Barry Boettcher; Sydney, to visit the bookshop where Joanne worked and to meet a friend of Murdoch's; and Canberra, where I'd made contact with a profiler who it was rumoured had done some work on the Falconio case.

While we drove, one of the puzzles that preoccupied us was what we called the 'dog factor'.

The tale of the dog seemed to begin in Alice Springs, when Peter noticed Rod Smith's blue heeler and asked what kind of dog he was. The next sighting of a dog was in the gunman's four-wheel drive as he pulled up.

Joanne told Martin Bashir, 'He put the sack over my head and pushed me through the passenger door of his vehicle … His dog was there, which didn't make a sound.' But something about this didn't jell. If the vehicle had bucket seats with a space between them (as she said) and the gunman had pushed her into the passenger seat, where was the dog sitting? On the handbrake? In the driver's seat? Up on the centre console? To have been visible when the man pulled alongside, the dog must have been on the passenger seat. So did he move over for Joanne before the gunman pushed her in? And to get to the space between the seats, she would have to push the dog out of the way – with her hands tied behind her.

I phoned Luke Hura, who has a business, training animals for TV and film roles, and owns a blue heeler himself. He told me, 'It would be a very unusual blue heeler that allowed her to push him around. Normally, blue heelers that travel with their owners are very protective, one-person dogs. It would be more likely to have a go at her than let her push it out of the way. It's the dog's space, as he sees it.'

Many people were incredulous that the dog did not find Joanne, but Luke said, 'Unless the dog was trained – for example, knew a command for "find" – it might have just jumped around, thinking it was some kind of game. But if it was trained to find, it would have found her in a flash.'

Another puzzling factor was the alleged lack of dog hair on Joanne's clothes. So far, no one had mentioned finding any dog hairs, even when pressed about it. Luke confirmed that heelers shed a lot of hair. Anyone wriggling across a seat where a dog had been would have to get hairs on their clothes. So why were there no hairs on Joanne's clothes, or on the sticky tapes from around her ankles and neck?

Near the bathroom at Barrow Creek she'd stopped to pat Cathy Curly's dog, also a blue heeler, and asked what kind of dog it was. Soon after, she described just such a dog to police. And what about Vince's jumper, which did have blue heeler hairs on it?

If there were blue heeler hairs on Joanne, that would seem to let Murdoch off the hook, because his dog was a Dalmatian.

During one of their visits to Joanne in England, the police had shown her a compendium of dog breeds of the world and asked her to pick out the dog she thought was similar to the gunman's. She said later in court that she'd picked the Australian cattle dog by its 'size, width, build, shape of face and ears'. Although the colouring of the dog in the book was 'not exact', being dark blackish brown with a black muzzle, it most resembled the dog she saw, which was 'brown and white with patches of dark colour'.

Finally, there was the question posed by the Aboriginal trackers –
why were there no signs of the dog? Dogs that travel long distances
are used to taking advantage of any stops by the roadside to relieve
themselves.

Luke told me, 'You would expect this dog, having been in a warm
car, being let out beside the road in the cool of the night, would pee
straight away. A male dog would mark the bushes as well, while he
was walking around.' So trackers should have found prints in the
sand, claw marks in the red dirt, or traces of hair on branches. But
they found nothing.

'That's really strange,' Luke said. John Daulby thought so too, and
said so to Scottish TV. So did Brian Bates, who is a dog person himself.
He told me, 'The investigators had difficulty with the dog – it was an
unknown, not a fact. We had to keep asking, what facts do we have?
How can we pursue those?'

David Jones had helped out from time to time at the Barrow Creek
pub, and knew the men from the Barrow Creek mob pretty well. They
told him they'd been out looking at the site unofficially on several
occasions and had never seen a single sign that a dog had been there.

We would just have to wait to see what came out at the committal
hearing. If there truly had been no dog hairs on Joanne's clothes, that
would add to the mystery, because Murdoch owned the Dalmatian,
which also sheds. If there were blue heeler hairs, they could have
been from Vince's dog, Cathy's dog or the gunman's dog, but not
Murdoch's. If there were Dalmatian hairs, Murdoch had some
explaining to do.

Late September on the east coast of Australia is notorious for
changeable weather. We arrived in Terrigal on a blustery afternoon.
I phoned the number I had for William Smith, the retired commando,
and got a message telling me the number was no longer connected.
We found his address, but neighbours told us he had moved a few

weeks before. There was no forwarding address, and no help at the post office, either.

I'd been intrigued by the details in the file I'd collected from Mark Twiggs. Mr Smith had written a number of letters or statements, supported by photos, vehicle number plates, detailed descriptions and little notes. Of particular interest to me was the description of a very tall man whom Smith claimed to have seen during August 2001, long before Murdoch had been arrested, but during a time when he'd dropped out of sight in Broome.

Smith claimed that on 30 August 2001 at about 9 am, he was sitting in his car above Terrigal Beach when he saw a young man answering Peter Falconio's description walking a black-and-white kelpie.

Smith said to the young man, 'You get a good view from up here, but I'm thinking it's too rough for fishing.' The man replied pleasantly and politely. He was wearing a Sloppy Joe with the letters FE on it; Smith later said it was the same top Peter Falconio had worn in a photo taken on top of Ayers Rock.

Then a man about six feet four inches tall, whom Smith described as looking like the photos published of the man in the truck-stop stills without the long hair and moustache, drove up in a white four-wheel-drive HiLux and got out. 'He said in an angry voice "What are you doing out here? Get in the car, quick."'

According to Smith, 'Peter' replied, 'Oh, he's all right.'

The driver repeated his instructions to get into the car, then picked up the dog and put it in the rear of the HiLux. 'Peter' got in, and they drove off. William followed at a discreet distance and noted the address where the car had parked. He later returned with his camera and took several photos of the car and the house, which were in his file. None of 'Peter', though.

We found the house in question. Smith had told me he'd spent several hours sitting in his car outside, observing 'Peter' there. Now, no one was home. Neighbours told me that a group of young people had lived there for a while, but they had moved on, and now there was a young couple and a small child. No one recognised a newspaper photo I showed them of Peter.

'Brr! I've got goosebumps on my suntan. What a waste of time,' I told Clive as I eased my damp body into the car.

'Well, we had to check, Rob. What if he had been here?'

'Oh, well. I'm looking forward to Sydney tomorrow. Bright lights, big shops, nice restaurants – I can't wait.'

Detouring via Newcastle, we caught up with Barry Boettcher. I was keen to find out how long DNA would last on a steering wheel, but I had to avoid giving the game away, so I framed a hypothetical question. 'If Clive and I took our car to be serviced and the mechanic drove it, could you pick up the mechanic's DNA a couple of weeks later?' 'Quite likely,' Barry replied. 'Skin cells could find their way into the cracks where the spokes join the wheel and stay there for quite a long time. And a mechanic would have roughish hands, which would be more likely to shed cells.'

The 'best spanner man in the Kimberley' would have rough hands, I thought.

I also told Barry that the DNA had been on the back of Joanne's T-shirt, and we speculated about how it could have got there.

'Being on the back makes it more likely that it could have been an accidental transfer,' Barry said. 'Someone could easily have brushed up against her in a crowd. Do we know if Murdoch went to the Camel Cup?'

'Not sure. Police trawled twenty-four videos for a glimpse of him, with no luck, I believe. He told me that Hepi might have given the police one of his shirts with his blood on it, and they could have wet it and dripped the residue on her shirt. Could DNA be transferred like that?'

'It could. It probably would,' Barry said.

'But that theory doesn't hold water,' Clive cut in, 'because we know they got the DNA within twenty-four hours of the incident, and

Murdoch wasn't named until ten months later. So how could he have been set up that way?'

And how did the same DNA get on that steering wheel? I telegraphed silently to Clive, who could tell exactly what I was thinking.

◆ ◆ ◆

The rotten weather followed us to Sydney, so shopping was off the agenda. Anyway, we still had no room in the car, although we'd left the folding chairs at Airlie Beach. I think our luggage breeds at night.

I went into town to look for Dymocks in George Street, fighting a wicked wind, horizontal sleet and traffic so murderous that it made me yearn for Barrow Creek and the odd wandering cow. I could see lots of books in a window display, but the store itself seemed to have disappeared. Then I spotted a doorway leading to a descending staircase. Dymocks at last!

Gary Sullivan was not expecting me, but he made time for a short interview in his office, which was tucked under the footpath. He spoke of how the media had ambushed Joanne when she returned to work; I could see it would have been hard to get past them down those steps. Photographers also camped out in the coffee shop behind the store, giving Joanne no respite.

Paul Falconio had been a great support to Joanne, and Gary's brother, who was overseas, had lent the two of them his house for a few weeks. Gary said Joanne's girlfriends had been very loyal to her and had refused all interviews; he added that they probably wouldn't talk to me either. I later found out he was right.

He described how Joanne had come to work there. 'She was determined to get a job here, although we were not looking for staff. She came in for a few days running, pestering me to give her some work. Finally, some of the younger men began pressuring me too! She was very well groomed and a bit of a party girl. She became very popular – and was good at her job too.'

He told me about Joanne's most recent visit, when she told him she'd chosen Martin Bashir because he'd interviewed Princess Diana. 'I don't think she's very pleased with him now, though,' Gary added. 'I think he dwelt a bit too much on the perceived discrepancies in her story for her liking.'

Gary was still in touch with Joanne, as were her other friends from the shop, but the barrier they'd erected around her showed no sign of cracking.

◆ ◆ ◆

One of my most important interviews was scheduled for Sydney – a session with Jazz, who'd worked with Murdoch and Hepi in Broome. Julie had put me in touch with her, and we'd arranged to meet at a shopping complex near Ryde, a middle-class suburb I hadn't visited for twenty-five years. A lot of new roads had been built during that time, and I soon got lost. I was trying to extricate myself from a freeway that was promising me an express journey to Wollongong when my mobile shrilled and I recognised Jazz's number. I was terrified she'd changed her mind, so I had to answer. With one hand on the wheel and all my fingers crossed, I cajoled her into keeping our appointment. After I parked, I risked an extra couple of minutes to buy her a big bunch of lilies, and that started us off on a happy footing. We got coffees and settled in for a chat.

Jazz was thin and tense. I couldn't estimate her age from her looks, but from her life history I put her in her early thirties. She told me how her itinerant lifestyle had taken her to Broome, where she got a job at the Divers Tavern. She soon met James Hepi, who was driving a taxi and was well known as a supplier of high-class hydro. Jazz was a smoker, and would often top up her supplies while catching his taxi home after her shift. Later, she and Hepi became closer friends, and she was a regular visitor at the Forrest Street house he shared with Murdoch.

She'd met Murdoch independently, outside the bakery where Julie worked. She said he rarely drank alcohol, but was a heavy smoker –

'PJ Virginias, I think.' He usually wore work clothes – Stubbies shorts and blue singlets, or cut-off Yakka shirts and thongs. 'He always wore thongs,' she told me. 'Probably found it hard to find shoes to fit his size-thirteen feet!'

On sultry Broome evenings at Forrest Street, she'd often share a joint with the two men, and eventually Hepi invited her to take over the drug distribution in Broome while he and Murdoch did the runs from South Australia. To acquaint her with the perils of the trip, he invited her along on the next run. She travelled to Sedan and back with Hepi between 26 August and 6 September 2001. 'I don't remember where Brad was at the time,' she told me. 'I'm not sure if he was in Broome or not. The trip took about forty hours, driving over two and a half days. We stayed for about four days in Sedan.

'I remember on the second night I was there, I got really cold. I asked James if he had any warm clothes, and he said there was a bag of his clothes in a corner in one of the rooms and told me to help myself. I went through a green garbage bag and found an XL white or pale blue fleecy windcheater. It was fairly old and faded, with a round elasticised neck and wrists. The waist was also elastic, but it was stretched out of shape. I didn't put it on, but I held it up to James and asked, "Whose clothes are these?" He said, "They're mine."

'I thought it was odd, because there was a faded logo of a red heart with two little hands and a caption in black writing under the logo that said, "Try hugs, not drugs".' She laughed. It certainly was a bit of a joke, considering.

I had a feeling I'd seen a photo of Joanne in a top with that logo on it. Did she and Peter have a matching set?

'What else was in the bag?' I asked.

'Well, the bag smelt really musty and mouldy,' she said. 'A lot of the clothes needed washing, and the sweatshirt particularly. It had like grease stains or reddish-brown stains like pindan [the red dirt of central Australia] on the front, and they went right through the material. There were a couple of other flannel shirts, cut-off sleeve woollen vests, pairs of jeans, jumpers and a brown suede wool-lined vest that I wore while I was in South Australia.' She said the New South Wales police had asked her about these clothes when she had made a statement after leaving Broome.

'I wasn't going to make any statements in Broome,' she told me.

'I don't trust anyone up there now. So they organised two cops from Ryde to come and see me when I got here.'

'So how long did you work for Hepi in Broome?' I asked her. 'About three weeks after that trip to Sedan, I moved into Forrest Street and took over the hydro sales and a few amphetamines they were selling. After that, Brad and James weren't at Forrest Street much. Only one would be there at a time, because they'd alternate on road trips. They'd stay three or four days, get the cars checked, collect the money from me and go again. But in the first week of October, for some reason, they were both there for about a week.

'One night, we were sitting in the kitchen having dinner and discussing the business. I said, "Why don't we do some Es?" [Ecstasy] because Es were popular in Broome. James got quite angry. I can't remember his exact words, but he said there'd been a f--k-up in the Northern Territory earlier in the year and he didn't want to go there again. Brad didn't say anything, so I dropped it.'

'Wait a minute! A "f--k-up in the Northern Territory"? Can you remember anything more about that? Did James or Brad ever bring stuff up the Stuart Highway?'

'Not that I can remember. They never made contact with me once they left Sedan. They could have driven by any route. And don't forget, I was only fronting for them for about three months, and soon after Billy Gibbs got done and James came and threw me out.

'But I do know I never saw Brad with a gun. He might have had one, but I never saw it. James had one, a .357 stainless-steel pistol with a rotating barrel. He gave me a spent cartridge and a live round that I've still got.'

The 'f--k-up' in the Northern Territory really interested me. I'd always thought Hepi looked more like Joanne's description of the gunman than Murdoch did. I wondered out loud if maybe Peter had been talked into carrying some drugs for Hepi, agreeing to the job without Joanne's knowledge and the handover had gone sour. Maybe Murdoch had been there, but not alone.

'I really don't know,' Jazz told me. 'One thing I have thought of. I can't remember exactly when, but James was stressing about a bed he'd ordered from a furniture place in Sydney. It was one of those fake antique iron beds, imported from Thailand I think, and he was worrying because the four corner posts were stuffed with drugs and the bed was delayed arriving. It did arrive eventually. Didn't Joanne and Peter come to Australia through Thailand? Maybe that's a link?'

I felt a bit prickly. Jazz probably didn't know that Peter had worked in at least one furniture factory in Sydney. Was this why the police had asked Paul Dale whether Peter had worked at another furniture factory? Perhaps they had discovered that he was working there from his tax return, which they had tracked down in a Darwin accountant's office.

'And one other thing,' Jazz said as we were getting up to leave.

'When I saw the announcement on TV of Brad being arrested in South Australia, the police laid out a lot of stuff from Barrow Creek, and I'm sure I saw that shirt.'

'What shirt?' I asked, my mind still full of iron beds.

'The shirt I found at Sedan. I'm sure it was the same shirt. Now, where would the cops have got that? Did Brad have it with him when they grabbed him? Or was it from Barrow Creek? I'm not sure.'

I hadn't seen that footage, but it was another detail to remember.

Chapter Thirty

LOOSE ENDS

It ain't over till it's over.

Lenny Kravitz

Bob*, the profiler we saw in Canberra, was not much help, mainly because he had worked (unofficially) on Joanne's interview tapes and did not want to be identified or quoted. The most interesting thing to come out of our discussion was the difference in our views about whether Murdoch was likely to have been the gunman.

Murdoch struck me as a careful, organised man who took big risks hoping for minimum consequences: the well-maintained four-wheel drive; the secret compartments; exchangeable number plates; reversible canopies; off-road routes; mobile phone silence – almost paranoid security. I had also been told that he was kind to women, did not engage in unusual sex practices, and was an all-round good bloke in the eyes of many.

In a letter to me, he'd said:

> *I know I have been a bit of a rat-bag at times and I know I have smacked a few people under the ear, only people that have deserved it though. I am a bit rough around the edges at times, but my principles are in the right place. I knew when you came to visit me in Yatala that you were not sure. You came to see a person of average size and shoulder length hair and were confronted by a 6'4", crew cut, fully tattooed arms, which to most people is intimidating. It is something that I have had to live with for many years and people that look past that find a gentle,*

kind person with some hard principles that won't stand for any bull.

Even the Broome police had told me he had never been in trouble up there. He claimed he'd been set up on the South Australian charges, and I was getting closer to believing him on that score. The Northern Territory police would not be pleased if he got off. If Murdoch was convicted in South Australia, there would suddenly be a 'pattern' of irregular sexual behaviour by a depraved predator who kidnapped and raped little girls – a prime candidate for attempting to abduct Joanne Lees.

I put it to the profiler that the crime seemed out of character for Murdoch. It did not seem opportunistic, because the intricate manacles must have been prepared in advance. Therefore, the gunman must have chosen her, followed them, lured Peter out, murdered him, tied her up so ineffectually that she was able to escape – while he busied himself doing something – and then left her. After all that trouble and risk, you'd think he'd persevere longer than an hour or so. And why take Peter's body? Why not leave it with the Kombi?

'Murdoch is a very careful man,' I said to Bob. 'He's not a risk taker. Why would he pull them over on a national highway, on a long straight stretch, and take one risk after another for a bit of sex? If it was Murdoch, he probably had a drug load on board – an even bigger risk. Not to mention hauling away the body.'

But as Bob saw it, the gunman was minimising risk. He would have deliberately chosen a long clear stretch of road where he could see approaching vehicles. He abandoned his search for Joanne because he wanted to reduce the risk of someone pulling up to check on them. He took the body so the bullet could not be identified, and probably disposed of it in a disused mineshaft or out on a track somewhere, which indicated a knowledge of the area and confidence in his ability to avoid detection. All very careful behaviour, in Bob's view.

'But the deed itself was crazy,' I persisted. 'Why interrupt his journey to take such a risk?'

Bob felt that Joanne's story might not fully reflect what had happened. After all, she was the only witness, and police had to take her at face value. One of his roles was to assess whether they should accept her version of events on that night. He had been the first person to raise the question of mental illness. He had watched the hours of taped interviews and told the Northern Territory police they should check on Joanne's background.

Some of the footage he'd watched included the three-and-a-half-hour interview done with Joanne when NT police still thought she may have been involved. In the months after the murder, Alice Springs police had struggled to cope with the enormity of the murder case – which mysteriously involved no body.

'We had nothing, some of it [Ms Lees's testimony] seemed a bit surreal, some of it didn't add up initially,' said a former chief investigator Colleen Gwynne on a *60 Minutes* program. And, like with the media in the absence of information you tend to start wandering off and having your own theories … [police] are human too.

The night before Ms Lees was due to leave Alice Springs, police called her in at 8.30 pm and interrogated her for three-and-a-half hours.

'I started to question myself and doubt myself, I guess that was a police tactic,' Gwynne said.

Joanne was furious about the interview. 'I think they were hoping I would confess to something I hadn't done. It was like a stab to the heart, how could they think that?' she told *60 Minutes*.

We headed home, not much the wiser. Having been on the road for three months, I now had a lot of 'desk research' to do. This meant preparing a list of things I needed to know and people who might tell me, then pestering the hell out of them on the phone. The groans from Clive's office when the phone bills came in were a measure of my enthusiasm for following up loose ends.

I'd sent all the truck-stop measurements to Gale Spring, but the camera's focal length was still a sticking point. I contacted Shane Ride, who had installed the cameras, but the details he gave me didn't help. The camera was an old one and could have had several different focal lengths. I wanted to find out for sure if the man in the truck-stop video was Murdoch, and I wondered if it might be possible to approach it another way. I'd been reading a book by forensic pathologist Bill Bass, who developed methods of estimating height by measuring long bones. Gale told me a Professor Henneberg at Adelaide University might be able to help, so I made contact and asked him if he'd be prepared to have a look, then asked Gale to forward the information to him.

I made contact with former Commissioner Brian Bates, who was celebrating his retirement by trekking around Australia in a caravan with his wife. He and I spoke frequently, and I pictured him answering his mobile beside a beach or a river, while I was back at my desk. We agreed to have lunch when he reached Melbourne. We met under the clock at Flinders Street station and wandered over the road to Young & Jackson's hotel.

'This brings back memories of the days when I was a young constable on the beat,' he told me. 'I used to patrol right outside there, in Swanston Street.'

He confirmed that the handling of the truck-stop video had been a bit of a stuff-up. 'Somebody wasn't astute enough to realise the importance of it,' he told me. 'We should have got the whole CCTV kit and kept the better photos, but it was too late after a few days. They'd been recorded over. Then we tried every method imaginable to get the ones we had enhanced, but you can't improve much on a basically lousy picture.'

He also confirmed that they'd had Joanne Lees under surveillance. 'In a very early briefing it was viewed as important that we maintained contact – as close as actually living with her. We got a listening device order a day or so into the investigation, by phone, I think. It's quite easy in the Northern Territory. That's why Libby Andrews moved into the motel. We also had Joanne under surveillance after she moved to Sydney.'

'What, actually being followed?'

He smiled. 'That's what surveillance is. And we monitored her calls, just in case she made contact with anyone – more to rule her out than rule her in. But she never did make contact with anyone suspicious. It was a fine line between not being sold a dummy story and taking her story at face value.'

'It is a fine line,' I agreed. 'If she'd been a shrinking violet, she would have attracted more sympathy. As it was, she was defiant and uncooperative, and people perhaps read more into that than they should have.'

'You're right. I'll never forget the first time I met her. I'd flown down to try to persuade her to appear on TV, and I walked into the coffee lounge where she was sitting with Kate Vanderlaan. She looked up and said, "I don't want to hear anything from you unless it's about how you're going to find Peter," and then she looked away and tried to ignore me.'

It sounded as if he'd been taken aback by her attitude. 'You couldn't talk to her like you and I are talking now,' he said.

'Although I explained to her the importance of having the victim involved with the public and using the media to spread the word, she did not once look me in the eye. She was twisting around, trying to see who was in the coffee lounge, never really paying attention. She clearly did not want to do it and was making her feelings quite plain. She was a strange girl. Very closed, very difficult to warm to.'

In the hope of finding out how much the investigation had cost, I contacted Mike Reed, the former Northern Territory treasurer and police minister. He confirmed that Brian Bates had been forced to seek additional funds from Treasury to cover the cost of the investigation.

This led me to believe that the cost would have been more than $1 million in the first six months, alone.

He said he had believed Joanne's story after being briefed by Bates. 'But I knew they'd had her under surveillance. I have no problem with that. I would expect as an individual and police minister that the police would conduct parallel inquiries if they thought it was necessary.'

I heard from the Freedom of Information Office in Darwin, saying I wasn't going to get my hands on the review report. Ongoing investigation, confidential information, subsection blah blah of Police Act. Daulby had already made selected passages public, but I knew they'd refuse to release the whole report. It had been worth a try, even if I'd lost the one-hundred-dollar deposit.

Chris Tangey had more luck with the Ombudsman, whose six-page reply finally arrived in February 2004. The report separated Chris's complaints into two broad areas – the treatment of the forensic examination of the Kombi and the treatment of Chris himself.

The Ombudsman explained that he was not going to discuss the forensic testing of the van. The DPP and the police commissioner had both expressed the view that the examination of the van was part of the ongoing prosecution of Murdoch, and it was not in the public interest to discuss the issue. The Ombudsman agreed, and said he would finalise Chris's complaints by providing his findings on the way Chris was treated by police.

He said he had taken sworn evidence from Bill Towers (now no longer in the police force), John Nixon, Kate Vanderlaan, John Daulby and Joy Kuhl. He had also called for various documents pertaining to Chris's complaint. He had formed the view that senior officers had given Bill Towers approval for Chris to film the van, and that this showed poor judgement:

Testing the capabilities of the low light camera to record luminol reactions should not have occurred on an unsolved high profile police investigation. In my view, it was incumbent on the police from the outset [to ensure] that the chain of evidence was protected and indeed, that police retained the prime evidentiary material.

His finding on this point was that the actions of police were wrong.

He then examined Chris's claim that he and Bill Towers had entered into a 'gentleman's agreement' that Chris could retain ownership of the video and use it as he wished after six months. It appears Bill Towers denied this, and the Ombudsman said the matter remained unresolved.

But the Ombudsman spent a page of his report saying that there should have been a clear written agreement about ownership of the video. He also felt it was a matter of concern that police had approached Chris to do the filming because they did not have the funds to carry out such an exercise themselves. It was 'unacceptable … that such an excuse should be used to carry out such a process', he wrote to Chris. 'The simple fact is that you would not have had any access … to videotape the forensic testing as it occurred unless you had been invited to do so by police. Police were entitled to and should have set appropriate conditions around such participation.'

His finding on this point was that the actions of police were wrong. He also took the view that the police had been 'overbearing and intimidating' in their attempts to obtain the master footage. He believed the threat by Kate Vanderlaan was probably prompted by her superiors ordering her to 'go and sort it out', and by her concern that public knowledge of the tape might lead to attacks on the credibility of the forensic examination.

The first call from Daulby, Commander Hardman and Dr Thatcher had been 'unnecessarily intimidatory', as had the second call from Daulby. He suggests the police used the 'bluff technique, which was never going to work with you'. (Though a lesser mortal would have crumbled.)

The Ombudsman felt the police actions demonstrated 'a breakdown in the chain of responsibility for the investigation itself', and concluded this part of his report by querying 'the lack of any definitive legal advice being obtained by senior police' as to what rights they had to secure the tape. His finding on this point was that the actions of police were unreasonable.

He had recommended to the commissioner that police who had been involved should be counselled on their responsibilities for ensuring a chain of evidence was protected. Chris should be sent a written apology for the 'intimidatory and unprofessional manner in which his senior officers had acted', and the commissioner should counsel them about their behaviour.

Before the report was sent to Chris, the commissioner had responded, saying the police had 'learnt a valuable lesson' and would 'ensure they don't make the same mistake in future'. He noted that Towers had left the police, and Daulby and Hardman were on 'extended leave without pay on overseas projects'. A copy of the report had been sent to Kate Vanderlaan, the only officer still on active police duty – unfortunately for her.

The Ombudsman concluded by telling Chris that he was recommending that 'should Assistant Commissioner Daulby, and/or Commander Hardman return to the Northern Territory Police, then they should be formally counselled on their return'.

He thought Kate Vanderlaan had been chastised enough, 'considering her involvement' and his inquiry was now at an end.

A victory for the independence of the Ombudsman's office – and for Chris Tangey.

◆ ◆ ◆

I decided it was time to get in touch with Murdoch's parents, to ask them about young Brad Murdoch before he grew into a big, tattooed man. Colin Murdoch was friendly and unstinting in his praise for his youngest son. He rambled through his recollections.

'He's never told a lie to us,' he said earnestly. 'I've got a idea in the back of my mind that Brad might know who did it. He told us, "The DNA is not mine. I was never within cooee of her." He told me he and Hepi were on the road that night – Hepi was driving about twenty minutes in front of him. It wasn't Brad who killed Falconio, but Brad thinks Hepi had something to do with it. He'd never say, though, because he's not a dobber – like some people,' he finished darkly.

I wrote in my notes: 'Both in the area at the time?? Were they? Did Hepi have something to do with Peter's disappearance? Was this the Northern Territory Ecstasy "f--k-up"?'

Murdoch had told me he'd stayed a few times at the Bolivar Gardens caravan park outside Adelaide, so I gave them a call. The manager said he remembered Murdoch. 'A pretty nice fellow, really, like a real Northern Territory outback type. He had a dog, that's one of the reasons he always stayed with us,' he told me.

'We're dog-friendly.'

'Do you remember what sort of dog?' I asked.

'Yeah, a Dalmatian. It was a very quiet dog, sat on the porch of the cabin he rented. That's why I got talking to him the first time. I was on my way past and admired the dog and we just chatted. I could never imagine him doing those things they say. I've followed the case pretty closely, you know. Peter Falconio and Joanne Lees stayed here too, so I was interested.'

'Joanne and Peter?'

'Yes. On their way up north. They camped almost outside my office window in their little red Kombi. I saw quite a bit of them while they were here. She was quite attractive, always well groomed.'

'How did they get on?' I asked him. 'Any arguments?' 'Not that I saw,' he replied.

'Could they have run into Brad Murdoch? Was he there at the same time?'

'I don't remember – and, before you ask, I can't look it up for you, because the South Australian police took all my records during the rape investigation. I still haven't got them back.'

'South Australian police, not Northern Territory police?' I repeated. Did the Territory police know about this possible convergence of the travellers' paths?

'Yes, I'm sure it was South Australian police. I don't know if Peter and Joanne met Murdoch. He wouldn't have been able to see her casually from his cabin – he'd be looking through at least two rows of cabins.'

I immediately shared this information with Clive.

'What if they did meet there?' I said excitedly. 'They were having trouble with their van – maybe he offered to have a look? He could've driven the van at the caravan park! That could explain the DNA on the steering wheel!'

'But why did he lie to you about Joanne, if that was the case?' Clive asked. 'He said he'd never set eyes on her. And he told his father the same thing.'

'But he might not have trusted me back then,' I said. 'And anyway, it might be the truth. Joanne might have been somewhere else that day. All along I've been thinking he knows something more about that night, but he's keeping his powder dry. Maybe this is it. He'd love to make the cops look silly.'

We put the FBI's list up on the whiteboard. 'If the intended victim was Joanne and the gunman was Murdoch, how would that list stack up?' I asked.

Clive starred several entries under the heading 'Organised':

> *Offence planned (police say) Victim is targeted stranger*
> *Restraints used*
> *Aggressive acts prior to death Weapons/evidence absent*
> *Transports victim (or tried to)*

But there were also quite a few stars for 'Disorganised':

> *Depersonalises victim (bag on head)*
> *Minimal conversation (instructions to Joanne Lees, talking to Peter Falconio)*

Crime scene random and sloppy (blood on road, open highway,
poor application of restraints, victim gets away)
Sudden violence to victim
Body left in view (Joanne left in bush)

'Six out of eleven for "Organised" and five out of eleven for "Dis-organised",' said Clive. 'If Murdoch is an organised, careful person, would he make so many out-of-character mistakes?'

'What if the intended victim was Peter? Or maybe not intended, but things got out of control, and then Joanne became the secondary victim – not even necessarily for sexual reasons, but to despatch her because she was a witness to Peter's murder. How would that look?'

This time, there were more signs of disorganisation:

Spontaneous → offence → Victim → or → location → known →
Minimal conversation
Crime scene random and sloppy sudden violence to victim
Minimal use of restraints

But there were still three entries under 'Organised':

Body hidden
Weapons/evidence absent
Transports victim

'That paints a different picture. It's much harder with two victims,' I sighed. 'There are so many different things to take into account, and we don't really know what we're doing.'

'Well, we'll just have to wait,' Clive said. 'You've done about as much as you can on your own. Now we have to see what the police have on Murdoch – and whether or not it stands up in court.'

Part Three

THE TRIALS OF BRADLEY MURDOCH

I was involved in getting my own skin off the line, but not in setting up Mr Murdoch.

James Hepi, Darwin, June 2004

Chapter Thirty-One

THE SOUTH
AUSTRALIAN STING

*This trial is a conspiracy of police in three
States against my client.*

Grant Algie, Adelaide, November 2003

Murdoch's trial on the abduction and rape charges began on 13 October 2003 in the South Australian Supreme Court. The defence team, funded by Legal Aid, consisted of Mark Twiggs, junior barrister, and Grant Algie, senior barrister. They made an unlikely combination.

Mark Twiggs is a robust man with prematurely greying hair and a clipped beard. He favours dark suits and conservative ties, and in court he has an avuncular appearance, reminiscent of Perry Mason. He is a passionate defence lawyer, although he spent the first half of his career working as a police prosecutor in Adelaide. In his early thirties, he figured that he was spending so much time in court he might as well become a 'proper' lawyer. Now his clientele is largely drawn from the alleged criminal class. He nearly refused the Murdoch case, exhausted from almost three years representing a defendant in the infamous Snowtown murder trials. To give Twiggs time to recuperate, Peter Longson stood in for him as junior to Grant Algie.

Grant Algie is a bit of a renegade by legal standards, coming from a family whose old school ties were probably recycled to tie up the roses. To start with, he's the son of a country shearer. His family had an acreage at the end of a little dirt road near Edithburgh, on the bottom of the Yorke Peninsula, about 250 kilometres from Adelaide. When Grant was twelve, he won a scholarship to Emmanuel College in Adelaide. A year later, when his family could no longer afford to keep him as a boarder, Grant's father called a family conference and decided their future, saying, 'Well, the boy's done his bit, now we have to do ours.' They moved to Adelaide, where his father took any work he could get, to ensure his son completed his education.

Now in his mid-forties, Algie wears his blond, wavy hair in a Wild Bill Hickok style, with a matching sandy-coloured beard, which he constantly strokes while listening to evidence in court. He asks his questions in a soft, slightly plummy and deceptively non-threatening voice. He appears in snappy suits, with carefully selected shirts and ties. He's quite fond of purple.

Since his arrest, Murdoch had spent plenty of time sitting in his cell reviewing the prosecution case-notes, and he was adamant that he'd been set up. Grant Algie supported this claim. He set out to show that the case was a 'conspiracy by police in three States' to stitch up his client.

The prosecution told the court that Murdoch had been staying in the 'granny flat' at Lurline's property when he discovered that the police were looking for him in connection with the disappearance of Peter Falconio. He then covered the windows of the granny flat with black cardboard and hid out there, taking large quantities of amphetamines. It was under the influence of the 'speed' that he committed the alleged rape and abduction.

Lurline told the court that after the abduction, Murdoch had met up with a truck driver to do a drug deal on the side of the highway. He changed over his number plates and drove to an isolated tyre dump, where he held her and her daughter for three days. He took more amphetamines, smoked dope and otherwise behaved erratically. Then, still incoherent and under the influence of drugs, he drove them to Port Augusta, where he seemed to experience a pang of remorse. He said something about them 'being in the wrong place at the wrong time' and set them free at a service station. 'Don't use the phone here,' he allegedly said. 'I'll be watching you, and my gun can shoot from a long distance.' He gave them one thousand dollars in cash to get themselves home.

Lurline said they walked along the road to a public phone, which was out of order, then returned to the service station. The owner called a local taxi (which just happened to be driven by an ex-cop) and they paid him about $350 to take them to Adelaide. They went to Frankie's bedside to tell him what had happened, then phoned Dags to collect them and take them all to Bolivar Gardens caravan park. There, Lurline helped her daughter to clean herself up and threw all the clothing they'd been wearing into the bin.

They all stayed at Bolivar for a while, making just one trip to Sedan to get clean clothes and feed the dogs. Eventually, Lurline contacted Senior Detective Constable Geoff Carson, a police officer stationed in Berri, hundreds of kilometres away, and told him her story. Detective Carson told me later that he'd met Lurline some years before, when he'd tracked down the killer of a baby whose mother was Lurline's friend. After Lurline phoned him from the caravan park, he drove down to meet the group at Sedan. When Lurline told him the whole story, it gradually dawned on him that the incident had parallels with the Falconio case, which he had been following through police briefings.

'This guy had used cable ties to tie the women up,' he told me, 'and put tape over the girl's eyes and mouth, and taped over the mother's mouth. He could easily have been on the road that night.

'I immediately contacted David Chalker in Alice Springs, but he scoffed at the idea. Wasn't interested. "This is your bloke," I told him, but he didn't think so. Then I contacted the Ds in Port Augusta, gave them a full description of Murdoch and his vehicle, warned them Murdoch was armed and probably dangerous and asked them if they could go to the servo where Lurline said she'd been freed and get any CCTV tape that would corroborate her story. Not long after, they radioed me and said they were following him in Port Augusta. They spotted him driving through town and tailed him.

'They followed him to the Coles car park and called for armed backup, got the place surrounded and nabbed him on the way out. He went for his gun, you know. Only a quick move by the guys, flipping him onto his face and getting his hands behind him, stopped him pulling it on them.'

He said that he and the Port Augusta police had prepared notes for a case conference in Adelaide, and David Chalker was invited to attend. Afterwards, Carson and Chalker were having a few beers.

'He's your man,' Carson insisted, but Chalker was still not convinced.

'You owe me a beer if he is,' Carson told him.

Later, when the Territory police checked Murdoch's DNA against that of the unknown male from Joanne's T-shirt, there was a match.

'Chalker still owes me a beer, the bastard,' Carson told me.

I didn't point out that Murdoch was innocent until proven guilty.

The time didn't seem right.

◆ ◆ ◆

Colleen Gwynne's confidence in the two females making good witnesses proved to be misplaced. Murdoch's defence challenged many key points in their evidence.

Much of the evidence was given in closed court, because Lurline's daughter was a minor. Even Julie, who'd travelled from Broome to support Murdoch in court, was left wandering around Adelaide, locked out and fed up.

Murdoch had told me his version of events at Yatala several months before. 'This is what really happened,' he said. 'I left their place a few days before they reported the so-called rape. I went to my place at Port Broughton and got my gear all packed up.

'Lurline, her daughter and Frankie came and stayed with me at Port Broughton for a couple of days before they took Frankie down to hospital in Adelaide. I told them I was so wild with Hepi, I was going to head north and maybe even kill him. Then I think Dags drove them and Jack up to Sedan and back to Bolivar Caravan Park and booked them all in for a few days.

'I went looking for Dags at his place a few times over the next couple of days, and when there was no sign of him or Jack, I got nervous and decided to take off. I thought he might have made himself scarce because he knew something I didn't. Actually, he'd collected the women, driven them down to see Frankie, checked Frankie out of hospital and gone to Bolivar to wait and see if I'd done over Hepi. I think Hepi put them up to the rape claim, the bastard.' The turning point in the trial came when defence lawyer Peter Longson contacted the caravan park proprietors, who told the defence team that Dags had indeed stayed there and booked another unit for Frankie, Lurline and her daughter, at the time when Frankie was allegedly in hospital and the females said they were being kept prisoner. The following morning, Dags had picked up Frankie and the females in Adelaide, driven them to Sedan, then taken them back to Bolivar, where they all stayed for a few nights.

Murdoch explained why they had been waiting for the outcome of his mission. 'If I'd done Hepi over,' he told me later, 'they didn't need to go to the cops with that rape crap, because I probably would've got done for whatever I'd managed to do to Hepi. But since they heard nothing, they fell back on Plan B.'

He was convinced that the reason for the set-up was that the police needed his DNA to compare with the DNA on Joanne's T-shirt and if he was charged with rape, he would have to provide a sample.

'But why would anyone put a girl through such an ordeal?' I asked.

'Money. Frankie wanted to apply for compensation, and they would have got about $70,000 between them. Frankie also got two of my vehicles, a Glock [pistol] and about $30,000 in cash. And he told someone about the hundred grand I'd put aside for Mum and Dad.'

I still wasn't entirely convinced, but it was possible.

Evidently, the jury thought so too. For days they struggled to hear the females' stories because the court's CCTV equipment kept breaking down. They watched Grant Algie cast doubt on the evidence presented by Dags, Frankie, Lurline and her daughter. The evidence given by the caravan park operators clinched the 'reasonable doubt' in Murdoch's favour. On 10 October, after only three hours' deliberation, the jury found Murdoch not guilty on all counts.

Julie rang me immediately, yelling just two words: 'He walks!'

I rang Glenn Morrison at the *Centralian Advocate*. 'He's been acquitted,' I said.

Glenn immediately phoned Colleen Gwynne for a comment. At first she didn't believe him, but Glenn reassured her that Murdoch's friend couldn't have got that wrong.

'Shit!' was the only response.

But Julie wasn't happy for long, and Murdoch didn't walk very far. After the verdict was announced, instead of leaving the dock a free man, he was returned to the cells. The Northern Territory police wanted to arrest him immediately on the Falconio charge and escort him through the assembled media to a police car waiting outside the front door of the Supreme Court.

Mark Twiggs argued with them, asking them to allow the warders to take Murdoch through the rear exit, back to Yatala, where they could make quiet arrangements for his transfer to the Northern Territory. But the police had waited a long time to capture him and were not going to be cheated out of the resultant publicity. Territory police officers detained Murdoch on the warrant for Peter Falconio's murder and manhandled him through the crowd to the footpath outside the court.

'It's f--ken illegal what they've done here,' Murdoch yelled to the swarming media. Grant Algie complained that the Territory police had illegally arrested his client before he left the court, but the police held on to their prize. Murdoch languished at the Adelaide lock-up for two days while legal arguments raged, but by Thursday 13 November the cuffs were back on and he was headed for the far north, to wait for his next hearing in a tough prison under the most draconian legal system in Australia. There he would be formally charged with the murder of Peter Marco Falconio and the deprivation of liberty and unlawful assault of Joanne Rachel Lees.

During the two-year investigation, police had assembled more than 300 files of material and 600 witness statements, amounting to 150,000 pages of documents. The trick would be to decide how much of this material would make it to court. There was plenty of time to decide, as the committal hearing was not expected to begin until the first half of 2004.

◆ ◆ ◆

As the time for the committal approached, I still had plenty of questions. Clive spent several hours sifting through the mountains of paper we had accumulated, trying to make sense of it all.

He compiled a time line culled from police reports, witness statements, Joanne's story, media releases and our own estimates. When we looked at the statements by passing motorists, two new inconsistencies stood out. First, at 7.45 pm, a witness had seen the two cars parked together, but no sign of people or activity. Yet this was supposed to be when the gunman was wrestling with Joanne while Peter lay dead on the road. With the four-wheel drive's door open, the interior light would have been on, which is why Joanne could see the dog so clearly. Why did the witness not notice any sign of a struggle – or see Peter's body?

Another witness saw a second vehicle (not the Kombi) 'leaving the scene' and driving north at 8.00 pm. This does not fit with Joanne's claim that the gunman drove the Kombi north through the bush, then walked back from where he'd left it, got into his vehicle, did a U-turn and drove south. Where did the 'second vehicle' – the four-wheel drive – go at 8.00 pm? Did it return later? It doesn't seem to have, as the next witness, passing at 9.00 pm, saw only a Kombi, 'off the highway and in the bush on the western side, and possibly a torchlight'.

The Kombi was probably being moved into its hiding place at that time, so the witness might have mistaken the bobbing headlights for a torch – but where was the gunman's vehicle?

Far from corroborating Joanne's story, the evidence from passing motorists raised more doubts. Clive wondered aloud whether Joanne could have still been inside the four-wheel drive when it pulled away from the scene, maybe to turn up the track 400 metres north of the incident site, where Vince said he had found fresh tyre prints. Did Joanne's attacker take her away from the road? Perhaps she escaped from there, and the man let her go and went back to hide the Kombi. But if that was the case, why hadn't Joanne said so? And where was Peter's body while all that was happening?

We also compared police media releases from the early days up until Murdoch's arrest. It seemed that the description of the gunman morphed to resemble Murdoch more and more closely once his identity was known. For example, a police report of 15 July 2001 described the man as 'medium build, with dark, straight hair to the shoulder with grey streaks, driving a four-wheel drive with canvas on the back with a clear open space at the rear. He is possibly accompanied by a blue heeler dog.' Two days later, the police added a 'chrome bull-bar' to the description of the four-wheel drive.

On 21 May 2002, before Hepi pointed the finger at Murdoch, Assistant Commissioner John Daulby said that, although 'in some ways' the man in the truck-stop video resembled the description given by Joanne Lees, 'there were some significant differences'. The man in the video was Caucasian, between forty and fifty years old, approximately 183 centimetres tall, with short- to medium-length dark hair. 'He appears to be wearing glasses and thongs and to have a thick droopy moustache. He is wearing a distinctive dark cap with a lighter-coloured oval logo on both the front and back of the cap. The cap also appears to have a lighter-coloured Velcro strap at the back and he's wearing a pullover with a large collar.'

In contrast, Daulby reported that the man described by Joanne Lees had 'long, straggly hair, appeared to be younger and was not wearing glasses'.

Furthermore, the police report listed several 'significant differences' between the truck-stop vehicle and the one Joanne had described.

'The bull-bar was chrome, not black, the vehicle did not have flared guards or a bug deflector [which could be seen in the truck-stop photo] and the truck-stop vehicle did not have a gap between the two front seats.'

Yet only a month later, after Hepi made his claims, a different story was being told. On 12 July 2002, the *Centralian Advocate* reported, 'The man on the video bears a remarkable likeness to the description of her attacker given to the police by Joanne Lees on the night she was attacked. Aside from the moustache and the baseball cap with a motif, the man's vehicle, a white Toyota 75 series ute with a canopy, matches the description given to police by Ms Lees and witnesses. And Ms Lees has identified the truck-stop man as her likely assailant.'

In November 2002, Colleen Gwynne went to England with a twelve-person photo-board, with Bradley Murdoch, sporting a droopy moustache, as number ten. Joanne identified him as the gunman. But by then, Murdoch's arrest had received considerable media coverage. Joanne later admitted in court that she had seen photos of Murdoch on the internet on 10 October 2002, well before police showed her the photo.

The description of the dog also seemed to mutate. It had been described (mostly by Joanne Lees) as 'a blue heeler', 'brown and white', 'a red dog', 'a reddish dog with grey and black bits', and 'brownish black and speckled'. Murdoch's dog has always been described as a Dalmatian or Dalmatian cross, never a blue heeler look-alike.

Joanne described the gun as a 'silver revolver'. Jazz had told me that Hepi owned a stainless-steel gun, possibly a .357 magnum. (Evidence supporting this was later given by a girlfriend of Hepi's in court). Had the police ever examined it? Could Murdoch have borrowed it? Where was Murdoch on the night of 14 July 2001?

Would the committal hearing provide any answers to the infuriating anomalies of this case?

Chapter Thirty-Two

TESTING THE EVIDENCE

Let's run it up the flagpole and see if anyone salutes it.

Reginald Rose

D arwin on 16 May 2004 was hot – 34 degrees Celsius, with ninety-five per cent humidity. It had been pouring every night, and the ground steamed in the morning sunshine. The locals told anyone who would listen that the rain was unseasonable. 'The dragonflies usually come out on 1 May and the rain stops,' they said wisely. If I'd been a dragonfly I wouldn't have come out in that weather. My wings would have been too soggy to fly.

I had obtained media accreditation for the hearing because I had heard that security was going to be tight. Before the hearing started, the media contingent assembled around a huge circular table in the soundproof jury room at the Supreme Court to be briefed on the behaviour expected during the three weeks of the committal hearing. The committal would be heard by Mr Alasdair McGregor, a relieving magistrate, but it was to be held in the Supreme Court, one of the most high-tech courtrooms in Australia, with plasma screens, special acoustics and electronic transcript recording. We all hoped it would work.

Grant Algie had already held a media conference, calling on the media to give his client 'a fair go'. He emphasised that Murdoch was entitled to a presumption of innocence. It was a committal hearing, not a trial; the magistrate would simply decide whether the evidence was compelling enough to try the defendant. Jane Munday, the DPP's media liaison officer, emphasised the same point at our briefing.

The briefing meeting hummed with anticipation. The media contingent numbered about a hundred, with representatives of all the big media outlets and stringers from *The Times*, *The Guardian* and all the London tabloids. Many of the journalists had been in Alice Springs three years before and saw this committal as closing the circle. Nearly all believed there would be a trial. Most were convinced Murdoch was guilty, although they couldn't say so in their reports. A witness list for the first week was issued: Paul Falconio, Joanne Lees, Vince Millar, Rod Adams, Cathy Curly. More buzz among the media.

There were almost as many photographers as journalists, and they would really feel the heat as they lay in wait outside in little marquees – erected in deference to health and safety regulations – hoping to snap witnesses coming and going. It was rumoured that Joanne Lees would use the rear entrance, so another group stood in the sun in the rear driveway, hoping for a glimpse of the star witness.

That morning I'd been to see Murdoch at Berrimah Prison, taking some new shirts from Julie, who was concerned about how he'd look in court. Berrimah was even more forbidding than Yatala, with razor wire everywhere and grim-faced guards who were not very polite to visitors. After a few delays, I was shown through for my two-hour visit.

I'd been warned not to discuss anything controversial or reveal any inside knowledge of the case, in case I was picked up from a distance by a hi-tech mike. I didn't want to become a witness for the prosecution. There was a sign on the wall saying that you might be taped during your visit. Can't say you haven't been warned.

Murdoch was looking well and relaxed. He had a new denture, which he found very uncomfortable, but it gave him a whole different look. I again wondered how Joanne Lees could not have noticed his missing front teeth. After a lengthy negotiation about whether Northern Territory Legal Aid would pay his Adelaide lawyers, the senior criminal lawyer at the Northern Territory Legal Aid Commission, Mr Ian Read, had joined his legal team.

Murdoch said they'd be seeking orders to suppress any

controversial evidence presented by the DPP. I guessed he had the DNA in mind. I asked him if he'd received the DNA evidence, because I felt with my knowledge about the additional DNA on the steering wheel, I'd been harbouring a guilty secret for months.

To my surprise, he hadn't received the evidence, although the committal was due to start next day. His lawyers had been asking for it for several months. He said Grant Algie had issued the DPP with a subpoena to get it, so I changed the subject. We talked about the rape case and about the gaps he said he'd identified in Joanne's three statements. He made a big fist at me across the cement outdoor table.

'See this? She reckons in her first statement that she was punched in the face with a closed fist while lying face down on the ground. Even the two female cops didn't believe her. They kept on at her about whether it was open hand or closed fist. If I'd punched her, she would've had a broken jaw. And gravel pushed into her face.'

I believed him.

'But she had no marks on her face whatsoever,' he went on. 'And what about the dog? She's still sticking to the blue heeler story.'

We were both looking forward to hearing her evidence in court – for slightly different reasons, I suspect. Murdoch already knew what she was likely to say, as he'd had her statements for some time. The visit passed quickly, and soon the guards were telling the visitors to leave. Prisoners in different coloured T-shirts signifying their status in the prison filed out to get their lunch, while we women and children thankfully headed in the opposite direction.

Fancy doing life in a place like this!

As we filed into court next morning, we were searched and zapped by security guards looking for mobiles and cameras (and maybe weapons). Court 6 was very small, and there was fierce competition for the twenty-eight seats in the public gallery, so the magistrate had given permission for selected representatives of the main media groups to occupy the jury box. They would be sitting right beside Paul Falconio and his elder brother, Nick. One of Peter's friends from his university days was here to look after Joanne Lees.

Both brothers were wearing black shirts and pants, and Paul's hair was shaved to a buzz cut, making him look uncannily like his missing brother. Nick looked quite different, more like their father. They both looked drawn and tense. They would be allowed to remain in the court throughout the hearing. (Usually witnesses to a committal must leave the court, because they may have to give evidence at a trial and so can't be exposed to other witnesses' accounts.) Paul was there to give evidence that his family had not heard from Peter since the day before his disappearance, although previously they had been in constant contact. As there was still no body, the DPP was hoping Paul's evidence would demonstrate that Peter must be dead.

Rex Wild QC is a highly qualified lawyer, having won the prestigious Robert Menzies Prize before he left the bar in Melbourne to work in the Territory in 1993. He has a patrician appearance, with a Roman profile, but, as he ruefully acknowledges, not much hair. In court, he wore a white shirt and conservative tie, but no coat. This would probably be the biggest case of his career.

His deputy, Tony Elliott, was in his early forties, but looked years younger. He was headhunted from Perth, where he was known as 'The Baby-faced Assassin' because of his youthful looks, his dogged questioning style and his enviable conviction rate. Dark-haired and smaller than Rex Wild, he too wore white shirts nearly every day.

Before giving his opening address, Mr Wild read a statement warning the media yet again about contempt of court and explaining the process upon which we were about to embark. 'It is a committal, not a trial,' he said, endorsing Grant Algie's point at his media conference. But we all knew it would be a brave magistrate who didn't send Murdoch to trial after they'd spent so much getting this far.

Mr Wild said his office had already received two media faxes offering Joanne Lees money for an interview. His tone indicated he thought this was pretty tacky and he didn't want to receive any more.

In the first few seconds of his opening address, the DPP told the court about the DNA on the steering wheel, as well as 'a weak and partial DNA profile from the gearstick' with several components that could be attributed to Murdoch. Reporters scribbled furiously, flicking glances at the glassed-in dock, but Murdoch looked pretty relaxed, wearing one of the shirts Julie had sent.

Mr Wild also informed the court that Joanne Lees had picked Murdoch as number ten from a twelve-man photo-board.

'This identification is contaminated by prior knowledge,' I wrote in my notes.

The DPP read on. 'Security footage from the Shell truck stop shows a vehicle that is very similar to the one described by Joanne Lees. The security footage showing the appearance of the man driving that vehicle not only fits the description given by Joanne Lees but looks similar to the man later identified as her assailant.' But I knew this was open to doubt. Even Daulby had said there were 'some significant differences'. And the man in the video looks nothing like her description of the gunman – Joanne said it wasn't him when she was first shown the photos, only days after the incident.

Mr Wild went on to detail the changes Murdoch had made to his vehicle in the twelve months after the incident, but he didn't list those he made before the incident, as a matter of course, to disguise his vehicle while running drugs.

The DPP also said the prosecution would demonstrate that 'the defendant was in the right area at the right time'. As well as the truck-stop video, they had a witness who met Murdoch on 19 June 2001, travelling from Perth to Adelaide across the Nullarbor. She described him as 'six feet tall; eighty-five to ninety kilograms; proportionate build; wiry thick cropped hair – about a number three or four; long grey moustache. He was driving a white Landcruiser with a green canopy. Inside the vehicle was a pure-bred white Dalmatian dog, with black or brown markings.' This evidence, the DPP asserted, 'puts the defendant in South Australia just before the killing'.

Was he serious? Unfortunately, I couldn't see his face. The Nullarbor is about 3000 kilometres from Barrow Creek, and this meeting occurred on 19 June, nearly four weeks before the incident. Murdoch had to grow his 'cropped' hair to collar-length (or longer) by then as well. It was beginning to look as if they'd taken a shortcut to the answer and then taken a long way round to build a case. If there was a case.

The next piece of evidence was no more conclusive: a registration receipt dated 10 July 2001 for a trailer in Murdoch's name, registered at the Murray Bridge office of Transport SA.

The DPP said there was evidence that Murdoch used the Tanami Track to Broome, arriving at Fitzroy Crossing at about 8.30 pm on Sunday 15 July 2001. Murdoch had phoned Hepi on his mobile in Broome about 4 am, and had purchased some glasses in Broome on 16 July, placing him where he said he was that week. So were these replacement glasses for the ones in the truck-stop video, or were they a red herring?

'Those time frames are not inconsistent with his being just north of Barrow Creek at the time of the killing,' Wild concluded.

Pretty nifty driving, I thought. I made a note to ask Clive to check the times and distances.

Immediately after the opening address, Grant Algie asked for the suppression of the DNA information and other content that could indicate Murdoch might have been the gunman. The magistrate warned the media not to 'run out and file material before I've issued an order', thus cutting off a mass exodus. I groaned inwardly. Here comes a legal argument, I thought.

The argument was long and boring, and resulted in the suppression of all reports about the DNA and the identification of Murdoch. Although Paul Falconio gave his brief evidence that day, saying that if Peter was still alive, he would have been in touch with his family – in a surprisingly broad North Country accent for such an Italian-looking young man – it was clear that Joanne Lees would not appear until Tuesday. All the photographers had been staking out the entrances in the heat in vain.

Chapter Thirty-Three

ACCESS DENIED

Joanne Lees is a victim, and she is entitled to her privacy.

Jane Munday, DPP Media Liaison Officer

On Tuesday, the court was silent as Joanne Lees appeared. She seemed to have had a DPP makeover, appearing demurely in a high-buttoned, white long-sleeved tailored shirt, tucked into a straight, black, knee-length skirt – and wearing virtually no make-up. Her hair was pulled back into a ponytail, held by an elastic band. She looked like a sales assistant from Harrods. She appeared much plainer in real life – or maybe it was the toned-down cosmetics. She walked tall, giving Murdoch a long stare as she crossed the court to the witness box. He looked at his notes and ignored her.

She gave her evidence in a clear voice, punctuated by a nervous cough, but sounded wooden, as if she'd been over-rehearsed. At times she was asked to speak up. Mr Wild seemed nervous too, rolling imaginary balls between his thumb and forefinger and sometimes repeating questions, even though Joanne had just answered them.

Joanne got impatient – 'I've already told you that,' she said. Murdoch and the media were making notes, and so was I. Some parts of her story had changed again.

The plane tickets found in the Kombi were explained at last. On the Friday before they left Alice Springs, Peter bought a ticket to travel to Papua New Guinea for a week. Joanne did not want to accompany him, and bought a ticket to Sydney so that she could spend a final week with her friends there before travelling on to New Zealand. Both planned to return to Brisbane, the departure point from Australia on their round-the-world tickets.

Mr Wild asked why they left Alice Springs so late on 14 July. 'We had no plan,' Joanne replied. 'We were just heading off.'

'Did you know where you were going?'

She shrugged. 'It's just one long road, heading north. We were on holidays. I didn't wear a watch and I didn't need to be aware of the time.'

She told the DPP matter-of-factly that she and Peter rolled a joint at Ti Tree and they shared it watching the sunset. 'The sky was clear, there were some clouds, it was warm,' she said. A roadhouse docket printed at 6.21 pm confirmed their purchases. Joanne said that Peter was feeling refreshed after his sleep. Since they had food with them, they intended to drive a while and probably sleep by the road.

She explained why she had not wanted Peter to stop when they encountered the fire beside the road. 'I said it could be a trap or a trick and asked him to drive on.' She did not elaborate on her reason for this suspicion.

She went on, 'We must have passed Barrow Creek, but I didn't notice it.'

I found this amazing. The joint was jumping that night, with cars everywhere, and it would have been the only lit-up spot since Ti Tree.

She said that after they were waved down, Peter got out and left the driver's door open, so the Kombi's interior light was on. Joanne could see the man at the back of the Kombi because he was standing on the road side of the van, talking to Peter, whom she couldn't see. She thought Peter was bending down looking at the engine. 'I can't remember if the four-wheel drive's headlights were on,' she said.

She described the man again, introducing new elements that could have been describing the man in the truck-stop photo. 'I saw he was tall, kind of stooping, hunched over, with lines on his face and droopy eyes with circles under them.' She said his face was about twenty to thirty centimetres from hers when he came to the Kombi door.

She couldn't remember how she ended up outside on the ground next to the passenger door. Her hands were secured behind her back and she was face down on the gravel. She said the man sat on her back, straddling her waist and facing her feet as he tried to tie them together. She kicked hard and tried to grab her attacker in the crotch with her tied hands.

She said after failing to tie her feet, the man 'came around to the front of me and punched me with a closed fist here', pointing to her temple.

The man pulled her to her feet and propelled her towards his vehicle, holding her upper arm and the back of her neck. She did not see Peter. She said when the man reached the four-wheel drive, he 'lifted up a loose corner of the canopy and brought out a canvas sack'.

This interested me, as Murdoch, his friends, and even Loi O'Dore had told me the canopy was a rigid structure of aluminium mesh, covered by fitted canvas.

After putting the bag over Joanne's head, the man pushed her into the passenger's side of the four-wheel drive and the bag came off. The 'blue heeler – a reddish dog with grey and black bits' was sitting in the driver's seat. 'It looked straight ahead and did not move or make a sound.' When asked if she had ever seen a blue heeler before, she said, 'No.'

'How did you know it was a blue heeler, then?' Mr Wild asked. Joanne said she later saw another dog at Barrow Creek that looked 'almost the same' and she was told it was a blue heeler. That must have been Cathy Curly's dog.

Joanne said she was in the front seat for 'seconds, minutes, I didn't time it', screaming and shouting for Pete. 'The man somehow pushed me into the rear of his vehicle through a space between the seats. I ended up on a raised area on something soft like a bed. The area was spacious, I couldn't feel anything else around me. My head was at the front and my legs were pointing to the back of the tray.'

I tried to visualise how someone being pushed through from a seated position with her hands tied behind her back could end up the way she described. Logic said she should have been on her back, head towards the rear of the tray, but a lot of things were not logical about this story.

She said the man was beside the four-wheel drive and she could hear gravel and scraping. She was calling out, 'Have you shot Pete?'

'No,' he replied.

The man was 'bending down and doing something with the gravel'. When she kept yelling, he came back and said he'd shoot her if she didn't shut up.

Then she described how she escaped, after he'd left her alone again. 'I slid to the back of the vehicle and looked around and couldn't see anything, so I jumped down.'

'Did you make a noise on the gravel?' asked Mr Wild. 'It sounded like a very loud noise.'

'How were you able to get out?' 'Easily.'

'Was the canopy tied down?'

'I couldn't see. I ran straight off to the right and ended up hiding under a bush.'

She said she was wearing sports sandals. The man chased her and then started looking for her with a torch. He came very near. She hid in the bush 'for hours'. She thought the man was shining the headlights into the bush to look for her, but later realised it might have been the four-wheel drive being turned around to head back towards Alice Springs. She believed the Kombi was driven north, and the man returned on foot. She then heard 'some dragging', and about twenty minutes later the four-wheel drive drove south. She brought her hands to the front when she heard the second car start up.

In her interview with Martin Bashir, she said she did this when the Kombi started up. 'While I was in the bush and I heard the man drive off in the vehicle the first time, I brought my hands to the front of my body.'

Her lip balm was in her shorts. She got it out and took the lid off with her teeth, then tried to use it to grease the ties and get them off her wrists.

She eventually emerged. 'There was no moon. It was pitch black. I didn't think it was safe, but I thought I'd have to be brave and get some help for Pete.'

She said when the truckies freed her, her wrists were 'cut, bruised and red raw'. (The photos of her injuries shown on the TV screens did not support this.) She was also 'freezing cold and had been for the past five hours'.

The court clerk produced a bagged black elastic hair tie with a brass clip that had been found in one of Murdoch's vehicles. She said it was identical to the one she'd been wearing before the attack. When she was found, her hair was loose.

'You can buy ten of those for two dollars in discount shops,' I wrote. It could have belonged to any woman Murdoch had ever given a lift to – or even a bloke with long hair. What significance could it possibly have unless Joanne's hair was attached to it? But there had been no mention of any hair.

She also identified her T-shirt, now tightly secured in a plastic evidence bag. Mr Wild asked her to read the words on a small printed sticker on the left front shoulder.

'The Australian Drug Awareness Foundation – Try hugs, not drugs,' she read. I felt a small prickle down my spine.

'What is that sticker?' Wild asked.

Joanne explained that it was the pass given to visitors at the 2001 Camel Cup to signify they had paid their entry fee. I felt pricklier. If Jazz was right about the blue windcheater, she'd found at Hepi's place in Sedan, could that have been Peter's? I'd never heard anything about what Peter was wearing on the night. Or was it Murdoch's, signifying that he too had been at the Camel Cup? Or did it belong to Hepi, as he had told Jazz? Was Hepi at the Camel Cup? Had the police investigated this link?

Mr Wild took Joanne through her evidence until she reached the safety of the Barrow Creek Hotel, then we adjourned for the day. Joanne walked out with her head up, flanked by several minders.

◆ ◆ ◆

We were all expecting Joanne to continue next day, but it was not to be. The media were challenging the suppression orders. Some said Mr McGregor did not have the power to make suppression orders; others just wanted to be free to publish as they pleased. Until they were sorted, we'd all have to wait.

We waited and waited. The legal arguments went on for five days, right up to the full bench of the Supreme Court. Meanwhile, Joanne Lees remained in hiding, and the other witnesses lived it up on the Northern Territory government, which was paying up to $400 a night for hotel rooms and supplying taxi vouchers, meals and most expenses. For some, it was the holiday of a lifetime.

Not for Joanne, though. She made two or three trips to court to wait out of sight in case the legal arguments were resolved, each time sparking a mad rush by photographers to follow her car, which was expertly and speedily driven by her TRG escorts. Channels Seven and Ten resorted to sharing the hire of a chopper to fly above the fleeing convoy while Joanne cowered on the back seat under a coat, but the driver simply headed into a 'no-fly' zone, and the airspace regulations foiled the chase.

Comments in the local paper were critical of this Pythonesque behaviour, prompting Joanne to offer the media 'one still shot' to prevent people from getting hurt in the scramble. We were summoned to reassemble around the jury table for a discussion. Concern was expressed about the speed at which the convoy shot along the Esplanade, where tourists amble back and forth on 'Darwin time', not expecting to encounter a high-speed car chase. Photographers also complained that some of the security guards were manhandling them.

The media rejected Joanne's offer. TV representatives wanted a 'walkie' shot, and made a counter-offer, suggesting two photographers behind a rope three metres from her – one still camera and one TV camera, which would share the footage, and no shouted questions. If she agreed to that, everyone would stop stalking her, most photographers would go home and there would be no more chases.

Joanne's response floored everyone. She said she'd agree, if a representative from every media organisation donated some money to charity. No figure was mentioned, but the Victims of Crime Support Group was – the UK organisation, not the Darwin mob. She said she 'wanted to give something back to those who'd helped her'. Someone was heard muttering, 'She could give them some of the money she got from the ITV1 interview.' Nevertheless, the media room burbled with spirited discussion. Some UK journalists couldn't commit until their editors woke up, while many Australian organisations said, 'No way! We don't pay for news.'

Finally, about $9000 was on the table, almost all from the UK contingent. Those paying said those who didn't pay couldn't share the image. Those not paying would not agree to stop chasing Joanne. Then it turned out that Associated Press, who had agreed to pay a hundred dollars, 'even though it is against our principles', normally supplied all media with their images anyway. It was a stalemate.

In the end, Joanne pulled the plug on the deal, explaining later in court that she thought the media offer was 'pitiful'. While the wordsmiths relaxed in bars around town, hot and frustrated photographers returned to trawling Darwin's better suburbs, swimming pools and shopping centres, hoping for a glimpse of her. Journalists who'd never taken a news photo in their lives bought cheap disposable cameras and kept them handy, just in case. The rumoured rate for a usable photo was about $20,000.

Everyone was bored, and the TV crews used footage of not much happening to put together a 'goof tape'. A betting tab was started on when Joanne might get back into the witness box. Mr McGregor's irritation was beginning to show as he periodically popped in to Court 6 to adjourn again. Downstairs in the Supreme Court, the legal arguments droned on.

To relieve the monotony, I was pleased to get a fax from Clive with his calculations. The vehicle left the truck stop at 1 am, he wrote:

> *Next seen with trailer at Fitzroy Crossing at approx. 8 pm Sunday 15 July (according to Brad's mate Paul when you saw him in Broome). Distance from Alice Springs via Tanami/Great Northern Highway 1337 kilometres. If averaging 80 kph (about 50 mph), with trailer, 16 hours 40 minutes non-stop travel time – after travelling an additional distance to the Barrow Creek site from an unknown location, killing Peter, chasing Joanne, etc. Does this guy ever sleep?*

Clive believed the travel time from Alice Springs could fit the sighting at Fitzroy Crossing, about twenty hours after the truck-stop photo. He also raised another question: 'What was Murdoch doing between 8.30 pm and 4 am?' The travel time to Broome from Fitzroy Crossing (482 kilometres away) is about four-and-a-half hours. This left three hours unaccounted for. 'Did he sleep in the car and wait for dawn to go into Broome? Get rid of body? Too early to call in on anyone.'

Clive's calculations gave me more food for thought. I wondered if Paul would stick to his version of sighting Murdoch at Fitzroy Crossing when he gave his evidence.

Joanne Lees finally made her second appearance, dressed in the same conservative outfit, this time with her hair in a tight bun. Led by Mr Wild, she completed her evidence in chief.

She said the canopy on the tray of the four-wheel drive might have been tied down, but a corner behind the passenger door was loose. A drawing of a four-wheel drive was shown on the big screen above her head, and Wild asked her to point out exactly where she claimed to have 'hung her legs over the tray, then dropped', She pointed to the rear of the tray in the centre.

Grant Algie's cross-examination compensated the media for their long wait. First, he homed in on the story she'd told Mr Wild. A few inconsistencies were apparent. Algie spent a long time on the length of the alleged gunman's hair in the photofit image. It seemed that Joanne and the police artist had developed nine images before she was satisfied they had an accurate picture, yet she'd told Mr Wild earlier that the hair in the photofit was longer than she now said the gunman's hair was.

Although the artist had made marginal notes of several changes suggested by Joanne, there was nothing about the hair being incorrect or too long during the process.

Algie asked for her to be shown a photo of Murdoch's dog. She described it as 'clearly a cross-breed … not a pure Dalmatian'.

'Have you seen that photo before?' Algie asked, knowing it had been taken by police at Sedan during the trial the previous November.

'Yes,' Joanne replied.

'Since you've been in Darwin?'

'Yes.'

'Who showed it to you?'

'Mr Wild,' Joanne said.

I wondered if anyone had suggested to her that it was a crossbreed – as she hadn't demonstrated much expertise so far in identifying dogs.

She was asked if she felt any heat from the muzzle of the silver revolver or smelt any gunpowder when it was pointed at her face, but said no to both questions.

Then Grant Algie produced a sensational series of questions. He cast doubt on Joanne Lees's version of her 'harmonious, loving relationship' with Peter. Although Mr Wild objected, Algie sought leave to pursue this line of questioning on the grounds that it might be 'highly relevant to the credibility of this witness'.

Mr McGregor allowed it, but said a bit crossly, 'I don't think it will get you anywhere.'

Grant Algie first asked about an alleged fight between Joanne and Peter in Alice Springs the night before they left, but Joanne denied it had taken place.

'So you and Peter were getting along fine, no problems at all?' 'Yes.'

Algie's next series of questions shocked everyone in the court, including Joanne Lees.

'Who is "Steph"?' he asked softly.

'I don't know.' Joanne's eyes widened and she stared at Rex Wild, who couldn't rescue her.

'Is not Steph a pseudonym, a false name, for someone you write to through email, called Nick?'

'Yes,' Joanne responded even more softly. It didn't matter, though. The court was so quiet, we would have heard her if she'd whispered.

'Who is Nick?' 'A friend.'

Algie's manicured hand and glinting signet ring chopped the air. 'A friend from Sydney, with whom you had a relationship?'

Joanne stared at him, appearing dumbfounded. 'No,' she whispered.

Rex Wild objected loudly and Mr McGregor saved Joanne by adjourning the court until the following day.

The suggestion that Joanne was 'having a bit on the side' was not damning in itself. But after a relatively soporific day in court, this evidence minutes before the adjournment sent the media into a frenzy. The inference was that while police were searching for her missing boyfriend, Joanne was sending 'secret' emails to Nick (disguised as a female correspondent called 'Steph') and arranging to meet him in Berlin at a later date. Algie became a star, having elicited this information just in time to provide sensational lead stories to meet news deadlines.

'She's lied to Fleet Street,' one journalist pronounced, 'and now we're going to get her.'

◆ ◆ ◆

The next morning, after a polite 'Good morning, Ms Lees', Grant Algie followed up a few minor matters to put Joanne off balance, then had another go at whether or not there was a secret relationship – 'Answer yes or no.'

Joanne obviously knew she had nowhere to go. By not introducing

Nick during his direct examination, Rex Wild had left Joanne vulnerable. She hesitated, drew a deep breath and then said carefully, 'I'm going to answer yes, but I wouldn't class it as an affair or a relationship.'

The atmosphere was electric. No one judged her for having a 'fling'. Young people do. But to deny it in the witness box cut deeply into her credibility as a reliable witness. And to continue corresponding with her lover while her boyfriend's body might have been lying out in the desert somewhere earned her no brownie points.

The damage done, Algie moved on, asking where Peter bought his drugs. Did he have a supplier in Sydney, or Adelaide? Joanne couldn't help him.

Then he asked if Joanne had used any drugs other than the dope they'd shared. She said that she did not use cannabis in Sydney, but admitted to taking 'half an Ecstasy tablet on one occasion'. She also denied having been in a Sydney nightclub when it was raided by the Drug Squad.

Algie had taken this series of questions from statements made by the police who were monitoring her calls and email use in Alice Springs, and from statements made by Joanne's friends in Sydney, so it seemed he must have some basis for his enquiries – but he chose not to press her at that time.

I had worked out that Nick was the 'friend' Paul Dale had mentioned to me. When Peter was concerned about the relationship, Paul had told him not to worry. Now it turned out some of Joanne's friends had known about 'Steph' all along, and possibly other aspects of her life that she would have rather not become public knowledge. That's the trouble with murder – it's no respecter of privacy.

Joanne finally squirmed off Algie's hook and left the court with a sigh of relief. If she thinks that was bad, I thought, just wait for the trial. I bet Algie has her in the box for two days.

All of us wondered how Paul Falconio felt. His face was stony, but the twitching muscle above his temple suggested some inner turmoil.

Joanne's TRG escort whisked her straight to the airport, across the tarmac and onto the plane to Singapore. Two photographers, Nigel Wright for the British press and Renee Nowytarger for News Limited (Australia), guessed she'd make a run for it and got there first. Finding out Joanne had received celebrity-style treatment to board the plane did not please them one bit. This would be their last opportunity for a photo after two frustrating weeks, and neither wanted to admit defeat.

News photographers rarely go anywhere without their passports. Both Nigel and Renee bought tickets to Singapore and jumped aboard the plane, only to discover that Joanne was sequestered behind curtains at the rear, in seating normally reserved for the cabin staff during their in-flight breaks. At Singapore airport, however, their persistence was rewarded. After waiting nearly an hour for Joanne to leave the plane and being told several times that she'd already gone, each secured a single shot of her being shepherded into a waiting vehicle by Singapore police. The photographers caught the next flight home – mission accomplished at last.

Meanwhile, the British and Australian press were scrambling to find a photo of newly (and reluctantly) famous Nick Riley, whom Joanne had met while he was serving coffee at Earl's Café behind Dymocks. It was said that Joanne had introduced Nick to Peter, and that sometimes Nick would join Peter and Joanne on their outings to bars around town.

Huge sums were offered for an image of the 'secret lover', and within forty-eight hours the *Sydney Morning Herald* won the race, paying $15,000 for a friend's snapshot of a good-looking, grinning young man, an IT specialist from England described as 'a bit of a lad' and a 'nice sort of guy'. The photo, taken at Kelly's Hotel in the inner western suburb of Newtown, was soon flashed around the world. Obliging colleagues revealed that Nick and Joanne met every Thursday night in the weeks leading up to Joanne and Peter's departure. They said Joanne slept upstairs in the front bedroom of Nick's Newtown house each Thursday night. Presumably, Peter thought she was having a girls' night out with Steph and her friends.

Chapter Thirty-Four

TICKET OUT OF JAIL

It wasn't me.

Brad Murdoch, 16 July 2001

During the next few days, the court resumed its former plodding pace. There was detailed evidence by police who attended at Barrow Creek describing their actions (and, in some cases, lack of action) in the days after the incident.

One officer, Sergeant Ian Kesbie, told us that he'd been responsible for photographing Joanne before her clothes were collected as evidence. Afterwards, he'd shown her a four-wheel drive outside the Barrow Creek Hotel belonging to a Mr Malouf. My ears pricked up. This was Chris Malouf, who'd admitted to being the man in the truck-stop footage and said he was camping near Barrow Creek that night. Julie had sent Grant Algie a copy of the *Broome Advertiser* with a full-page photo of Malouf looking the image of the gunman photofit.

Algie asked Ian Kesbie if Joanne had seen Chris Malouf as well as his vehicle.

'Yes, and she made no comment about his appearance,' he replied.

'How did he appear?' Algie asked.

'Short dark hair and clean shaven.'

'Did you take his number plate?'

'No,' Kesbie replied.

Sergeant Kesbie also told us that a white dog hair was 'located on the body of Miss Lees'. Was that after her clothes came off? And how did it get there? The hair had been given to a Crime Scene Investigation officer.

A dog hair at last! Only one, though. Could it belong to a Dalmatian? More importantly, does it belong to Jack? We didn't find out, because Kesbie said he didn't think it had been tested yet.

Vince Millar came into court in a wheelchair, recovering from yet another operation. He gave his evidence in his usual deadpan way, diverging from his three earlier statements only on one important point. He was adamant that Joanne had not 'crawled' under his trailer, although he'd said so in all three statements. He now believed the cuts on Joanne's knees and elbows had not been caused by crawling under his truck.

During the cross-examination, Algie asked Vince if he'd seen Joanne since the incident. After a short hesitation, he said he'd seen her in Darwin.

Then Algie read him the three places in his statements where he'd said Joanne crawled under the truck.

'She didn't crawl, but came crab-style, bent over,' he insisted. I'd heard that when Joanne arrived in Darwin, she'd asked to see Vince, to thank him at last. Being pretty peeved with her, he had refused. But then, while he was at the DPP's office being briefed, Joanne burst in and ran to him. They hugged and a few tears appeared, and Joanne thanked Vince for saving her from the perils of the outback.

Having a nasty suspicious mind, I wondered if the DPP's office had engineered this meeting to ensure that Vince didn't say anything negative about her when he gave his evidence.

Rod Adams was not as supportive as Vince. When Algie asked if he had seen Joanne since then, he said a little bitterly, 'No. We were just the taxi drivers to her. If we hadn't come along … We saved her life.'

◆ ◆ ◆

As the audience thinned and the media scrambled for something to write about, Mr Wild produced his own sensation. Late one afternoon, he called Murdoch's former girlfriend, Beverley Anne Allan. She was slightly built, with lots of blonde hair that she flicked nervously over her shoulder from time to time. Murdoch watched her with stony-faced contempt.

She squirmed a little in the witness box, avoiding his gaze, while Mr Wild took her through some pretty damning revelations. She said she was 'close to' Murdoch during the period it was alleged he murdered Peter Falconio. She was shown a peaked Pennzoil cap and agreed she'd given it to Murdoch. She told the court that in mid-July 2001 he returned to Broome 'strung out' after a trip from South Australia. 'He told me that it hadn't been a good trip. [There'd been] a few dramas. He believed someone was following him, and he had to deal with it.'

She also said Murdoch told her he'd encountered a roadblock as he came home 'the long way'. This was significant information, if it was true. The Tanami Track was the 'short way', and no roadblocks were set up on that track. So, if the man at the truck stop had been Murdoch, he'd ambushed the British couple, headed south to Alice Springs, fuelled up and gone north again along the Stuart Highway, on through Fitzroy Crossing and back to Broome. A very long way indeed – 2444 kilometres at eighty kilometres per hour would take more than thirty hours non-stop.

Ms Allan said that she recognised Murdoch when the stills from the truck-stop video were published in a Western Australian paper on 7 August 2001. Murdoch also told her his father had phoned him that morning, thinking the man in the truck-stop photo might be his son. She said Murdoch had vigorously denied it and pointed out various differences between his four-wheel drive and the vehicle in the photo. He also told her he had been pulling his trailer on that trip, so the vehicle in the photo could not have been his.

Ms Allan told the court that Murdoch's Dalmatian rode on his own cushion in the front seat, or in the rear of the four-wheel drive when Murdoch had a passenger. Jack was 'very well trained', but always barked at strangers. She also confirmed several differences between Murdoch's four-wheel drive and the vehicle Joanne Lees had described. Murdoch's vehicle had never to her knowledge had a crawl-through or any space behind the seats; the fire extinguisher was in a different position from the one shown in the drawing of the four-wheel drive from Joanne Lees's description; the rear of the canopy on Murdoch's vehicle was fixed, and there was no access to the tray from the back, only the sides. Furthermore, although Murdoch had shaved his moustache in mid-July, his hair had never been shoulder-length; in fact, it was already very short before he shaved it to a 'number one'.

So if Jack always barked at strangers, it's unlikely that he would have sat 'staring straight ahead' and 'not making a sound' if he'd been in the four-wheel drive on the night in question. Also, Joanne Lees couldn't have dropped off the end of the tray in the way she'd described – not from Murdoch's truck, anyway.

Evidence was given about the changes Murdoch had made to four different vehicles he'd owned. The information seemed long-winded and not very interesting. Besides, Paul and Brett had told me that he was always modifying his vehicles. 'He had one old blue truck that I reckon he rebuilt at least twice from scratch,' Paul had said.

The next witnesses were police officers Jeanette Kerr and Helen Braam, who told the court about their interviews with Joanne and their role as 'chaperones'.

Under cross-examination by Grant Algie, Jeanette Kerr told the court that police had challenged several aspects of Joanne's story during a three-hour confronting interview on 7 August. She outlined their list of concerns – fourteen in all. Shown a lip balm in a plastic heat-sealed bag, she identified it as the one she'd found during her only visit to the incident site in October 2001. Algie asked her to look into the tube to confirm it was the one she'd discovered.

I knew why he asked this question. Murdoch had told me that he thought the lip balm and the bits of bitten-off tape had been planted by the police.

'That lip balm isn't shrivelled up. It has no bits of vegetation or dirt sticking to it,' he asserted. 'If that had been out in the open, night and day for three months without a lid, it wouldn't be in such pristine condition. And what about those two little bits of black tape, just sitting there waiting for Kerr to pounce on them?' he snorted contemptuously. 'How come the trackers didn't spot them when they sussed out the site?'

Outside the court I chatted briefly with Jeanette Kerr, who was a warm and friendly woman. I thought Joanne had been lucky that Kerr was allocated to interview her, even though her questions may have been difficult to answer.

'The interview was just to fill in the gaps,' she said. 'We always felt there was some information missing from her story, for some reason. Perhaps something else did happen out there, something she initially didn't want to tell us and then, having told the first story, she stuck to it. But she was never a suspect for Peter's murder. I'm certain Murdoch is the man.'

I agreed with her comments about the gaps in Joanne's story and relayed some comments by my friend Tim Watson-Munro, a forensic psychologist, who said that people can tell a story so many times they come to believe it themselves. It's like confabulation, although it's not very common in severely traumatised victims. They usually either have horrifyingly total recall, like a replaying video, or try to blot everything out.

In court, Jeanette Kerr, who is a trained negotiator, had mentioned that linguistic experts asked to review Joanne's statements had unanimously agreed that 'vital information was missing'. I told her I'd interviewed the profiler in Canberra who had suggested that Joanne might have a history of mental illness or a narcissistic personality disorder.

'Yes, a DSM IV, Cluster B. My personal opinion.'

This correlated with other professional assessments of Joanne's personality. The DSM IV is an international measure of personality style and disorder. Cluster B is characterised as 'anti-social, borderline, histrionic, narcissistic, emotional/erratic behaviour'.

Some time earlier, I had sent the videotape of Joanne's interview with Martin Bashir to Dr Clifford Boland, a forensic psychiatrist in Sydney who specialises in pre-sentencing evaluation. He emailed me the following comments on 12 December 2003:

> 'The doco was most interesting and obviously raises more questions than answers due to the numerous inconsistencies outlined in the program. How she managed to get out of the van while her alleged assailant was round the front appears a bit farfetched, since doing so would have taken a lot of time.
>
> 'She only became stressed when talking about the loss of Peter Falconio.
>
> 'It is also unusual for individuals who have been severely traumatised by events to be able to return to the scene of the crime, even for a reconstruction of the event.
>
> 'In summary, her clinical presentation is not in keeping with someone who has been severely traumatised by an event, making me question whether the events which she reported are true. There are so many inconsistencies in her story that one cannot but question the credibility of the statements she made at interview.'

Maybe that night was worse for Joanne than she'd told anyone. She'd refused to be examined for sexual assault at the hospital, and had no counselling. Perhaps she felt guilty that she'd lived and Peter had died. Many professionals found her distant and difficult to relate to in the days after 14 July. Was she suffering post-traumatic shock?

◆ ◆ ◆

James Hepi's turn in the witness stand was eagerly awaited. While he was being ferried in through the back way, we heard evidence from a young man called Ben, who grew up calling Murdoch 'Uncle Brad'. Ben said that in mid-2002 Murdoch had taken the chassis and compliance plates from Ben's old four-wheel drive and attached them to the cabin from Murdoch's vehicle, which had a twisted chassis.

Probably the one Hepi bent, I thought.

Murdoch asked Ben to register the car in his own name, which he did on 3 July 2002, and then sell it to Murdoch for $10,000 cash, effectively giving Murdoch a 'clean' car.

Shortly before the sale, Ben overheard Murdoch talking to his mother.

'Uncle Brad came in after tea in May or June 2002. He looked awful, grey-faced and not well. He said to Mum, "I've done something wrong. I've never done this before." He said he'd dobbed in his Kiwi mate. He was upset with him, and there were drugs in his car.'

Could that be true? Was it Murdoch, not the Coffin Cheaters, who rang the Broome police? I would certainly ask him during my next visit.

Although Hepi was a convicted criminal, he was given TRG protection from the media cameras, which didn't impress anyone much. He had dark curly hair and dusky skin and looked nuggety and tough in a blue-grey T-shirt that had seen better days. He faced Murdoch defiantly from the witness box, his dark eyes burning above a heavy black moustache.

His evidence was pretty damaging, although the defence made light of it outside court. He said Murdoch had 'collar-length hair and a handlebar moustache' in July 2001. He went on to confirm everything Jazz had told me about the vehicles they owned and the routes he and Murdoch used for their 'business operation', as Rex Wild euphemistically described it.

'Was Mr Murdoch doing trips as well?' Wild asked. 'Yes.'

'Did you discuss with Mr Murdoch the routes he was using?' Hepi outlined several routes from Sedan to Broome – not including the Stuart Highway – and said they were the ones he used, according to whim and weather.

'Don't know about Brad. We timed our arrival in Broome early – around 4 or 5 am – to blend in with the traffic going in from Twelve Mile.'

He was shown a peaked Pennzoil cap with a logo on the back, and he agreed Brad had worn it.

Perhaps Hepi's most harmful revelation was that he and Brad had been working in the Sedan shed together when he noticed Brad was fashioning some 'handcuffs' from cable ties and hundred-mile-an-hour tape. Journalists scribbled furiously. I looked over at Murdoch, who was vigorously shaking his head inside his glass showcase.

Hepi continued, 'On 16 July 2001, around 4 am, a phone call came to the house from Brad. He said he was in the yard at Kimberley Diesel, that the four-wheel drive needed some work done on the gearbox and he needed to be picked up. I can't remember if me or the Sheriff [one of their offsiders] went to collect him.

'Brad was edgy, more so than usual, and during that day I saw him shave off his moustache and shave his hair back to a number one. Later on that day, the news about the missing man came through on the TV and Brad volunteered, before I asked him, "It wasn't me."

'Following that day his vehicle was heavily modified – new canopy, new exhaust, turbo – it cost quite a lot and the four-wheel drive's appearance changed dramatically. Brad couldn't do any trips for a couple of months while the car was being fixed.'

But I knew he had taken his four-wheel drive on an overnight fishing trip with Paul ten days later. I would later have the photos to prove it.

Hepi went on to tell the court, 'On 7 August I saw a front-page photo of a four-wheel drive and a man I thought was Brad at the Alice Springs truck stop.' When confronted by Hepi, Murdoch argued, saying the car was not his, as he'd been pulling a trailer and other features didn't match.

Wild showed Hepi the truck-stop stills. 'Do you recognise that vehicle?'

'Yes. It's Brad's.'

'Do you recognise the man in the picture?' 'Yes, it's Brad.'

'How do you know?'

'He's wearing the glasses we used for disguise – we had round and square ones – his stance, his moustache, everything.'

'Did you have a conversation about ways to hide bodies after this incident?'

'Yes. Brad said you could put them in a spoon drain and cover them with dirt – soft digging …' He faded out as Murdoch caught his eye.

'What did you say in response?'

'I didn't think I needed to kill anyone to continue to do what I was doing,' he replied firmly.

Hepi said that around Christmas 2001, he and Murdoch had a falling out over some money Murdoch owed him. They'd eventually met in a car park in Perth, and Murdoch had said he'd been unable to keep earlier appointments because he thought the police were watching for him at the border.

Everyone expected Algie to take Hepi apart, but he'd decided to whack him a couple of times where it hurt and save the 'king hits' for the trial.

'Have you been given any immunity about being prosecuted for any of your activities in return for giving evidence in this case?'

'No, I have not.'

'This set-up of Mr Murdoch provided you with a great opportunity to get out of serving a lengthy sentence, when you were convicted in May 2002 for a serious crime, did it not?'

'Yes.'

'In fact, you saw Mr Murdoch as your ticket out of jail, didn't you? And there's a two-hundred-and-fifty-thousand dollar reward for giving evidence that leads to a conviction. A combination of saving your own skin and the reward has led you to make false statements to the police, about the handcuffs, the "body in the drain" discussion, Mr Murdoch's appearance?'

'That's not correct.'

'You wouldn't be involved in setting up Mr Murdoch?' Algie asked in silken tones.

'I was involved in getting my own skin off the line, but not setting up Mr Murdoch.'

'Does a man called Steve Middleton sometimes stay on your Sedan property?'

'Yes, he does.' Hepi shifted a bit in his seat.

'In June or July 2002, before Mr Murdoch's arrest in South Australia, did you arrange for Steve Middleton to collect Winfield cigarette butts from your Sedan property and post them to you in Broome, along with photos of some property that had been damaged?'

'Yes.'

It sounds as if Hepi was after Murdoch's DNA from the butts, I thought.

Algie asked, 'Did the police ask you to do this? Did you pass the butts on to detectives?'

'No, I did not. I took it upon myself to get those butts, but I was told by Detective Jenal in Broome that DNA evidence could not be taken from a cigarette butt.'

If Jenal really had said that, I wondered which detective school he went to.

'I planned to hand them to the police, if they could get DNA from them, to see if they matched the T-shirt,' Hepi continued defiantly.

If looks could kill, Hepi and Murdoch would both be leaving the court in body bags, I thought.

Having made the point that Hepi was not a very trustworthy business partner, Algie let him go. The South Australian set-up was looking more likely to me now, and the odds on Hepi having a hand in it had shortened.

Young Ben told me later that he'd travelled home on the same plane as James Hepi. 'I was shocked that someone who has done so many wrong things was allowed to walk around so freely.'

We were supposed to hear from 'the Sheriff', but he didn't show. There was media speculation he'd been 'silenced' or was in hiding, and

I spent all afternoon humming 'Who shot the sheriff?' Mr McGregor adjourned proceedings until 9 August. The next day I ran into him outside the Supreme Court.

He said, 'I suppose we'll see you back for the rest of the evidence?' I told him, 'Apart from the DNA evidence, I'm not sure if I'll bother coming back in August.'

'Mmm,' he replied. 'Neither am I.'

On my last visit to Brad Murdoch before leaving Darwin, I asked him if he'd been involved in getting Hepi arrested. His craggy face softened into an almost bashful grin.

'Well, as a matter of fact ... I did have a hand in it. See, he'd set up a couple of mates of mine, and there was some other stuff going on at Sedan where I realised, he was ripping me off and lying to me.'

He explained, 'I found some money, about thirty thousand dollars, in the woodpile and hidden in stashes around the house. It was done up in four-hundred-dollar lots, not five hundreds, the way the bank does them, so I knew they weren't ours. We always did the money exactly like the bank, same rubber bands even, so if you got pulled over you could bluff that you'd just made a big withdrawal.'

I remarked on his attention to detail.

'Yeah, well it was my business, not a game,' he replied. 'I had to go and pick up some hydro from a guy I hadn't met before, not far from Sedan. When I did meet him, he told me he was surprised I'd consider doing business with Hepi – said he'd had some bad experiences with him a few years before.

'When I heard what he had to say, a lot of the recent shit started to make sense – Hepi missing for days on a run to Broome; taking my vehicle and bending the chassis on a sand dune so it would be off the road; the Ecstasy deal he said went wrong in the Northern Territory; people getting dobbed in; short loads of gear – that kind of stuff. You develop a very sharp sense of danger in my business.

'I decided to get to Perth as quick as possible and join Billy Gibbs and fly into Broome to front Hepi. I took the money I'd found and all the hydro I'd already collected and drove to Perth, but I heard on the CB network there was a fruit-fly inspection at the border, so I detoured through the bush to avoid the roadblock. That was an extra seventy or eighty kilometres.'

'Are you saying you bush-bashed for seventy kilometres to avoid a fruit-fly inspection?' I asked, surprised.

'Didn't bush-bash, I used my topographical map. The army does maps – first they take an aerial photo, then distil it down to show tracks, houses, dams and so on. I've got them all. The tracks are quite passable in my vehicle. The reason I don't like border inspections is that they sometimes record number plates. I don't like people having a record of my movements, especially across borders.

'So, anyway, I missed the plane. Billy was on it, though. I had to drive to Broome, but before I left, I contacted Billy and told him I was coming in. Lucky I did. While I was on the road, Billy warned me that there was a random roadblock stopping white Toyota four-wheel drives on the highway into Broome. They were probably just still looking for the arsehole that did Falconio, but I was loaded up, and Hepi would've known it. He knew about the roadblock too and didn't try to reach me, the bastard. He figured it would be worth losing the load to get rid of me – and who knows what deal he had going with the cops?'

'So did you and Billy front him when you got in safely?' I asked. 'No, he took off. Too scared to face me, I reckon.'

Soon after this, Billy Gibbs was dobbed in to the police, and the relationship between Murdoch and Hepi soured beyond repair.

'I never did another run from Sedan after that one,' Murdoch told me, 'and he was wild as hell when he got back to Sedan and found I'd taken all his money. He wanted to meet me to get that money back, but it wasn't safe to travel across borders in my vehicle when the cops were searching so intensively for the Joanne Lees Special, so I headed south to Port Broughton and laid low for a while.'

He said that when they eventually met in the car park in Perth, he accused Hepi of double-crossing him, told him he was not getting his money or his hydro, and warned him to watch his back. At this, Hepi 'slunk off'.

'So how did you have a hand in his being caught in Broome?' I asked.

'Oh, that wasn't the end of it. That was just the warning. He'd lied to me, so I put out a bulletin on him.'

'What's that?'

'I contacted all my truckie mates, described Hepi and his vehicle, and asked them to contact me on the CB radio if they saw him on the road. That way, I could track his journey. Once he did a run, I knew which way he'd go into Broome. It was more a matter of when.

'So eventually, I got these reports – he's in Marla, then Alice Springs, then Billiluna and so on – and I knew he was heading north, loaded up. I phoned a mate of mine in the Cheaters up north and told him he could either ambush Hepi and blow out his tyres and take the hydro, or just dob him in as he came into Broome. I didn't care, really. My mate had to pick up one of his kids from school on the first afternoon Hepi drove in, so he just watched out for him the next day and rang the cops from the Roebuck roadhouse outside town.'

I replied, 'Hepi does the dirty on you, then you get him arrested, but now you're in jail and he's not. Looks like it's your move, mate.'

Chapter Thirty-Five

THE ODDS SHORTEN

I wouldn't have missed it for quids.

Magistrate Alasdair McGregor, 18 August 2004

Back home in Melbourne, I contacted more people who might shed light on my nagging questions. I was still confused. After this much research, I'd usually have a good grasp of what might have happened. This time, truth seemed to be eluding me. I still had doubts about the credibility of the evidence presented so far. I was not convinced that the forensic evidence directly linked Murdoch with the murder of Peter Falconio. And where was any provable link between Murdoch and the aggravated assault of Joanne Lees?

Bill Towers had retired, and I tracked him down in Queensland, thinking he might be more willing to speak to me now. He was a bit defensive, and I didn't mention Chris Tangey – or the criticism Towers had received in the Ombudsman's report. Instead, I asked him about police procedures after the Barrow Creek incident.

'Forensics has done its job,' he assured me. 'We had a good bit of a look around at the scene and for three-and-a-half kilometres on either side of it, picking up bits of tape and other rubbish, none of which proved to be of any value.' They searched for the spare set of Kombi keys, which Joanne said were missing. Eventually, they combed both sides of the highway for a hundred kilometres in each direction, but turned up nothing useful. It was interesting that no cigarette butts were found at the scene, because both Peter Falconio and Brad Murdoch smoked.

Towers was certain Joanne had seen a dog. 'A blue heeler – or red heeler. There was dog hair found in the dump at Tanami Roadhouse,' he told me seriously.

But what did that prove? The roadhouse was more than a thousand kilometres from Barrow Creek. Did the hair match anything? He couldn't say. Didn't know if it was tested. But he also said that five days later a 'large brown mixed-breed dog' had been found shot in the bush a few kilometres from the incident scene. 'It didn't match Joanne's description,' he told me, 'so we had a look, but didn't collect the bullet or any hair samples.'

Still on the trail of the elusive, silent dog, I spoke to Dr Andrea Taylor, an anthropologist at Monash University, about testing dog hairs. I remembered one of the key forensic pointers to the abductor of Sydney boy Graeme Thorne in 1960 was the long dog hairs found on a blanket wrapping Graeme's body. If they could link hairs to dogs then, why couldn't Jack's hairs be analysed now?

Dr Taylor told me that it would be almost impossible to identify a dog from one shed hair. 'Most shed hairs do not have a bulb – it dies, which is why the hair falls out. But there is a slight possibility of identifying the dog from skin cells adhering to the shaft, or even from oil from the dog's skin.' She said it depended on how carefully the sample had been handled.

I asked about identifying the breed.

'It could be possible,' she agreed, 'but only the mitochondrial genome could be isolated from any loose cells and these contain the mother's DNA. So if the dog was a cross-breed, say a staffie mother and a heeler father, the dog would appear as a staffie. Having said that, most breeds are very similar, even though they can look so different.'

Dr Taylor put me on to Dr Barbara Triggs, one of Australia's experts in hair morphology. She also said that dog breeds are very similar, although she can detect differences between a poodle and a dingo, for example. Australian native species are a different bundle of fur and they are simple to isolate.

I wondered if investigators were aware of Jack's current address. To find out, I rang Sergeant Carson again and obtained Lurline's contact details. Frankie had succumbed to his illness and, after his death, Lurline had sold up the Sedan property and gone into hiding, taking Jack and her daughter with her. She told me she was terrified of Murdoch and Hepi, although until Murdoch had abducted her she had never been afraid of him. She was not so kind to Mr Hepi.

'He is an evil, evil man,' she told me in a shaky voice. 'Frankie couldn't swim, and Hepi told him he'd take him to the river and drown him. Or chop off all his fingers. He used to try running us off the road when I was taking my daughter to school. I had to get a restraining order out against him. He was totally drug-f--ked.'

She didn't think much of the South Australian justice system, either. 'They ignored all the DNA evidence in our case,' she went on.

'Those jurors and lawyers thought it was just too bizarre that anyone could do something like that, because they live in their own perfect world. They treated our case like a traffic infringement. My daughter still has her bad days, she's on antidepressants. So am I. If you want to say I'm pissed off with the system, well, that's an understatement.'

Frank Thorne, a British journalist who'd been covering the Falconio case for various British tabloids, told me later he'd interviewed Lurline after the South Australian trial. 'The poor woman's terrified,' he said. 'Every time a car pulls up or the phone rings, she thinks it's something to do with this situation. You couldn't sit opposite her and not believe her fear is very real.'

Another woman who'd known both Hepi and Murdoch well would be called to give evidence at the second part of the committal. Her name was Rebecca Weaver*, and she'd been Hepi's girlfriend for a couple of years. She'd lived for a time at both Hepi's and Lurline's properties. She told me that during the first week of the July 2001 school holidays, Murdoch had phoned her to say he was near her house at Nuriootpa, in the Barossa Valley, and would call in for a coffee.

'Brad often called in if he was in the area,' she told me. 'I can pinpoint the date exactly, because I'd just got my kids back from their father's custody. Brad arrived looking very tired – more so than usual – wearing jeans, a flannelette shirt and a suede wool-lined vest. He had one of those Merv Hughes moustaches and a couple of days' growth, but no beard. He did have a full beard in January 2001, but he'd long since shaved that off. And his hair was reddy-grey and always very short – clipped to a number one or two.' I remembered the suede wool-lined vest Jazz had worn in Sedan to keep herself warm. Could it have been the same one?

Rebecca said on one occasion she'd travelled in Brad's car to Western Australia to meet Hepi. She was certain that Brad's vehicle had bench seats, no crawl-through and 'no aluminium mesh that I can remember. It might have gone on later. Brad was very, very tidy. Really fussy about everything being in its place. Not like James,' she giggled. 'He was a bit messy.'

Around the end of August 2001, Hepi had given Rebecca her marching orders. 'He never explained why, just told me to get lost, basically. I found out later from gossip that he'd been told I'd been cheating on him with Brad and the Sheriff! Absolute rubbish, but I haven't seen James since.'

She could not recall ever seeing Murdoch making 'handcuffs' at Sedan, but she wanted to reassure me on another point. 'If I can say…' she began hesitantly, '… well, I knew Frankie pretty well, and I wouldn't trust every word that came out of his mouth. I never believed Brad did anything to hurt Lurline and especially her daughter. He and James loved kids. I met James through my daughter's callisthenics coach. James used to baby-sit my kids, before I was in a relationship with him. He and Brad were both real gentleman, although James had a very dark look if he was angry – like *Once Were Warriors*. But if he saw an old lady struggling with shopping or trying to cross the road, he'd stop and help. I've seen him do it. They were both very polite to women.'

I contacted the South Australian Education Department and found that the 2001 mid-year holidays ran from 6 July to 23 July. So Rachel must have her dates right, I thought, because Murdoch had said he was in Sedan in early July and in Broome from 16 July. But he couldn't have grown shoulder-length hair in the few days between his visit to Rachel and 14 July.

I also got back to Paul, Murdoch's friend from Fitzroy Crossing, and asked him if he was certain Brad had been pulling a trailer when he refuelled on the night of 15 July. He confirmed this, and also told me he had photos of a fishing trip he had made with Brad and a friend on 25 July 2001. 'My friend keeps a meticulous diary,' he told me, 'so Brad's car couldn't have been off the road for months after 16 July like Hepi said. I'm going to send a set of photos to the DPP to prove it. I'll send you a set too, if you like.' I agreed – but I put in a bid for the negatives, saying I'd print my own. I thought Gale Spring might be able to enhance them. Paul demurred, but before we hung up, in the interests of fair play, I suggested he send a third set to Grant Algie.

The photos showed that Murdoch's vehicle had a solid metal sheet behind the driver's cabin. But there was no sign of an aluminium mesh frame, just posts in each corner supporting roll-up canvas sides. Had the frame been removed? And if so, when?

Part two of the committal started on 9 August 2004. Murdoch had now been in custody almost two years. I visited him with some questions from our Melbourne whiteboard.

I was interested in why he'd taken almost eight hours to cover about 480 kilometres between Fitzroy Crossing and Broome in the early hours of Monday 16 July.

He was a bit pissed off. 'You city people think you're so smart,' he said. 'I had a meal with Paul. Then I had a bit of a sleep in the truck. Then I dodged cattle and roos, so I wasn't driving fast. And I timed my arrival into Broome for around 4 am, when the cops were coming in from their patrols, tired at the end of night shift and waiting to knock off. Just my normal behaviour.'

Suitably rebuked, I asked, 'I'm interested in when you found out about the roadblocks. Did you tune in to the police radio band in your truck? Beverley Allan said you took the long way round, implying you were avoiding roadblocks. What was the 'long' way?'

'I did carry a 400-band radio on my trips, but a lot of the time you don't get any reception in the desert. I first found out about the incident when I got petrol at Fitzroy Crossing. Paul told me. I was glad I hadn't run into any roadblocks along the Tanami Track, because I had twenty-five pounds of hydro on board. No body, though,' he grinned.

◆ ◆ ◆

Court 6 was more subdued this time. The media contingent was sparser and not as excited as when Joanne Lees was there. Only about half the jury box was occupied by media, although the public gallery was nearly full every day. Good theatre, air-conditioned and free.

The first two days saw a procession of people testifying about the changes Murdoch had made to his vehicles over several years. It quickly became obvious that he made a habit of changing the looks and specifications of his many vehicles. Partly because, as one witness said, because he could – it was 'his hobby' – and partly, as he'd told me, because of his 'business'.

'There's a family out on the Tanami,' he'd told me, 'who run a local heavy vehicle business. I drive past them and their depot often, but if they were asked, they might only say they see me occasionally, because on other runs, they don't recognise the vehicle. It always looks different.'

Several police witnesses, including Loi O'Dore, seemed to become less certain of themselves when cross-examined by Grant Algie. All said there was no crawl-through in any of Murdoch's vehicles, but not all could agree on exactly what his truck looked like on 16 July, when it was altered, where and by whom, and if it was the one at the Shell truck stop.

Murdoch's friend Brett was an uncomfortable and unwilling witness. He answered the DPP's questions in monosyllables and volunteered little. Shown a photo of a tray-back canopy frame that police had confiscated from the yard of his workshop, he admitted it had once been on Murdoch's truck, and was probably the one that was replaced after 16 July. When asked if he knew the whereabouts of the aluminium mesh, he said no.

Brett admitted that Murdoch had spent about $20,000 on his Toyota during the last half of 2001. But he told me later, 'He was always spending money on his cars. They were his livelihood. What else is he gonna spend money on?'

Reporters were beginning to mutter about 'a pretty circumstantial case', and Grant Algie looked more relaxed every day. Some journalists who were convinced of Murdoch's guilt seemed worried he might get off if this was all a jury would hear. But a jury would actually hear much more, especially from Mr Algie, who was saving his best questions for the trial.

Murdoch's former mate 'Dags' was questioned very gently about cars and dates by Tony Elliott, who prefaced at least three questions with 'This may sound like a silly question ...'

Finally, Dags had had enough. 'That's it!' he yelled. 'I'm not answerin' no more silly questions. I'm outta here.'

Mr McGregor mumbled something about silly questions too, but quickly put on his stern face, picked up a little book from his desk and told Dags that he'd be in contempt of court if he refused to answer the questions. McGregor had been so laid back throughout the proceedings that it was a surprise to hear his gruff instructions. After a bit of shuffling in his seat, Dags agreed to continue. As if by some tacit agreement, Mr Elliott did not warn us of any sillier questions.

The media settled back in their seats too, disappointed that a potential headline – 'Witness defies court' – had melted away. It looked as if Dags's outburst might be the highlight of the day.

The witness I'd been waiting for was Carmen Eckhoff. Some said she might be giving evidence for a couple of days. Her credentials took Tony Elliott a few minutes to rattle off, as he paused from time to time to ensure we were all aware of her expertise in DNA and other forensic tests.

In his rather nasal voice, Elliott took her through her evidence step by step. She estimated the amount of blood on the road at between 100 and 250 millilitres – less than a cupful. She was at pains to describe the care they'd taken.

Elliott asked if she'd conducted a full test of the steering wheel. She said she hadn't. After she'd done a preliminary swab, 'I saw a police officer touch the steering wheel with an ungloved hand.' For a person of her qualifications to have to say that must have been a real downer.

Page after page of DNA results were flashed onto the electronic screens in front of us, all peaks and troughs and a few little blips caused by power surges. A totally foreign landscape to the untrained eye. The most interesting thing I saw was that a lot of the DNA tests had been quality checked by JK – Joy Kuhl, who'd told me she'd had nothing to do with the case after Carmen returned from Alice Springs. Carmen gave evidence that Joy Kuhl was team leader at the time.

Most conspicuous was the lack of results: no DNA from the lip balm or the black bits of tape allegedly chewed off the handcuffs by Joanne; no DNA from a print inside the driver's door; no results from the tape tests on the seats; no gunshot residue; an XY (male) result on the black hair tie identified by Joanne as hers; no human blood on or in the Kombi; no forensic evidence of any struggle, inside or outside the Kombi; no Murdoch DNA on the handcuffs, only Vince Millar's and Joanne's; no useful results from the single white dog hair; nothing from Joanne's pants or sandals – only one tiny speck on her T-shirt which eventually matched Murdoch.

'This is 640 billion times more likely to belong to Bradley John Murdoch than any other male in the Northern Territory,' Carmen assured Mr McGregor, who was struggling with the maths, like the rest of us. But we all understood they were big.

Grant Algie surprised most people by not asking many questions. He concentrated on the lack of bench space in the lab in July 2001. He hammered the fact that the former lab was not accredited, to Carmen Eckhoff's obvious irritation.

'It was not accredited for occupational health and safety reasons,' she explained. 'If there had been a fire, the staff would have had to jump out a small first-floor window. This did not affect the quality of our work.'

Algie was foreshadowing a mix-up or a stuff-up. I couldn't blame him – that DNA was the only real bit of evidence the DPP had.

Although I hadn't met him, I was certain the 'old copper' sitting outside the court was Bill Towers, and I wandered over for a chat. He told me he was not amused about having to interrupt his retirement; perhaps he was anxious about being questioned about the Chris Tangey episode. I thought he'd be safe enough, as the Ombudsman's report had not been made public. In fact, I thought his evidence would be boring, but I was wrong.

He started describing where he'd found the red dog that had been shot. 'It was found about a week later,' he told the court, 'off the road into Neutral Junction Station. About ten to fifteen metres to the left off the road that continues on to Neutral Junction community. The body was alongside the creek-bed that crosses that roadway.'

Exactly where we'd spent two back-breaking days looking for Peter's body! Could this just be another coincidence? Towers was asked if he'd retrieved the bullet, but he said he hadn't. 'The dog didn't fit the description of the dog we'd been given.' I felt like getting on the phone to Chris Tangey and sending him out with his metal detector. Would the skeleton still be there? Unlikely. Rain, animals, decay would have all taken their toll.

I asked Tony Elliott if I could look at the photos Towers had taken of the dog.

'No problem. They're of no significance to our case,' he said. The photos only showed the rear view of a dead red dog. There were none from the side or the front. But what if that was the staring, silent dog, now silenced forever?

I felt unsettled for the rest of the day. The next witness, David Stagg, did nothing to alleviate my misgivings.

Stagg is an Art teacher in Alice Springs. On the morning of Monday 16 July, he'd been asked to present himself at Alice Springs police station to assist with an 'important case'. He sat in the waiting area for about an hour and then saw a young woman enter the room, escorted by Kate Vanderlaan, Max Pope and Paula Dooley-McDonnell. 'I instinctively knew this must be Joanne Lees,' he said. He was told that the police artist was on leave, and was asked if he could render Joanne's description of the vehicle into a drawing for the media. Although he had never done anything like this before, he was happy to 'do his best'.

They started with the exterior. He said Joanne had noticed 'simple square headlights' before obtaining 'the briefest glimpse of the sides before being pushed into the passenger seat'. I wondered: was this before or after the bag came off her head?

'The canopy was attached to the vehicle in a zigzag fashion, like rope, not clipped to the bar.' (I had thought Loi O'Dore had said that the truck at the Shell stop had clips, though.) 'She described the cabin interior as predominantly grey, with aqua and light blue trims,' Stagg said.

It was a tedious process, requiring several sketches for each aspect of Joanne's recollection, all of which were shown in sequence on our little viewing screens. There was carpet on a shelf behind the fabric-covered bucket seats. I noted that there was no crawl-through on the drawing she signed off, and apparently no crawl-through was discussed. Mr Stagg said that from time to time, one of the police would leave the room and return with more information about details such as where the fire extinguisher might be kept. Everybody chipped in to help with the final outcome. An impression created by a committee, I wrote. No wonder Australia could have been looking for the wrong vehicle for weeks!

The gun was described as being 'shiny', with 'an engraved barrel'. Then the dog made his appearance. Stagg had rendered a child-like dog drawing with pointed ears. 'I asked her if it was a blue heeler,' Stagg said. 'She said, "I don't know. It was a dog. A bush dog – a Territory dog." She was very confused about the dog. We couldn't get a clear description. We asked for a dog book, and she went right through it. She couldn't say what sort of dog it was. It was sitting on the driver's side. It was very unusual; it sat there looking straight ahead, very passive.'

Mr McGregor asked if Joanne had said it had pointy ears, like the drawing he was looking at on screen. Mr Stagg couldn't reassure him about that.

'So you gave it pointy ears to indicate this was a dog?' McGregor asked.

'Yes.'

Tony Elliott asked the witness to explain how the shape of the interior of the canopy was determined.

Mr Stagg said that Joanne had felt around in the dark and had detected a vinyl-covered mattress, tall sides and a curved top. She felt something like 'drab army canvas' and a 'round, circular shape'. Although he'd earlier stated she could see nothing in the dark, he said now 'she got the briefest glimpse of a hexagonal shape' and then 'she sat up and brought her still-manacled hands to the front and used her hands to feel the interior of the canopy.' After that she'd slid out of the back of the tray and run into the bush, without detecting a towbar during her drop to the ground.

Grant Algie sat up and raised his eyebrows. He leaned over to Mark Twiggs for a little whisper. I sat up too. This was the third version from Joanne Lees of how and when she'd brought her hands to the front. It made much more sense than the other two, because if she'd fallen with her hands tied behind as she slid from the rear of the truck, she'd have been a goner. It's virtually impossible to rise to your feet from a prostrate position with your hands tied behind you. And difficult to run too, because your balance is off.

Algie was deceptively nice to Mr Stagg. He told me later he could have pulled him apart, but it would have served no purpose. The man had done his best under difficult circumstances. Nevertheless, Algie asked some pointed questions.

He asked if Stagg had realised that his drawing would be the one all of Australia would use to help the police. He ensured the magistrate got the point that Mr Stagg was inexperienced in this work and that his rendition was augmented by the police.

Then Algie held his hands together in the air and checked with Stagg that this was how Joanne had felt around the interior of the canopy, after she had brought her hands to the front. Stagg confirmed this was so.

Algie asked him about the methodology of developing the sketches.

Stagg replied that he was used to developing a rapport with students. He had a long career in teaching, and he mixed counselling with his creative role during the six hours and forty minutes he spent with Joanne.

'There was a degree of empathy involved. I had to tread carefully,' he said.

'Were there any systems in place to prevent empathy interfering with the outcome?' Algie belted back.

Stagg was clearly taken aback and struggled to reassure us that the process had been objective at all times. 'No, I'm sure it … Joanne did not OK something, it was not put in,' he said firmly.

After asking if the process was videoed and hearing it wasn't, Algie let him off very lightly, but the points were made.

I got the feeling Mr McGregor's favourite witness was Janie McDonald*, the woman who'd met Murdoch on 19 June 2001, travelling from Perth to Adelaide across the Nullarbor. The magistrate told me later he'd found her 'a breath of fresh air'. She was very attractive, slim and tall, with long brunette hair and wearing a pretty sundress. Her voice was throaty and she spoke clearly and openly – which was paradoxical, considering what she had to say.

I didn't think I'd be interested in her evidence, as Murdoch had told me his version of what happened, but she looked so different from what I'd expected that I stuck around to see how her story tallied with his. He'd told me he'd first met her when she worked as a 'tits and bums' waitress at the Broome Coffin Cheaters Club. In mid-June 2001 they ran into each other at a roadhouse in Western Australia after he'd been to see his parents in Perth. Murdoch was travelling to Sedan to collect gear for another run. This tallied, as three weeks later he admitted to heading north, loaded up.

He was driving his big Toyota and she was in a small Suzuki Vitara. He said she could slipstream behind him to the border – he would drive in front with headlights and spots full on, while the smaller car would drive behind, just overlapping the centre line enough to take advantage of the clear view, while being pulled along in the wake of the front vehicle. As Ms McDonald described it, it's a companionable way to drive.

She told the court in her cheerful way that she drank at least a dozen stubbies while she drove and they stopped every so often to 'snort a line of speed and share another beer'. They travelled like this for hours.

'I was a heavy drinker in those days,' she explained. Mr McGregor was captivated, registering mild astonishment at each admission.

'I'm a little unsure about this. Were you actually driving side by side?' McGregor asked at one point.

'Oh no!' she smiled at him. 'That would have been very dangerous!'

'Mmm,' was all he could muster. The rest of us nearly laughed out loud.

She told how they stopped to camp a few hours before dawn at Top of the Bight, and shared a few more beers and lines. She told Murdoch she'd 'always wanted a ladies' gun. A little one, with a pearl handle.'

'How did that subject come up?' McGregor wanted to know. 'It just did, as it does when you're chatting,' she assured him. 'Just came up . . .' he noted. 'Mmm '

She kipped down in her swag on top of a big flat rock and Murdoch slept in his truck, with his 'very well-behaved pure-bred Dalmatian'. Next morning, she said, he showed her a silver ladies' gun, but she didn't like it.

'What didn't you like about it?' McGregor asked, fascinated. She swivelled her chair to face the bench and leaned towards him.

'It had a wooden handle. I wanted a pretty one. If you're going to have something like that, it might as well be pretty, don't you think?' She's flirting with him! I wrote. I couldn't hear what Mr McGregor said, but he left the questions to Mr Elliott after that.

Elliott's final question was, 'During the time you spent with Mr Murdoch, how did he treat you?'

She gave a pretty dimpled smile at the prisoner and said, 'At all times he was a perfect gentleman.'

I'm not sure if that was the answer Tony Elliott was after, but apart from the gun episode, it was exactly the same story I'd heard from Murdoch.

◆ ◆ ◆

Poring over the thousands of pages of the brief, Murdoch had discovered the statements from Robert Brown and his wife Melissa in Bourke. The defence asked that the couple be called, partly because of the content of their statements and partly because, as Murdoch pointed out to me, the Oodnadatta Track, which led from the Stuart Highway to Bourke, was one of the potential escape routes not roadblocked by police.

The couple provided the British press with headlines after they appeared by video-link from Bourke affirming that they had served Peter Falconio at the family roadhouse on 22 July 2001. Mr Brown seemed a nice, earnest young man.

Later that day, I fielded a call from Yorkshire Radio, wanting to interview me about the possibility that Peter Falconio might still be alive – or had been sighted seven days after he disappeared. I was reluctant, aware that Peter's mother might be listening. Eventually I said, 'I'm certain Mr and Mrs Brown believed every word of their testimony. They were in no doubt their customer was Peter. But it is possible they may have been mistaken.'

And I think they were. Peter Falconio is surely dead. But who killed him?

The last witnesses were husband and wife Pamela Nabangardi and Jasper Jimbajimba. They live at Ti Tree, an Aboriginal settlement about sixteen kilometres west of Ti Tree roadhouse. On the night of 14 July 2001, on their way back from visiting family members at Ali Curung, they passed by the site of the Barrow Creek incident at around 9 pm, although Ms Nabangardi could not be precise about the time. She told the court that she saw the headlights of a vehicle pulling out from the verge onto the highway ahead of them. The car, a white Toyota or similar vehicle, passed them at speed, travelling north. They drove past the orange Kombi, which was dark and stationary on the side of the road.

The car pulled out before they reached 'the track off to the west that leads through Neutral Junction to the waterholes'. (This was the track 400 metres north of where Peter Falconio's blood was found on the highway). Tony Elliot asked her how she knew the white car had not entered the highway from the side track, since it was very dark and she only had the headlights to go by.

'No dust,' she said flatly, as if it was one of his 'silly' questions. They took a bit over an hour to get to the Ti Tree turn-off, after a short stop to pick up some friends at Barrow Creek. It was possible the vehicle had done a U-turn further up the highway and gone past while they were at Barrow Creek, but she said no vehicle of any description passed them in either direction after they saw the four-wheel drive.

I was calculating in my head. If they didn't turn off until after 10 pm, it would be cutting it fine for the perpetrator to get to Alice Springs by

12.45 am. And who moved the Kombi into the bush, if the perpetrator had left the scene? The idea that there was more than one perpetrator kept nagging at me. Ms Nabangardi had told me when I'd interviewed her that she saw no lights behind them after they'd passed the Kombi and no sign of life (or death) around the van. Her husband supported all her evidence.

A policewoman, Megan Rowe, was the final witness and then the committal was over. Rex Wild stood up and said quietly, 'That is all our evidence, Your Worship.'

No summing up from the DPP, no reiteration of the strength of the case against Murdoch, a sense of apology rather than conviction in the DPP's voice. No rabbits were appearing from DPP sleeves. That was all there was.

McGregor asked Murdoch if he had anything to say. Murdoch stood up and said firmly over his glass enclosure, 'I am not guilty of any of the allegations, Your Honour.'

In spite of this, McGregor found a case to answer, and Murdoch became the defendant rather than the accused.

◆ ◆ ◆

More interesting than the revelations during the committal were the unanswered questions raised.

Crime scene investigators were unable to explain why, after finding a lip-balm lid under a bush where it is thought Joanne Lees hid, a 'shoulder-to-shoulder search' by trained police officers (and a subsequent search by trackers) had overlooked the lip-balm container and two pieces of black tape that may have come from Joanne's efforts to bite off her restraints. These were discovered three months later under some leaf litter in exactly the same place. The court was told that each group expected the other to search that 'significant' area properly, but neither did.

Specialist police also admitted that they did not wear covers on their boots while they were line-searching the area the morning after the incident. Trackers were not brought in for a week, and by then the area was contaminated with hundreds of prints. This raises questions about how 'three partial shoe prints' said to match Joanne Lees's sandals could definitely be identified. In fact, apart from photos of the prints in situ, there seem to have been no further examination of these prints.

Then there was the argument about the testing – or not testing – of the rear of the Kombi for gunpowder residue and blood spatter. If Peter Falconio was shot at close range, there was likely to be some gunshot residue or body matter on the Kombi. Crime scene investigators explained that gunshot residue 'doesn't hold too well' on surfaces like oxidised paint, and that the 'fingerprinting process might brush it off'.

Almost two years after Peter Falconio disappeared, the officer who collected the relevant samples still had not submitted them to be tested, because forensic services in Darwin had told him to 'hold on to it' until further notice. Grant Algie asked the officer scathingly:

'How many years do you think you might have to hang on to it?' No blood spatters were found on the van, and no blood inside. The belief that Falconio met his death by gunshot injury was based on two premises. First, there was blood, later identified as his, on the road, although no one seems to be able to confirm that the amount would have been a lethal bleed. Secondly, Joanne Lees said she heard a 'bang', like a car backfiring, or a shot. But what if the noise she heard was not a gunshot? It appeared that Lees's assumption of a shot had been accepted as fact. Furthermore, no one so far had been able to identify the revolver Joanne Lees described. It appeared to be a one-off. Where was the trailer Murdoch was supposed to be pulling at Fitzroy Crossing, but which was absent in the truck-stop footage? Had Peter Falconio or Joanne Lees ever met Murdoch or Hepi? Who owned the blue sweatshirt Jazz saw at Sedan – Hepi, Murdoch, or Peter himself?

While there was no question of Joanne Lees being involved in the disappearance of her boyfriend, the fact that she avoided the full truth on several occasions under cross-examination raised the question of what else she might be hiding.

The case against Murdoch relied heavily on her testimony and the discovery of Murdoch's DNA, both on her T-shirt and in the Kombi van. Yet DNA analysis is a useful servant but a bad master. It had been shown to be fallible in several recent cases, and the Kombi results were likely to be ruled out at the trial due to incomplete testing and lack of proper procedures.

Finally, there was the confusion about the dog. Joanne Lees identified it as an Australian cattle dog. But Murdoch had a white dog with black spots. How could Joanne confuse the two? Police had taken a mouth swab from Murdoch's dog and put it on the Northern Territory animal database. So far it was the only specimen there. Alasdair McGregor joked, 'Did you say starter base or database? Perhaps it should be known as a barker base?'

And there was that single white hair. What had happened to that? Was it from Jack? Tests had been inconclusive.

The only definite conclusion that could be drawn so far was that the fat lady was still practising her scales. Key witnesses' evidence against Murdoch was faulty, the truck evidence sketchy, the weapon evidence irrelevant. There was no body, no weapon and no demonstrable motive for Peter's murder or the assault on Joanne.

Chapter Thirty-Six

'THE FRONTIERS OF DNA EVIDENCE'

*The prosecution's submission is just theory, speculation and
guesswork.*

Ian Barker, QC, 7 April 2005

In February, with the trial only three months away, I decided to
return to Darwin and Broome to seek a few more answers to the
outstanding questions that still plagued me. I planned to visit Brad
Murdoch in Darwin, then fly to Broome to see Jan, Loi O'Dare and
anyone else who'd talk to me, such as Bev Allen, friends/foes of
Murdoch, police, and so on.

It was about the worst time of the year to go to the Deep North, and
the temperature and humidity in the visitors' breezeway at Berrimah
Prison was almost unbearable. I shuddered to think what the cells
must be like – small, concrete and no air-conditioning.

Murdoch was in good spirits and counting down to the trial. He
was a little anxious about some new DNA evidence the DPP seemed
to be working on, but otherwise filled my head with snippets from the
PROMIS file.

He said I should try to find the police officers who drove Joanne
south from Barrow Creek. 'Their statements say that Joanne kept
talking about "they" did this and you catch "them". She repeats
"they" in her own statements at times too,' he told me. Of course this
interested me because I'm not alone in thinking there may have been
more than one perpetrator at the scene. I planned to follow this up
with Col Hardman, who expressed similar views.

Murdoch said that his old nemesis, Detective Chalker, had done a test run with the Kombi van from Alice to the incident site to check the accuracy of the Kombi speedo. 'Apparently it was right, not fourteen kilometres out.'

'I wish I'd known that before,' I said. It would have saved us a lot of digging!'

'Yes, but it was backfiring and missing. Kombis are one of the few vehicles that backfire because of their air intake. Most people haven't even heard a car backfire, modern cars don't. Anyway, it got as far as Aileron on the way back and conked out. Had to be towed back to Alice.' He chuckled at the thought of Chalker stuck at Aileron, waiting for a tow.

He gave me a knowing look. 'Have you been to Aileron?'

'Not recently. We stopped in on our long trip in 2003, but only for a look. We didn't question anyone.'

'Maybe you should've,' he replied. But he wouldn't be drawn on this cryptic statement. I wondered if I'd missed something important. One of the British journos had been very interested in Aileron, and he wouldn't say why either.

I decided to risk a hard question.

'Do you think it's possible that James Hepi could have been travelling up the Stuart Highway that night? If this was the four-wheel drive seen by the Aboriginal couple heading north at around 9 pm, could he have got back to Broome in time to take that phone call from you at 4 am?'

He gave me a hard look in return.

Calculating before he answered, he finally said, 'The timing is possible. It's all bitumen that way. I haven't told you this before, but when he came out to open up the gate for me that morning, while we were unloading the hydro, I noticed his whole car was hot. Not warm, like from a dawn run down to Cable Beach, but hot. I didn't attach any importance to it then, but I've thought about it a lot since.'

'But Hepi doesn't look much like the drawing that Joanne produced,' I said.

'Neither do I,' he re-joined, quick as a flash. 'Maybe it was an accomplice?'

He said he didn't think the DPP would call the psychologist who'd hypnotised Joanne as a trial witness, because she'd put in two reports, one for each session, and in the second one she'd said it was possible that Joanne was not actually responding to the hypnosis technique, although she appeared to be. 'If she was just giving the same story she'd learned by heart, she might believe it, but how do we know it's the true story?' he asked.

I told him I'd like to check and asked him for the psychologist's name. She'll get a hell of a shock when I phone her, I thought, but I can't rely solely on his information – although it's hardly ever been wrong. But I only hear the bits from him that support his case, as you would expect.

He said seventeen unknown fingerprints had been identified in the Kombi, none of them his. 'She's never said the man was wearing gloves, so how could that be? It's not as if it's been wiped down, because they later ID'd some prints belonging to the mechanic, Rod Smith, who was in the van well before the attacker.'

Our visit was over in no time. He seemed pretty confident that the case against him was circumstantial – an obvious stitch-up. *There is that dratty bit of DNA to explain though*, I thought as I walked through the soggy heat blanket to the haven of the car air conditioning. It was found within two days of the attack and it's a dead-cert full match with Murdoch's.

As I drove off, I wondered what 'new DNA' the DPP was looking for. Was it a better match on the gearstick or steering wheel, or something even more incriminating?

◆ ◆ ◆

Broome was hotter than Darwin, if you can imagine it. Forty-two degrees and humidity in the high eighties. My sluggish brain classified this little expedition as 'extreme research'.

Jan greeted me at the airport with a new hair colour. I'd been yakking to her on the phone the night before while she'd had the colour in, and she'd been worried that if I didn't hang up, all her hair would fall out. Fortunately, it hadn't.

We had a good catch-up and she told me she'd been racing around trying to obtain documents certifying the pedigree of Jack the Dalmatian from his parents' owners, and getting a set of the unique canopy ties from Tropical Upholstery to take to Darwin. She'd also been keeping Brad's parents' spirits up. His dad was very sick and wanted to go to Darwin to see Brad, but Brad had said no. He didn't want his father to see him in prison. Late in the afternoon I drove off to see Loi O'Dare. I didn't phone first, and he was nervous the minute he saw me. I'd timed my arrival at closing time again and, because he's a nice, polite man, he very reluctantly stayed a little while and chatted.

I wanted to know if he'd ever been shown any enhanced photos of the truck-stop vehicle, so that he could more accurately identify the canopy as his – or not. He said he'd been shown some just before his appearance at the 'pre-trial' last year and they had raised serious doubts.

'But those photos were not produced at the committal, were they?" I said, certain I couldn't remember any.

'No, I was just told they'd be asking me questions about my statement. Not to worry about those photos. But I have worried. A lot. And I've heard other things here in Broome and now I'm worried that an innocent man might go to jail because I made a mistake. I'm not sleeping. I just want this trial to be over!'

Join the queue, I thought.

I asked him about the 'things' he'd heard and who he'd heard them from but he got evasive and refused to say any more. He wanted to close up shop.

'There's no need to worry,' I told him as I left. 'All you have to do is tell the truth in the witness box. You won't lose sleep over telling the truth.'

At the Satay Bar I ran into an Aboriginal friend of Murdoch's who told me what a champion good bloke Brad was and how he wouldn't hurt a fly. Known hydro dealer, yes – murderer, no way. This was interesting coming from an Aboriginal, considering Murdoch was supposed to be a racist. I said 'Hullo' to Hepi's lawyer who was there too, wearing a tropical shirt and a long, grey ponytail down his back. I wanted to interview him, but not in front of the barflies. Over the phone would be better. Bev Allen was in hiding and none of my usual tricks flushed her out.

Next day I tried the police. Detective Pete Jenal was in Perth, most of the other officers were away, and I was referred to the Area Commander because there was still a very tight lid on the case. He hadn't been there at the time, so that was a fizzer too.

It had been a long trip without much result, but sometimes you just have to try. I headed for home, telling Jan I'd see her in a few weeks.

Soon after I returned to Melbourne, Murdoch's much-loved father, Colin, died. Murdoch was devastated and thought about asking permission to go to the funeral under guard. But he wanted a prison-guard escort, not a police escort.

'The police case is so weak against me,' he told Jan on the phone, 'that if they could they'd shoot me in the back "trying to escape" and save it being tested in court. And save a lot of money'. So he stayed in jail.

The trial date of 3 May was coming up fast. Jan quit her job and made arrangements to stay in Darwin, despite a few dark mutterings on the phone from Murdoch, who'd told her some trouble was brewing. My friends Mark Wilton and his wife, Traci, had generously offered me a room, so I made plans to leave Clive and the Pekes for the expected six weeks.

On 21 April the *voir dire*, which would decide which bits of contentious evidence could be led at the trial in the hearing of a jury, commenced before the new chief justice, Brian Martin, who would preside over the trial. The hearing would be held in the ten days leading up to the trial itself. I debated about going up earlier, but thought it would only be boring legal argument, so I didn't. Wrong!

Overseas DNA experts had been hard at work on Carmen Eckhoff's samples. And now the DPP planned to test the results in court. If the judge allowed them to produce the allegedly damning results, they could be very damaging to Murdoch's defence. Ms Eckhoff's previous orthodox forensic testing on the mixed DNA on the gearstick and steering wheel produced such poor results that they are inconclusive and therefore inadmissible in court. But if the new tests could place Murdoch in the van, he'd have a hard time talking his way out of being at the crime scene.

Murdoch's defence team were furious when they heard of the new DNA evidence, which had been suddenly sprung on them only the day before the *voir dire* began. Nervous about what might be produced, Grant Algie had asked Ian Barker, QC, the lawyer who'd made Lindy Chamberlain tremble and crumple in the witness box, to appear pro bono for their client. Mr Barker loves a good stoush and he accepted. He knows the way the legal system works in the Deep North.

And in another, more sensational development, the Crown announced they had new DNA evidence linking Murdoch with the cable-tie manacles.

When Tony Elliot sprang the new DNA surprise about the manacles, Mr Barker said in a loud aside to Mr Algie, 'He'll be showing me a signed confession next!' This indicated the frustration of the defence at this latest development so near to the trial date, after the forensic people had had the materials for four years.

The new evidence about the DNA traces on the gearstick and steering wheel was to be presented by UK expert Dr Jonathan Whitaker, whose world-first low copy number (LCN) DNA testing technique had allegedly identified fragments of DNA belonging to Murdoch at the crime scene. He would then allege that the same kind of fragment tests done in Australia had shown Murdoch's DNA on the cable ties for the first time.

Proclaiming an ambush by the prosecution, Mr Barker made an immediate application to have the legal hearing stopped and the trial date, a week away, pushed back to enable the defence to do their own testing.

Commenting on the new development, Judge Brian Martin told Deputy DPP Tony Elliott, 'the evidence you propose to lead, if accepted by the jury, would inevitably place the accused not only at the scene, but having handled the ties used to tie up Miss Lees. It is critical.'

In another body blow, Team Bradley was informed that, in order to provide his LCN DNA findings, Dr Whitaker destroyed all three samples of the mixed DNA from the gearstick and steering wheel, leaving none for the defence to have analysed by an independent laboratory – if there is another lab doing this sort of testing anywhere else in the world.

DPP Rex Wild told the court that Dr Whitaker's unique work was 'pushing the frontiers of DNA evidence'. Mr Barker was not a bit impressed, countering with the argument that the new evidence was 'of tremendous prejudice to Mr Murdoch'.

Mr Barker advised His Honour, 'You cannot and should not proceed with this case a moment longer.'

But Justice Martin wanted to hear evidence from both Dr Whitaker, who had flown in from his base in Wetherby, Yorkshire, and from forensic scientist Carmen Eckoff. He told Mr Elliott to have Ms Eckhoff in court the next day. She was unable to attend and sent a sick note. Unimpressed, the judge indicated he still wanted to hear from her. When she attended, the court heard that in March 2005, only a month before, Ms Eckhoff took three samples of human DNA material to England to be tested by Dr Whitaker at his agency, the Forensic Science Service.

Dr Whitaker and his colleague Dr Peter Gill are well known in

England for their involvement in a number of high-profile appeal cases, including the one involving a convicted criminal who spent twenty years in jail for a crime he did not commit.

Dr Whitaker had limited success with two of the Australian samples, but made a request to Ms Eckhoff to test the third and last remaining tube of material taken from the Falconio van, in order to get a result that would stand up in a court of law. Ms Eckhoff gave her permission.

The results matched the DNA of Bradley John Murdoch by odds of 1 to 19,000, leaving the defence in rather a deep hole.

Mr Barker pointed out that at the outset of the Falconio incident, Ms Eckhoff's superior was Ms Joy Kuhl, who had destroyed evidence of blood in the infamous Lindy Chamberlain case.

Ms Eckhoff said she was aware Ms Kuhl was attacked for destroying blood samples and that the Chamberlain case had changed the way blood was dealt with throughout the forensic community in Australia.

Mr Barker suggested Ms Eckhoff knew that when she gave Dr Whitaker permission to use the third DNA sample it would yield positive results for the Crown case.

'You knew the practice in Australia was to preserve samples,' said Mr Barker.

Ms Eckhoff: 'Yes, where possible.'

Mr Barker: 'And this was a case where the sample should be preserved. You took it upon yourself to have the evidence destroyed.'

Ms Eckhoff: 'Used to obtain a scientific result.'

When Dr Whitaker gave evidence later, he was asked by His Honour how long it would take him to do further DNA fragment tests on the cable ties used to restrain Miss Lees. Dr Whitaker said it would take him no more than two weeks.

Chief Justice Martin then had to decide whether or not to postpone the trial. Later in the day, following submissions from Team Bradley, Mr Martin ruled that in fairness to both the prosecution and the accused, he must abandon the 3 May trial date so that further testing could be carried out.

Chapter Thirty-Seven

THE 'TRIAL'
OF JOANNE LEES

This is not 'The Trial of the Century' – it's my trial!
Bradley John Murdoch, Darwin, 16 October 2005

Anticipation was high as we assembled at the Darwin Supreme court for a media briefing the day before the 'Trial of the Century' would begin. It was Sunday afternoon and the hundred-strong media contingent attended the formal court surroundings in casual tropical gear, looking like raggedy trimmings for Carmen Miranda's hat. It was more like a high school reunion than a pre-trial briefing, everyone comparing hairstyles, weight loss (or gain!) and other places they'd been during the long wait for today.

We'd been told security for Joanne would be high, but she'd be walking in the front door like every other witness this time – no TRG escorts and mad media chases. She had arrived in Darwin the previous Friday at 4.30 am, met by a selected number of media representatives who'd photographed a tired and drawn young woman, much slimmer than she'd been last year. Murdoch had told me yesterday during my visit with him at Berrimah that he was very relieved to read the reports of her arrival in his morning paper. The jurisdiction of the Northern Territory Supreme Court does not extend to the UK, so strictly speaking, she could have refused.

If she hadn't come, he told me, 'I reckon I would have walked free in a few days, but I always would have had that stigma hanging over me. Now I say, "Bring it on." I'm really looking forward to the whole thing.'

As we all were. I'd heard on the already-active grapevine that Chief Justice Brian Martin had personally briefed court security guards and told them Murdoch's trial was to be conducted like any other – no special treatment for the accused or witnesses. No one would be sneaking in and out of his court. Security had been increased and four new applicants for guard positions had been specially selected by the sheriff himself. Airport-style security had been installed in the foyer, and a guard would be on duty at the door of the court at all times. Guards would not be permitted to sit in the court in uniform, however, in case their presence implied to the jury that trouble was expected. The Chief Justice was bending over backwards to ensure that nothing happened to abort the trial.

Much of the media briefing was taken up with how the media would be allowed to film the start witness. Ropes would keep them back, effectively providing Joanne with a walkway to the front door. She and her phalanx of friends, Witness Support people and DPP minders would arrive in a government-funded black limo with darkened windows. The only thing missing will be the red carpet, I thought. She would do no interviews. We were reminded of her victim status. After several admonishments about not publishing any material that might prejudice a fair trial, or worse, cause a mistrial because the jury had access to speculative or prejudicial stories, we all wandered out into the glaring heat of Darwin. Visitors from 'down south', like me, can't comprehend how anyone can live here all year round. Perhaps the Noel Coward song should be amended to 'Mad dogs and Territorians…' Not for the first time, I cursed the long delay since May.

Murdoch had been pretty flat after the postponement too. He's said as much when I'd visited him on Friday, seeing him for the first time since my visit in February.

'At first I didn't give a shit,' he said. 'Just lay about in my cell, feeling really depressed. Then I got my second wind and I've been hard at work ever since.'

His 'work' had been to trawl the rich mind of the PROMIS file, looking for little gems that might assist Team Bradley in his defence. Few defence barristers in Australia can have had such a dedicated and committed researcher, I thought. Why not, when it might mean the difference between a life on the road or a life sentence in Berrimah?

Beside Murdoch in his single cell sat a hard-won computer (modified to 'read only') along with boxes of disks containing the entire police brief of over 150,000 pages of evidence, reports, statements, photos, conjecture and more than a few surprises. It is virtually unheard of for prisoners to have access to the entire police brief and a computer to research it, but due to the evidence given by police at the committal hearing in 2004 as they constantly referred to 'the file' to be produced. The magistrate then stipulated this privilege.

'I've perfected a way of matching up handwritten notes,' he told me conspiratorially. He was referring to the various notes that had been scanned into the file, usually written by a police officer, but sometimes not dated or signed.

'You look at the letter "e", how that's formed is usually quite distinct and it's the letter that occurs most often in writing. If you can match that letter with similar-shaped "e" in signed notes or a signature elsewhere in the file, you've got a match.'

I reflected on how much talent seems to be wasted in prisons around this country. Pity some of it has not been put to more productive use.

Murdoch's purpose in matching up notes with formal statements was to try to identify any differences or anomalies with which the witnesses could be challenged. Murdoch seemed pretty pleased with the outcome of these endeavours and promised a few surprises during the trial. He was less pleased about the proposed evidence from the British world expert in DNA, Dr Jonathan Whitaker. Murdoch didn't accept that a tiny trace of a partial match to his DNA could be detected on the inside layers of one ring of the black tape manacles allegedly used to restrain Joanne Lees. He was convinced it was planted to seal his fate and, using our empty potato chip packet, he showed me a model of the manacle construction and where the trace of DNA was located.

'How could my DNA only get on one inside bit of those manacles?' he challenged me, 'when if the tape was so sticky and I'd manufactured them, there should be my DNA on all of the sections, not just that one that conveniently got sent to the UK. And how come they didn't send it until four years after the alleged incident?' He leaned across the table and whispered, 'They've found DNA that fits Falconio inside the manacles as well.' He sat back with a smirk.

Once more I was cursing at not being allowed to bring in writing implements. There was always so much to remember after a prison visit.

'How do you know it was Peter's DNA?' I whispered back. Could he be kidding me?

'There's just as much match with his DNA as there is with mine,' he asserted. 'Neither was a full profile, but if mine was there, they had plenty of opportunity to plant it there,' he concluded.

If Peter Falconio's trace DNA was found on the manacles it put a whole different light on what might have happened at Barrow Creek.

Murdoch also told me about Joanne's movements in Alice Springs on the day Peter was last seen. He said they'd gone early to the library where Peter left Joanne to email her friends while he went to make inquiries about his tax return. He enjoyed finding references to Joanne Lees. After all, her evidence against him was one of the reasons he was sitting in that stinking hot concrete box with little prospect of ever seeing his family again.

'My father and one brother have already been buried without me,' he said intensely. 'My mum is in her eighties – she'll be next, this is killing her anyway, then my older brother. If I'm locked up in here, my whole family will probably die before I get out. I will leave this place a bitter, angry man.'

It didn't seem a good time to say he might never leave this place, in view of the Northern Territory government's recent debates about refusing parole (even after twenty years) to all murderers doing life.

A politician's proclamation of 'Life means life in the Northern Territory' is a proven vote catcher in the Deep North.

Murdoch continued telling me about the morning of 14 July 2001. He said that after the argument, Joanne decided she would go back to Sydney for a week once they reached Brisbane and Peter would travel from Brisbane to Papua New Guinea, returning to join her so that they could leave Australia from Brisbane together as planned. They went to buy her ticket that day, but did not arrange to buy one for him.

So much for all the air tickets in his name rumoured to have been found in the Kombi, I thought. Although there might have been tickets to Thailand – Murdoch couldn't remember. I'd seen on Chris Tangey's video that all their possessions from the Kombi had been piled haphazardly in a corner in the police compound where the Kombi was stored, so anything could have gone missing anyway.

I was looking forward to hearing it all from Joanne herself. I ran into Grant Algie at the Sailing Club that evening. The sunset as disappointing and so were his responses to most of my probing. He reminded me of my mother, saying 'Wait and see' so often I gave up.

The jury selection from a pool of eighty-five was held in a big courtroom downstairs. Murdoch had told me he was allowed twelve challenges and that his preferred jury was middle-aged women and young black men, if possible, 'who know how the police can stitch you up'. He didn't want 'management types' or young women who might identify with Joanne Lees. Using eleven of his twelve challenges, he got pretty much the jury he wanted – a jury of six men and six women, with three spares in case anyone had to retire.

Mr Wild may have cottoned on to this strategy, because he used several of his challenges as well, to even things out a bit.

The jostling and lobbying for seats in Court 4 was fierce. Public queues stretched through the lobby and a special TV screen had been set up in Court 2 for the overflow. Selected media organisations were allocated one seat each in Court 4, and I was relieved I had asked Jan to arrange a reserved seat next to her for me, otherwise I'd have been watching on a TV screen, after all that time and all those kilometres. Anyway, I'd figured she'd need a bit of moral support to get through the trial and I didn't see anyone else volunteering.

A whole front row was reserved for Peter Falconio's parents and his brothers, Paul and Nick. Joanne and her various minders would sit behind them once she'd given her evidence. There were only five seats left for the taxpayers, who were funding the trial. It became an interesting contrast as the trial progressed, with Joanne and the Falconio family, quite rightly receiving extensive support from court counsellors and members of the DPP's staff, while Jan, innocent of any misdemeanour except believing in Bradley, sat alone day after day, a solitary and somewhat sad figure, hoping against hope for an outcome that would allow her to drive off into the sunset with the bloke she'd stood by for many years.

Joanne made her entrance in the same black-and-white outfit she'd worn at the committal, albeit probably a couple of sizes smaller. Her hair was longer and pulled back into a ponytail. It became apparent as soon as she'd sat in the witness box that she had received extensive preparation on how to present her evidence. 'Not from our DPP either,' I wrote in my notes. 'She hasn't been here long enough to become this polished.' She gave her answers in a clear voice, addressing most of the replies directly to the jury, the way expert witnesses are trained to do. She smiled at them often.

She said they did go to the library, then went to the Camel Cup for two or three hours, leaving around 3 pm, then they travelled through Alice to the Stuart Caravan Park where they took turns to have a clandestine shower (having checked out already). Pete first, then Joanne. She said she rang her friend Amanda in Sydney to tell her she'd changed her tickets to come to Sydney and said Pete was 'in the shower'. After her shower, Joanne did not change the shirt she'd worn at the Camel Cup. Peter was dressed in a pale blue short-sleeved shirt and khaki knee-length shorts. I realised this was the first time I'd ever heard what he'd been wearing that day. I remembered that Jazz had told me of finding a man's blue shirt at James Hepi's place in Sedan, with the 'Try hugs, not drugs' logo. But she had said it was long-sleeved. Could she have been mistaken?

After showering they went to Red Rooster to get something to eat for Pete, and left to drive north between 4 and 4.30 pm. This was new information. Before this she'd said they left the Camel Cup after seeing the Beauty Pageant ('if you could call it that' she joked to the jury) and drove north from there. Never any previous mention of showers or Red Rooster. The latest they could have left Alice Springs was about 4.30 pm or they would not have had a receipt for petrol saying 6.21 pm, as she told the court the top speed of the Kombi was about eighty kilometres per hour.

She said she didn't recall passing Aileron (a large roadhouse on the way to Ti Tree). Pete was reading *The Catcher in the Rye* before he fell asleep in the back, and she was listening to Texas on CD. 'It's the driver's privilege to choose the music,' she said, smiling at the jury.

Her familiar story continued, with a few extras to fill in some gaps. She estimated the incident began at about 8 pm. She told Mr Wild that the car that pulled alongside them was 'brightly lit up against the dark of the night, with its interior light on'. The vehicle had a bull-bar, silver or chrome, but she added that 'could have been due to the brightness of the light'.

She remembered that the lights of the vehicle parked behind them were on when Peter got out of the car. She wasn't sure if she was revving the car or not when she heard the bang. 'At first I thought it was a backfire,' she said. 'It was not until later I thought it could be a gunshot.'

Her smile vanished and she told the tale of her ordeal with the gunman. He wrestled with her on the gravel, trying to tie her legs together. He punched her on her right temple (which she pointed to as she looked at the jury) and the blow 'stunned me but did not knock me out'. Murdoch shook his head, with a sardonic grin.

She described wriggling down the mattress in the back of the four-wheel drive – hands still tied behind her, not brought to the front as Mr Stagg had testified at the committal – and reaching an opening at the rear of the canopy. 'I hung my legs over the edge, then I just ran,' she whispered to the jury. They were swivelled in their chairs to face her, every one of them enthralled, hanging on her every syllable. I'd heard the story so often that I'd forgotten how engrossing it must be the first time a new audience hears it.

She said having her hands tied behind her impeded her, so she ran 'not very long and not very far'. She stumbled and could hear the man behind her. 'I knew I could not outrun the man, so I hid, trying not to breathe.'

When Joanne finally emerged, having brought her hands to the front of her body, she tried to remove the handcuffs by 'mushing up my lip balm on the palm of my hands'. She then explained how she got under Vince's truck 'crouching or bending over to cross under the trailer'.

When the judge asked her how she felt through her ordeal she said she'd realised she was more scared of being raped than being shot by the man. 'The realisation hit me that he might have killed Pete.' She hiccupped back a little sob. Mrs Falconio, listening intently, seemed close to tears too.

Joanne described meeting Cathy Curly at Barrow Creek and said Cathy's blue heeler was 'of similar breed to the dog I saw'. She also vaguely remembered being shown Chris Malouf (the Broome itinerant gunman lookalike) and his four-wheel drive out the front the next morning, but said she did not examine the vehicle, merely 'glanced at it'.

The jurors were shown some photos taken of Joanne at Barrow Creek the next day. Although Helen had told me Joanne's feet 'didn't have a mark on them' I could see on the electronic screen that she did have a few scratches on her legs and deep grazes on her knees and elbows. But her three-quarter-length shorts were not bloodstained around the knees. Surely if she'd been curled up tightly in the bush and she had already sustained those injuries, the knees of her pants would be stained. But if she'd grazed them crawling under the truck...?

Joanne was shown the drawings she worked on with Mr Stagg, the Art teacher in Alice Springs. She now claimed they were 'not accurate'. She said many of the comments written around the sketches were not her directions to him, just notes made by the artist. Others she said she couldn't remember if she said or not.

But the major departure from her previous evidence about the vehicle came when she was asked how she got into the back of the four-wheel drive. Since the committal, perhaps Joanne had become aware that not one vehicle in Australia was found answering her description of a 'crawl-through' from the cabin to the tray. She told the court: 'I don't know how I got to the back. I'm not sure if he put me from the front or the back, or around the side' This made His Honour sit up. He asked what she meant by this new evidence.

'Perhaps because we had front to rear access in the Kombi – now I've had time to reflect – and as I landed on my stomach in the back, it's possible he might have pushed me in through the side.'

'A bob each way,' I wrote in my notes.

'Is the man that attacked you in court?' asked Mr Wild. She turned to stare across at Murdoch.

'Yes, I'm looking at him.'

Murdoch shook his head vigorously.

She nodded emphatically in reply, her mouth partly open in that slightly surprised look she sometimes has.

Mr Wild went on to ask her a series of questions about the rear of the four-wheel drive. She firstly said there was 'natural' light coming in through the rear of the canopy, which was open, although outside 'it was pitch black, but there was light'. She said when the man lifted the canopy to get the sack out to put over her head, she could see the canopy was green from the interior light of the cabin.

She said the reason the drawing of the man had longer hair than Murdoch was 'because I felt pressured to get a photo out there so that people could be looking for the man. I wasn't satisfied, I said the hair wasn't quite right.'

Wild gave her a lead by reminding her she'd told police when shown the truck-stop video that the man was 'too old'.

Joanne's new ease with presenting evidence, which was very noticeable to those who'd seen her at the committal, became more apparent with her reply.

'Police were later able to show me a better-quality picture and now, after four years, I say, "That is the man who attacked me."' She admitted that on 10 October 2002, before Northern Territory police went to see her with a photo-board on which she identified Murdoch, she had seen a photo of the alleged suspect, identified as Murdoch, on the internet. But she insisted that when she saw that internet photo, she immediately thought, 'That's the man.'

She also agreed that when shown a photo of Cathy Curly's brown and grey blue heeler, Tex, she had told police that Tex 'looks like the man's dog'.

Under cross-examination, the nervous cough she'd displayed at the committal returned. And all of us who'd followed the case for so long thought she had cause for anxiety. Murdoch's entire defence rested heavily upon Mr Algie being able to discredit Joanne Lees as a witness. If her reliability was questionable, then so was the Crown case.

She said when the man put the gun to her temple, she felt no heat and smelled nothing. She said that the man had the gun in his right hand and she saw no handcuffs or tape in his left hand. Joanne said she'd been wearing the glasses that she usually wore for driving as an aid to watch out for kangaroos and that the man removed them before he put the handcuffs on.

'Wonder if there were any prints on those,' I wrote in my notes. 'And why was the guy so polite?' Murdoch had told me during one of my visits that the police inventory showed that her glasses had been found in the Kombi in their case on the dashboard.

'I was moving and screaming and struggling the whole time,' she told the jury. She said she didn't look for Peter as she was taken between the vehicles. 'I was concerned for my own life.'

Mr Algie pushed her hard on the front to rear access.

She told the jury that she believed at the time she was forcibly pushed between the seats into the rear of the vehicle.

'Police later told me there was no such vehicle and that has put doubt in my mind. It's a possibility the man lifted the flap where he got the bag out and I was put in there.'

She had no recollection of getting out of the cabin and no recollection of being put in the side.

Mr Algie read her a passage from her interview in Alice Springs on 7 August 2001:

> *Detective Henrys: There was no other possible way?*
> *You definitely went in through the seats?*
> *Detective Kerr: And you're quite sure it's over the seats?*
> *Joanne: In between the seats.*

She told Mr Algie that, 'I can't remember police telling me there was no such thing as front to rear access. It's possible I could have got from front to rear by some other means.'

She repeated her assertion from the committal that her head was at the cabin end, feet pointing towards the back – a strange way to end up if pushed backwards through a space between the seats. She also denied telling Stagg about bringing her hands to her front and feeling around in the tray of the four-wheel drive.

Mr Algie was visibly annoyed by her well-rehearsed answers. He moved on to the dog. He had been very cranky at the committal that Mr Wild had shown Joanne the photos of Jack (looking very white-with-black-spots) outside the court and told her he was Murdoch's dog. She'd identified it shortly afterwards in court as the dog she saw in the four-wheel drive. He asked Joanne to repeat this information to the jury. His Honour interrupted and asked, 'You say you looked at a photo knowing it was a photo of a dog belonging to the accused? When you saw this photo, did that knowledge influence your identification of the dog?'

'No,' replied Joanne. 'I was not influenced by that knowledge. The similarities are clear.'

I was blowed if I could see how they were similar, but I was not in the witness box.

When Mr Algie took her through her account of the afternoon in Alice Springs, further anomalies appeared.

Mr Algie read her a statement in which she said they ate at Red Rooster and headed north from Alice Springs at around 2 to 2.30 pm.

'Did you see Mr Murdoch at Red Rooster?' Mr Algie asked. 'No, why would I?' she flashed back.

I noted, 'Must ask Murdoch if he got Red Rooster. Maybe he bumped into her in the queue!'

She said they did not stop at Aileron or anywhere else. It took three and a half hours to get to Ti Tree (195 kilometres).

'So if they got there around 6 pm they must have left at 2.30 pm', I wrote. 'What's going on here? The times keep changing.' Regardless of this confusion, it was the fact they bought fuel at Ti Tree at 6.21 pm and the Kombi speedo showed they had travelled 107 kilometres since then, which at about eighty kilometres per hour put them at the incident site between 7.30 pm and 8 pm.

Grant Algie then challenged her identification of Murdoch. He pointed out she had not said anything to Mr Stagg about the hair length of her attacker in the drawing and asserted she was mistaken about Murdoch being her assailant. Upon getting the stern reply 'I would recognise him anywhere', Mr Algie said, 'No further questions' and sat down.

'Joanne sailed through with flying colours,' I wrote. 'Whoever coached her has certainly scored a few goals for the prosecution. Mr Algie's anger at her replies was barely concealed, and it's my guess he's decided that she's so well trained he's not going to score without making himself look like a bastard for berating the victim and giving Joanne further brownie points. His only recourse it to attempt to highlight the anomalies in her version of events through the evidence of other witnesses.'

The media room was gloomy. Many people thought she 'got off lightly'. No major headlines. No illicit love affairs. No demolition of the star witness. That's what it all came down to for the editors – who's kicking goals?

Chapter Thirty-Eight

WITNESSES FOR THE PROSECUTION

The truth is rarely plain and never simple.

Oscar Wilde

After the almost anticlimactic appearance of Joanne Lees, media pencils were re-sharpened in the hope that the rest of the witnesses would provide a steady stream of front pages.

Before going on with Vince Millar, His Honour took up an offer made by Joanne to demonstrate to the jury how she brought her hands to the front. She returned to the court in a designer tracksuit and performed the feat in two seconds flat.

Vince didn't add much to the evidence he'd given at the committal. He stuck firmly to his assertion that there was a good metre of clearance under his trailer dolly and that Joanne had 'crab walked' underneath, not crawled.

'She had a fair bit of bark off her when I first saw her,' he told the jury. They seemed to understand, but not familiar with truckies' vernacular, His Honour needed clarification. This judge is asking a lot of questions, I thought.

We heard from Dr Matthew Wright, who was on call at Alice Springs Hospital on the night Joanne was brought in. He said Joanne was 'pretty subdued', and he obtained most of the history from the police officers accompanying her. He said her 'small lacerations' were dressed by nursing staff and that she made no mention of having been hit in the temple.

His 'attention was not drawn to any lacerations on her wrists or her face or body', and he did not observe any other injuries. He did not conduct a full physical examination of Joanne.

Les Pilton was his usual cheerful and expansive self, repeating his claim to fame as the publication of the now famous Barrow Creek Hotel for the last time in court, although pub patrons will no doubt hear it for years to come. His Honour asked Les if he was present when Joanne was shown Malouf and his four-wheel drive. Les said he was outside watching.

'Did you see what she did?'

'They opened the canopy, but she did not climb in. They also opened the cab, driver's door, and she looked in there as well.'

Mr Algie followed this lead by questioning if Joanne got into the vehicle.

'She looked into the truck; she did not get in,' Les told the jury. Cathy Curly's new contribution came from the fact that she'd mentioned three men whom she knew as truckies who all looked like the Comfit photos and who all drove white four-wheel drives, only emphasising the size of the task faced by the Northern Territory police in those early days.

We heard from a police witness, that dog hair had been found on the manacles and pieces of tape from Vince's rocker box. Could that have been Hartley's hair or did it belong to the offender's dog? The tape had been sent off for analysis.

At the beginning of Day 6, Mr Algie got up before the jury came in and addressed Chief Justice Martin. He said that he had an 'issue of concern' regarding the way His Honour had been asking questions of witnesses during both evidence in chief and cross-examination. He said in his opinion the intervention of judges should be relatively rare, when something was left unclear. Mr Algie said the jury might think that the influence of his high office placed greater weight on the questions asked and he concluded, 'I invite Your Honour to refrain from the approach you have adopted.'

Chief Justice Martin listened politely and then answered abruptly. 'I don't agree.' He said he would continue to ask questions and that he was certain the jury would put the appropriate weight on his lines of inquiry. Later in the morning, he instructed the jury to do just that.

Murdoch had been active in his glass box with his red pen as well as the blue pen. He'd told me during a visit that he was 'keeping a record with his red pen' every time the judge 'interrupted'. He was assembling material for an appeal already.

Pamela Nabangardi and Jasper Jimbajimba, the Aboriginal couple who were very credible witnesses at the committal, were just as believable today. The evidence I was most interested in was the white four-wheel drive they saw going north at about 9 pm. For quite some time I'd been convinced there had been more than one offender at the scene and that possibly one of them might have been James Hepi, because Murdoch had told his father that he and Hepi were 'both on the road that night and James was about twenty minutes ahead of me'. Although he was in Broome at 4.30 am to take the call when Murdoch arrived, he could have beaten Murdoch to Broome, travelling on sealed roads nearly all the way. Could this have had something to do with the 'Ecstasy deal gone wrong in the Northern Territory in 2001' he'd told Jazz about?

I'd also been told by a police officer since I'd been in Darwin that Hepi had been seen in Kununurra on the Sunday during the day, with his dog and Murdoch's, which was unusual. If that was true, he could have easily made it to Broome that night. The same person had told me that the Kombi had been searched more ruthlessly in Darwin, with the new panels installed by Peter Falconio and Paul Dale pulled out and found to have hidden a bag of Ecstasy tablets. So far, I'd been unable to confirm this, but if it was true there could be the real motive for the attack. And if Peter was giving the Ecstasy a 'lift' and Joanne knew nothing about that, it could be the reason they'd been pulled over. Perhaps the fire they'd seen earlier, where Peter wanted to stop, was a signal fire? There were so many unanswered questions still.

While I was thinking this over, we had completely new information from the owner and two staff of the roadhouse at Aileron. All three stated categorically that Joanne and Peter had stopped for a short black coffee, a Coke and toasted sandwiches.

The owner of the roadhouse gave the most colourful account.

'It was about 3.30 pm, and I was a bit stuffed workin' outside. I start work when the sun's up, go home when the moon's risin'. So I decided to go in and make a cuppa and smoke a coupla joints. I saw a van outside and thought it was a load of ferals. I was gunna give 'em a mouthful, but Mick [the manager] pointed out a young couple at the table. They were well dressed and clean, not hippies. I watched them talkin' and goin' through paperwork. The woman looked pretty all right, slim, dark hair, a Pom. He looked Italian or Greek, short cropped hair, wog-style complexion, accent. They were there about forty minutes.'

He said the girl was wearing a dress. 'Couldn't have been Joanne,' I wrote, 'unless she changed.' When asked if the woman had a ponytail, he couldn't remember.

'I didn't perv on her that hard,' he said with a wide grin. He agreed that he was shown photos of Peter and Joanne by Jeanette Kerr about two weeks later.

'Same people,' he told the jury. 'Definitely them. Otherwise they got a good set of twins in Australia.'

What were we to make of this? If they were there at around 4 pm, they could still have been at Ti Tree at 6.21 pm, but they would have had to leave Alice Springs much earlier than 4.30 pm.

The manager of the Camel Cup told us that the Beauty Pageant, which Joanne had said she'd seen, took place at 2.30 pm and the Camel Cup ran at 4.15 pm. Then they still had to have a shower and go to Red Rooster. The timelines were all over the place. Murdoch had been plotting these timelines for months, and I was starting to see what he meant when he told me they didn't compute.

◆ ◆ ◆

A procession of police witnesses went over the old ground, giving evidence about the aftermath of the incident and the activities around Barrow Creek. We heard about a metal-detector search for Peter's watch, his keys and a religious medallion, none of which were found. Two officers who experienced vigorous questioning were Constable Tim Sandry and Constable Ian Spilsbury, who were the Crime Scene Examiners on the spot. They found the lip-balm lid, but did not look any further, which Mr Algie implied was very strange, suggesting that as detectives – and specially trained crime scene detectives at that – if they'd found one half of an object, they'd be likely to at least 'have a poke around' for the other half. But they didn't. The discovery three months later of two little bits of tape sitting in plain view on top of the leaf litter with the bottom part of the lip balm nearby raised a lot of speculation about why these vital bits of evidence had not been found during the first search. Mr Algie suggested to both witnesses that the items were 'planted', which of course they denied. The media ran with the 'Police Planted Evidence?' headline, nevertheless.

Tim Sandry's evidence was not over, though. His next involvement was that he'd been called out after hours on 18 October 2002 by Dr Peter Thatcher, head of the Forensic Services in Darwin, to take a brown paper bag containing the cable-tie restraints down to Adelaide. Murdoch had been arrested by this time and Sandry gave evidence that he was instructed to take the bag to Adelaide and deliver it to Superintendent Colleen Gwynne, who intended to confront Murdoch with them during an interview at Yatala. Despite his misgivings about transporting the originals of the cable ties rather than a photo or a mock-up, Sandry was outranked and he did as he was told.

He says he checked the bag in to the Adelaide police forensic custody storeroom, which was locked with restricted access. The problem from Mr Algie's position was that this storage room was where all the stuff impounded from Murdoch's arrest, covered in his DNA, was kept. Days of prosecution evidence were then elicited from Mr Sandry, to demonstrate that no contamination could have occurred accidentally. The jury's eyes were glazing over, as were everyone's. Even Sandry became angry at the endless and tedious questioning from Mr Elliott, taking out his frustration several times by punching a wall outside the court during one of the lunch breaks when he didn't know he could be seen. Sandry repeatedly assured the court that no contamination could have taken place, as the brown paper bags containing the manacles were never opened.

It seemed amazing to me that this brown paper sack, allegedly containing the actual manacles used to restrain Joanne Lees, had travelled from the Darwin Forensic Centre to the Adelaide police storeroom, to Yatala prison, back to the storeroom and home again on a plane without one person even peeking inside the bag to have a look – or show South Australian police colleagues. This was sensational and vital evidence in a high-profile case. More to the point, how did they all know the manacles were in there? 'Could have been a Christmas cracker,' I wrote in my notes. In addition, he told the court that he 'didn't ask Superintendent Gwynne what she was going to do with the manacles' and 'only found out later' that the plan was to produce them at Yatala. The bag was definitely not opened in Adelaide.

Further evidence was given about Sandry's trip to Berrimah Prison to photograph Murdoch to obtain his height and take video footage of him walking. These photos were the ones objected to during the *voir dire* and were to be used to assist the prosecution experts in attempting to prove that Murdoch was the man at the Shell truck stop. Sandry reported that Murdoch was 196 centimetres, or six foot five inches, tall. We heard in endless detail about how the manacles had been frozen to remove the effect of the stickiness and then pulled apart. Mr Elliott wanted Sandry to give his opinion about some cut ends of the manacle tape displayed on the board, but Sandry said that particular examination had not been done. For a minute I thought we might have to adjourn for a couple of days when he froze it and checked it out, but the judge was not impressed, saying that if the comparison was so important, it should have been done months ago.

Sandry looked relieved to complete his evidence in chief, but he was not off the hook yet.

The defence began canvassing the possibility of deliberate contamination. This was obviously going to be their strategy for the case. Sandry told us that was impossible. He said every precaution was taken to prevent contamination. He dismantled the manacles and placed them on a storyboard in little plastic bags, save for one link, which was sent to the UK to Dr Whitaker. He also told about a trip to Sedan where he'd taken several photos of Jack the dog: 'a very well-behaved dog, although a bit shy.'

Murdoch had told me that a vet had gone along on one of the police visits and had provided a report to the police that started off: 'I saw a dog of Dalmatian appearance...'

We heard next from a Dr Woodford who was an expert in gunshot wounds to the head. He said a .22 bullet would not necessarily exit the skull – 'it could lodge in the thicker part of the skull, or leave a person unable to make a sound by lodging in the larynx.' Mrs Falconio left the court in tears.

Why are we getting all this evidence about a .22 gun, I wondered, when it has not been proved that a shot was even fired? Or if you accept there was a host, how do we know the assailant used a .22?

Colleen Gwynne, looking even leaner than when I'd last seen her, said her original intention was to show Murdoch the manacles at Yatala. The bag was not opened. 'I was told it was the manacles, but I never actually looked to confirm it.'

Carmen Eckhoff, the Acting Chief Forensic Scientist in the Northern Territory due to Dr Thatcher's illness, was more organised in her presentations than previously. During my most recent visit to Berrimah, Murdoch had told me that Team Bradley had recruited a forensic specialist from Adelaide who would be sitting in the public gallery taking notes. He said she actually knew Carmel and had worked with her. Her job was to help develop the cross-examination questions.

Carmen's chief task was to present most of the DNA evidence against Murdoch and demonstrate it was forensically sound and had not been exposed to any contamination. Her evidence would be pivotal; if she could successfully demonstrate that Murdoch's DNA was found on Joanne's T-shirt, the steering wheel, the dashboard and the link of the manacles, to put it in a nutshell, he was in deep shit.

She gave evidence for a couple of days, detailing the collection of samples from the Barrow Creek scene, from Joanne at the hotel and the Kombi at Alice Springs, to all the subsequent testing. Each garment, item, sample was detailed. She affirmed that the 'unknown male' DNA sample was identified on Joanne's T-shirt within thirty-six hours of its return to Darwin, within three days of the alleged attack on Joanne Lees. She said two other samples had been taken from the middle back of the T-shirt, that tested positive for blood but were never tested for DNA. This was the sample that over a year later was found to be an exact match to Bradley Murdoch, once she had compared the SA sample sent to her from Yatala. She detailed how the other samples were taken from the gearstick and the steering wheel, partial matches to Murdoch, with, in her opinion, a very high likelihood of placing him in the van. Then the coup de grace, the report from Dr Whitaker to identify Murdoch's DNA on the manacle link.

She vigorously denied any possibility of accidental or deliberate contamination of any samples, although she was forced to admit that the DNA of her then head of forensics, Dr Peter Thatcher, had been identified on the manacles. Mr Algie asked her how this could have happened, and she said he'd have to ask Dr Thatcher. He immediately called for Dr Thatcher to be produced, despite his absence on sick leave.

'He's got a few things to explain,' muttered Jan, beside me. Carmen said the exhibits were kept in stapled brown paper bags, because plastic sweats and can degrade DNA. 'First we've heard mention of staples,' I noted. 'Everyone else says the bags are rolled shut.'

Arguments raged for days about the likelihood of this and the numerical significance of that. I learned that cigarette butts are in fact a good source of DNA – not from saliva, but from the skin cells that slough off lips as they are smoked.

Commander Hardman's email about properly examining the manacles and 'dismantling them if necessary, to get the DNA from them' was read out by Mr Algie.

Carmen said she did not dismantle the manacles and that this was done months later by forensic expert Tim Sandry. She said she had peeled the tape back in some areas to try to find any DNA.

Taken overall, her evidence was damaging to Murdoch, although it also highlighted a few forensic glitches. Murdoch was never going to overcome the perfect match on Joanne's T-shirt. While I have always maintained that technically this only places him next to the T-shirt, not necessarily next to Joanne at Barrow Creek, if he continued to deny meeting Joanne anywhere else and he didn't bump into her at Bolivar Caravan park, or the Camel Cup, or Red Rooster in Alice, Barrow Creek was looking good. But not for Murdoch.

Dr Jonathon Whitaker was younger and leaner than I'd expected. He recited his impressive credentials, then explained to the jury that his task had been to construct a DNA profile from anyone who might have handled the gearstick, the steering wheel or the link he received from the manacles. He described the 'quite intricate' construction of the loop, then explained he had gone 'right to the heart of the cable-tie construction' and tested the inner layer of tape. 'It's not rocket science,' he told the jury. 'I didn't test the outside because I recognised it may have been contaminated.' He said his opinion was that the outer layers had formed a complete barrier, allowing the inside to reveal scientific results.

All the samples he was sent produced DNA results. Tony Elliott took Dr Whitaker through the testing techniques in the minutest detail, earning a direction to 'get on with it' from the judge and a big cheer from the media room.

The steering wheel, the gearstick and, most damaging, the inside of the manacles, all revealed some degree of Murdoch's DNA.

Dr Whitaker went further. 'Bradley Murdoch appeared to be the major contributor to those sites.'

'Is it anyway significant if the last person to have driven the car was the offender and before that was Peter Falconio?'

'I think that's what you'd expect to find,' Dr Whitaker said.

His evidence went for a long time – layer upon layer of detail about how Murdoch's DNA was found on those three items. As the judge had said at the *voir dire*, 'this analysis inevitably places the accused not only at the scene, but having handled the ties used to tip up Miss Lees. It is critical.'

And DNA is the 'fingerprint' evidence of the twenty-first century. Viewed by most lay people as infallible. Things were not looking good for Murdoch if Mr Algie couldn't shake him.

Although Algie did his best to break him down, he turned to the jury and said firmly, 'I can assure that the interpretation is correct.'

A couple of police officers who attended at Barrow Creek gave evidence next. One of the officers said that when he took possession of Joanne's sandals, one of them 'had ash on them'. Carmen had said she'd seen ash on Joanne's sandal too. I've seen photos of the Kombi in the bush surrounded by the remains of a grass fire. Could Joanne have ventured nearer the Kombi hiding place than she realised? He also told us about the red heeler dog that had been shot, found on Neutral Junction Station. No significance was attached to this newly deceased dog, even though it resembled Joanne's description more closely than Jack.

Boot and shoe prints were photographed but not matched to any specific shoe print, including Joanne's sandals. Murdoch told me that the boot prints did not match any known print sold in Australia.

'That shows they must have been a foreigner's shoe. Could have been Falconio's prints?' he'd suggested to me. 'Anyway, they weren't mine.'

Dr Harold Wroebel is a Victorian Forensic Science Institute expert on close-range gunshot evidence. He told the jury about the composition of gunshot residue and how traces are left on the shooter's hands. He also told how the propellant can deposit itself on flat surfaces in front of the muzzle. He did not find it significant that no gunshot residue was identified on the back of the Kombi because the surface was vertical and the Kombi had been exposed to overnight dew, possibly raindrops, a long trip down the highway, and other forensic examinations.

Under cross-examination he agreed that gunshot residue from the attacker's hands could have transferred to Joanne's clothes, but Mr Wroebel said he thought it unlikely that Joanne would have smelt gunpowder or experienced any sensation of heat from the muzzle because only one shot was fired, and in the open. Any small amount of heat or smell would dissipate immediately. Mr Algie also obtained Mr Wroebel's agreement to the proposition that finding gunshot residue on the steering wheel would be consistent with the last person who drove the vehicle being a person who'd just fired a gun. No gunshot residue was detected.

We heard the forensic people had tested the four hairs or hair fragments from various locations. One was a white hair, definitely from a dog, that could have come from any breed. The one from Joanne Lees's body was more like a cat hair. The others were of no use. 'Looks like Jack is in the clear,' I wrote in my notes.

The visiting area at the prison was thick with humidity. The damp atmosphere reflected the oppressiveness of the surroundings as Jan and I arrived for our weekend visit. Murdoch's orange remand T-shirt was becoming threadbare and I suggested he should ask for a new one.

Murdoch responded, 'No, the new ones are too hot – too thick. I like this one. But I think I'll be changing it for a red one and moving to

B Block [the high security prison area] soon. I'm resigned to doing my seventeen years.'

I think, he's already done three, so he expects a sentence of twenty. But what about the Territory's rule of an extra five years for 'special circumstances'? Would the assault on Joanne constitute those circumstances? It didn't seem a good time to raise this.

Jan looked dismayed.

'I don't want to go there,' she said with a tremble in her voice. He gave us a thumbnail sketch of what to expect from the next witness, Superintendent Jeanette Kerr.

'You should read the affidavit she swore to get the listening devices on Joanne's phone,' he said. 'Said Lees was still involved in a "deep and passionate relationship" with Nick Riley and that she was making arrangements to meet him in Berlin. She even said that if they had a child together and it was a girl, they should call it Stephanie.

'And there was a memo from some police brass that said if Joanne didn't cut down on her spending, they'd cut off her credit.' This must be the one Brian Bates had told me about months ago, I think.

He said Kerr had sent an email to her police colleagues regarding her concerns about the forensic investigation.

'In another email she suggested they go again and search the place Joanne Lees hid,' he said, 'and when they did, hullo, hullo! They found the lip balm. What do we make of that?'

Next day, Jeanette Kerr was under the gun. Murdoch had indeed found the email and Mr Algie read it to Ms Kerr. It was dated 24 August 2001, about five weeks after the incident at Barrow Creek:

> Forensic, everybody knows about this, I have serious concerns about the way the manacles have been handled, and also there appears to be serious problems with the measurement of them, i.e. they appear to be incorrect. We really need to get on top of the forensic side of things, we need greater consultation. If we can't get this, I will be asking for a review of the handling of all forensic exhibits from an outside source if necessary.

It seems the police I'd interviewed last year were not alone in their concerns about the integrity of the evidence. Here was a senior police officer confirming in writing what I'd already been told by the troops.

She said she had made a number of copies of the manacles using the same type of tape, 'getting sticky stuff all over my fingers and arms. I thought DNA should be all over the tape on the inside of the originals, but DNA was eventually found only on one of the loops, not all.'

It emerged that a fingerprint belonging to Jeanette Kerr was found in the Kombi, indicating that in spite of her forensic concerns, she had not worn gloves when she came in contact with a potentially important source of evidence.

Chapter Thirty-Nine

WHEN FRIENDS FALL OUT

Brad had to be there at that time, he was on a run home.

James Hepi, Supreme Court, Darwin 2005

James Hepi's entrance into court caused a frisson of excitement. Dark and menacing, he passed within inches of my feet, glaring at Murdoch and muttering 'Maggot!' as he passed.

He told Mr Wild that he and Murdoch had 'run drugs around the country from Sedan to Broome'. It was obvious from the way they stared venomously at each other across the courtroom that their relationship had soured beyond repair.

He also said that others, including Jazz, accompanied them on their trips from time to time and that Jazz later lived in the house in Broome from which they distributed drugs. I was still wondering if the prosecution were going to call Jazz as a witness, since she'd seen the blue jumper with 'Try hugs not drugs' at Hepi's place. Each day had been a witness lottery, a new list being issued every morning, so we didn't know who was yet to come.

Much of Hepi's evidence in chief related to the various computations of Murdoch's vehicles. First, he had an F100, which was not suitable for the long hauls, so he changed it to a 75 Series Land Cruiser. Then Hepi detailed all the changes made to that vehicle. His evidence was very damaging to Murdoch. Every other aspect was covered – the return at 4 am on 16 August looking stressed out; immediate alteration of his appearance; removal of the mesh sides on the vehicle before the date of the incident; saying 'it wasn't me' without being prompted; Brad denying it was him at the truck stop when Hep believed it obviously was. 'That's Brad's car,' Hepi told the jury. 'I've spent a lot of time with that car. I've driven it round the country myself.'

He said they used caps to shield their faces from cameras – 'Brad had a Pennzoil cap' – and glasses as a disguise when travelling.

'Glasses can change your appearance.' He indicated that the man at the truck stop 'held his arms in a specific way like Brad, so no one could get close to him'. He said the man in the truck-stop photo was 'wearing my shirt'.

He told the jury he'd seen Murdoch making manacles in the shed at Sedan 'before Mr Falconio died – if he's dead,' he added very softly. Nobody except the transcribers picked up this sotto voce comment, so unfortunately, he was not cross-examined on why he'd said it. He repeated his committal evidence that Murdoch had told him he could hide a body in a 'spoon drain in the desert'.

A conservative-looking lady in the jury drew a deep breath and stared balefully across at Murdoch. Mrs Falconio was weeping quietly. It must be so hard for the family, I thought, but they've hardly missed a minute.

Mr Wild steered Hepi to the reasons for the demise of their relationship. He said that after July 2001, 'Brad changed his routines, he became paranoid, wouldn't cross borders at all. We had a vehicle built to go hard and fast across the desert and it was sitting in Broome doing bugger all. There was about twenty pounds of dope missing and quite a lot of money.

Murdoch half rose from his chair and said, 'You f--king liar!'

'Get f--ked!' Hepi yelled back. The whole court drew an inward breath but the exchange went no further. If they'd been outside, I thought, the outcome would have been very different.

He said they'd ended their relationship in a car park behind a hotel in Perth and that he'd done nothing since then to 'set up Murdoch for anything to do with the Falconio matter.'

Mr Algie thought otherwise.

He accused Hepi of collecting cigarette butts to get Murdoch's

DNA for the police, dobbing him in to get his get-out-of-jail-free card and fabricating evidence to save his skin.

Hepi looked contemptuous.

'My skin's already saved, mate. I'm sitting here, he's sitting there.' Pretty much what I'd said to Murdoch months ago.

Hepi said he'd surprised Murdoch in the shed making handcuffs and asked him what he was doing. '"Just mucking around" he said. I was outside pumping water and I didn't want it to overflow so I went out. I think he made several sets and threw some in the bin.'

Hepi described the manacles pretty accurately, but he agreed that during his interview to Broome police officer Pete Jenal he didn't mention seeing this important event. 'I wasn't asked,' he told Mr Algie. We took a much-needed break. The tension in court was electric.

Hepi walked down to the far end of the foyer pacing back and forth, his back to the curious crowd, also stretching their legs. I wandered down towards Hepi with the idea of asking him if he would speak to me after he'd given evidence. Before I could reach him, one of the female guards approached him, asking if he was OK and if he'd like a cup of coffee.

When we resumed, Hepi told the court that Murdoch had ripped him off $125,000 and twenty pounds of dope.

'Bullshit!' Murdoch said in his glass box.

'What about the possibility of squaring off for your perceived ripping-off by dipping into a reward of $250,000? If Mr Murdoch is convicted, you'll be making application for it, won't you?'

'I haven't yet, but if he's convicted I will.'

He told Mr Algie that Murdoch carried a '*Dirty Harry* gun', which he identified from a photo of items Murdoch was carrying in his vehicle when he was arrested. 'After he had abducted and raped children, this photo shows all the stuff he had in his trailer when he was on his way back to Western Australia to have a go at me.'

Having inflicted the maximum amount of damage, he sauntered out, muttering 'piece of shit' in Murdoch's direction as he passed. Joanne

Lees actually smiled at him. I followed him and gave him my card. 'I'd like to talk to you,' I told him. 'Could you phone me?' His eyes were dark glowing coals under heavy black brows. I felt distinctly uncomfortable and thought I wouldn't be sorry if he didn't call and wished I'd thought twice about giving him my number.

Next morning, in the absence of the jury, Mr Algie asked for a mistrial based on Hepi's 'abducting children' remark. The judge denied this application. Later that morning His Honour instructed the jury that they should disregard Hepi's outburst and we continued.

Of course Hepi wouldn't change his story, I thought. If he did, something might be done about his suspended sentence.

Bev Allen, the self-styled former girlfriend of Murdoch, gave the same evidence she'd delivered at the committal. She was followed by Dr Peter Thatcher, who had been recalled from sick leave in Victoria to explain the embarrassing news that his DNA had been detected on the manacles. He couldn't. He said he always wore gloves, couldn't remember handling the manacles unprotected. Maybe he coughed on them during a teleconference where he put them on a coffee table in clear view.

He said he'd been opposed to the manacles being taken to South Australia and leaving forensic control. 'We don't own the exhibits. We can only express opposition or disappointment about any decision the police might make.'

He also told the court that 'there was no scientific evidence of a gun, no cartridge case, no weapon, no evidence it was fired in the direction of a Kombi.'

The trial was entering its third week. I had a good look at the photo of Joanne's green pants. As far as I could see, there were no bloodstains on the knees.

One of the prosecution's star witnesses appeared next. She was petite and attractive and seemed pretty smart, too. She had obtained her doctorate in forensic anatomy, facial identification and facial recognition, and Dr Meiya Sutisno now proceeded to introduce us to the intricacies of body and facial mapping – a relatively new forensic process. She had done an extensive forensic consultancy job on the truck-stop photos and various other footage available of Murdoch, some from media film and other footage filmed by Sandry at Berrimah.

She showed the court graphic examples of how she evaluated the photographic evidence available to her. Poor quality footage from the truck stop, clearer shots of Murdoch, demonstrating on storyboards with overlays how Murdoch's face and physique matched the person of interest, or POI, at the truck stop. As I've always suspected that Murdoch was the POI, I didn't take much convincing. Dr Sutisno was a good witness, talking directly to the jury and explaining her methods in great detail. She said she detected a concave region of the upper lip in the front view and profile (Murdoch has no front teeth) and said the hairline was the same in the left profile.

'No two men have the same hairline,' she told the fascinated jury.

She then demonstrated her craft on the computer, using the same photos. As the images of Murdoch slid across the images of the person of interest, I heard indrawn breaths behind me. The public gallery was convinced too. Just then, the court light flickered and dimmed. 'It's witchcraft,' I wrote in my notes, unaware of the electrical storm raging outside.

'This is not morphing, this is an anatomical match. I can see this clearly and I'd like you to see what I can see.' Most of the jury looked sold to me.

Her conclusion, after a lengthy explanation about notable features and distinguishing features, was that, 'The multiple number of features match, and distinctive identifiers indicate that this is the same person.'

Team Bradley had imported their own anatomical expert, the very same Professor Henneberg I'd contacted months ago to see if he could help me determine the height of the man at the truck stop. He was vigorously note-taking, shaking his avuncular head and leaning forward from time to time to pass notes to Mr Algie to use in his cross-examination. Mr Algie pressed Dr Sutisno on the poor quality of the footage: 'No precise identification is possible, is it?'

'I disagree.'

'The thickness of the moustache does not allow you to make an assessment of the concave lower lip?'

'I disagree.'

After several similar exchanges, Mr Algie produced a CD and asked Dr Sutisno to look at the images on it, which were also displayed on the courtroom screens. The photos show a 'suspect' man in the same poses as the POI in the truck stop, then each 'suspect' image automatically slid over the POI image, matching the shape and stance. All except one image was from behind, but the last one revealed the 'suspect' was our benign-looking Professor Henneberg. Dr Sutisno was slightly surprised to see it was him, but not convinced her technique was open to discussion. She said the professor was smaller and had been enlarged to fit over the POI images. She assured Mr Algie she was an expert in this field and magically produced her PhD from under the shelf – with both hands – and fanned through it. It was almost two inches thick, complete with colour pictures.

'It took almost forever to complete,' she said winningly to the jury. Most of them looked impressed.

Mr Algie is a pragmatist. He sat down.

I challenged Grant Algie about the truck-stop footage after court the next day, saying, 'Why doesn't Brad come clean about being at the truck stop?' He told me, 'We've given him every opportunity to say it was him, but he denies it, so that's how we're running our case.'

On my next visit to the prison, Murdoch was jubilant. He thought Professor Henneberg's magic picture show had gazumped the young doctor. But privately, I couldn't agree. I'd thought all along he'd been denying it was him because it put him too close for comfort to the scene of the crime. In criminal law, an effort to hide actions is called evidence of consciousness of guilt. Conduct after a crime has been committed is admissible as 'post-offence conduct' only when it provides circumstantial evidence of guilt. Murdoch may not have been aware of this, but he was smart enough to know that guilty or innocent of the Barrow Creek incident, it would not do his case any good to be the POI in the truck stop.

But had he done himself more harm by denying it?

The trial seemed to go on and on. I felt so sorry for Peter's family, listening day after day. At times the graphic descriptions were too much for Mrs Falconio and she left the court. And Jan was not happy either.

Mr Staff, the Alice Springs Art teacher, delivered one stunning new bit of evidence. He said he was 'mistaken' that Joanne Lees brought her hands to the front of her in the four-wheel drive. 'I made a mistake. I got it confused.' Mr Algie made the point that he'd said that in his sworn statement to police and under oath at the committal, but he was adamant. 'On that aspect of my evidence, I don't think I got it right.'

Mr Algie was clearly cranky about this unpredicted about-fact and accused the prosecution of pulling a swiftie. Mr Wild told the judge he had 'no idea Mr Stagg was going to alter his testimony'. Stagg had been just as adamant before, though, demonstrating with his hands over his head the way Joanne felt about in the back.

After Andrew Head gave his evidence about serving that night at the truck stop, I ran out to say 'Hullo' before he left the court.

'I don't know if that guy did anything up at Barrow Creek,' he told me, 'but he was definitely my customer.'

'What do you mean? You remember serving Murdoch that night?'

'Yes, absolutely. He had a mo, but that was my customer.'

I shook my head. Neither of the counsel had thought to ask him to identify Murdoch. Or perhaps they had, but each for their own reasons didn't want the answer.

Libby Andrew, a fresh-faced young policewoman, was questioned about her chaperoning role with Joanne in the days after Barrow Creek. She made lots of notes, even using a brown paper bag when she had no paper, and Murdoch had found several inconsistencies in these during his trawl through the file. In particular, there was a set of notes that recorded Joanne's description of shelves in the attacker's vehicle. Murdoch was triumphant because he said his vehicle did not have shelves and anyway, if the shelves were behind the driver's seat, how could there be a crawl-through?

The notes said:

> *Wood, not deep, dark, medium brown, bottles on the shelf, something red maybe, car cleaning, the shelves are narrow, divided by bottle height, maybe three shelves. Shelves didn't come with car, don't match in. It's the bottle shelves. Whole height over cabin, maybe something else that is blue. It's not a bottle, maybe cloth or rag, don't know, can't see. Shelves start behind seat. Not bit. Not wide. Narrow.*

Libby Andrew said that she took these notes during the compilation of Stagg's drawings, but that didn't wash with Mr Algie, because firstly, there was no mention or depiction of shelves in the drawings and, secondly, the notes were signed off by Andrew and Joanne, and dated two days after the day the drawings were done.

Mr Algie read some more, at the judge's direction:

> *I let myself fall to the ground. Bed goes right to the end, legs are out, no can't feel anything underneath. No joins, it's all smooth and level. From moment I land in cabin to my legs out, it's all smooth. I have a strong feeling something going on there, shelving from top to bottom.*

This set me thinking. It sounded much more like notes taken during a hypnotherapy session than notes of the session with Stagg. I decided to phone the psychologist, whose name I discovered, to ask her if she did the session on 22 July and if the notes rang a bell. She kindly agreed to check her lengthy transcript of the two sessions, which she said took place on 2 and 3 August, not 22 July. She rang me back to say that Joanne did not mention the shelves during either session, so I got that wrong and so did Murdoch. Perhaps it was just Libby Andrew's own shorthand, or maybe Joanne was trying to re-visualise the events of the night and Libby was just taking notes as Joanne spoke.

◆ ◆ ◆

The roll call of witnesses went on and on. We'd been told eighty-five were to be called and the trial looked set to last till Christmas.

Mr Wild told the court he intended to play some recordings of phone calls Murdoch made from prison, some of them to Jan. She was horrified that her private calls would be broadcast to the entire court and reported in the media. She fled from the courtroom.

The media were excited. At last they would hear Murdoch in his own words. Murdoch didn't want to hear the recordings, though, as he'd been warned he would hear his dead father's voice so he was excused.

There were seven calls: two to Jan, one to Paul Jackson and four to his parents. The reason these calls were selected was that Murdoch sounded as if he might have been trying to persuade Paul to stick to the 8 pm arrival time at Fitzroy Crossing and that Jan had told Paul what Murdoch wanted him to say to the police. But Paul had actually already given his statement to the police by the time this call was made. Murdoch did finish his call by saying, 'I've said to everybody, just tell the f--king truth.' He told his mother that it was 'impossible' for him to have 'done 1700 kilometres in twenty hours through some of the roughest bloody dirt in Australia'. But prisoners know that calls are recorded, so they are always aware of choosing their words carefully.

The media consensus was that Murdoch was surprisingly articulate and that hearing the calls has 'humanised' him more to everyone – 'Especially the way he said "ta ta" to his mum,' one girl said.

Mr David Ringrose is an expert in 'cleaning up' the 'white noise' that blurs and distorts low-quality film footage, especially CCTV footage. He explained his technique to the jury and then told them how, with the clearer images, he was then able to use measurements of known objects taken at the truck stop to attempt to calculate the height of the POI. The measurements he used were pretty much the same ones I'd obtained for Professor Gale Spring about two years ago – size of floor tiles, height of camera, marker by the door, other known objects that were still in the same position. Additional measurements taken outside around the diesel bowsers enabled him to get a pretty accurate measurement of the POI was 191 centimetres tall, plus or minus three per cent, which put Murdoch squarely in the frame. He also provided the jury with detailed estimates of the canopy and tray of the four-wheel drive, which would later be examined by a Toyota expert. The prosecution had done their job pretty thoroughly.

After a couple more minor witnesses, Loi O'Dore took the oath. I wondered how he planned to square off his conscience with the evidence he knew the prosecution wanted him to give. He told the jury he was 'not sure' about the canopy at the truck stop being one he made. 'We don't generally use blue rope, and the little diamond-shaped logo we usually sew on the bottom-right rear corner is not there,' he said. 'When I saw the image on TV, I thought it was Brad's canopy,' he continued, 'but it's been a long time since. I got doubts.' Two of his staff confirmed his doubts.

We heard evidence about Murdoch's bull-bar being the same as the one on the truck-stop photo and more evidence from police and road maintenance people about the condition of the Tanami Track on or about 14 July 2001. They were in accord that Murdoch could have easily driven the Tanami leaving Alice Springs around 1 am and arrived in Fitzroy Crossing the following evening around 8 pm. It would've been a snack for a tough, off-road driver like him.

Next time at Berrimah I asked Murdoch again about this journey he made that night. 'I've always told you I was on the road that night, doing a run,' he replied. 'But I had my new camper trailer with me. Paul Jackson remembers me pulling in to Fitzroy Crossing with it. So where was it at the truck stop? Or Barrow Creek, for that matter, if I was supposed to be there?'

He told Jan and myself that he'd unearthed a memo by Constable Sandry that would be the subject of a recall for him. Poor old Tim Sandry, I thought. Bet that will make his day. 'It's a file note he made about an examination of the manacles he and the South Australian police, one Mr Paul Sheldon, did on 12 October 2002 at 0945. They took them out of the secure lock-up, out of the bag and examined them together. So they were opened in South Australia!' he crowed. 'Sandry lied.'

'Well, perhaps he forgot?' I countered.

'Oh, yeah, right,' re-joined Murdoch.

Changing tack, I asked him if he'd be able to get all his property back if he was acquitted. There was quite a haul at police HQ, various vehicles and parts, the famous camper trailer, a motorbike, the four-wheel drive he'd been driving when he was arrested.

He grinned. 'I don't know if I'll get that one back or not,' he said. 'That was stolen for me by a mate in WA, so I could put those compliance and number plates from young Ben's old 75 Series on. The four-wheel drive I rebuilt from young Ben's 75 Series was still in the shed when I was arrested. I've told you all along, there were more vehicles than the cops worked out.'

That was something new. So the four-wheel drive he was arrested with was not the same as the one he'd allegedly changed to look different to the one he'd been driving on 14 July. Twists and turns. How many more?

Back at the court I had another surprise. The tough young guard who'd been checking us in and out of Court 4 had been replaced. I was told that he'd gone back home to care for his kids.

'And he's a Gypsy Joker. His job was to keep an eye out for Murdoch.' Well, well. I supposed he thought he might get a guard job sitting with Murdoch in the dock. But because of his history as a bounder, he'd been given the door. I wondered if Murdoch knew his mates were looking out for him.

Eventually, we heard from Mr Sheldon by video link from South Australia. He didn't know about Sandry's file note and Sandry had not yet been recalled to tell the jury about it. Sheldon looked tense, his hands crossed on the table in front of him, thumbs twirling. He admitted that the South Australian police security lock-up access records show he accessed the room at 0915 on 12 October 2002. He said he had 'No recollection of that examination. An examination like that would involve me becoming involved in the chain of evidence. If it did [take place], it would have been informal – "Here, have a look at these" – and I would not deem it necessary to make notes.'

Mr Algie challenged him vigorously, but he didn't budge. When excused, he left so fast he forgot his backpack and had to come back for it.

We heard from all the Broome police involved in Hepi's arrest, and they reassured the jury that no special promises were made to Hepi for 'dobbing' in Murdoch. They definitely did not ask him to supply any cigarette butts. It seemed no police did.

Julie-Anne McPhail told me in the court coffee shop that she had originally approached the police because she thought Murdoch was not guilty. But her evidence did not help him much, and Mr Wild made good use of her frank and open way of telling her story about getting the speed from Murdoch and the guns Murdoch was carrying. She lost her cool when Mr Algie challenged her about Murdoch showing her a little handgun, but apart from that she was a good witness for the prosecution.

Murdoch's former mates, the Sheriff and Dags, told of changes to his vehicles and how hard and fast he drove on his various drug trips. Both of them had travelled with him. Little Rebecca Weaver told her story of Murdoch 'lifting the canopy to put her bag in his vehicle – no mesh' and how she'd come upon Hep and Murdoch sitting at a table in Sedan with a 'big silver John Wayne-style gun on the table between them'.

Slowly but surely the prosecution was building a pretty strong circumstantial case.

Murdoch's mates from Broome, Paul Jackson and Brett Duthie, tried to say as little as possible that would land him in more trouble, but it was obvious from Mr Wild's demeanour that he viewed them as reluctant witnesses. They had already had a session with him before they appeared, both losing their cool and not accepting some of his suggestions about how they should answer their questions. Paul and his father were quizzed about the Barred Creek camping trip, both agreeing that there were no visible mesh sides in those photos they'd sent the DPP all that time ago.

Murdoch told me on my next Berrimah visit that he was certain their rooms had been searched while they were in court.

'Why would anyone do that?' I asked him.

'Rex was convinced there was another camera or more photos,' Murdoch said.

'Well, if they were searched by professionals, they shouldn't have been able to tell,' I said.

'Oh yes. They set their bags up. You know, a folded sleeve here, a comb there, they were searched all right.'

Paranoia does fester in prison, I thought. Nothing else to think about.

◆ ◆ ◆

Mr Algie asked His Honour to have Joanne recalled to tell us about those shelves. She was furious when Tony Elliott looked over his shoulder and indicated the judge had agreed. She left the court immediately, with her friend in tow. Next day, her black-and-white outfit and nervous cough re-appeared in the box as she was sworn in again.

She looked at Libby Andrew's notes and agreed, 'They are my initials, but I can't remember signing them.' She said she never said anything about shelving. 'I never had any memory of shelving in the four-wheel drive,' she said. She added that she might have mixed them up with the Kombi shelves: 'They were wooden with lots of bits and pieces on them.'

She didn't remember any conversation with Libby Andrew and said of the notes on the brown paper bag and the other notes she'd initialled, 'I don't remember saying that. It wasn't a statement, it was on a brown paper bag. I made lots of official statements, had lots of conversations.' She looked appealingly at the jury, 'I was trying to get the man caught.'

Mr Algie was limited to asking her about the shelves only, so she was excused. She walked to sit next to her friend, looking very relieved and blowing a 'whew' breath as she sat down. Mrs Falconio leaned over for a little word and Joanne smiled. It was all over for her now, until the verdict.

Tim Sandry was also recalled. This was the third time. He too was not happy. He looked pale and bit his bottom lip from time to time. Sitting with his hands clasped in front of him like Sheldon had, he said he had forgotten about examining the manacles with Sheldon when he was giving his evidence earlier. But he did say that he'd given a copy of his briefing notes about the detailed examination, in the next room under a microscope, to both Detective Chalker to Dr Thatcher. Both of them had forgotten to mention this fact during their evidence too.

After hearing from a couple more police, the Crown case was over. Would Mr Algie forfeit his right to make his closing submission last by calling any witnesses? Would Murdoch speak on his own behalf?

We wouldn't have to wait long for the answers.

Chapter Forty

THE LAST WORD
FROM MURDOCH

I didn't think I would come across any shit like this.

Brad Murdoch, Supreme Court, Darwin 2005

'I call Bradley Murdoch.' With those words, Mr Algie assured the media of a few more headlines and ended speculation from everyone about whether Murdoch would tell his own story. He unfolded his 195-centimetre frame and walked across the court, still flanked by his two escorts. Jan was almost overcome with emotion and her wish that he would do well in the box. I bet Algie hopes so too, I thought.

There was a very visible police presence in court. The Falconio family was surrounded by many of the Regulus investigators in plain clothes and the mild-mannered guard who'd replaced the Gypsy Joker at the court door had stepped up his body and bag searches, too.

After telling the jury about his early association with Hepi and the routes by which he usually carried the drugs on runs from Sedan to Broome, Murdoch told his story of the events leading up to 14 July 2001.

'I'd bought an off-road camper trailer in Adelaide and registered it on 12 July. This was just another way of making the vehicle look different, just plodding along like Tommy Tourist, towing my gear. I left Sedan on the thirteenth in the dark. They're all acreages out there, so you don't want to broadcast you're leaving your place unattended. It was raining hard when I left and very cold. I stopped at Marla to air out the camper trailer because I'd closed it up wet at Sedan. I camped overnight and rolled into Alice Springs round the 10.30 to 11 am mark on 14 July.

'I went to buy some Red Rooster for myself and some nuggets for Jack – he's very fond of nuggets – and then I sent around to Kiddles [the Toyota dealership] to use the car-wash hose out the back to wash the limestone mud off the underneath of my rig.'

He explained that the limestone around Sedan makes white, sticky mud that clings to the underside of vehicles when you drive through deep puddles as he had done. That mud dries on and is hard to shift. Because the dirt around Broome and through the Centre is red pindan, any observant person would know from the mud that he had travelled from interstate. Just another precaution in a drug runner's routine.

'I went to the Repco shop at about 1 pm and bought two water tanks for the trailer, a dash mat and a few other bits I needed. Then I fuelled up at BP on the way out of town. I usually get BP if I can because it's clean fuel. A bit past that I went into a little shopping area and bought small goods – milk, bread, dry goods, and set off, reaching the turn-off to the Tanami Track at about 3.30 to 4 pm.'

Murdoch had told me during my previous visit to Berrimah that on that trip he had been planning to go home by the Stuart Highway because the Tanami had been closed recently due to washouts and flooding. Seeing no 'Road Closed' sign, he decided to check out the Tanami, since it was his preferred route. A semi driver emerged soon after he'd turned onto the bitumen road leading to the Track, and Murdoch asked him what the road was like. The man said he'd have no trouble in the rig he was driving, so he kept going.

Pity he couldn't have found that bloke to verify his timing, I thought. But Murdoch tried so hard to look like 'Tommy Tourist', would he have remembered anyway?

He told the court he pulled over before starting on the gravel and put all his purchases in their designated places in the back. He also let his tyres down a bit.

'I travelled at fifty to sixty kilometres per hour on the rough bits,' he said. 'Any faster than sixty-five to seventy can blow a tyre.

'I stopped once for about an hour because I was having trouble with the axle on the camper trailer. It was coming loose and the mudguard was scraping and I had to stop to fix it up. At 8 pm I was near Yuendmu. I did not have anything to do with Joanne Lees. I got to the Granites around midnight to 1 am, and because I was having the same trouble with the trailer I camped there until daylight. I got to Halls Creek about 3 pm – twenty-four hours after leaving Alice – then on to Fitzroy Crossing, arriving about 8 pm. I spent an hour or so with Paul, catching up on things, having a steak sandwich, filling up the vehicle, and went on to Broome, rolling in there about 4 am as usual.'

He said he'd been planning the changes to his four-wheel drive for months before 14 July and had ordered various canopy and steel components already. On the fishing trip to Barred Creek he'd already stripped out most of the back, including the mesh, leaving only the fuel tank in place, in readiness for the planned alterations.

He assured the court of his innocence. 'Hepi is setting me up. He stole clothes from me with my DNA on them. I wasn't at the Shell service station. I wasn't at Barrow Creek. There is supposed to be my blood on the back of her shirt. I don't know if I crossed her path in Alice Springs. Maybe I bumped into her at the Red Rooster.'

He said he had hair ties in his vehicle because they lasted longer than 'lackie' bands, which perished. He also had hundred-mile-an-hour tape. 'Everyone on the road carries it.'

'How could it be that your DNA is on Joanne Lees's T-shirt?'

'I don't know.'

'Did you know your phone calls from prison were being recorded?'

'Yes.'

'If you had left Alice Springs at 1 am, could you have reached Fitzroy Crossing by 8 pm the following evening?'

'No.'

'Did you kill Peter Falconio?'

'No, I did not.'

Algie sat down. 'Good presentation,' I wrote in my notes, 'but the slow trip with all the stops was a bit out of character for Murdoch. When he's carrying a load, he puts his foot down, from what I know.'

Mr Wild rose for his long-awaited crack at his quarry.

'Where did you bury Peter Falconio?' he thundered. The question caught everyone off guard, including Murdoch. He sat there stunned, not replying, giving Grant Algie time to get to his feet and object.

'That's objectionable. It implies an answer that is simply not proved. A bit like, "When did you stop eating your wife?"' he said. But Wild was off on a different tangent, determined to get his question answered.

'You know places to bury bodies, don't you?'

'No.'

'You've buried one, haven't you? Mr Falconio.'

'No, I have not.'

'How did your blood get onto Joanne Lees shirt?'

'I don't know.'

'You do know.'

Mr Wild abandoned this exchange because he only had one hour before the adjournment for the day, and I guessed he'd want to lock Murdoch into the version he'd just given of the trip, so he could take it apart, kilometre by kilometre, the next day. He elicited from Murdoch that he was a very fastidious man and then asked why he'd been so careless as to take a brand-new trailer on a rough track like the Tanami. 'It was an off-road trailer, Mr Wild. That's why I bought it.' After Murdoch said again that he had not removed the mesh sides earlier than 14 July, we heard the story of the trip once more and then it was time to go home. I thought Jan took a breath for the first time since Rex Wild had stood up.

◆ ◆ ◆

Plenty of headlines were expected as Murdoch resumed his seat in the witness box. Sure enough, Mr Wild inched along the trip from Sedan to Fitzroy Crossing, challenging every metre and every minute.

He's very thorough, I thought. It must be the QC in him.

He asked Murdoch if he'd heard the police officer giving evidence about taking his family on a holiday trip, towing a trailer along the Tanami in June of that year, travelling up to 120 kilometres per hour and easily maintaining a speed of eighty to ninety kilometres per hour.

'Yes, I did, and I'm shocked that a police officer would expose his wife and children to such reckless behaviour,' re-joined Murdoch. He disagreed that vehicles should be driven at speed over corrugations, as the police officer had said. 'You obviously don't do much four-wheel driving, Mr Wild.'

Mr Wild asked the same questions I'd asked: 'Why did it take seven hours to drive the 400 kilometres from Fitzroy Crossing to Broome?'

He got the same answer: cattle, roos, best time to roll in was 4 am – not in a hurry.

Then Mr Wild took Murdoch painstakingly through every aspect of the changes the police alleged he'd made to his four-wheel drive after 14 July. Murdoch repeated he was always changing his vehicle – nothing suspicious about it. Wild asked him why, if the camper trailer was in Broome when he went on the fishing trip to Barred Creek, he didn't take it to camp in.

'Because, Mr Wild, I took the boat, so I could go fishing,' Murdoch replied with elaborate sarcasm. 'Even I can't pull two trailers at once.'

Then came all the details of the four-wheel drive at the truck stop. 'Tell us about the differences to your vehicle.'

Then, 'Tell us about the similarities.'

Murdoch was tiring and getting tetchy. From time to time, Wild scored an angry response – a glimmer of Murdoch's temper showing through.

He showed Murdoch the Pennzoil cap. 'Is this the cap you wore at the truck stop?'

'I was not at the truck stop.'

'Your own father thought it was you at the truck stop, didn't he?' Mr Wild asked. This was the first time the jury had heard this, although

Bev Allan said it at the committal. Wild had slipped it in because it was not given in direct evidence. 'He saw the newspaper and rang you.'

'I was not at the truck stop.'

By the time they got to the hair ties, hours later, Murdoch was cranky and Wild was still unrelenting. He'd waited a long time for this. Murdoch examined a packet of hair ties allegedly found in his four-wheel drive.

'They are not my property,' he spat contemptuously. 'These are sun-kissed. They have been sitting in the sun, not stored in a box at the police station for two years.'

'Are you suggesting a conspiracy?' Wild shot back.

'I'm saying they are not mine.' Mrs Falconio, who had been watching Murdoch get wound up, left the court, very upset. I wondered if it was because she thought Murdoch was guilty and she was imagining him getting aggro with Peter, before he died. Mr Falconio leaned over to Nick, probably suggesting he go look after his mother, because he left too.

Finally, after having Murdoch nearly all day in the box, Mr Wild went in for the kill.

'You're a meticulous man, aren't you, Mr Murdoch?'

'I am. Fastidious.'

Wild put it to him that, to avoid getting blood in his vehicle, he wrapped Peter Falconio's head in Joanne's denim jacket, put his body in the four-wheel drive, covered the blood on the roadway and kept Joanne's hair tie as a souvenir. Murdoch denied this and the series of direct questions about whether he'd killed Peter Falconio. Mr Wild sat down.

The reaction in the media room was mixed. Some thought he'd 'humanised' himself by telling his story, others thought he'd sealed his fate.

The next defence witness was the counter clerk from Repco, who confirmed that Murdoch had bought all the items he said he'd bought on 14 July at 1.15 pm. The police had known this since November 2002.

Dr Katrin Both was a middle-aged lady who looked the part of a former Science teacher, which she had been years ago. She was not a very eminent scientific expert and had been the consultant who'd been in court noting Carmen Eckhoff's answers for Mr Algie. She told the jury that LCN DNA testing was still in its infancy and was not accepted in many jurisdictions, including the FBI in the USA. She said that Dr Whitaker was the only person in the world doing LCN testing, and because 'it is his baby' there was no opportunity for peer review or independent testing. Therefore, it was suspect. The technique was fine for identifying people from bone remains, for example, but if the outcome was going to send a man to jail for life, it was too dangerous to use in criminal cases.

'The media likes to play up that we're always trying to get the bad guy. Most of our work is exclusionary,' she said. 'We don't include someone at a certain level, but can exclude someone at a lower level. You can only be missing one number to be excluded, but you need all alleles to include someone.'

His Honour interjected with a little gift for the Crown.

'Is it any different from any new techniques in science, being subject to intense scrutiny until accepted [by the mainstream]?'

She agreed this was the case. It seemed that Dr Both was arguing caution about blindly accepting a new technique, unable to be subjected to peer review or independent testing, and warning the jury about the scientific methodology employed to reach the conclusion presented by Dr Whitaker. She challenged the validity of the LCN process, going as far as to say that to accept his results would be 'very dangerous'. After a break, Tony Elliott came in carrying a book entitled *Forensic DNA Evidence Interpretation.* He must have been doing a crash course over his coffee, I thought. I also thought he was quite rude to Dr Both. He heckled and yelled at her and was so pedantic in his questions that even Mr Wild leaned back and told him to back off. Putting a defence witness on the spot doesn't mean you have to heckle them. However, he scored a couple of points. All his reading paid off when he elicited agreement from Dr Both that this type of testing had been done in the UK since 1999; that there was another lab in the UK that could do independent testing (although Dr Both said it was run by privately funded graduates of Dr Whitaker's government-fun facility); and that if push came to shove, she could independently test the results herself.

'But I wouldn't,' she managed to get in, 'because I think the process is scientifically unsound.'

She started off well as a credible witness, but Elliott's full-frontal attack unsettled her and she became a bit dithery, as most would under such an unexpected assault from a young man with a sweet face.

Professor Henneberg would have been more than a match for Tony Elliott, which is probably why Mr Wild asked the questions. The professor was very charming and entertaining, and the jury all loved him. He was full of anecdotes and little stories and delightful illustrative examples of his craft, which was pretty much the same as Dr Sutisno's. Maybe the field attracts a certain kind of personality, I mused. He told the jury how he'd been responsible for catching this bank robber by the shape of his ear and that half the men in the jury, and 'if I may say so, the learned judge' all had exactly the same hairline. In a trial where we were all so worn out, he was delightful and engaging. He went through several of the truck-stop images in detail and told the jury that Dr Sutisno could not have seen anything like the detail she claimed to have seen, due to the poor quality of the photos and the unsound anatomical basis for her conclusions.

I wasn't sure if the jury believed him, but they certainly enjoyed him.

The final defence witness was my old mate, forensic photography Professor Gale Spring from RMIT University in Melbourne. I was very surprised to see him in the court foyer. No one from Team Bradley had told me he was coming. His job was to convince the jury that the poor quality of the truck-stop images was due to the smaller number of pixels that caused the images to be grainy and unreliable. It's tough being a technical expert and the eighty-fifth witness in a nine-week trial.

He told the jury it would be dangerous to rely on the footage. Quality is always lost when it is copied, unless it is copied from digital to digital format. In fact, when material is lost, the system can create artefacts to fill in spaces left by the transposing process. Then the simple act of printing images and the type of paper they are printed on can further diminish the image.

At last the case was over. All the evidence was in. The submission from Algie, Wild and His Honour would be presented over the next week and then the jury would have the unenviable task of sifting the evidence from both sides, ninety witnesses, over 300 exhibits and their own observations. Which way would the jury find? Was Bradley John Murdoch guilty or not guilty of the murder of Peter Falconio, and the abduction and aggravated assault with a gun of his girlfriend, Joanne Lees, on 14 July 2001, at Barrow Creek?

During the weekend I visited Brad Murdoch, probably for the last time. For those two visits I was allowed to take in my notepad, so that I could faithfully record his plans for the future, whichever way it went.

'I'm prepared for a guilty verdict,' he told me. 'When you're facing twenty years you've got to prepare for it mentally. Why wouldn't I be found guilty – I've been paraded round the country like a prize catch, on every media outlet you can be on for years. No other case has had a dedicated media officer like mine, even the really wicked crimes, like those arseholes who bashed those women and tied them up and threw them live to the crocodiles didn't have this kind of media. Why not? My case is all about everyone making money – selling papers, selling tourism in the North Territory. The Northern Territory government has a vested interest in this case. The British High Commission is represented at court most days – what kind of other case has that sort of pressure? It's something I've had to go through, but I would've liked to have done it quietly. It's tough enough in here. When you walk out that gate, we still have to go that way,' he said, inclining his head towards the cell block.

'It's been the hardest part, knowing all my friends and family are worried and concerned about this case. That's worried me more than looking after myself. Not that I don't appreciate it.' He reassured Jan.

'But doing it by yourself is sometimes easier.'

Was that a message to Jan? I wondered. Would he tell her to go home and forget him if he's found guilty?

'But you do wonder how they convict on all this f--ken bullshit,' he went on. 'No body, no motive. They said I was after "Miss Lees" I had a wad of money. If I was that way inclined, I could've called in to every whorehouse on the way. If I was that way inclined,' he repeated, with a glance at Jan. 'If they do convict me, I don't want to live out there. It's too sick a society.'

Jan nodded. 'How can they convict on what they've heard?' she asked. She has such unwavering faith in Bradley that I'm worried about how she'll take it if he's found guilty.

'Will you go straight to B Block [maximum security]?' I asked him.

'Yep, once I'm sentenced. I'll get a red T-shirt and they'll put me there for a while. How long you stay depends on how you behave. B Block is a sort of evening-out process for all high-security prisoners. If you work hard and do the right thing, you move on to a better part of the prison.'

'Is there work?'

'Yeah, there's a few jobs. I can't tell you much about what it's like, because it may be seen as a break of prison security. When it all comes down to it, you're still living if you're in jail. It's just a different kind of life. It's an easy life really – no rent, three squares a day, no tax, no parking fines. You work a couple of hours a day, then watch TV, read a bit. I won't have to worry about being late for work,' he laughed. We all did.

'Is life on the outside any easier?' he continued. 'At least I don't have to worry about what I'm going to do each day.'

I said I thought he had a pretty calm attitude about the possibility of doing twenty years without air con.

'Jail time is only what you make of it. The people who do it hard are already soft in the head. You keep your mind active, do a bit of reading, help the others with their paperwork – half those poor buggers can't read or write, and everything in prison is paperwork. Requests for this or that – all have to be in writing. If I do the time, I'll be a 63-year-old fitness freak and eligible for a pension when I get out.'

That made us laugh again. He was in good form, I thought.

Mentally preparing for the worst.

I decided to change the subject. 'What if you get off?'

'Firstly, if they come back and say, "Not guilty", I'll probably say "Shit!" I'll need to sit down, take a deep breath and wipe my forehead. Then I'll walk out of that box and down those front steps a free man.

'Not really very free,' he corrected himself. 'I'll be watched – and looked at. Thanks to your media mates, everyone knows what I look like. I'd like to know how people think they can judge me when all they've been told is crooked, one-sided stories by the media. The truth doesn't sell papers.

'I probably won't even have a drink in case I get charged with something. But I don't care what other people think. My close friends and associates know the truth and I'll be living my life with them. Firstly, I want to go home and do my family duty and look after my mum. She's had a terrible time. She's a lovely old lady, clutching a jarrah box filled with my father's ashes. And if any media come near us, they'd better watch out. I want to be left alone to try to live a normal life. I believe in showing respect to old people. Not like Mr Wild,' he added darkly.

'Later on, Jan and I will go on the road, camp by the sea. I've camped in places that city people would pay eight hundred dollars a night to stay – beautiful, unspoiled coastline. I don't need many possessions. All I need is down the road at police HQ. And if I get off, I get it all back.

'Or we might maybe rent a little farm, grow some vegies. Live a simple life. We've got all this land around us here,' he swept his large arm outwards. 'No farming, no vegies, not even any proper gardens. What a waste! It's pathetic!

'My prediction is, by Wednesday night this court case will be over. Whichever way it goes, I'm ready. I've done three years and four months. It's all the same. I'll just count 'em down: sixteen, fifteen, fourteen. When it all boils down, I've chosen the road I went down and I'm stuck with it.'

The judge finally completed his summing up, half a day ahead of schedule. He sent the jury out with their heads full of instructions and their arms full of over-stuffed folders. The 'court groupies' (locals who were at court nearly every day), lawyers, media, Joanne and the Falconios all filed out but didn't go far. They wanted to be handy whatever time the jury returned. Paul was overheard saying he was 'a nervous wreck'.

Although the Falconio family and Joanne Lees presented a united front at the trial, they had not been staying at the same hotel and did not socialise after hours. Relations between Joanne and Peter's two brothers had cooled considerably since her clandestine fling with Nick Riley became such public property at the committal. At a time when Mrs Falconio had been obviously upset, Joanne had not attempted to comfort her – that task had fallen to the court-appointed witness support lady. And Mrs Falconio, apart from her brief aside to Joanne after her recall, had made no move to be close to Joanne either. They seemed to be doing it hard, but in isolation from each other.

In the foyer outside Court 4, Luciano and Joan Falconio were standing near the entrance, as if they wanted to be first back in to the court when the jury returned. The sign 'Court in session' above the door of Court 4 remained lit, indicating that the court was still open for business, while we all waited for the news that the jury was returning.

The wait is over. The judge calls the jury back at 8.45 pm to tell them that they can knock off and go to the hotel, to complete their deliberations in the morning. All the onlookers who have sat through the last nine weeks are scrambling for a seat. Team Bradley and the

DPP team are in position, half-frocked up, adjusting their wigs, lining up behind the bench, waiting for the judge. Members of the media can't all get a seat and several of them stand at the back, despite the rule of No Standing Room in the court.

But when the jury files in, the foreman moves from his usual seat to the one nearest the judge, the one traditionally occupied by the person delivering the verdict.

I lean over to Jan. 'Brace yourself. I think we've got a verdict.' The court settles down, the outward calm required by His Honour in his courtroom belying the undercurrent of excitement. Jan is so tense, I'm sure she is trembling. Mr and Mrs Falconio also look very anxious. Joanne is seated behind them next to Paul Falconio, gripping his hand as if welded to him. His arm is around her shoulder. The judge is told the jury has a verdict. His associate puts the charges to the foreman.

'Guilty or not guilty on the charge that on 14 July 2001 near Barrow Creek in the Northern Territory of Australia the accused murdered Peter Marco Falconio?'

'Guilty.'

'Guilty or not guilty on the charge of the deprivation of liberty of Joanne Rachel Lees?'

'Guilty.'

'Guilty or not guilty on the count of unlawful assault of Joanne Rachel Lees and threatening her with a gun?'

'Guilty.'

Murdoch grimaces at Jan, shrugs and then his face goes blank. His Honour faces Murdoch. He does not ask him to stand up to receive his sentence, so Murdoch continues to lean back in his chair. The judge says that the mandatory sentence is life and the minimum sentence before parole is twenty years. He passes a sentence of twenty years, to commence on the date of his arrest. He says it is at his discretion whether parole is granted after twenty years and that he will make a decision about that in two days, when the victim impact statements from Mrs Falconio and Joanne are heard in the court. He also says he agrees with the jury's verdict – an amazing admission from a judge.

Jan remains stony-faced, staring at Bradley. Joanne recovers her composure, flicks her hair back and looks straight ahead, not at Murdoch. Mr Falconio reaches behind him and shakes Joanne's hand. As soon as Murdoch is taken to the cells, Jan flees the court and disappears through a secret exit. The Falconios are embraced by dozens of well-wishers, including the police and the court groupies. Many people are crying. No one even notices the judge leaving the courtroom.

I speak to Mr and Mrs Falconio and Paul, wishing them closure and the ability to now move forward with their lives. Joanne is surrounded, so I don't even try to reach her.

The Falconios and Joanne Lees, flanked by plain-clothes police and TRG members, have to pass through the media as they leave the court. Mrs Falconio seems stunned by the assembly of about a hundred media representatives waiting on the front steps with cameras, mikes and tape recorders. Staggering a little before bracing herself and leaning on her husband's arm, flanked by her sons, she moves forward. This is her final hurdle. After nine weeks, it's over and she and her husband can go on a planned holiday together.

Prepared statements from Joanne and the Falconio brothers are ready. Peter's father says he is 'very happy' at the result. All of them urge Murdoch to tell them where he has hidden Peter's body, his guilt now accepted and endorsed by the jury's decision. Nick Falconio tells a reporter: 'We'll go out there and look for him.' What can Peter's parents say that will bring Peter back? What can Joanne say that will bring back the last four years of her life? Now it's all been said one way or the other.

We are all going at last – except for Bradley John Murdoch. He got twenty-eight years without parole, so for at least the next twenty-four years he will make his home at Berrimah Prison, wearing a red T-shirt.

EPILOGUE

After his conviction, Murdoch sought leave to appeal his heavy sentence – 'I got twenty years mandatory and eight years on top because the judge said I was 'a coward' and 'a liar' and because of the impact statements from Lees and the Falconios' he told me – and the identification issues. To some people's surprise, leave was granted.

In January 2007, his counsel, including high-profile Australian barrister Ian Barker QC appearing pro bono, addressed the Appeal Court on several grounds relating to the identification issues regarding the evidence given by Joanne Lees. These included:

- The identification of Murdoch on a picture board after Joanne had seen his photo, identified as Peter's killer caught at last, on the internet days before
- The evidence she gave about a 'crawl-through space' between the seats of the four-wheel drive, which, after physically examining over 4000 white four-wheel drives around Australia, the police had not found possible
- Joanne's subsequent story change to the jury regarding the crawl-through space
- Her identification of Murdoch at the trial as the man in the famous 'truck-stop video', when days after the incident she'd rejected him as a suspect as he was 'too old'
- Her identification in court of a photo of Murdoch's Dalmatian as being the 'brownish black cattle dog' she'd described to police the morning following the incident.

The appeal was dismissed.

On 22 June the same year, Team Murdoch sought leave to appeal that decision in the High Court. Former NT DPP Rex Wild QC, who'd retired from the NT DPP's position after the 'Trial of the Century', acted for the prosecution, telling the court in his summing up that Ms Lees's identification had not been central to the 'overwhelming' case against Murdoch, which had hinged upon DNA evidence linking him to the crime. Her evidence was 'ancillary and additional', Mr Wild told the High Court. 'In our submission, there was no miscarriage of justice.'

High Court Justices John Heydon, Murray Gleeson and Ian Callinan agreed. Within five minutes they had dismissed the application as having 'insufficient prospects of success.'

Another issue raised its head less than six months after Murdoch was sentenced, but before his attempts to appeal. He wrote to me and asked me to come to Darwin, as he couldn't discuss anything on the phone. Going to Darwin from Melbourne is not like popping up to the corner shop. The distance is 3148 kilometres, and the cost is considerable. But this story had intrigued me for years, so what was too important and confidential to be said on the phone or in a letter? Planes from 'down south' get in around midnight, so after a kip in the car (parked in the car park of the hotel I would register at later on, to save the cost of a night's accommodation), I headed straight for Berrimah. I had allowed three days in Darwin and hoped that was enough. Murdoch's information was explosive. Put bluntly, he alleged that his judge's daughter, Joanna, was 'in a relationship' (well not quite how he put it!) with a juror during the trial. Murdoch wanted me to confirm this rumour, brought into the prison and told to a fellow inmate by a visiting social worker.

Readers need to know that it is an offence for people like me to know the identity of a juror. Or to attempt to discuss the trial with them, during or after. This put me in a terrible spot. I was shocked at the implications and, to be honest, gave little thought to the possibility of breaking the law. I was more concerned about the impact such a relationship may have had on the outcome of the trial. The opportunities for 'pillow talk' seemed obvious and damaging.

Joanna Martin had worked in a community legal service near the Supreme Court. So, next day, I visited to see if her workmates knew anything about the alleged situation.

Joanna's boss, an older Aboriginal woman, knew quite a bit about Joanna's friendship with Joanne Lees. This was even more disturbing news. The woman was reluctant to discuss the matter at work, so she invited me to her house after work, for a chat.

When I arrived about 6 pm, everyone was sitting outside in a breezeway around a picnic ice-chest full of cold drinks.

'Too hot in the house,' the lady said. (Even though Aboriginal people on remote settlements are often provided with basic housing, they rarely live in the houses. They socialise and even sleep outside. Too hot in the houses.)

Joanna's boss told me she'd had to reprimand Joanna on several occasions for spending too much time at the court and neglecting her workload. They were a small legal service and heavily committed to the community. 'She spent time sitting in court with that Joanne Lees,' the lady told me, 'instead of coming to work. Gave her presents. Lees wanted T-shirts to give her UK friends, so Joanna got her some with Aboriginal designs on, from our supply.' I asked her what Joanna looked like and her description matched a young woman I'd seen coming and going with Joanne and sitting with her on several occasions.

She confirmed Joanna was on maternity leave, but didn't want to discuss the details. Too frightened she might lose her job.

After three days of research, I was able to establish the following facts:

• Chief Justice Martin's daughter, Joanna Martin, was in a relationship with a juror who sat on Murdoch's trial.
• A boy was born to the couple, allegedly in the first week of May 2006. The trial ended on 13 December 2005. Another child, a girl,

has been born since then and the CJ has retired.

- Joanna Martin did befriend Joanne Lees and sat with her quite often during the trial and gave her some gifts.

On the third day, I headed back to Berrimah to tell Murdoch what I had found out. The whole thing had me fairly worked up. I thought the potential for a mistrial was high. I'd never heard of anything like this in all my court attendances and research over many years. However, I had no idea what to do about it. I asked Murdoch to authorise his Legal Aid lawyer in Darwin to let me speak to him on Murdoch's behalf. 'You'll need to ring him as soon as I leave here and tell him it's OK to hear what I have to say,' I told him. 'I'll go and see him on my way to the airport.' Which I did.

The lawyer was jumpy as a grasshopper. He kept asking me what he was supposed to do with all the information I'd given him.

'Investigate it further,' I said. 'My resources are limited, but you are Murdoch's lawyer. You can get documents and get verifications I can't.'

'But Robin, this is the Chief Justice,' he kept saying. 'It's the *Chief Justice*!'

'Well, I'm not alleging he's done anything wrong, but it might be relevant if he knew about the relationship during the trial...'

My pleas were swamped by the stress of the revelations. The lawyer was having conniptions and I had a plane to catch.

A journo I tipped off sought an interview with the Chief Justice who asked for questions in advance. The journo provided them, to be told the Chief Justice knew nothing and that a relationship, *if* it existed, commenced after the trial.

So that was it – until 20 December 2007.

In mid-2007, Bradley Murdoch was transferred to Alice Springs Correctional Centre. There were all sorts of rumours – he was dobbed

DEAD CENTRE

in for planning a prison breakout; he wouldn't tell where he'd hidden Falconio's body, so he was being punished by being sent to a prison with a largely Aboriginal population; he wanted a transfer to WA to be nearer his mother and he was being sent as far as possible from his mother travel-wise, and so on. The official reason was that the Berrimah facility was overcrowded. In any case, four boxes of his personal property were left behind in the Berrimah Property Room. His brother Garry collected those boxes, full of all the material from Murdoch's case. Garry didn't know what to do with all of the stuff, so he stored it safely with a mate.

On 20 December 2007, Sean Hoey, a man charged with the Omagh bombings in Ireland, was acquitted. In his judgement, Judge Weir accused the police of 'deliberate and calculated deception'. The DNA evidence that was central to the case was rejected. It is unclear whether this was because of a cross-contamination risk, the LCN DNA testing technique used, or both. He said that LCN DNA evidence did not belong in a British court.

Evidence against Sean Hoey was given by Dr Jonathan Whitaker of Britain's Forensic Science Service, using the same controversial LCN DNA technique he'd presented at Murdoch's trial. At Hoey's trial in Belfast, several experts said the LCN DNA technique used to identify the accused was unreliable and the judge was highly critical in his assessment of Dr Whitaker's evidence.

Two forensic experts, one of them Professor Allan Jamieson, Director of the Forensic Science Institute in Glasgow, testified that LCN could give a distorted result and was not scientifically reliable. Moreover, the miniscule amount of material used makes LCN DNA easily susceptible to tainting and contamination. Giving evidence for Hoey's defence, Professor Jamieson said that, in his opinion, the less DNA being tested, the less chance there was of a reliable result.

Following the Omagh trial, British police suspended use of the LCN DNA technique in over a dozen trials, but it has since been resumed for use following a review by the Crown Prosecution Service, which concluded that 'the CPS has not seen anything to suggest that any current problems exist with LCN'.

These findings, however, have been questioned by other forensic experts, including Allan Jamieson. He says that the CPS investigation was not fully independent and the validity of LCN has not been demonstrated. He has a lot more to say in a five-page report he released after the findings were announced. (see http://netk.net.au/DNA/DNA24.asp)

Some time after this, I became aware that Garry had all the trial material in Geraldton, so I travelled to WA and spent three days going through more than 20,000 pages of documents, photos, DNA graphs and statements on a huge wooden table on Garry's back verandah. On my way home to Melbourne I stopped over in Perth to see West Australian QC Tom Percy to acquaint him of my misgivings about the use of LCN DNA evidence to convict Murdoch, when it is perhaps a useful tool, but a bad master and still poorly understood by scientists, never mind juries.

Based on the material I gave him, and mindful of the outcome of Hoey's trial, Tom Percy agreed to conduct a review of the LCN DNA evidence presented at Murdoch's trial. Tom is a barrister of great standing, and an expert in 'fresh evidence' cases – the most famous being the cases of Daryl Beamish and John Button, for whom he obtained pardons with the help and support of WA journalist Estelle Blackburn. Estelle won a Walkley for her work on these cases. Tom Percy said he would conduct the review pro bono, as he believes that evidence may have emerged that was not available to the defence at the time. Allan Jamieson, a world-recognised expert on LCN DNA, supports this view. He told me that Sean Hoey's defence was also told no further testing could be done on Whitaker's tests, and Professor Jamieson was forced to subpoena the results he knew were available, to enable him to conduct tests for Hoey's trial. But three years earlier and half a world away, Murdoch's lawyers had no possible knowledge that further tests could be conducted. Could we subpoena Whitaker's test results on Murdoch? I wondered.

Professor Jamieson undertook a preliminary review of Dr Whitaker's reports to the DPP, which were sent to him on Murdoch's behalf. These were the reports the Crown relied on during Murdoch's trial. Jamieson also provided further material for Murdoch and his legal team to consider. The professor has indicated a willingness to conduct additional investigations on Murdoch's behalf. Physical evidence cannot be wrong, only its interpretation can be mistaken.

On Friday 7 June 2008, Murdoch was informed that NT Legal Aid would act as instructing solicitors to Tom Percy. As at March 2020, no one from Legal Aid has visited Murdoch. The wheels of justice turn slowly. Tom Percy is flat out daily, with cases just as important as this one. Professor Jamieson is kept busy jetting round the world, giving expert evidence and presenting at conferences and I get on with my writing and research. Murdoch is not going anywhere any time soon. So this new bid for a 'fresh evidence' appeal could take years, but we are all in for the long haul. Murdoch is contributing to costs where he can, which is a good attitude for a heavy smoker with twenty-plus years to go in the slammer.

With yet another anniversary of Peter Falconio's disappearance coming up, I thought I'd have another look through the big box of paperwork and files I brought home from Garry's place. To my surprise, I found a CD I had not looked at before, tucked into an inside pocket of one of the files. When I opened it up, I found a full copy of the report from Dr Whitaker to the DPP's office in Darwin, along with a photographed Chain of Evidence maintained by his laboratory, Forensic Science Services when the manacle link arrived in the UK. Dr Whitaker had told the jury that the outer tape on the manacle he'd received 'formed a complete barrier' which would have prevented contamination, 'allowing the inside to reveal scientific results'. Tim Sandry, a forensic police officer in the NT, tasked with several episodes regarding the manacles, had also testified before Dr Whitaker at the trial and had shown the jury on a whiteboard how thoroughly the forensic team had obeyed a senior officer's instructions to tear the manacles apart to test for DNA. He said this was done in the weeks following the incident, 'save for one link, that was sent to Dr Whitaker in the UK'.

But they were doing the tests, freezing the links to make them easier to pull apart, in July 2001. In those frantic weeks after the next big thing since the Chamberlains, did they save one link intact, just in case an expert might present himself in 2005? I don't think so. But this is what the jury heard, from both Sandry and Whitaker.

However, the photos attached to Dr Whitaker's report told a different story. The big buff OHMS envelope was logged in on 4 May 2005 and photographed. This in itself was interesting, as Murdoch's trial had been scheduled to start on 3 May. During a *voir dire* preceding the trial, beginning on 21 April, the defence was first hit with the news that Dr Whitaker's magic process was being used on some partial samples of DNA found on the gearstick and steering wheel in the Kombi. If proven to be Murdoch's, this would be a severe setback. It could place Murdoch in the Kombi. But a greater hurdle to a successful defence was announced by the prosecution. They thought they might be able to link Murdoch's DNA to the actual manacles, which would place him at the scene. Ian Barker QC, appearing pro bono for Murdoch, muttered, 'They'll be producing a signed confession next.' He was not amused. Sure enough, Dr Whitaker arrived from the UK and told the court his testing had indeed identified Murdoch's LCN DNA from an undamaged ring sent to the UK by the DPP. Magic indeed. Pretty speedy too, for intricate tests. The ring was received on 4 May and all possibility of verifying the tests had gone up in the puff of electronic testing. No more left. And on 22 May the Chief Justice Brian Martin actually announced that the trial was likely to be delayed until October. Intriguing.

What really grabbed my attention in the series of photos of the manacle ring with the 'complete barrier' was the condition in which it was received. They are reproduced in this book, so perhaps readers should make up their own minds. But it doesn't look intact to me.

The Murdoch/Lees/Falconio story just keeps on giving, like *The Magic Pudding*, a famous Australian story about a pudding that replenishes itself every time a slice is taken. Rumours become facts. Facts are overlooked or swept under the carpet. Stories abound, continuing to give life to a story that has no end.

In Melbourne's *Age* newspaper following Murdoch's trial, a report appeared about a truck driver, Geoffrey Gerard Atkins of Merrigum near Kyabram in Victoria, who in a written statement to police said that Bradley John Murdoch told him that Joanne Lees had offered Murdoch $2600 to "pop off" her boyfriend Peter Falconio. This may have been bravado by Atkins, but his name keeps popping up and he does look as much like Joanne's 'gunman' description as Murdoch did.

An alternative suspect surfaced again in the UK *Sun* on the tenth anniversary of Peter's disappearance, as told to the intrepid Frank Thorne, who says:

> '...new questions are being asked about whether the real killer could still be out there.
>
> 'An Aussie truck driver has told The Sun he believes he may have met the real killer near the scene of the crime the morning after the shooting. After Joanne raised the alarm, armed police pounced on a man at Barrow Creek, because he matched her description of the attacker.
>
> 'He had the same droopy Mexican-style moustache, was the same height with rough, thin facial features and wore the same sort of black baseball cap and a black and white checked shirt.
>
> 'The suspect also drove a four-wheel-drive Toyota Land Cruiser with a square green canopy similar to one driven by the assailant. But when police paraded the man in front of Joanne hours after the attack, she said he was not the gunman because he did not have a dog.'

Phil Cook, a regular trucker up and down the Track, made a sworn statement to a detective in Alice Springs about a week after the incident, later saying that he thought the man he'd met and spoken to 'was a real weirdo. I definitely thought this man could be the killer and I still have my doubts to this day. He could have done it.

'He was a dead ringer for two of the first police photofits they put out from Joanne's descriptions. It was him to a tee.

'He also looked identical to the man caught on CCTV at the Shell truck stop in Alice Springs on the night of the shooting. I never thought that man was Brad Murdoch, who was much taller.

'But I would swear it was the man I met in the Barrow Creek Hotel on the morning after the shooting and who I caught up with several times on the road north to Darwin later that day.

'I didn't trust the stranger from the moment he wandered up to me at the roadhouse and told me he had just been cleared by the police.'

The man told him he'd made camp only fifty yards from the murder scene on the night of the incident – and that he had buried his stash of cannabis before police cordoned off the area.

Cook said that he'd told the man he was lucky he didn't have a dog, to which he replied that that was easy – you could just shoot the dog and get another one down the Track.

The police search of the area the next day revealed a makeshift campsite nearby and a mixed-breed brown cattle dog shot dead in a dry creek bed. As Deputy DPP Tony Elliot told me later, that dead dog was of 'no importance to the investigation', as it did not match Lees's description.

The two men later met up at another truck stop at Elliott, further north. The man boasted to Cook that he had been given a written indemnity by a police sergeant to inform other police that he had been checked and eliminated from their enquiries.

Mr Cook said: 'He showed it to me. He told me how he was stopped by two armed cops, who dragged him out of his car before he was able to show them the card. I told him I thought he was lucky not to get shot. He also told me that he had shaved off his moustache. He felt it was drawing too much attention to him.'

When they arrived almost at the same time at another truck stop at a place called Dunmara, the shop assistants locked the doors and called the police.

Again, the man went free and was never investigated.

Mr Cook said that Murdoch was continuing to protest his innocence. And he that felt there was still a lot more to the story.

'I think it needs a lot more looking into. It's nagging at me that there's a lot more to this crime than meets the eye.

'But once I made my statement to police, I felt I had done my bit and it was up to them to make of it what they would.'

He said that he was not surprised they have not found Peter's body after ten years.

'The outback is a big place and he could be down a big hole somewhere, covered up and will never be found.

'It's one of those outback mysteries which will continue.'

Was this man Chris Malouf? Or Gerard Atkins? Or another of the hundreds of moustachioed, truck-driving drifters at large in the NT? Was the dead dog important after all? It was closer to Lees's description than Murdoch's dog – a Dalmatian.

In December 2016, another story surfaced in the *Northern Territory Times*. The manager of the Aileron Roadhouse, Greg Dick, said he believed another man is the killer. Mr Dick said he saw Ms Lees jump up and start speaking to the man at his Stuart Highway roadhouse, 100 kilometres north of Alice Springs, on 14 July 2001 – the same day Falconio disappeared. He gave evidence to this effect at the trial, but it was brushed off, as Joanne said they did not stop at Aileron, a roadhouse before her first designated stop, Ti Tree, another 100 kilometres north.

Mr Dick said that the man looked like a person who could live in the bush, or live off the land. 'A very clean, neat fella. He was going to a good place where he could have disposed of the body.'

Although he remembered seeing Joanne speak to this man outside the roadhouse, 'I didn't take any notice of them until well and truly after that.' He recalled some specific details including how the man complained over the price of a bottle of Coke and bought a meat pie for his dog.

He says he is certain about one thing – the man he saw Ms Lees speaking to was not Murdoch. 'I still reckon they've jailed the wrong man,' he said. Mr Dick believes the man convicted of the murder has no idea of the whereabouts of Falconio's remains. He believes Peter's body could be up in the ranges of 'Policeman's Waterhole' in Davenport Range National Park. He said that the area contains many mineshafts and was reportedly where the mysterious man was heading to camp.

Could Joanne have identified (or described) the wrong man so soon after her shocking night and in a state of traumatised stress? There's no doubt *something* bad happened to her out in the bush near Barrow Creek and now she has told her version of that so often, it's unlikely the full story will ever be told. Did 'the gunman', reluctant to cause another death, threaten her, tell her to make herself scarce, keep quiet, give him a head start? Was the dead dog important after all? An examination of its stomach contents may have revealed Red Rooster nuggets, or a meat pie? Or the bullet used to kill it may have been found, possibly from the same gun that allegedly killed Falconio. Could the ashes around the camper van have been those left from a campsite the previous night? Was the killer within grasp of the police the very next day, but still slipped through their fingers?

Within a week, Joanne was being watched day and night by police officer Libby Andrew under the guise of 'chaperone', and they were cooped up with each other in a hotel room. Although informally 'jailer' and 'prisoner' back then, Joanne and Libby have remained close friends since. More than ten years after the incident, Joanne visited Australia with the objective of trying to find Peter's remains and erecting a monument to him on the Track near Barrow Creek. She said she was determined to honour her partner's memory by confronting the awful past. She said she loved him then and 'still loves him'. She says now that his story has 'got a little lost', in all the drama about her and Murdoch. Appearing on current affairs program *60 Minutes*, still impeccably groomed, she is shown driving along the Track in the NT on a 'courageous journey tackling unfinished business'. She stayed with Libby at her ACT home and used Libby's close connections to Yuendemu to obtain some artwork from Aboriginal artists to raise funds at a charity auction in Melbourne. Unfortunately, whether it was due to scepticism from the proposed buyers or administrative reasons, the auction never took place. When contacted, the Alice Springs Council appeared mystified about the project, saying they had not been consulted about the location of a memorial on the Track.

Peter Falconio has never been found and Joanne says she wants to 'search for him and take him home to England'. It sounds like a mission impossible in the vast Australian outback, especially since so many have searched so widely for years. She says she 'wouldn't wish what she has been through on anyone'.

When the man stopped them, Peter was grateful. 'Who would expect this was a gunman who would kill him?' Joanne asks. 'Pete even thanked him, "Cheers mate, thanks for stopping us". We had no idea this was going to happen.'

Joanne says it's been hard to live with, thinking she was the target, with the DPP's theory that Murdoch (or the gunman) having spotted her in Alice Springs and followed them all that way. She has also said she never wanted to come back to Australia again – never again wanted to hear an Australian accent – after the trauma.

However, she has been back, several times. Lees always believed she was an only child, brought up by her mother alone in Huddersfield, Yorkshire and later by a stepfather. On one trip, she discovered that she and a half-sister, Jess, who lives in Sydney, shared their Australian father.

'It has been really amazing and kind of emotional,' Lees said about this amazing discovery.

She says the resemblance is almost like looking into a mirror. 'We saw each other and it was just instant. It was amazing.' They are uncannily alike.

'It's so neat when someone says, "Oh, you can tell you're sisters" to us the novelty definitely hasn't worn off, we're still in celebration mode of finding each other.'

Lees also says that she will be applying for Australian citizenship and now wants to spend a lot more time in Australia.

Jess has said she had no idea that Joanne was her sister and did not know about Falconio's death. She was travelling overseas at the time of the incident.

Joanne now feels less alone in the world. 'When wonderful things happen, I want to share them with Jess. It is kind of mind-blowing.'

60 Minutes reporter Liz Hayes had never met Lees before filming the special program they did on Joanne's return to look for Pete.

'I didn't know what to expect from her. When I first met her, she was definitely very suspicious of me and of all media. She was very distrusting. In her mind there is no such thing as a good journalist. I had no doubt in my mind that this is a woman who has suffered a terrible crime. She is without doubt the victim of a horrendous attack and lucky to be alive,' she said.

'I came away appalled by the suspicion that she was treated with. I can't imagine what that was like. Think about it – you've been attacked, you've almost died, your partner's been murdered and not only do people not believe that, but they think you're some part of it.

'I was devastated when she said to me, "I wish I'd died out there because living has been sheer hell".'

There are as many opinions about this story and Joanne Lees as the number of people involved. A couple of important ones to end with are one from Colleen Gwynne, who told the media after the dust settled that police tried everything they could for a confession from Murdoch, and to find Falconio's body, which would clear Ms Lees once and for all.

She said that when she visited Murdoch in jail, she walked up to him and lifted up her shirt. 'Look,' she said. 'No wires. I just wanted to ask you, tell me where the body is. This isn't permissible as evidence. Just tell me.' For a moment, Murdoch looked at her. Their eyes locked. She held her breath. Then his eyes slid away. He said nothing. She realised that, even if he were proved to be the killer, he still might never tell. It was a moment straight out of *The Silence of the Lambs*.

'His image has never left my mind,' Gwynne said. 'There's something about him. I've never let anyone get to me like that. I was glad to get out of there, basically. I've interviewed murderers, rapists, paedophiles but this was worse, somehow. I couldn't get his face out of my mind.'

Rex Wild QC, DPP and prosecutor had more to say about the case ten years later. Lees had frustrated the prosecution because they believed she was a heroine who had made a remarkable and courageous escape. 'We believed her,' he said. Because of the prevailing negative attitudes towards her, they couldn't get that across. Wild says Lees sat back, imperious, radiating disdain toward the 'northern cowboys'.

When she finally wept after the judge asked her to try and describe the terror she felt that night, they felt vindicated. After all the late night phone calls she'd made from England saying she would not come to the trial, after paying for her to stay in a secluded apartment, providing victim support, TRG transport and security to and from the airport and the court, and paying for her 'Harrods makeover' to make her acceptable to the jury, Mr Wild was disappointed by Joanne's attitude expressed towards his team in her subsequent book. They were barely acknowledged after they'd spent two years preparing for the trial.

'I was not surprised, but disappointed,' he told News Limited.

'She dismissed the work we'd done in the case in one short sentence. That was pretty hurtful. Towards the end of the book, she said: "I suppose I should thank the prosecutors. But then again, they were only doing their job." Full stop.'

Joanne Lees is now in her forties. She has not married. She has not had children. Her life has stalled. If she is going to move on, she's running out of time.

On 13 July 2016, the *Northern Territory Parole Amendment Act 2016* was passed by Parliament and became operational soon after. The Act brought the Northern Territory in line with numerous other State jurisdictions, which either already had, or were considering, similar legislation. Known as 'No Body, No Parole', this legislation is intended to prevent people convicted of murder from being able to qualify for parole unless they provide police with the location of the body (or remains) of their victim/s.

Murdoch, despite years in prison, still refuses to disclose what he did with Peter's body. This law could keep Murdoch in jail for at least twenty-eight years, until he is seventy-four, and then until he dies – unless he reveals the location of Peter's remains. His sentence then becomes a life sentence, which represents ethical and legal problems as it exceeds his sentence of 'mandatory life' (twenty years).

The Attorney General John Elfernick said that parole is a privilege, not a right. He further said, 'One of the final dignities a family can afford to a loved one who is a victim of a violent crime that ends their life is the celebration of that life, which includes the ability to lay their loved ones' remains to rest. Conversely, the location of a body is a matter that an offender can hold over a victim's family's head for the sole purposes of extending their suffering. It is a clear sign of a lack of contrition and remorse.'

Which is all very well. But as Stuart Tipple, Lindy Chamberlain's barrister, said, '... laws do not take into account the possibility that some people convicted of a crime may be innocent'. If the offender does know and is withholding the information, that's one thing. But Murdoch maintains his innocence to this day, which is why I call this bill 'The Murdoch Amendment'. Murdoch is probably one of the only, if not *the only*, person imprisoned in NT under these circumstances. What if he really doesn't know? Is that justice?

I am often called a 'Murdoch supporter' in media and other reports. For the record, I am a supporter of truth and justice, no matter to whom it applies. In this case I believe the whole truth has not been told and, therefore, justice has not been done. Murdoch has been demonised in media photos and footage. Up close, he's not all that lovable either. He's a hard man and he's lived a hard life. He has engaged in many criminal activities, most of which he has told me about during five years totalling sixty hours of visits. He has always denied being the attacker at Barrow Creek. After his legal options had been exhausted, before he had any inkling there might be a sliver of light beyond the bars of Berrimah, he could have opted for a softer life in a garden-style WA prison near his mother, by disclosing the whereabouts of Peter Falconio's remains. He continued to insist he didn't know. Murderers have status in prison. If he was looking at another twenty years, why not go the soft option?

If I'd been in the dock during that trial, I would have felt the wheels of justice crushing me. One police officer told me during an adjournment, in the presence of the head of Supreme Court security, that, *'We know Murdoch wasn't the shooter, but he's going down for it.'* In this country, between one and two per cent of people in prison, some who perhaps should be there for different reasons, are serving time for crimes they did not commit. [This percentage translates to 1000 inmates across Australia.] Criminologist Professor Paul Wilson and academic Juliette Landon conducted a longitudinal study over fifteen years, which determined some of the reasons for this are poor police conduct; the use of suspect expert evidence; prejudicial media coverage and flawed trial processes. A thousand doesn't sound like all that many, unless you are one of them.

Bradley Murdoch does not inspire warm, fuzzy feelings. He's quite a bad crook in his own way. But just as you would demand it for yourself, he deserves justice.

Further reading
The full judgement of Justice Weir in the Hoey trial can be found at:
www.courtsni.gov.uk/NR/rdonlyres/79D8BE5E-3EE8-4D4C-827F-
E98B5401B815/0/j_j_WEI7021FINAL.htm

TIMELINE

Countdown to Murder

- 15 November 2000: Peter Falconio and Joanne Lees leave England for a trip of a lifetime – round the world.
- 16 January 2001: After travelling through Asia, they arrive in Sydney on the Australian leg of their holiday.
- June 2001: Peter and Joanne leave Sydney in a thirty-year-old orange VW camper (Kombi) van, travelling through Canberra, Melbourne, Adelaide (where they stay on the outskirts in the Bolivar Caravan Park), Port Pirie, Coober Pedy and Alice Springs.
- 13 July 2001: Several people claim to have overheard a bitter row between Peter and Joanne at the Mataranka Hostel that night.
- 14 July 2001: After several days in Alice Springs, during which some necessary repairs are done on the Kombi, they spend their last day with Peter visiting an accountant, and Joanne spending time on the internet, before they attend the annual Camel Cup. They leave around 4.30 pm to continue their journey north up the Stuart Highway (the Track).
- 14 July 2001, 6.20 pm: They stop at the Ti Tree roadhouse, 195 kilometres north of Alice Springs, to buy fuel and watch the spectacular red centre sunset while they shared a marijuana joint.
- About 100 kilometres or so up the road, Joanne later relates, a man in a white four-wheel drive waves down the Kombi – and Peter disappears, believed shot dead.
- Joanne says she is threatened with a gun, punched and restrained with cable-tie handcuffs before she manages to escape and hide in the scrub for several hours, until she waves down a passing road train.
- Sunday 15 July 2001, around 1 am: Truck drivers take Joanne about eleven kilometres south to use a phone at the Barrow Creek Hotel, to call police.

- Sunday 15 July 2001: NT police launch a search for Peter and the gunman. They find a pool of blood covered with dirt beside the highway near Barrow Creek.
- Sunday 15 July and for several days: Police trample and search the area around where the Kombi is found hidden off the road, seriously compromising the site.
- 15 October 2001: Senior police officers on an orientation visit to the site discover black tape used to restrain Ms Lees and her lip gloss tube – apparently overlooked during the police search three months before.
- Early 2003: Some 2500 people have been identified during the lengthy police investigation as 'persons of interest'. A nationwide search ensues for the gunman and a four-wheel drive with a crawl through between the seats.
- 28 August 2002: Broome mechanic Bradley John Murdoch is arrested at gunpoint in Port Augusta, SA, charged with detaining a woman and raping her twelve-year-old daughter.
- 10 November 2003: NT detectives waiting outside the South Australian District Court in Adelaide arrested Murdoch, who had just been acquitted on the rape charges.
- 14 November 2003: Murdoch is charged and faces Darwin Magistrates Court over Peter Falconio's murder.
- 17 May 2004: A three-week committal hearing into the charges is heard in Darwin Magistrates Court, adjourned for a further two weeks in August 2004.
- 18 August 2004: Murdoch is committed to stand trial in the Northern Territory Supreme Court on charges of murder and assault.
- May 2005: Authorities send a portion of the cable-tie restraints to the United Kingdom for specialist DNA testing, which finds a DNA sample 100 million times more likely to have come from Murdoch than anyone else.
- 17 October 2005: Bradley Murdoch's trial begins in the Northern Territory Supreme Court.

- 13 December 2005: Murdoch is found guilty of murdering Peter Falconio, assaulting Joanne Lees and depriving her of her liberty. He is given a mandatory life sentence (twenty years) with a minimum twenty-eight-year non-parole period.
- 12 December 2006: Murdoch's lawyers run a three-day appeal against his conviction and sentence in the NT Court of Criminal Appeal in Darwin.
- 10 January 2007: Murdoch's appeal is unanimously dismissed by three NT Court of Criminal Appeal judges.
- Murdoch's subsequent application to the High Court for leave to appeal that decision is denied.
- 13 July 2016: The *Northern Territory Parole Amendment Act 2016* is passed by Parliament. Known as 'No Body, No Parole' (and, to me, the 'Murdoch Amendment') this legislation is intended to prevent people convicted of murder from being able to qualify for parole unless they provide police with the location of the body (or remains) of their victim/s. Since Murdoch still refuses to disclose what he did with Peter's body, this law will probably keep him in jail for life.

GLOSSARY OF AUSTRALIAN SLANG

Chuck a uey – do a U-turn.

Pommie or Pom – semi-affectionate term for a British person, thought to have derived from the convict days of Prisoner Of Mother England!

Spewing – throwing up, being sick, or just being anxious and feeling sick, as in, 'I was spewing because she didn't let me know where she was.'

Tinnie – a beer can or sometimes a small aluminium runabout boat.

Mozzies – mosquitos.

Sunnies – sunglasses.

Lackie bands – rubber bands (from elastic bands).

Tata – baby talk for 'goodbye'. Sometimes carried into adulthood!

Benzos – benzodiazapam tablets, often taken by truckies (illegally).

Pulling a swiftie – getting around a difficulty in a swift movement, or sudden change. E.g., 'he pulled a swiftie on the court when he skipped bail.'

Dob, dobber – To dob someone in is to tell on them. A dobber is a 'dog' or a 'scumbag', i.e., not highly thought of.

Bunging it on – putting on a show or playing something up to an audience.

Rooted – exhausted.

Crook – can mean criminal, as in 'he's been a crook all his life', but also means not good, as in 'feeling crook', or 'she was a bit crook about that'.

Kooks – weird people.

Ocker – an Australian.

Never within a coo-ee of her – cooee is a call made by Australians out in the bush if they are looking for someone. It's a high-pitched, loud, long-drawn-out call as in 'coooo—eeee'. It travels and indicates a human presence in the location. A return cooee indicates someone has heard.

Servo – petrol service station.

TRG – Tactical Response Group.

A fizzer – a failure, a non-starter, as in a firework that fails to ignite

A good stoush – a stoush is an argument, not always unfriendly, just a firm differing of opinion about something, as into 'they got into a stoush about politics'.

'A fair bit of bark off her'— this refers to Joanne's skinned elbows, looking like a tree trunk with the bark scratched off.

Conniptions – anxious reaction to something, or at times can be angry as well, depending on context.

Thongs – flip-flops, sandals.

Kombi – VW camper van.

Gave me the irrits – annoyed me, as in made me irritable.

Jake – 'But he was just jake about it' – happy or agreeable about something, as in 'she'll be jake'.

Rollie—a cigarette you roll yourself.

Windcheater— fleece-lined or thick cotton top, worn over a lighter weight one.

NORTHERN TERRITORY SEASONS

The Dry – The Dry is from about May to October. Barely any rain falls and the heat is intense – 40+ degrees and desiccating. However, in about late September to October, the climate changes to:

The Build-Up – for most 'whitefellas' this is a terrible period. It's hot and super humid, causing heavy sweating and short tempers. Blackfellas don't like it much, either! Relief comes with:

The Wet – November to April, when it pours and pours with rain. Humans relax, animals enjoy standing out in the rain and dry creek beds become raging torrents. Many rivers are swollen into deep and dangerous obstacles pouring across outback roads, which become impassable, cutting off properties and even townships. It's a rugged country!

ABOUT THE AUTHOR

Robin Bowles is Australia's leading female true crime writer. In 1997 she closed her successful sixteen-year-old PR business to concentrate on investigating the death of a young country housewife whose story she'd read in a newspaper. The result of that research was a book, *Blind Justice*, which initiated a new career as a creative non-fiction investigative writer.

Since the release of *Blind Justice*, Robin has written fourteen more best-sellers and numerous short stories and obtained a Swinburne Uni Diploma in Investigation (PI) along the way. She teaches writing and is an active campaigner for injustice.

Robin lives in Melbourne with husband Clive and a Brussells Griffon called Chewie.

www.robinbowles.com.au
robinbowles@bigpond.com